FUN FOR KIDS IN SINGAPORE

KAREN J. RENNER

Marshall Cavendish Editions

Design and illustration by Lock Hong Liang
Special thanks to Wildlife Reserves Singapore for the use of the Night Safari and Jurong Bird Park logos on the cover.
3rd Edition updates by Karen J Renner and Yong Jui Lin

Fun for Kids in Singapore first pubilshed in 2003 by Times Media Private Limited

Reprinted in 2004, 2008 by Marshall Cavendish International (Asia)

Published by Marshall Cavendish Editions
An imprint of Marshall Cavendish International
1 New Industrial Road, Singapore 536196

Other Marshall Cavendish Offices:
Marshall Cavendish Ltd. 119 Wardour Street, London W1F 0UW, UK • Marshall Cavendish Corporation. 99 White Plains Road, Tarrytown NY 10591-9001, USA • Marshall Cavendish International (Thailand) Co Ltd. 253 Asoke, 12th Flr, Sukhumvit 21 Road, Klongtoey Nua, Wattana, Bangkok 10110, Thailand • Marshall Cavendish (Malaysia) Sdn Bhd, Times Subang, Lot 46, Subang Hi-Tech Industrial Park, Batu Tiga, 40000 Shah Alam, Selangor Darul Ehsan, Malaysia

National Library Board Singapore Cataloguing in Publication Data
Renner, Karen J., 1963-
Fun for kids in Singapore / Karen J. Renner. – 3rd ed. – Singapore : Marshall Cavendish Editions, c2011.
p. cm.
ISBN : 978-981-4346-42-9 (pbk.)

1. Outdoor recreation for children – Singapore – Guidebooks.
2. Family recreation – Singapore – Guidebooks. 3. Singapore – Guidebooks. I. Title.

GV191.63
796.5095957 – dc22 OCN719409733

Printed by KWF Printing Pte Ltd

For Daniel and Matilda Leng

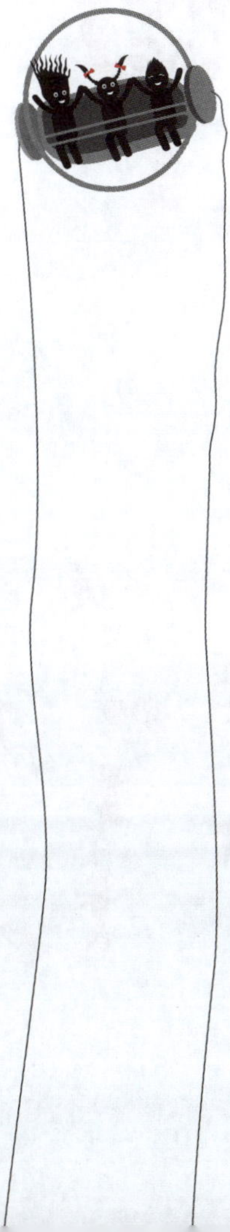

I ♥ SG

ACKNOWLEDGEMENTS

It has been wonderful to develop what started as an idea when I was at home with two pre-schoolers. From its initial publication in 2003, *Fun For Kids in Singapore* has proven a popular and key guide for both families living in and visiting Singapore.

This third edition would not have been possible without the encouragement and opportunity given to me by my publisher, Marshall Cavendish and my editor, Stephanie Pee. I would like to thank them and all those people who have contributed information, quotes and feedback. And to the reader, a "thank you" as well — I hope you enjoy discovering Singapore with your family as much as I have!

CONTENTS

Introduction 11
Where Is It? 11
Getting Around 12
A Quick Guide to Information 14
Special Needs 15
Getting Together 16

Chapter 1: Back to Nature 23
Fast Facts 23
National Parks Board 24
Singapore Botanic Gardens 33
Chinese and Japanese Gardens 35
HortPark 36
MacRitchie Reservoir 37
Camping 38
Picnic Time! 38
Natural Habitats 41
Singapore Zoo 43
Night Safari 45
Jurong BirdPark 46
Farm Tours 48
Underwater World Singapore 53
Butterfly Park and Insect Kingdom 53
Crocodiles 54
Pets 54

Chapter 2: Adventure Singapura! 61
Adventure Clubs 61
Adventure Sports 65
Other Adventure Activities and Venues 68
Bukit Timah Nature Reserve 71
Camping 71

Diving with Marine Animals 73
Dolphin Encounters 73
Island Hopping 74
Singapore Ducktours 76
Ghoulish Trails 77

Chapter 3: Sports 79
Fast Facts 79
Sports for All 81
Sports Instruction 84

Chapter 4: The Performing Arts 128
What's On? 128
Where? 130
Special Needs 133
Memberships 133
Drama 134
Cinema Venues 144
Music and Movement 147
Fast Facts 148
Dance 148
Music 157
Special Events 171
Other Things to Do 175

Chapter 5: Arts, Crafts and Cooking 176
Classes 176
Fast Facts 177
Venues and Exhibitions 188

Chapter 6: Where to Go? 192
Museums and Infotainment Venues 192
Fast Facts 193
On Your Doorstep 201
Out and About 202
World War II — A Journey into the Past 207

A Cultural Investigation 209
Sentosa 215
Theme and Amusement Parks 221
Cruising 224
Something Different 226
Playtime 226

Chapter 7: Annual Events 233
Fast Facts 233
Festive Celebrations 234
Special Events 240
Open Days 243

Chapter 8: Shopping Distractions and Culinary Delights 246
Fast Facts 246
Shopping Distractions 247
Childminding 265
Culinary Delights 267

Chapter 9: Reading and Resources 280
Fast Facts 280
Libraries 281
Bookshops 285
Children's Books about Singapore 290
Singaporean Websites for Children 293
Special Events 293

Chapter 10: Long School Break Activities 295
Fast Facts 296
Art 298
Music 301
Speech and Drama 302
Sports 303
Variety Programmes 308
Holiday Camps Away 313
Special Events and Venues 315
Shopping Centre Activities 316

Children nowadays are tyrants. They contradict their parents, gobble their food and tyrannise their teachers.

Socrates (c. 470–399 BC)

INTRODUCTION

Welcome to *Fun for Kids in Singapore*! This is the latest guide to everything children, predominantly between the ages of 3 and 18, can do or enjoy in Singapore. It is written for all families, whether you are new to Singapore or if you've been here for a number of years.

Things don't stand still in Singapore — it is a place of great change and there are always new venues being constructed, classes opening up and the old making way for the new. As a result, it is wise to check websites, keep a lookout for events in newspapers and periodicals and call ahead if you are planning something special. Everything in this book was correct at the time of going to press but obviously some information (such as prices) should be taken only as a guide. That said, *Fun for Kids in Singapore* is a comprehensive guide about where to go, what is available and how to find out more about just about anything that may occupy or entertain your children. Have fun with your children in Singapore!

WHERE IS IT?

Publications

The *Singapore Street Directory* (published by Mighty Minds) at $12.90 is a good investment. It is a useful aid for any taxi journeys you may take, especially to any of the smaller streets and roads. While many taxi drivers do have their own directory at hand, a number don't so I usually make a rough sketch of my destination in preparation for such situations.

Websites

www.streetdirectory.com

This is an easy and quick tool for finding out where places are.

www.asiamaya.com/singapore

Look here for a map of Singapore that is sectioned into 4 different levels of detail.

www.gothere.sg

An easy-to-use website that will provides directions whether you are driving or using public transport. All you have to do is key in your start and end points!

GETTING AROUND

Publications

Look out for the annual *TransitLink Guide* (published by Transit Link Pte Ltd) at $2.50. It is available at newsagents, some bookstores and MRT customer service counters. Inside you'll find all you need to know about how to use the bus, LRT and MRT services. It's an essential guide for anyone who uses public transport.

Web: www.transitlink.com.sg

Website

This eGuide provides a convenient one-stop information guide on point-to-point bus and train services.

www.transitlink.com.sg/eguide2.html

Buses

More than 300 bus services cover all parts of Singapore, providing an inexpensive, mainly air-conditioned and relatively convenient means of transport. However, bus journeys can take a long time during peak hours and for parents with strollers, be prepared to have a child in one arm and the buggy in the other. Buses do not have designated baggage space so keep bags to a minimum.

Child/student concession fares range from $0.33 to $0.45 (ez-link card) and $0.45 to $0.65 (cash) for non air-conditioned buses and $0.36 to $0.58 (ez-link card) and $0.55 to $0.75 (cash) for air-conditioned buses. Children up to 0.9 metres in height travel free (if they are with an adult). Concessionary fares are also available for those between 0.9 and 1.2 metres without a concession card. For those above 1.2 metres, concessionary fares are given on production of a valid concession ez-link card.

Web: www.sbstransit.com.sg / www.smrtbuses.com.sg

Note: As drivers do not carry money, make sure that you have the exact fare in small change if you are not using an ez-link card.

MRT

The Mass Rapid Transit (MRT) provides a frequent, clean and efficient rail network system that covers the whole of Singapore. There are four main lines running North-South from Marina Bay Station to Jurong East Station via Woodlands Station; the East-West line which runs from Pasir Ris Station to Joo Koon Station; the Circle Line which runs from Dhoby Ghaut to Marymount Station and the North-East line which runs from Harbourfront Station to Punggol Station. Other lines including the Downtown Line are currently in development. Train intervals are between 3 and 8 minutes from 5.30 a.m. to 1.00 a.m. Fares range from $0.36 to $0.58 (child/student). Be prepared to stand during peak periods.

Web: www.smrt.com.sg

LRT

The Light Rail Transit (LRT) system provides three feeder services to the MRT network. Each of the three lines serves an HDB public housing estate. Services operate from about 5.30 a.m. and usually end before 1 a.m. daily, with frequencies of approximately 5 minutes.

Web: www.smrt.com.sg

Ez-link Card

The stored value ez-link card offers the convenience of travelling on the MRT, LRT and by bus without having to pay cash for every trip. Cards can be bought at any TransitLink Ticket Office for $12 (includes a deposit and a stored value). Special cards are available for children. Cards can be topped up in value by paying cash at any TransitLink counter. Alternatively, you can use the GIRO-Link (if you have a DBS/POSB account) or Auto Credit Card facilities to top up. If you lose your GIRO ez-link card, you can invalidate it by calling the TransitLink Hotline (see below). To use the card, tap it on the fare gate upon entry to your preferred mode of transport and tap it again when you alight.

Tel: 1800 2255 663 (TransitLink Hotline)

Web: www.ezlink.com.sg

Singapore Tourist Pass

This contactless smart card may be purchased from $18 (inclusive of a $10 card refundable deposit and one day pass) for the payment of public transportation fees. The card can be purchased at selected Transit Link offices and Singapore Visitor Centres.

Taxis

All taxis are metered. Taxi fares begin at $2.80 – $3 ($3.20 for limousine cabs) inclusive of the first kilometre or less. Fares then increase by $0.20 every 385 metres thereafter or less up to 10 km and by a further $0.20 every 330 metres thereafter or less after 10 km. Every 45 seconds of waiting time is charged at 20 cents. There is no extra fee for flagging down a Mercedes cab. From midnight to 5.59 a.m. a 50 per cent surcharge over the meter fare is applicable. Surcharges of 35 per cent of the metered fare are also incurred during peak hours i.e. 7.00 a.m. to 9.30 a.m. from Monday to Friday and 5.00 p.m. to 8.00 p.m. from Monday to Saturday. Additional charges are also incurred when travelling to and from Changi Airport, Seletar Airport and Singapore Expo Centre, on the eve of and on certain public holidays and for trips originating within the Central Business District (CBD) area between 5.00 p.m. to midnight from Monday to Friday. Where applicable, reimbursement of Electronic Road Pricing (ECP) charges will be sought.

A surcharge of $2.50 (non-peak) or $3.50 (peak) is payable for current bookings and $5.20 for advance bookings (at least 30 minutes in advance). The surcharge rates are higher for limousine services at $8.00 for current bookings and $16.00 for advance bookings.

Web: www.taxisingapore.com

There are a number of taxi companies in Singapore:

Comfort and CityCab

(Blue and yellow taxis)

Tel: 6552 1111

Email: feedback@cdgtaxi.com.sg

Web: www.cdgtaxicom.sg

Comfort also operates a limousine service (Tel: 6552 2828).

Premier Taxis

(Metallic silver cabs)

Tel: 6363 6888

Email: feedback@premiertaxi.com

Web: www.premiertaxi.com

Premier Taxis also runs the SilverStar service.

Trans-Cab Services

(Red-and-white cabs)

Tel: 6555 3333

Email: transcab@singnet.com.sg

Web: www.transcabservices.com.sg

SMART Cabs

(Light green taxis that have TV screens)

Tel: 6485 7777

Web: www.smartcab.com.sg (under construction)

SMRT Taxis

(White taxis)

Tel: 6555 8888

Web: www.smrt.com.sg/taxis.html

SMRT also runs a limousine service.

Note: It is often difficult to get a taxi during peak hours, when it rains and at around midnight.

A QUICK GUIDE TO INFORMATION

Newspapers

Popular daily newspapers include:

The Straits Times

Look at the Life section for information on entertainment and events.

Web: www.straitstimes.com

The New Paper

This tabloid format paper is particularly noted for its coverage of sports news. There is also reasonable focus on matters relating to entertainment and fashion.

Web: www.tnp.sg

Lianhe Zaobao

The leading Chinese newspaper in Singapore, *Lianhe Zaobao* covers business news, current affairs, culture and the arts.

Web: www.zaobao.com.sg

Today

This popular daily English-language

newspaper (there is no edition on Sundays) is free. It is a useful guide to what is on.

Web: www.todayonline.com

Periodicals

Expat Living Singapore

This $6.50-monthly magazine focuses on features about family life and home furnishings. It also publishes an annual guide on child-related matters. The website is worth checking out.

Tel: 6259 0058
Email: info@expatliving.sg
Web: www.expatliving.sg

The Finder

This free monthly periodical is a useful guide to what is on and where. It has lots of advertisements and plenty of information for families with children.

Web: thefinder.com.sg

IS Magazine

This free publication appears fortnightly and has features on dining, shopping and travel. It also has a useful listing of what's showing at the cinema and theatre and what exhibitions are running. While it is not child-orientated, teenagers may find its shopping features interesting. It is one of the most up-to-date sources for entertainment listings and features some good reviews.

Web: www.is.asia-city.com

Time Out Singapore

Launched in early 2007, this is the 18th international edition of one of the world's leading listings of arts and entertainment. Priced at $3.95, it covers music, nightlife, performance, sport, art and anything and everything relating to Singapore's arts and culture. There is also a section specifically for children. The writing team does not shy away from expressing personal opinions, abiding by the guiding principle of *Time Out* to remain independent and uninfluenced by advertising.

Location: 89 Neil Road #03-01, Singapore 088849
Tel: 6324 2386
Web: www.timeoutsingapore.com

Juice

This glossy free magazine will appeal to teenagers with its emphasis upon music and fashion related matters. It is published monthly and lists all music events including updates on the clubbing scene.

Email: ask@juice.com.sg
Web: www.juice.com.sg

SPECIAL NEEDS

There are various organisations in Singapore that offer fun activities and courses specifically for children with special needs. I've included a section on this in the chapter on

Sports (*see* pp. 82–84) and for those interested in the arts, the Very Special Arts Singapore organisation (*see* The Performing Arts, p. 133) is well worth contacting.

For families seeking advice or information on care and support, the following associations may be able to help:

- ***Autism Association of Singapore***
  Tel: 6774 6649
  Email: autism@singnet.com.sg
  Web: www.autismsg.org

- ***Down Syndrome Association (Singapore)***
  Tel: 6278 3907
  Email: nalia@downsyndrome-singapore.org
  Web: www.downsyndrome-singapore.org

- ***Movement for the Intellectually Disabled of Singapore (MINDS)***
  Tel: 6479 5655
  Email: minds@minds.org.sg
  Web: www.minds.org.sg

- ***Singapore Association for the Deaf***
  Tel: 6344 8274
  Email: aa@sadeaf.org.sg
  Web: www.sadeaf.org.sg

- ***Singapore Association of the Visually Handicapped (SAVH)***
  Tel: 6251 4331/ 6252 9116
  Email: enquiries@savh.org.sg
  Web: www.savh.org.sg

- ***Society for the Physically Disabled***
  Tel: 6579 0700
  Email: information@spd.org.sg
  Web: www.spd.org.sg

- ***Spastic Children's Association of Singapore***
  Tel: 6585 5600
  Email: spastic@pacific.net.sg
  Web: www.spastic.org.sg

- ***Asian Women's Welfare Association (AWWA)***
  Tel: 6511 5200
  Email: AWWAHQ@awwa.org.sg
  Web: www.awwa.org.sg

GETTING TOGETHER

Associations

Various organisations provide activities that may be of interest to all children in Singapore. Some groups help expatriate families meet others from their home country, which can be particularly useful when new to Singapore. Most of the associations also offer associate membership to other nationalities.

American Women's Association (AWA)

The AWA offers activities for children, a monthly newsletter, resources for parents and children and playgroup contacts. Children's first aid classes are also offered through the AWA and a preschool list is available for perusal.

If you or your spouse is an American or Canadian citizen, you qualify for regular membership ($125 per annum). If not, you can still become a member with associate status ($125 per year).

Tel: 6734 4895
Email: office@awasingapore.org
Web: www.awasingapore.org

Asian Women's Welfare Association (AWWA)

The members of this association are active in voluntary work and fund-raising. The AWWA also runs TEACH ME, an integration programme that enables physically challenged children to attend mainstream schools. The AWWA Special School caters to children with multiple disabilities and autism from 6 to 18 years. An Early Intervention Programme for Infants and Young Children (EIPIC) is also available to children with special needs from birth to 6 years old.

Tel: 6511 5200
Email: AWWAHQ@awwa.org.sg
Web: www.awwa.org.sg

Australian and New Zealand Association (ANZA)

This organisation conducts sporting activities such as netball, soccer and athletics among many other activities, for children. Membership is open to all nationalities, not just Australians and New Zealaners. The annual membership fee is $130 per family. Additional registration fees may be incurred for sporting activities.

Tel: 6733 1215
Email: info@anza.org.sg
Web: www.anza.org.sg

British Association of Singapore (BA)

The BA has a Parents and Tots group that meets on Thursdays at The Playhouse at Rochester Park. It will also help you find playgroups in your locality. Annual family membership is $150.

Tel: 6339 8229
Email: info@britishassociation.org.sg
Web: www.britishassociation.org.sg

Canadian Association of Singapore (CAS)

The CAS has a weekly playgroup, conducts various events for children and hosts several junior ice hockey teams. Family membership fees are $90 per annum for all nationalities.

Tel: 6622 5485
Email: info@canadians.org.sg
Web: www.canadians.org.sg

Chinese Development Assistance Council (CDAC)

The CDAC is a self-help, non-profit organisation set up by and for the Chinese community in Singapore. It runs a subsidised tuition programme for those who qualify and Student Service Centres for children aged 6 to 18. These centres have libraries and computers and offer supervised homework groups as well as various enrichment programmes and workshops.

Tel: 6841 4889
Email: feedback@cdac.org.sg
Web: www.cdac.org.sg

Japanese Association

This organisation runs courses, activities and workshops for children. The sports committee is particularly active and hosts tournaments and competitions throughout the year.

Tel: 6468 0066 (General Office)
Email: info@jas.org.sg
Web: www.jas.org.sg

People's Association (PA)

The PA is at the core of Singaporean society. It is responsible for fulfilling community needs in the areas of education, recreation and leisure through activities organised at Community Centres/Clubs and Residents' Committee (RC) centres.

Tel: 6344 8222
Web: www.pa.gov.sg

Singapore American Community Action Council (SACAC)

SACAC is open to all families. It offers a comprehensive sports programme for children aged 4 and above and well-established counselling and community programmes. You need to pay an annual family membership fee of $160.50 to participate in all SACAC activities and programmes.

Tel: 6363 6454 (Sports Office) / 6733 9249 (Counselling and Community Programmes)
Email: sacac@sas.edu.sg (Sports Office) / admin@sacac.com (Counselling and Community Programmes)
Web: www.sacac.com

Singapore Council of Women's Associations

This is an umbrella body for women's organisations in Singapore. It aims to promote and improve the status of women, particularly in education, economic participation, social and community involvement and participation in culture and sports. It is a useful starting point when seeking family-related advice or contact with a variety of other women's associations.

Tel: 6837 0611
Email: scwo@scwo.org.sg
Web: www.scwo.org.sg

Singapore Indian Development Association (SINDA)

SINDA organises educational and youth development programmes as well as family services for the Indian community. It runs Reading Centres for children aged 4 to 9, computer courses (4 years and above) and Project Victory for Primary school students (designed to raise self-esteem through a fun and interactive programme). SINDA also supports a youth mentorship programme called the Kaki Klub that matches children in Secondary 1, 2 or 3 to an older, trained mentor.

Tel: 6298 5911
Email: feedback@sinda.org.sg
Web: www.sinda.org.sg

Yayasan MENDAKI

MENDAKI provides support for the Malay/Muslim community. It offers educational instruction through its Read-With-Me and M-Power! (intensive maths) programmes as well as basic IT instruction, tutoring and befriending schemes. It also organises various events for children (such as soccer clinics).

Tel: 6245 5710
Web: www.mendaki.org.sg

Young Women's Christian Association of Singapore

This association runs Child Development Centres and a Nursery/Kindergarten, a Student Care Centre and other community services. It also organises various activities, e.g. Kid's Baking Programme.

Tel: 6223 1227
Email: admin@ywca.org.sg
Web: www.ywca.org.sg

Young Women Muslim Association

This association organises events and provides various services including kindergartens, YWMA Child Development Centres, a Single Parent Family Centre and the YWMA-MENDAKI Family Service Centre.

Tel: 6744 0258
Email: info@ppis.sg
Web: http://web.ppis.sg/

Clubs

As well as local Community Centres/Clubs, Singapore also has a number of private clubs that offer a range of facilities for all the family. To join, you need to make a one-off payment (minimum fee of $8,500+) and a monthly fee thereafter (usually $150+ for families). Many clubs also offer one-year short-term memberships. The expatriate clubs hold a number of events and celebrations unique to each community but membership is not exclusive. Some clubs are more child-orientated than others, so do visit them and ask about facilities and policies. Favourites with families include the British

Club, the Hollandse Club and the Swiss Club.

American Club

21 Scotts Road, Singapore 228219
Tel: 6737 3411
Email: info@amclub.org.sg
Web: www.amclub.org.sg

British Club

73 Bukit Tinggi Road,
Singapore 289761
Tel: 6467 4311
Email: enquiries@britishclub.org.sg
Web: www.britishclub.org.sg

Community Centres

You will find Community Centres (CCs) in all neighbourhoods throughout Singapore. These offer a wide selection of activities at very reasonable prices (an expensive membership fee is not required).
Contact: For individual centres, look in the Buying Guide section of the Singapore Yellow Pages.

Web: www.pa.gov.sg /
http://one.pa.gov.sg (search under keywords "PA Kiddies" for children's activities and courses)

Hollandse Club

22 Camden Park,
Singapore 299814
Tel: 6464 5225
Email: reception@hollandseclub.org.sg
Web: www.hollandseclub.org.sg

**Orchid Country Club*

1 Orchid Club Road,
Singapore 768162
Tel: 6755 9811
Email: membership@orchidclub.com
Web: www.orchidclub.com

Singapore Cricket Club

Connaught Drive, Singapore 179681
Tel: 6338 9271
Email: ssc@org.sg
Web: www.ssc.org.sg

**Singapore Island Country Club*

180 Island Club Road, Singapore 578774 / 240 Sime Road Singapore 288303
Tel: 6459 2222 (Island Club Road) / 6466 2244 (Sime Road)
Email: enquiry@sicc.org.sg
Web: www.sicc.org.sg

Singapore Polo Club

80 Mount Pleasant Road,
Singapore 298334
Tel: 6854 3999
Email: enquiry@singpaorepoloclub.org
Web: www.singaporepoloclub.org

Singapore Recreation Club

B Connaught Drive,
Singapore 179682
Tel: 6338 9367
Web: www.src.org.sg

Swiss Club

36 Swiss Club Road,
Singapore 288139
Tel: 6466 3233
Email: admin@swissclub.org.sg
Web: www.swissclub.org.sg

Tanglin Club

Location: 5 Stevens Road,
Singapore 257814
Tel: 6622 0555
Web: www.tanglinclub.org.sg

* Clubs that have a golf course

Other Useful Information Resources

Covenant Family Service Centre

This centre provides a range of services for families and individuals regardless of race or religion. Its services for children include a tuition scheme, school holiday programmes, a computer library and a reading programme. A youth mentoring scheme is also available as well as a Parentline, which provides advice on child development and other family issues. Counselling services are also available.

Opening hours: 9.00 a.m. to 5.00 p.m. (weekdays) / 9.00 a.m. to 1.00 p.m. (Saturdays)

Tel: 6282 8558 (general queries) / 6289 8811(Parentline)
Email: admin@covenant.mws.org.sg
Web: www.covenantfsc.mws.org.sg

New Mothers' Support Group

This is a very useful contact for mothers new to Singapore or/and those with babies and preschoolers. Membership is $25 per year (plus $5 for attendance at the monthly socials at Gymboree). Members receive a bimonthly newsletter and have access to meetings, social gatherings and a library. A coffee club is held twice monthly and as well as a monthly walk through the Botanic Gardens there is an organised monthly talk at the Camden Medical Centre.

Email: info@nmsg-singapore.com
Web: www.nmsg-singapore.com

Singapore Homeschool Group

There are over 100 families, both expatriate and local, involved in this group. There is no membership fee. Activities are educational, social and cross-cultural. They include Mandarin classes, football, field trips, picnics and curriculum talks.

Web: www.singaporehg.byehost13.com

Websites

Regardless of whether you are a resident or tourist, check out the following websites if you have children:

www.livelife.ecitzen.gov.sg

Collectively owned by seven government agencies, this site offers a one-stop portal for accurate and comprehensive information about lifestyle activities and programmes. Here you'll find information pertaining to heritage, the arts, recreation and sports. Facilities also include a range of e-Services, including online registration and payment of courses and performances, library services, booking options for sporting and recreational facilities as well as details about the latest events in town.

www.entersingapore.com/ www.expatsingapore.com

Both of these websites provide act as useful guides for expatriates living in Singapore. The latter has an excellent message board on which you can post queries about anything relating to life in Singapore (it is a great place to seek other people's opinions about schools, classes, dining venues and where to go).

www.mumcentre.com

Look here for regular updates about shows, festivals, events and other activities. A comprehensive list of children and family service providers, as well as informative articles, can also be accessed.

www.singaporeforkids.com

Here you'll find information and links to things that may interest your child as well as a guide to holding a birthday party.

www.yoursingapore.com

Packed with information, this site has advice on where to eat, what to do, how to get around and the latest events on in town. If you want to find out more about Singapore, look here.

– Chapter 1 –

BACK TO NATURE

In this chapter, I have suggested some of the ways in which you and your child can experience Singapore's rich and diverse zoological and botanical heritage. Some children will prefer man-made animal and plant venues while others will prefer the real thing, depending on their taste (or distaste) for adventure, age and interests. If you're thinking of spending time with animals or plants, in any form, this chapter is for you.

FAST FACTS

National Parks Board

NParks Helpline (toll-free number): 1800 471 7300

Web: www.nparks.gov.sg

Nature Society (Singapore)

The Nature Society (Singapore), or NSS, is a non-governmental, non-profit organisation dedicated to the appreciation, conservation, study and enjoyment of the natural heritage in Singapore and the surrounding regions. There are special interest groups such as a bird group, a butterfly interest group and a marine conservation group. There is also an education group that organises Kids Fun with Nature programmes every month and has its own dedicated blog at http://funwithnature.blogspot.com/. Membership is open to anyone and there is a special junior category for those under 18.

Location: 510 Geylang Road #02-05

The Sunflower Singapore 389466

Tel: 6741 2036

Email: contact@nss.org.sg

Web: www.nss.org.sg

NATIONAL PARKS BOARD

The vision for National Parks Board is to make Singapore a garden city for all. It manages about 2,773 hectares of parks, park connectors, open spaces and nature reserves. In an island with a land area of only 704 square kilometres, that's a lot of greenery! The Board's role is primarily to develop, manage and promote these parks as valuable resources for recreation, conservation, research and education.

As a golden rule for enjoying these natural resources, remember: TAKE NOTHING BUT PHOTOS, LEAVE NOTHING BUT FOOTSTEPS.

Parks

In this section, I've concentrated on some of the most popular parks for children — but it should be noted that virtually every park in Singapore has facilities for all the family. For a listing of all the parks and some of their key features, please refer to the tables on pages 57–60.

Bishan Park

This large, beautiful park fronts Kallang River and features a number of lakes and bridges.

Location: Ang Mo Kio Avenue 1

Highlights for children: A cycling track, shady walks and an inline skate rental outlet. The concrete canal has also been turned into a natural meandering river, and there are three new playgrounds, each with a distinctive theme. Habitats have also been created for wild species to settle and thrive.

East Coast Park (Recommended!)

This is the largest and one of the most popular parks in Singapore. It is situated in shady parkland with extensive cycling tracks and pedestrian walkways. Within the park, there are cafés and restaurants inside the Marine Cove complex as well as bowling and arcade and snooker facilities.

Location: Along East Coast Parkway

Highlights for children

Sandcastle Building: Want to find out more about building sand sculptures? At weekends from 3.30 p.m. to 7.00 p.m., free lessons are available from Castle Beach, which is located in front of Car Park E2, next to East Coast Food Village.

Email: Alvin@castlebeach.org

Web: www.castlebeach.org

Cable Skiing: SKI360° is Singapore's first cable ski park, a sport in which participants are pulled by an overhead cable instead of a boat. A 1-hour ski pass is $30 on weekdays, with a reduced rate upon production of a student pass. Head for Car Park E1.

Tel: 6442 7318

Web: www.ski360degree.com

Sports rental: Bicycle, scooter and inline skate rental are all available. Bicycles for children cost from $2 an hour and baby seats and even tandems are available. Inline skates come complete with protective elbow/knee/wrist pads for about $7 an hour. There is an extensive bike/rollerblade track between Marine Cove and the sea.

An extreme skateboarding park has just been built beside carpark F1. Children will enjoy watching skateboarders perform their stunts. There is also a rollerblading track, and lessons are conducted every weekend by Inline Culture (call Benedict at 6844 5522).

Seaside: The park is bordered by a man-made beach which is great for children to play on although the water is murky. Changing rooms, toilets and showers are all at hand.

Other family facilities:

- Barbecue pit rental is available.
- Water sports are available from the National Sailing Centre (Tel: 6444 4555) and the People's Association's Sea Sports Club (Tel: 6444 0409 / www.seasports.org.sg), both of which are located at East Coast Parkway.
- Playground@Big Splash which was once a water theme park is now a recreation complex housing fast food, upmarket restaurants and recreational facilities such as Lilliput minigolf and children's gymnastics. There is even a hot yoga studio.

Note: At weekends and on public holidays, this park can get very busy, especially the cycle tracks. It is a good idea to get there early if you have specific bicycle demands, e.g., baby seats or bicycles with stabilisers.

Fort Canning Park

I've included this park because it is a blissful oasis in the city and it really does deserve mention because it is the site of the original Botanic Gardens. The historical heritage of this park will interest older children.

Location: Cox Terrace (adjacent to the Registry of Marriages)

Highlights for children:

The Battle Box: This preserved World War II British military command centre offers a fascinating record of the momentous day in Singapore's history when the British command surrendered to the Japanese. This venue is one of the best museum exhibits in Singapore and is suitable for children aged 8 and above. For more information, *see* Where to Go? (pp. 204 – 205).

19th Century Walk of History trail: This trail links the various historical sights of the park. Plaques and signboards explain the key features.

Nature: You will probably smell the Spice Garden long before you see it! It now has a collection of over a hundred species of plants! Fort

Canning Park is also home to some lovely heritage trees. Download the Trees of Fort Canning Walking Trail from the Fort Canning Park website.

Other family facilities:

- The park is an ideal location for a picnic. Outdoor events held in the park are preceded by picnic time. "Ballet under the Stars", an annual event held by Singapore Dance Theatre in the park, is where ballet is performed for picnickers by moonlight.

Labrador Nature Reserve

Although this is a small nature reserve and park of just over 16 hectares, it is rich in history and also has a diverse variety of flora and fauna. This pleasant, seafront spot overlooking Keppel Harbour is well worth a visit.

Location: Labrador Villa Road, off Pasir Panjang Road

Highlights for children:

History: This park contains relics of World War II, including bunkers and tunnels. Unfortunately, these are closed until further notice.

Nature: For young nature lovers, there are interesting things to spot and nature trails to follow. Key vegetation to note includes the *Draceana maingayi* which is thought to be more than 80 years old, the horse mango and the creamy, scented flowers of the Jambu Air Laut. More than 70 species of birds and 11 kinds of butterflies have also been recorded here.

Other family facilities:

- There is a short stretch of beach front, a playground, barbecue pits and cycle paths.
- For those who enjoy fishing, you can join the anglers along the promenade and jetty.

There has been a 1-hectare extension to the park called ComChest Green. It has a promenade area, lookout deck, shelters and seating area.

Note:

- This park has two car parks. If you have children aged 9 and below, head for Car Park B as it is much nearer to the seafront and playground.
- Most of the picnic tables overlooking the promenade are well shaded and the nearby toilets are very clean. This makes it an attractive venue for a quiet family outing. Currently there are no snack kiosks so take plenty of refreshments and light snacks. A café and a restaurant is located near Car Park A.

Marina Barrage

This is actually a dam in Singapore built across the mouth of the bay, between Marina East and Marina South, creating Singapore's fifteenth reservoir. It is open 24/7, and the water level in the Marina Basin is kept constant, making it ideal for all kinds of water recreational activities, such as canoeing and kayaking.

Location: Marina South

Highlights for children:

- There is a large fountain play area where children will have plenty of fun running in between the water jets and getting wet.
- This is THE area in Singapore to fly kites on the green roof with the Marina Bay area and Central Business District in full view. Younger children may enjoy making their kites beforehand — sticks, cellophane paper and crêpe paper can be readily obtained from most stationery shops and make for a simple yet effective kite.
- For dining, have a picnic or try the restaurant or café.

Note:

• For dining, a picnic is the easiest solution if you have young children. The view really is breathtaking and one can see the Singapore Flyer in the background. At night, the Flyer's changing lights are a sight to behold.

Pasir Ris Park (Recommended!)

This is a super park for anyone with children. It is situated by the seafront and has plenty of tree cover.

Location: Elias Road

Highlights for children:

Children's Adventure Land: This playground is usefully segregated into three play areas according to age, i.e., below 4 years, 5 to 9 years and 10 to 15 years. It is, as its name states, an adventure playground, with wooden equipment and no soft-fall covering. However, don't let this deter you — it really is a fun venue with lots of space and plenty to do. Key attractions include the two-way cable and Giant Spacenet. You'll find the playground between Car Parks D and E — you can't miss it.

Fisherman's Village: Situated on the seafront, this village has many restaurants and bars offering everything from seafood to satay and steamboat. The atmosphere is informal and families are welcome. You can sit here while younger kids play in the sand or just enjoy watching the boats together.

Bicycle and inline blade rental: There are bicycle and inline blading kiosks at Car Park C and Car Park D. Children's bikes start at $3 to $4 for 2 hours and adult bikes at $4 to $6 for 2 hours. Baby seats are charged extra. The kiosk at Car Park C is open from 8.00 a.m. to 8.00 p.m. daily (Tel: 6582 4297).

Mangrove Forest: Use the boardwalks to explore the 6-hectare mangrove forest where you will see mud crabs, gigantic mud skippers and the aerial roots of the mangrove trees. There is also a 3-storey-high bird watching tower.

Maze Garden: There is a maze made up of bushes that children will really enjoy running around in.

Pony riding: Go to Gallop Stable (Tel: 6583 9665), near Car Park C, for rides or lessons. There is a one-time registration fee for new enrollments, and regular riders need to purchase the proper riding attire. Ad-hoc rides around the paddock cost $10. The café serves an American breakfast.

Other family facilities:

- There is a People's Association Holiday Complex cum Water Venture Club featuring water sports such as kayaking next to Car Park E.
- If you prefer an outdoor DIY dining experience, rent one of the barbecue pits. Camping facilities are also available.

Note: If you are travelling by public transport, you'll need to get bus 403 from Pasir Ris MRT Station. This service usually operates every 30 minutes.

West Coast Park

This park has a marsh garden, a couple of snack kiosks and a large McDonald's café and restaurant. There are also go-karts available for rental.

Location: Next to West Coast Highway

Highlights for children:

Adventure Play Area: Segregated into age-specific sites (although you should expect some overlap), this park has one of the largest playgrounds in Singapore. There is a towering rope pyramid, flying fox, pirate ship, slides, swings and climbing equipment. The sites for younger children have soft-fall covering.

Other family facilities:

- There is a bird sanctuary, a marsh garden and a sand play area.
- Barbecue pit rental is available.

Woodlands Waterfront

This 9-hectare park to open up is the newest in Singapore.

Location: Location of Woodlands Waterfront lies slightly north to the junction of Admiralty Road and Admiralty Road West.

Highlights for children: There is also a huge playground for children and an exercise park for senior citizens. There is a newly opened trail where visitors can enjoy a scenic view of the entire coastal park and the Straits of Johor from high vantage points.

Other family facilities: There is a 1.5 kilometre waterfront promenade and a 700 metre jetty. You can see the Johore Bahru skyline and, sometimes, the Malaysian navy's boats patrolling the Straits. You can go fishing and crabbing from the jetty.

Note: Try to visit the park in the morning or evening, as the trees are not fully grown yet and it can get very hot. Take an umbrella. If you do drive, make sure you put a parking coupon. The car park is big and spacious, but there are hefty fines for coupon-less cars (and the CISCO traffic wardens are extremely conscientious).

Nature Reserves

Bukit Timah Nature Reserve

see also Adventure Singapura!, p.71

Nature enthusiasts could do little better than visit Bukit Timah Nature Reserve. Here you will find Singapore's only genuine patch of (untouched) primary rainforest, only 16 kilometres from the city centre. Within the reserve are Singapore's highest hill, Bukit Timah Hill, and an astonishing range of flora and wildlife. Look out for butterflies, macaques, giant forest ants, pangolins (rare) and even the occasional pit viper. You can reach the top of Bukit Timah Hill by using the windy, tarred road or taking the steeper but shorter route — the popular, staired Summit Path. Both these options are really only suitable for children aged 5 and above. Some accompanying adults may need to be prepared stamina-wise too! An orientation visit to the Visitor Centre beforehand is recommended. Here you can view an exhibit of the reserve's native flora and fauna. There is also a restroom, a bookshop (which sells cold drinks and snacks too) and telephones.

Younger children will enjoy the play area which is reasonably shaded, with drinking water dispensers and taps at hand. It is an adventure playground with a gritty, sandy base and an assortment of wooden equipment. To find it, follow the Hindhede Nature Walk, which is clearly indicated from the Visitor Centre. If you continue along this walk, you'll find a picnic area and more trails that are decidedly easier than the trek to the top of the hill. For parents seeking a workout, try pushing a double buggy (plus kids) to the top of the hill! I have witnessed this but have no intention of trying it.

Opening hours: 8.30 a.m. to 6.00 p.m. daily (Visitor Centre)

Price guide: Free admission.

Location: At the end of Hindhede Road, off Upper Bukit Timah Road.

Tel: 64717361 (Visitor Centre) / 0468 5736

Web: www.nparks.gov.sg (look under Nature Reserves)

Note: Free guided walks are held on the 2nd Saturday of every month at Dairy Farm Nature Park at 9.30 a.m. Private tours of Bukit Timah Nature Reserve are also available (for a fee).

Tips:

- For trekking, wear closed shoes and carry a water bottle. Remember your insect repellent!
- Get a map of the reserve from the Ranger Counter in the Visitor Centre.

Pulau Ubin

see also Chek Jawa under the Natural Habitats section featured later in this chapter and Adventure Singapura!, pp. 72-73 & pp. 74-75. If you and your family like the idea of a rapid foray into a rustic retreat, Pulau Ubin might just be the place for you. Be prepared with sun lotion, mosquito repellent and a bottle or two of water — it is not part of the sanitised, air-conditioned mainland.

To reach Pulau Ubin, take a bumboat from Changi Point. This will probably cost you $2.50 for a one-way trip. Alternatively, if you can't wait for the boat to reach capacity (12 or so passengers), you can hire it for about $30. If you're taking your bicycle along, be prepared to pay an extra $2 per trip. The boats operate from 6.00 a.m. to 8.00 p.m.

Upon reaching the island, head for the Information Kiosk which is to the right of the jetty. Here you can get a map of Pulau Ubin.

Once on the island, you can trek, cycle or enjoy some seafood. There are a number of places that hire out bikes in the village near the jetty from about $8 for the day. Child seats and children's bicycles are also available. Do ensure that your child is kitted out to cope with the heat and for what can be a tiring, albeit adventurous, day out. Food and drinks are sold in the village but do take along extra snacks.

Tel: 6542 4108 (Information Kiosk)
Web: www.nparks.gov.sg (Look under Parks & Gardens)

Sungei Buloh Wetland Reserve

Sungei Buloh Wetland Reserve is set in 130 hectares of mangroves, mudflats, ponds and secondary forest. Throughout the year, you can expect to see mangrove wildlife such as mudskippers, crabs, shellfish, water snakes, birds, spiders, moths and monitor lizards.

The reserve is popular with bird spotters because resident species like herons, bitterns, sunbirds, coucals and kingfishers can be found here. It is also a wintering ground for migratory birds, which can be seen from September to March while flying along the East Asian Migratory Flyway.

Features include a mangrove boardwalk, theatrette, cafeteria, nature gallery, butterfly trail, information kiosk and observation hides from which to conduct bird spotting. Check out the reserve's calendar of events on its website (see p. 31).

Free guided tours (usually around the mangroves) are held on Saturdays at 9.30 a.m. At times, these may be replaced by other tours like Marine Fish or PrawnWatch. Private tours are also available (for a fee).

The reserve also operates the Young Naturalists Programme whereby badges are given for completion of certain tasks. These tasks include nature activities for children such as Nest Builders, Wetland Craftsman and Creature Feature (Saturdays between 11.15 a.m. and 11.45 a.m.).

Opening hours: 7.30 a.m. to 7.00 p.m. (Mondays to Saturdays) / 7.00 a.m. to 7.00 p.m. (Sundays and public holidays; ticket sales close at 6.00 p.m.). An audio-visual show runs at 9.00 a.m., 11.00 a.m., 1.00 p.m., 3.00 p.m. and 5.00 p.m. (Mondays through Saturdays). It runs hourly from 9.00 a.m. to 5.00 p.m. on Sundays and public holidays.
Price guide: Free on weekdays. $0.50 for children / $1 for adults (weekends, public holidays and school holidays.)

Location: 301 Neo Tiew Crescent,
Singapore 718925
Tel: 6794 1401
Email: info@sbwr.org.sg
Web: www.sbwr.org.sg

Note:
• Watch out for mosquitoes. Take repellent and/or wear long trousers.
• Watch out for the *kampong* dogs that are prone to hanging out inside the bus shelter.

Tip: If you have the energy, follow with a visit to Aero-Green Technology Farm, which is just opposite the entrance to Sungei Buloh.

Activities

The National Parks Board operates an all-year-round calendar of activities in its parks and nature reserves. Many, if not all, of these will appeal to children (according to their age). These quality, value-for-money (often free) activities take place in picturesque surroundings and are run by professionals.

There are also a variety of children's educational activities that offer a fun, interactive learning experience away from the classroom. Many of these will probably be coordinated through school groups but occasionally you can join them as an individual participant, especially for school holiday activities. Check out the National Parks website for an up-to-date listing of activities.

As well as being pleasant venues, the parks are also the sites of numerous educational workshops and courses for children, especially during the school holidays. Most of these take place within the Singapore Botanic Gardens, which is also managed by the National Parks Board.

Educational Programmes

These tours, which are held at the Singapore Botanic Gardens, are usually group events that require a minimum of 20, or a maximum of 25, participants. Topics covered include pond life, the eco-garden, heritage trees, herbs and spices, the rainforest, orchids and even a treasure hunt. Depending on the tour, children aged 5 and above can take part. You can register online or contact:

Educational Outreach
Singapore Botanic Gardens
National Parks Board

Cluny Road, Singapore 259569
Tel: 6471 9961

Holiday Workshops

During the school breaks, notably during November and December, a number of 1-day workshops are held within the Singapore Botanic Gardens. These workshops cover a variety of topics such as palms, the rainforest, Fruits for Thought, My Hari Raya and Christmas Garden and Herbarium — A Library of Plant Collectables. The workshops are usually targeted at children from K1 to P6, with the cost varying from $50 to $75 (including materials and refreshments). Register on the National Parks Board Website or contact the Educational Outreach division.

Other Outreach Programmes

Various informative activities are held throughout the year, which you can register for individually. In the past, these have included a Native Plant Hunt and a Plant Walk at Bukit Timah Nature Reserve. For activities specifically targeted for children, check out Sungei Buloh Wetland Reserve (e.g., the Dragonflies of Sungei Buloh nature trail) and the Singapore Botanic Gardens (e.g., the Singapore Botanic Gardens — Our Heritage tour).

Free Nature Appreciation Walks

Guided walks are conducted on a regular basis in some of the Parks and Nature Reserves:

Bukit Timah Nature Reserve

see p. 29

Fort Canning Park

Recognised as Heritage Trees, some of the majestic trees in Singapore's parks have taken decades and, in some cases, more than hundreds of years to mature. You can join a guided tour at this park to learn more about them.

Contact: 1800 471 7300 (Helpline for information about the scheme) / 6332 1200 (tour information)

MacRitchie Reservoir

The walk in MacRitchie is held every second Saturday of the month.

Contact: Ms Neo Lay Cheng (PUB) at 67313276 or email her at neo_lay_cheng@pub.gov.sg.

Singapore Botanic Gardens

see pp. 33 – 35

Sungei Buloh Wetland Reserve

see pp. 30 – 31

Note: Check the National Parks Board website (www.nparks.gov.sg) for any changes in schedules or call 1800 471 7300.

Other Events

In addition to these programmes, musical, dance and theatrical events are held from time to time at various park venues, but particularly at the Singapore Botanic Gardens (Tel: 6471 7361) and Fort Canning Park (Tel: 6332 1200).

The best way to keep up-to-date on up-and-coming events is to go to the News & Events link and look at the Calendar of Events section on the National Parks Board website (www.nparks.gov.sg). Alternatively, check the entertainment listings in *The Straits Times* or contact the venues direct.

SINGAPORE BOTANIC GARDENS

Some of my earliest memories from my preschool days were about flowers, insects and fish in big drains. I remember fallen flowers from the Angsana trees outside our home. I collected and kept them in a tin box. By the road there were the bright pink flowers of the prickly 'touch-me-not' Mimosa. They were so pretty and fresh in the mornings and I could always see lots of honeybees feeding from them. Sometimes we played in drains from where we could catch little fish that we kept in bottles.

When I grew older, I became aware that we shared the world with plants, insects, birds and other animals.

The world of nature is full of wonder, magic and many strange and interesting plants and animals. I learnt that all life on our planet Earth depends on plants. We enjoy plants and animals but we also have a responsibility to look after them.

–Dr Chin See Chung,
Director of the Singapore Botanic Gardens

In the Singapore Botanic Gardens, you can see primary rainforest, exotic, manicured gardens and tree-lined pathways. The site is divided into three cores: Tanglin, Central and Bukit Timah. It is a beautiful venue and one the whole family can enjoy. Young children can run around freely.

Opening hours: 5.00 a.m. to midnight. The National Orchid Garden is open from 8.30 a.m. to 7.00 p.m. (last ticket sale at 6.00 p.m.)

Price guide: Free (Admission to the National Orchid Garden is free for children (under 12 years) / $1 for students / $5 for adults.)

Location: 1 Cluny Road (Visitor Services Desk)

Note: The major entrances to the Gardens are at the Visitor Centre at the junction of Cluny and Nassim roads; Tanglin Gate at the junction of Holland and Napier roads; Cluny Park Gate along Cluny Park Road and Burkill Gate along Tyersall Avenue (with access to the National Orchid Garden and the Ginger Garden).

Tel: 6471 7361

Web: www.nparks.gov.sg (see under Parks & Gardens) / www.sbg.org.sg

Features:

Plant life: If your children aren't already interested in botany, this is a good place to start. Look out for Singapore's National Flower—Vanda Miss Joaqium in the National Orchid Garden (*see* next column). Visit the Sun Rockery, Palm Valley and enjoy the Park's Heritage Trees and primary rainforest.

Swiss Ball Fountain (Tanglin Core): Younger children are often fascinated by this 700-kilogramme ball as it spins around covered in trickling water. Nearby is the charming Lady on a Hammock sculpture and the Sundial Garden.

Swan Lake (Tanglin Core): This 15-hectare lake can be found near the Tanglin Gate entrance to the park. Your children can have fun spotting the swans, turtles and fish. At the Ecolake (in Bukit Timah Core), you can also see black swans.

Symphony Lake (Central Core): Besides ornamental fish, water plants such as water lilies abound here. The lake is also the setting for the Shaw Foundation Symphony Stage, a leading outdoor venue for musical performances in Singapore.

Evolution Garden (Central Core): A wonderful venue to walk around. This 1.5-hectare site offers a journey through time, showing the development of plant life from the Earth's beginnings through the dinosaur period and into the modern world. Look for some unusual footprints!

The National Orchid Garden: There are 1,100 orchid species and more than 2,250 orchid hybrids growing here, all of which provide a riot of colour. It is a pleasant venue to visit with children and even the younger ones can enjoy walking around the winding pathways.

Children's Garden: The Jacob Ballas Children's Garden, is in the Bukit Timah Core. It is a fun and fantasy garden dedicated to children with the theme, "All life on Earth depends on plants". Through play and exploration, children are be able to learn about the importance of plants and conservation. It is the first garden of its kind in Asia and there are a number of specialised programmes for young children held in this garden.

Dining: The Gardens are a wonderful picnic venue but there are also a number of food outlets within the grounds. Casa Verde (Tel: 6467 7326)

at the Visitor Centre is a convenient outdoor stop for families, with a taxi stand and toilets close by. Try the wood-fired pizza. It also serves breakfast and is open from 7.30 a.m. to 11.00 p.m. The Halia Restaurant (Tel: 6476 6711) at the Ginger Garden does a weekend brunch that is worth trying. Here you can eat in air-conditioned comfort or alfresco.

Another alternative is the food court at the Tanglin Gate. It is open from 7.00 a.m. to 10.30 p.m. daily and offers a wide selection of local food fare. Inside is air-conditioned.

If you just need refreshments or quick snacks, try The Garden Refreshment Kiosk (Tel: 6476 6711) near the Ginger Garden.

For a special treat, Au Jardin Les Amis (also near the Visitor Centre) has a Sunday brunch between 11.30 a.m. to 2.00 p.m. Call 6466 8812 for reservations.

Special Events: Keep a look out for some of the excellent outdoor entertainment events conducted within the Gardens. These are usually free and prove to be good family occasions. Previous events include Christmas Fiesta in the Park, Jazz in the Park and performances by the Singapore Symphony Orchestra.

Free guided tours of the Heritage Trees, the Rainforest, Evolution Garden and The National Orchid Garden are also held on a regular basis (some of these are conducted in Mandarin and Japanese). Check out what is on by visiting the Calendar of Events section on the Gardens' website.

Note: The Education Outreach Department of the Singapore Botanic Gardens conducts workshops and tours for children, particularly during the longer school breaks. For more information, go to www.sbg.org.sg and look under the Education section.

CHINESE AND JAPANESE GARDENS

These two scenic gardens are situated side by side. The Chinese Garden (also known as Jurong Gardens) features pagodas, huge weeping willow trees, curved bridges, courtyards and fountains while the Japanese Garden is more restrained and minimalist in its approach, with goldfish ponds, stone lanterns and hillocks.

Opening hours: 6.00 a.m. to 11.00 p.m. daily (Main Garden) / 9.00 a.m. to 6.00 p.m. daily (Bonsai Garden and Garden of Abundance)

Price guide: $4.50 for adults and $2 for children. Live Turtle and Tortoise Museum ($3 for children below 6 / $5 for adults) and the Garden of Abundance ($1 for children below 12 / $2 for adults), which also includes admission into the Bonsai Garden. An entrance fee to both Gardens is usually applicable during the Chinese

New Year period and when the Mid-Autumn Lantern Festival is on.

Location: 1 Chinese Garden Road, Singapore 619795
Tel: 6261 3632

Features: Unless otherwise stated, the features listed below can be found in the Chinese Garden. The Japanese Garden is designed to be much quieter, with koi-filled ponds spanned by bridges.

The Live Turtle and Tortoise Museum (Chinese Garden): This museum is worth visiting (open 10.00 a.m. to 7.00 p.m.). Here you can view about 50 different turtle species (including a two-headed turtle) that have been collected from around the world for over 30 years. There is an entrance fee (see Price guide).

Tel: 6268 5363
Web: www.turtle-tortoise.com

Bonsai Garden: Containing over 1,000 carefully manicured plants, this is the largest Suzhou-style bonsai garden outside China. There is an entrance fee (see Price guide).

Dining: As well as drink stalls, there is the Bamboo Grove Teahouse and a restaurant at the Stone Boat Lake. You can also have a picnic in either of the gardens.

High-rise Pagoda and 7-Storey Pagoda: For those so inclined, you can enter and go to the top of these pagodas — it's one sure way of tiring out the kids!

Garden of Abundance: Located by the lakeside, this peaceful garden has the added attraction of various statues (including the 12 Chinese zodiac characters) and a plethora of flowering and vegetative plants.

Note:

- One of the best times to visit the Gardens is during the Mid-Autumn Lantern Festival in September when the Chinese Garden is lit up at night.
- Umbrellas are available for loan at the main entrance or from the Bonsai Garden.
- A children's fairground with a merry-go-round and various rides is set up in the Chinese Garden at certain times of the year, notably during festive periods.
- Toilet facilities are available at the Stone Boat Lake Restaurant, the Bamboo Grove Teahouse and the Main Arch Building (all within the Chinese Garden).

HORTPARK

Spanning 23 hectares, HortPark is a one-stop gardening lifestyle hub. It is the first park in Asia to bring together gardening-related recreational, educational, research and retail activities under one roof within a park setting. Located in southern Singapore, the park links Telok Blangah Hill Park and Kent Ridge Park. It aims to promote gardening as a hobby for everyone, through hands-on educational and interactive activities and gardening events.

Features: 20 theme gardens, including a Herbs and Spices Garden with traditional, medicinal and culinary herbs found in Singapore and a Formal Tree Garden that uses flowers, manicured borders, tall hedging and an array of trees in the style of an English garden. The butterfly garden, featuring several rare species of butterflies, opens every last Saturday of the month from 9.00 a.m. to 12.00 p.m. Admission is free. This is quite an amazing sight as there are 500 butterflies in a small greenhouse. One might even land on your hand!

There are also three different playgrounds for children catering to different age groups. Children adore the playgrounds (my own son did not want to leave).

Activities: HortPark hosts year-round activities for everyone, including guided tours, plant fairs, gardening talks and workshops and educational activities.

MACRITCHIE RESERVOIR

This peaceful and attractive destination is managed by the Public Utilities Board (PUB). There is plenty of space for little ones to run around and things to see for older children who are interested in nature. It's hardly wild but it does offer a suitable distraction from the hurly-burly that so often constitutes life in Singapore. Here you can jog, walk or picnic. There are monkeys, turtles, butterflies, dragonflies, skinks, monitor lizards, birds and pitcher plants to see. Recreational fishing is also available. There is a snack bar near the main turtle area and a playground near the main entrance. There is also a "green" parking lot with 300 carparks.

Price guide: Free

Location: Upper Thompson Road

Features:

Free Nature Appreciation Walks: These are held once a month (*see* p. 32).

The HSBC TreeTop Walk: Suitable for older children, this is the highlight of several long hiking routes in MacRitchie that brings you through different stages of mature secondary forest. This free-standing suspension bridge connects the 2 highest points (Bukit Peirce and Bukit Kalang) in MacRitchie and offers a bird's eye view of the community of plants and animals that live in the forest canopy. The total length of the walkway is about 250 metres. This walkway can get crowded at weekends and on public holidays.

Opening hours: 9.00 a.m. to 5.00 p.m. Tuesdays to Fridays / 8.30 a.m. to 5.00 p.m. weekends and public holidays

Location: The HSBC TreeTop Walk is accessible from MacRitchie

Reservoir Park via the MacRitchie Nature Trail or from Venus Drive, off Upper Thomson Road.

Note: The distance to the entrance of the TreeTop Walk is approximately 4.5 kilometres (1½- to 2-hour walk) from the reservoir park and 2.5 kilometres (45 minutes to 1-hour walk) from the car park at Venus Drive. Therefore, a round trip including the TreeTop Walk is about 7 to 10 kilometres (3 to 5 hours depending on your walking pace).

Tips:

- An alternative for younger children is the 280-metre canopy walk at Kent Ridge Park. This bridge links the park to the museum, Reflections at Bukit Chandu. The walkway is accessible from Vigilante Drive followed by a 5-minute walk from Car Park B or from the end of Pepys Road.
- Don't feed the macaques. They will pursue you without remorse if they suspect you have available titbits. This can be frightening for adults as well as children.
- The nearby garden centres of Thomson Road are also worth a visit. If you are feeling hungry, try Peach Garden (Tel: 6451 3233) in Thompson Plaza for excellent dim sum (only a couple of bus stops away).

CAMPING

see Adventure Singapura!, pp. 71 – 73

PICNIC TIME!

Nothing beats eating alfresco in the great outdoors with family and friends. This can take many forms, ranging from the sophisticated, stylised vision of gingham cloth, wicker hamper and bottles of bubbly to an informal barbecue. Take your pick...or better still, ask the kids what they want!

Preparation and a pleasant venue are the key ingredients to any picnic. Here I've suggested a few venues and ideas that may inspire you and your family to try having a picnic. I haven't ventured to suggest what food to include — that's really up to you. However, I have included a checklist and tips about food storage and preparation.

Checklist

- Ice packs are useful. These can easily be made in advance at home, using seal-lock bags filled with ice cubes.
- Utensils, cutlery, paper napkins, plates and cups are a must. Paper plates and paper/plastic cups make for an easy picnic and are more child-friendly.
- If you're sitting on the ground, take a blanket or mat. Try putting talcum powder around your ground mat to deter ants. It may be messy but the smell and texture will keep them away.

- A garbage bag to clear up the mess is a must.
- Insect repellent, sunscreen and wet wipes are essential.
- Check if you need a corkscrew or bottle opener.
- If you have younger children with you, emergency entertainment packs are useful. Include items such as an inflatable ball, a bottle of bubbles, etc.
- Avoid soggy food! Pack sandwiches and toppings separately (this includes fillers such as lettuce and cucumber). The same applies for salads.
- If you are barbecuing, don't forget charcoal, matches, lighter fluid and serving utensils. Baking soda is a useful temporary fire extinguisher. Don't forget to check whether a pit booking is necessary or the park supports Bring Your Own Pit (BYOP).

Eating Wisely

Food safety is a consideration whenever and wherever you eat. In a hot and humid climate like Singapore's, the old adage to 'keep hot foods hot and cold foods cold' becomes even more pertinent.

- Food must be kept cold enough to prevent bacterial growth. Therefore, if you have a car, don't put the cooler in the boot/trunk. Instead put it inside the air-conditioned car. Once at your venue, keep the cooler in the shade.
- If you have takeaway foods such as fried chicken or barbecued beef, eat them within 2 hours of purchase as meat and poultry products can spoil very quickly. Similarly, sushi and sashimi should be eaten as soon as possible.
- Repeatedly opening a cooler that contains perishable food is not advisable. It is probably a good idea to store drinks separately.
- Avoid contact between raw meat and cooked food. A double set of tongs is a good idea.
- Meat and poultry products can contain bacteria that are only destroyed if they are cooked at sufficiently high temperatures (and then held at temperatures that are either too hot or cold for further bacterial growth). Hamburgers should be cooked until their centre is no longer pink and the juices are clear. They should not be partially grilled for further cooking later.
- Precooked meats should be heated until they are steaming hot.

Picnic Venues

National Parks

Popular venues include Pasir Ris, East Coast, West Coast, Marina Barrage, Fort Canning, Labrador, Bishan and Singapore Botanic Gardens.

Barbecue pits are available at Changi Beach, East Coast, Labrador, Pasir Ris, Punggol, Sembawang and West Coast. You can either book a barbecue pit by contacting NParks or through AXS Stations islandwide (www.axs.com.sg) or simply visit the NParks website for online booking www.nparks.com.sg

Offshore

Kusu and St John's islands

Picnics-to-go

The following vendors can help supply you with a picnic:

The Coffee Bean & Tea Leaf

Coffee Bean's party packs feature mini quiches, scone sets, mini pizzas, sandwiches, canapés and cakes. A particularly good bargain is $26 for 20 mini pizzas, puffs, quiches, sandwiches or mini tarts. A minimum of 4 days is required to prepare your order and pick-up is preferred.

Tel: 6272 0036

Web: www.coffeebean.com.sg

Délifrance

Délifrance offers a range of sandwiches, savoury snacks and sweet bakery items. Prices start from $16 for 12 assorted mini pizza baguettes. There is a $15 delivery charge for orders below $100, except Jurong Island and Tuas (the delivery charge is $30 for orders below $100 to these areas).

Tel: 6324 4333

Web: www.delifrance.com.sg

Kyo Cakes

You can order excellent value sandwich sets from $4 to $5.50 per set. These sets contain fruit, cakes and pastries, etc. The company also does party sets, cakes and high tea sets (latter for larger groups only).

Tel: 6556 1311

Web: www.kyo.com.sg

Note:

- Minimum order of $50
- $10 delivery charge for orders below $100
- Additional $2 delivery charge for CBD area
- Subject to acceptance for delivery at weekends and on public holidays

Marmalade At Home

Marmalade offers an extensive range of canapés and desserts, from which you can select seven items for $25+++ per person, as well as sandwich platters (20 pieces) from $22+++. A delivery charge is applicable.

Tel: 6883 2258

Web: www.themarmaladepantry.com

Something To Go (at the Regent Hotel)

Enjoy a fantastic range of takeaways including picnic baskets, party platters, salads and desserts.

Tel: 6725 3244

Email: somethingtogo.rsn@fourseasons.com

Sakae Sushi

For those who fancy some Asian finger food, Sakae Sushi does deliveries as well. They have lovely party trays starting from $43. A minimum order of $30 is required for every delivery and there is a delivery charge of $4. Note that sushi ordered in sweltering Singapore should be consumed within 2 hours to prevent it turning bad.

Tel: 6338 8383
Web: www.sakaedelivery.com

Othor Options

Apart from the above vendors, try Cold Storage supermarkets or the Swiss Butchery for marinated meats. City Satay can supply sticks of uncooked pork, chicken, beef and mutton satay, chicken wings as well as satay rice. Try any BreadTalk outlet in Singapore as well for its amazing buns.

Swiss Butchery: 30/32 Greenwood Avenue / 56 Tanglin Road, #01-02, / Coronation Shopping Plaza, #01-05 587 Bukit Timah Road,
Tel: 6468 7588 (Greenwood Avenue) / 6235 8080 (Tanglin Road) / 6463 8080 (Coronation Shopping Plaza)
Web: www.swiss-butchery.com.sg/)
City Satay: 326 Tanjong Katong Road
Tel: 6345 6676
Web: www.citysatay.com)

Special Events

If you really do need an excuse, the following events all lend themselves nicely to a picnic:

- WOMAD
- Ballet under the Stars (Keep a look out for other special events that take place in Fort Canning Park.)
- Just about any musical, theatrical or dance performance that is held at the Singapore Botanic Gardens

NATURAL HABITATS

Chek Jawa (Pulau Ubin)

One of the highlights of visiting Pulau Ubin is the fragile marine habitat that constitutes Chek Jawa. Chek Jawa is made up of mangrove swamps, mudflats and seagrass beds. The area is rich in marine life and there is an enormous variety of colourful sea sponges to be observed at low tide. Here you may also see flying foxes, stick insects, junglefowl, dog-toothed cat snakes, wild pigs, otters, seashore nutmeg trees, sea anemones, sea cucumbers, cow fishes, octopuses, starfish, horseshoe crabs, sea urchins and sea grasses. A boardwalk, a viewing jetty and a 21-metre viewing tower has been built to facilitate visitors to this wetland paradise. Do check the tide times on the NParks Chek Jawa page and time your visit to coincide with low tide to see the myriad variety of marine life.

Location: Southeastern corner of Pulau Ubin (You will need to get a bumboat across from Changi Jetty to Pulau Ubin.)
Tel: 6542 4108 (NParks Pulau Ubin Hotline)

Visiting Chek Jawa

To find out more about how to get a bumboat to Pulau Ubin, *see* Pulau Ubin under the National Parks Board section featured earlier in this chapter.

- If you would like a more intimate guided tour of Chek Jawa and not just walk on the boardwalks you need to visit the NParks website to do a booking. Tours are popular and are taken up to 6 months in advance, so book early to avoid disappointment. You'll be given a booking number which you need to register with the officer on duty at the basketball court, opposite Pulau Ubin Community Centre, on the day of your visit.
- You can then cycle or take a 20-minute trip by local taxi-van to Chek Jawa. The vans have PU license plates and can be found near Ubin Jetty. It costs about $2 for a one-way trip.
- Upon reaching Chek Jawa, guides take visitors for a 45-minute walk along a designated route to see the marine life at the mudflats.

Tips:

- Wear closed shoes with hard soles.
- A change of clothing is useful (there are no rain shelters).
- Pack insect repellent and sunblock.
- Take a water bottle.

Note:

- There are no toilet facilities – Ubin Jetty is your nearest stop!
- As it is an outdoor habitat that can get very hot, it is not a suitable venue for children below 5.

Mangroves

Nature enthusiasts will welcome the opportunity to visit the rich and important habitat that makes up a mangrove. Here you will see a great diversity of animal and plant life and the unique characteristics that enable mangrove trees to survive in levels of salt and low oxygen.

Two areas of Singapore's remaining mangrove forests are conserved: Sungei Buloh Wetland Reserve and Pasir Ris Park. These areas are recommended for visits as they both have facilities.

Tips:

- Wear light cotton clothes and comfortable walking shoes.
- When visiting these areas, take sufficient water, snacks, an umbrella (for rain or sun), mosquito repellent, binoculars, camera, hats and a change of clothing.
- While mosquito repellent is an advisable precaution, liberal doses may drive away insects that you wish to observe.

Note: Mangrove swamps are not the best places to take young children. The swamps can get very hot and the mud can be slippery in places. However, older children will undoubtedly find the strange tree roots and the tree crabs, mudskippers, mud lobsters, monitor lizards and other wildlife fascinating. If you can, investigate with your child what a mangrove is and what you can expect to see before venturing forth.

SINGAPORE ZOO

This is a first-class open zoo and the regular destination of many stroller-pushing parents. There are some 2,530 animals across 315 species in this 28-hectare site that are housed in landscaped areas, separated from visitors by primarily natural barriers, such as dry and wet moats. Although it will appeal to children of all ages, the Zoo is really a superb facility for younger ones and I'd recommend becoming a Friend of the Zoo if you have children below the age of 12 (*see* Price Guide).

Opening hours: 8.30 a.m. to 6.00 p.m. daily

Price guide: $ 13 for children (3 to 12 years) / $20 for adults / free for Friends of the Zoo. The Friends of the Zoo scheme includes various benefits such as a quarterly newsletter (which will appeal to children 8 years and above) and notification of special events and discounts at various outlets in the Zoo. Annual membership costs $192.60 (after GST) for a family of 2 adults and 3 children (3 to 12 years) or $85.60 for an individual.

Location: 80 Mandai Lake Road, Singapore 729826
Tel: 6269 3411
Web: www.zoo.com.sg

Features: Some of the Zoo's key attractions for children and their families include:

Rainforest Kidzworld: This attraction incorporates all the fun for kids in one place. There is a water play area themed like a wet animal wonderland with a massive bucket that tips over and splashes the kids ever so often (children love this). There is a dry play area as well themed the "Rainforest Challenge" with a flying fox and a dinosaur walk. Pony and horse carriage rides are also available. Pony rides are $6 a child (aged 3 to 12 years) and horse carriage rides are $6 a person. There is a petting zoo with goats, bunnies, guinea pigs and falabellas (the world's smallest breed of horses) and a Kampung House with creepy crawlies in the drawers. Watch out for the grooming sessions and feeding times at the kids zoo!

Important: To avoid disappointment, do check on the zoo's website that the water playground is not scheduled for maintenance on the day you wish to go to the zoo.

Animal Feeding Programme: There are token feedings of the animals and live commentaries given by their keepers throughout the day. Popular highlights include the contact sessions with the giant Aldabra tortoise at 1.15 p.m. on Sundays and the Komodo Dragons (at 2.00 p.m. on Sundays). Times can change so it is advisable to request a schedule upon arrival at the Zoo.

Animal Shows: Animal shows are held daily but request a schedule upon arrival at the Zoo as show times do change occasionally. The shows are:

- Rainforest Fights Back Show (12.30 p.m. and 2.30 p.m.) at the Shaw Foundation Amphitheatre
- Splash Safari Show (10.30 a.m. and 5.00 p.m.) showcases marine animals. It is held at the Shaw Foundation Amphitheatre as well.
- Elephants at Work & Play (11.30 a.m. and 3.30 p.m.) at the Elephants of Asia exhibit.

Fragile Forest: This man-made rainforest offers an experience like no other. Here, you can find sloths, tamanduas, fruit bats, mousedeer, tree kangaroos, parrots, tree ducks, pigeons and rufted lemurs co-existing peacefully. If you are wearing a brightly coloured T-shirt, expect to become the landing site for numerous butterflies! Children below the age of 3 may be a little frightened of the close proximity of the butterflies but older ones will love it.

The Wild Discoverer Tours of the zoo: ($25 per adult and $15 per child) will take you behind the scenes of the Fragile Forest and Reptile Garden and you will experience a Great Rift Valley of Ethopia feeding tour (imagine tossing a baboon its favourite treat!).

Reptile Garden: There is something about snakes that both fascinate and frighten children. My son insists on visiting the snake enclosure every time we visit the Zoo and has done so since he was very small! Here, you can get up close to a King Cobra, corn snake and pit viper, among others, with only a glass panel between you. For the more ambitious, there is also a walkway where the reptiles move around freely.

Other animal exhibits include Australian Outback, Wild Africa, Hamadryas Baboons, Cat Country, Elephants of Asia, various underwater exhibits and the world's first orangutan free-ranging area.

Animal Rides: The opportunity to ride a pony or elephant always finds plenty of takers! Elephant rides are available from 1.00 p.m. to 2.00 p.m. and 4.30 p.m. to 5.30 p.m for $8 per child. Pony rides are from 10.00 a.m. to 5.00 p.m. at Rainforest Kidz World for $6 a child.

Horse-carriage rides are held every day from 10.30 a.m. to noon and 1.00 p.m. to 4.00 p.m. It's $6 per person.

Tram Ride: The Zoo can get hot during the day and walking around can become tiring. These factors can present a challenge at times for those with young children. Fortunately, there is a tram service from the entrance that does a circuit of the Zoo, stopping at three points after the point of departure. You can join it at any of these stops. It costs $3 for children (3 to 12 years) and $5 for adults for unlimited tram rides.

Dining: The Zoo has several food outlets. Snacks and drinks can be purchased at the Cheers minimart near the entrance or you can eat fast food before you enter the Zoo and at Children's World Playland. There are food and drink kiosks near the Fragile Forest and the Elephant rides.

In the centre of the Zoo are its Restaurants in the Wild, which offer a selection of eating venues. Choose ice cream from Ben & Jerry's Ice Cream Scoop Shop or enjoy the forest-themed ambiance of Ah Meng Restaurant, which offers local fare.

Located at the Zoo entrance is a pizza outlet, where individual slices can be purchased. There is also an Ah Meng Kopi outlet, which is a coffee and kaya toast outlet.

There are drink dispensers throughout the Zoo and at times a mobile stand dispenses free cold Milo. However, I'd still recommend carrying a water bottle.

If you are seeking a unique animal-dining experience, check out the Zoo's Jungle Breakfast — with Wildlife. This is held daily at 9.00 a.m. You can watch the elephants being bathed from a distance and meet the orangutans. It costs $16 per child (6 to 12 years old) and $25 per adult (excluding admission to the Zoo).

Tips:

- You can rent a stroller for $9 at the entrance or a wagon for $18. For the more adventurous, you could rent a motorised scooter. Locker rental is also available for $3.
- My favourite time to visit the Zoo is around 9.00 a.m. to 9.30 a.m., soon after the animals have been fed. You'll be able to view them more easily as most will still be at the front of their enclosures eating their breakfast. It's also not too hot then and when it comes to going home, you should avoid the taxi queues.

Note: The Zoo organises a lot of popular special events for children. These include Lantern Festival celebrations, Halloween fun, Christmas events, World Animal Day contests and Chinese New Year activities.

NIGHT SAFARI

The Night Safari is the world's first night zoo. Through the use of subtle lighting techniques, visitors are able to view over 1,000 nocturnal animals across 115 species in spacious naturalistic habitats. You can explore it by foot or take a tram ride.

Opening hours: 7.30 p.m. to midnight daily (ticket sales end at 11.00 p.m.)

Price guide: $21 for children (3 to 12 years) / $32 for adults

Location: Next to the Singapore Zoological Gardens, Mandai Lake Road
Tel: 6269 3411
Web: www.nightsafari.com.sg

Features:

Animals: The Night Safari has various animal exhibits. Highlights include the tapir and elephants of the Asia Riverine Forest, the majestic Gir lions of the Indian subcontinent and the giant anteater of the South American Pampas.

Walking Trails: There are three walking trails — Fishing Cat, Leopard and Forest Giants (primary forest) — each of which is approximately 0.5 km long. These trails are connected by walkways.

Shows: Look out for Creatures of the Night at 7.30 p.m., 8.30 p.m., 9.30 p.m. and 10.30 p.m. (10.30 p.m. shows only on Fridays, Saturdays and eve of public holidays) at the Entrance Plaza.

Dining: Choose from Bongo Burgers next to the Night Safari entrance or indulge in your favourite ice cream from Ben & Jerry's Ice Cream Scoop Shop. You can dine at Ulu Ulu Safari Restaurant, which serves local cuisine and other Asian fare. Food is available à la carte or from an extensive buffet. Nightly cultural performances are also held in the restaurant. Light refreshments are also available at the East Lodge.

Tram Ride: This ride takes about 45 minutes to complete. A live commentary is given for the duration of the ride and there is one stopover at the East Lodge. The tram ride is complimentary with entrance to the Night Safari. The last train leaves Station 1 at 11.15 p.m.

JURONG BIRDPARK

A popular venue with families, Jurong BirdPark is Southeast Asia's largest bird park and home to more than 4,600 birds representing 380 species from around the world. The BirdPark's exhibits and aviaries are specially designed to closely resemble the natural habitats of their inhabitants. Lakes and paddocks are built to display water birds and other large flightless birds such as ostriches, rheas, emus and cassowaries.

Opening hours: 9.00 a.m. to 6.00 p.m daily

Price guide: $12 for children (3 to 12 years) / $18 for adults (Discounts are available from time to time so watch out for offers/tokens in newspapers as well as notices on the BirdPark website. Special family packages are also an option and combo packages include entry to the Singapore Zoological Gardens/ Night Safari.)

If you and your family are regular visitors to the BirdPark, you should consider taking out membership under the Feather Friends scheme. This membership will give you unlimited access to the park as well as various other benefits. It costs $192.60 for family membership (2 adults and 3 children below 12 years) / $85.60 for individual membership.

Location: 2 Jurong Hill, Singapore 628925 (off Jalan Ahmad Ibrahim)
Tel: 6265 0022
Email: info@birdpark.com.sg
Web: www.birdpark.com.sg

Features:

Panorail: $3 for children (3 to 12 years) / $5 for adults. (Because of the heat, I'd recommend including this in your visit if you have young children in tow. However, it can get very crowded as the day goes on, especially at weekends.)

Shows: The BirdPark has an excellent programme of shows that runs throughout the day. I've not listed times here because they do change so your best bet is to pick up a schedule upon arrival at the BirdPark or refer to its website. Don't miss the Birds of Prey (at 10.00 a.m. and 4.00 p.m. at the Fuji Hawk Walk) and Birds 'n Buddies (at 11.00 a.m. and 3.00 p.m. at the Pools Amphitheatre) shows. Also look out for the children's parrot show (at 1.00 p.m. at the Pools Amphitheatre) during which the birds mimic and a cockatoo named Picasso draws using his own easel. Another highlight is the daily thunderstorm inside the Southeast Asian Birds Aviary. On cue at midday, it rains and there are special thunder effects.

Bird Exhibits: Penguin Parade, Parrot Paradise, Birds of Paradise, Southeast Asian Birds Aviary, Hornbills and Toucans, World of Darkness (nocturnal birds), The Riverine, Jungle Jewels, Swan Lake and the spectacular Waterfall Aviary. The Lory Loft is a must-see. This walk-in aviary has an elevated boardwalk, suspension bridges and a two-tiered central feeding tower, from which you have the opportunity to feed birds by hand with nectar. There are over 1,000 lories, including the stunning Rainbow Lory.

Playtime: As well as a pleasant, covered soft-fall children's play area near the main restaurant at the Lodge, there is a super adventure playground next to the picnic area (behind the Fuji Hawk Walk). Purporting to be Singapore's only wet and dry playground without a splash pool, the Splash 'n' Slide station is great fun! It has a very large, soft-fall adventure playground, with slides and bouncy rides. Next to this is the water play area that features water cannons, jet sprays and geysers. This playground offers a welcome respite from the heat of the Park that your children are unlikely to resist! (Don't forget to take a change of clothing.) There is also an excellent changing facility that has baby changing tables, children's toilets and showers.

Special Events: Past events for children have included Hocus Pocus Night, Scarecrow Carnival and Children's Day celebrations. Such events are tremendously popular and usually include free goodies. Admission fees are often discounted. Find out more by looking under Promotions and Events in the Calendar of Events section on the BirdPark website and in the daily newspapers.

Dining: Options include the Hawk Café at the park entrance which incorporates a Ben & Jerry's Ice Cream Scoop Shop and the African-themed, fully air-conditioned Bongo Burgers, which has a breakfast menu at weekends and on public holidays from 8.30 a.m. to 11.00 a.m. Visitors who purchase a breakfast from Hawk Café will receive a complimentary ticket to the Early Bird Breakfast Show.

Snack kiosks and refreshments are also available throughout the park, including good coffee at the entrance to the Lory Loft!

Education: The BirdPark's Learning Centre conducts a number of programmes that will fascinate children of all ages. Most of these are available to school groups but you may be able to join some as an individual participant. There are half-day and overnight camps, conservation programmes, special 1-hour tours as well as a 30-minute programme for preschoolers.

Others: Observe the world's tallest man-made waterfall, ride on the cool, air-conditioned panorail or browse around the souvenir shop where there are some colourful children's T-shirts and a selection of soft toys.

Tip: The BirdPark can get very hot, so it is advisable to carry a water bottle and apply sunblock. If you have the energy, a trip to the swimming/water complex at Jurong East makes for a fun, cool ending to the day.

FARM TOURS

There are a number of farms in Singapore that are open for public viewing. These farms are educational and interesting venues away from the shopping malls, precincts and general construction of Singapore. However, I would note that they are usually highly specialist in nature. Therefore, a farm visit here should not be compared to those farms in Australia or Europe, where you can expect to see a variety of animals, pick your own fruit or enjoy a farmhouse tea, etc.

Farm visits can get very hot, so do carry a bottle of water and don't forget sun protection. Younger children (below the age of 6) may find the visits very tiring and you really need to join a tour group or have a car to get around. That said, a farm visit or two is definitely worth planning. It helps that many of the farms are in the same area, off Neo Tiew and Lim Chu Kang roads in northwestern Singapore. This area is the largest Agrotech Park in Singapore and occupies 858 hectares, about 16 times the size of the Singapore Botanic Gardens!

Kranji Countryside Association

A number of farms are members of the Kranji Countryside Association, which has been set up to promote awareness and an appreciation of Singapore's countryside and natural environment. These farms have a genuine interest in educating the public.

Member Farms:

- Aero-Green Technology
  (Tel: 6792 4298)
- Bollywood Veggies
  (Tel: 6898 5001)
- Fire Flies Health Farm
  (Tel: 6793 7875)
- Hausmann Marketing Aquarium
  (Tel: 6792 1318)
- Hay Dairies
  (Tel: 6792 0931)
- Jurong Frog Farm
  (Tel: 6791 7229)
- Kin Yan Agrotech
  (Tel: 6794 8368)
- Max Koi Farm
  (Tel: 6862 6363)
- Nyee Phoe
  (Tel: 6793 6500)
- Thow Kwang Industry (this amazing pottery is further away.)
  (Tel: 62686121)

Features:

- Most of these farms sell their produce on site. Admission is free but a small charge is applicable for guided tours.
- You can stop off for something to eat at the Poison Ivy Bistro at Bollywood Veggies (Tel: 6898 5001) or Pedals & Leaf Bistro at Nyee Phoe (Gardenasia) (Tel: 6793 6500).
- The Kranji Express bus service operates daily from Kranji MRT Station between 9.00 a.m. and 5.00 p.m. A round trip costs $1 per child / $3 per adult and will take you to all member farms of the Kranji Countryside Association.

  Email: info@kranjicountryside.com
  Web: www.kranjicountryside.com
  (you can request a bus timetable)

Recommended Farms

There are a lot of farms to visit but my family's highlights include:

Aero-Green Technology

As Singapore's first commercial

aeroponics farm, this enterprise offers pesticide-free vegetables from a 5.3-hectare site. I'd recommend the guided tour as our host was informative and didn't ignore his younger audience.

Features: You can see rock melon, long beans, okra (Ladies' fingers), cherry tomatoes, etc. At weekends, you can harvest your own vegetables for a reasonable cost. Potted plants, vegetables, fresh lettucinno juice and starter kits are available for sale as well as snacks and refreshments.

Opening hours: 9.30 a.m. to 4.30 p.m. daily for public visits

Price guide: Admission is free. Guided tours for groups are available at cost (booking required).

Location: Plot LCK, 114 Neo Tiew Crescent (in Lim Chu Kang Agrotechnology Park), Singapore 718925

Tel: 6792 4298

Web: www.aerogreentech.com.sg

Note: While being a very active commercial enterprise, this farm is also well geared towards visitors. Children aged 8 and above will enjoy visiting this farm.

Bollywood Veggies

Organic fruits, vegetables and herbs are grown on this 10-hectare farm.

Features: Poison Ivy Bistro, the on-site restaurant, uses produce from the farm and is worth visiting.

Opening hours: 9.00 a.m. to 6.00 p.m. (Wednesdays to Sundays and public holidays)

Price guide: Admission is $2 per person. Guided tours for groups are available for a fee. Booking is required.

Location:100 Neo Tiew Road, Singapore 719026

Tel: 6898 5001

Web: www.bollywoodveggies.com

Farmart Centre

This farm places its emphasis on retail but for younger children it offers an instant farm mall. Kids can stroke the goats and rabbits, fish for small koi in the ponds or feed the turkeys.

Features: The farm boasts Singapore's only bee farm, fishing ponds, pet shops, a petting zoo, food outlets and produce shops.

Opening hours: 10.00 a.m. to 8.00 p.m. Mondays to Saturdays / 9.00 a.m. to 8.00 p.m. Sundays and public holidays (It is best to arrive after 11.00 a.m. when everything should be open.)

Price guide: Free admission. Guided tours run from Tuesdays to Saturdays (call 9450 0752).

Location: 67 Sungei Tengah Road, Singapore 699008

Tel: 6767 0070

Email: farmart@singnet.com.sg

Web: www.farmart.com.sg

Note: Have a phone at hand to call for a taxi afterwards. Alternatively, a shuttle bus runs from Chua Chu Kang Bus Interchange to the farm.

Green Circle Eco-Farm

This is an organic, vegetable farm that does not use artificial chemicals. There is no vegetable shop in the farm. Home delivery is available or customers can pre-order and collect from the farm. Delivery is free for orders of $6 and above.

Features: Visitors are welcome but guided tours are available for groups only (for about $6 per person for groups of 30). The farm also organises home-organic farming courses and health-related activities, which may involve a tour of the farm, harvesting some vegetables and a cooking lesson. Student education programmes are also available for school groups.

Opening hours: 9.00 a.m. to 6.00 p.m.

Location: 41 Neo Tiew Road
Singapore 719028
Tel: 6861 9286
Email: soo@pacific.net.sg
Web: www.greencircle.com.sg

Hay Dairies

At Singapore's only goat farm, there are about 1,000 goats of mixed breed that produce milk for sale.

Features: The farm a welcomes visitors on organised excursions or family outings (call to confirm). An educational tour is also available for $3 per person. Milking sessions last from 9.00 a.m. to 11.00 a.m. so visitors are encouraged to come in the morning. Milking demonstrations and briefings are held at 30-minute intervals at the following times: 9.00 a.m. 9.30 a.m., 10.00 a.m. and 10.30 a.m.

Opening hours: 9.00 a.m. to 4.00 p.m. daily

Location: No. 3 Lim Chu Kang Lane 4 (off Lim Chu Kang Road),
Singapore 718859
Tel: 6792 0931
Web: www.haydairies.com.sg

Jurong Frog Farm (JFF Pte Ltd)

Features: There are some 30,000 bullfrogs here! You can also see tadpoles and buy frogs for consumption.

Opening hours: 7.00 a.m. to 6.00 p.m.

Price guide: Admission is free. Guided tours that last 38 minutes are available for $2 per person / $3.50 with a bottle of bullfrog essence or an educational booklet.

Location: 56 Lim Chu Kang Lane 6 (off Lim Chu Kang Road),
Singapore 719764
Tel: 6791 7229
Web: www.jurongfrogfarm.com.sg
Email: sales@jurongfrogfarm.com.sg

Lian Wah Hang Farm

This is the only farm in Singapore that specially breeds game birds and produces meat and eggs for the local and overseas markets.

Features: Here you can see quails, partridges, guinea fowl, pigeons, turkeys, ducks and chickens. You can sample as well as purchase cooked and fresh quail eggs. Herbs and quails that are used to make various herbal tonic soups are also available for sale and you can taste the different types of herbal soups on Sundays. The friendly owner, Uncle William, specialises in farm tours of Singapore as well. His website is at: www.unclewilliam.biz/history.html. and he can be contacted via his mobile phone at 9450 0752.
Opening hours: 10.00 a.m. to 4.00 p.m. (Mondays to Saturdays) / 11.00 a.m. to 4.00 p.m. (Sundays)

Location: 5 Lim Chu Kang Lane 6F (within Lim Chu Kang's Agrotechnology Park), Singapore 718918
Tel: 6792 1366

Oh Chin Huat Hydroponics Farms

Oh Farms was the first company to supply fresh local herbs to the Singaporean market. It also grows temperate climate vegetables such as butterhead lettuce. All produce is notably pesticide free.
Features: The farm specialises in the hydroponic (soil free/ nutrient solution growing medium) production of leafy produce. You can purchase potted herbs, pesticide-free vegetables and starter kits. Guided farm tours can be arranged by advanced booking at $2.50 per person. There are two different tours: the Hydroponics Farm Tour and the Herb and Spices Tour.
Opening hours: 9.00 a.m. to 5.00 p.m. daily.

Location: 14A Bah Soon Pah Road (within Nee Soon Agrotechonology Park), Singapore 769970
Tel: 6753 8011
Email: ohfarms@singnet.com.sg
Web: www.ohfarms.com.sg

Orchidville

Covering 43 hectares, Orchidville is Singapore's largest tropical orchid farm just outside the Singapore Zoological Gardens.
Features: This farm grows over 2 million orchids plants producing over 10 million orchid sprays a year. Educational workshops are run for school groups. There is a rainforest-themed restaurant — Forrest — that offers Chinese cuisine.

Opening hours: 8.00 a.m. to 5.00 p.m. (weekdays and Sundays) / Closes at 10.30 p.m. on Saturdays / Closes 3.00 p.m. on public holidays
Price guide: Admission is free.

Location: 10 Lorong Lada Hitam (within Mandai Agrotechnology Park), Singapore 778793
Tel: 6552 7003
Email: orchid45@singnet.com.sg
Web: www.orchidville.com.sg

Qian Hu Fish Farm

This is a high-technology, factory-style ornamental fish farm that breeds many species of fish, including the endangered South American catfish and the exclusive Southeast Asian Arowana (Dragon) fish.

Features: This farm has about 200 species of fish and you can purchase koi and goldfish. Children will enjoy longkang fishing at the Agro-Education Centre.

Opening hours: 9.00 a.m. to 6.00 p.m. (Mondays to Thursdays) / 9.00 a.m. to 7.00 p.m. (Fridays to Sundays)

Price guide: Free admission. Guided tours are available at a cost.

Location: 71 Jalan Lekar, Sungei Tengah, Singapore 698950
Tel: 6766 7087
Web: www.qianhu.com

Note: A free shuttle bus service operates between Choa Chu Kang and Boon Lay MRT stations and the farm.

Kranji Nature Trail

If you are visiting farms in the Kranji vicinity, why not make a day of it and go to Sungei Buloh Wetland Reserve (*see* pp. 30 – 31) or Kranji Nature Trail? The latter is a 2-kilometre rugged nature trail that links two wetlands — Kranji Reservoir Park and Sungei Buloh Wetland Reserve. Here you can see grassland, secondary rainforest, mangroves and the seashore. Look out — a crocodile was once spotted in the mangroves!

UNDERWATER WORLD SINGAPORE

see also Sentosa under Where to Go?, p. 217

Opening hours: Underwater World and Dolphin Lagoon — 9.00 a.m. to 9.00 p.m. daily (last entry at 8.30 p.m.)

Price guide: Children (3 to 12 years) $17.60 / Children (under 3) Free / Adults $25.90 (entry to both Underwater World and Dolphin Lagoon). Packages are available, check the website for details.

Location: Siloso Point (Underwater World) and Palawan Beach (Dolphin Lagoon), Sentosa
Tel: 6275 0030
Web: www.sentosa.com.sg / www.underwaterworld.com.sg

BUTTERFLY PARK AND INSECT KINGDOM

see also Sentosa under Where to Go?, p. 216

Opening times: 9.00 a.m. to 7.00 p.m. daily

Price guide: $10 for children / $16 for adults

Location: Imbiah Lookout, Sentosa
Phone: 6275 0013
Web: www.jungle.com.sg

CROCODILES

If crocodiles fascinate your children, why not visit a crocodile farm besides the Zoo and the Night Safari?

Singapore Crocodile Farm

Features: Established in 1945, this commercial farm breeds crocodiles and other reptiles for their skins. For individual visitors, a free tour can be provided upon request (please call beforehand to confirm). The farm can also organise special educational packages for schools.
Opening hours: 9.00 a.m. to 6.00 p.m.
Price guide: Free

Location: 790 Upper Serangoon Road Singapore 534660
Tel: 6288 9385
Email: tmh@pacific.net.sg
Web: www.singaporecrocfarm.com

PETS

The Centre for Animal Welfare and Control (CAWC)

The CAWC offers a number of services related to animal welfare and control. It also has a strong animal welfare education programme that may interest your child, whether you have a pet or not or plan to get one. You can visit its resource centre which comprises a seminar room, library and pet poster gallery. Here you can listen to talks and watch pet-related videos (CAWC will also give outside talks to groups). Library use is currently by appointment. There are also a number of free publications available pertaining to pet care.

The theme of the resource centre is 'Towards Responsible Pet Ownership'. The goal of the centre is to provide pet owners with information on pets and pet care. By doing this, CAWC aims to ensure that pet owners understand and meet the responsibilities that come with owning a pet.

Location: 75 Pasir Panjang Road, Singapore 118507
Tel: 6471 9987

> *Pets can make wonderful companions but we must remember that a pet is a life-long commitment. They require our care and companionship for the rest of their lives and we must always remember that they have feelings too and are capable of feeling pain and suffering. If you want to own a pet, you must consider whether or not you have the time to look after it, otherwise the animal could end up neglected or unwanted.*
>
> **–Deirdre Moss, Executive Officer, SPCA (Singapore)**

Email: ava_cawc@ava.gov.sg
Web: www.ava.gov.sg (look under Animals & Pet Sector/Sales of Pets.)

Animal Concerns Research and Education Society (Acres)

Acres hosts a number of animal welfare campaigns both in Singapore and throughout Asia. It also works to raise awareness on a variety of animal welfare issues by giving talks and conducting road shows in schools, at public events and at other venues. The Acres office is open from Mondays to Fridays from 9.00 a.m. to 5.00 p.m.

Location: Acres Wildlife Rescue Centre 91 Jalan Lekar Singapore 698917
Tel: 68929821 / 9783 7782 (Wildlife Crime Hotline)
Email: info@acres.org.sg
Web: www.acres.org.sg

How to Adopt a Pet

If you've decided to get a pet, why not consider adopting an abandoned animal? A good place to visit is the Society for the Prevention of Cruelty to Animals (SPCA).

Alternatively, try Action for Singapore Dogs (ASD), the Cat Welfare Society (CWS) or The House Rabbit Society of Singapore (HRSS). You can also look at notice boards in supermarkets and apartments/condominiums. For further choices and other pets, there are plenty of pet shops around.

For those concerned about moving and taking a pet overseas, it is possible to do so as long as your pet meets certain requirements. A basic requirement is that your pet has lived with you in Singapore for more than six months. Most countries will also require proof that your pet is rabies-free. Allow plenty of time to check the regulations of the country you're moving to, as these will vary, including the length of the quarantine period.

Society for the Prevention of Cruelty to Animals (SPCA)

The SPCA runs the largest animal shelter in Singapore and receives over 1,000 unwanted animals each month. This registered animal charity is very active in promoting the care and needs of all pets through education and adoption. Adoption of animals is free of charge but you have to pay for compulsory medical expenses such as sterilisation. A counsellor is at hand to answer queries and provide information.

Opening times: 10.00 a.m. to 4.00 p.m. (Mondays to Saturdays, except Thursdays when it is closed) / 11.00 a.m. to 3.30 p.m. (Sundays and public holidays.)

Location: 31 Mount Vernon Road, Singapore 368054
Tel: 6287 5355

Email: education@spca.org.sg
Web: www.spca.org.sg

Action for Singapore Dogs (ASD)

This non-profit organisation finds new homes for animals that have been abandoned, are homeless or at the request of people who genuinely have to give them up.

Tel: 61002737 / 9259 0698
Email: info@asdsingapore.com
Web: www.asdsingapore.com

Cat Welfare Society (CWS)

The Cat Welfare Society is a non-profit organisation that is run entirely by volunteers who want to improve the welfare of stray cats in Singapore.

Email: info@catwelfare.org
Web: www.catwelfare.org

Mdm Wong's Shelter

A shelter for abandoned animals, this organisation is helmed by a kind lady named Mdm Wong. The shelter is kept running by her and her team of volunteers. They rescue abandoned animals (some of which are sick or abused), provide care for them and then try to re-home them. Check out their website for adoption and volunteering opportunities.

Location: 18 Pasir Ris Farmway 2 Ericsson Pet Farm Block 14 Shelter
Email: mdmwongshelter@hotmail.com
Web: http://mdmwongsshelter.wordpress.com

The House Rabbit Society of Singapore (HRSS)

The HRSS is an all-volunteer, non-profit organisation dedicated to rabbit welfare and awareness. It works closely with the SPCA to facilitate the adoption of rabbits in SPCA's care and also runs its own foster programme. The HRSS thoroughly screens potential adopters. Expect them to be more active in the coming Year of the Rabbit when sadly, people consume more rabbit meat.

Web: www.hrss.net

City and Heritage Parks			
Park	**Location**	**Size**	**Key family facilities / activities**
Dhoby Ghaut Green	Adjacent to Dhoby Ghaut MRT Station, opposite the Park Mall Shopping Centre	1.1 hectares	Amphitheatre, Café, Activity Plaza
Esplanade Park	Along Connaught Drive, opposite Padang and City Hall	2.4 hectares	History trails
Fort Canning Park	Bound by Hill Street, Canning Rise, Clemenceau Avenue and River Valley Road	18 hectares	History trails, the Battle Box, trekking, picnics, the Spice Garden, Outdoor performances
Istana Park	Bound by Orchard Road, Penang Road, Penang Lane and Buyong Road	1.3 hectares	Festival Arch, Trellis, Shelters, Pond, Benches
Pearl's Hill City Park	Pearl's Hill Terrace	9 hectares	Trekking and Nature Walks, Lotus Pond
Tiong Bahru Park	Bound by Henderson Rd, Tiong Bahru Road and Lower Delta Road	3.9 hectares	Adventure Playground, Pond pavilion
War Memorial Park	Bound by Nicoll Drive, Stamford Road, Beach Road and Bras Basah Road	1.4 hectares	Cenotaph ("The Chopsticks") War Memorial
Youth Olympic Park	Raffles Avenue. Junction of Raffles Avenue and Bayfront Bridge	0.4 hectares	Broadwalk to Marina Promenade, Helix Bridge to Marina Bay Sands Integrated Resort, Interactive Artwork

Community Parks			
Ang Mo Kio Garden (East)	Junction of Ang Mo Kio Ave 3 and 8, behind Ang Mo Kio MRT Station	5 hectares	Chess garden, children's playground
Ang Mo Kio Garden (West)	Opposite Ang Mo Kio Town Library, along Ang Mo Kio Avenue 6	21 hectares	Children's playground, trekking, nature walks, inline skating
Bedok Town	Bedok North Ave 3. Bound by Bedok North Road, Bedok North Avenue 3 and the Pan Island Expressway	14.6 hectares	Children's playground, campsites, running track
Choa Chu Kang	Beside Kranji Expressway and along Choa Chu Kang Drive	5 hectares	Toddler's playground, adventure playground, galaxy playground, multi purpose court, restaurant
Clementi Woods	Clementi Road next to Kent Vale, along West Coast Road next to Ginza Plaza	12 hectares	Playground, nature walks, restaurant

Park	Location	Size	Key family facilities / activities
Jurong Central Park	Jalan Boon Lay junction with Boon Lay Way	8 hectares	Snakes and Ladders playground and Ludo Garden, grand lawn, running track
One-North Park	Situated in the Northern Zone of one-north, near the ministry of education	16 hectares	Waterwalls and plazas
Punggol Park	Junction of Hougang Avenue 8 and 10	16 hectares (with a 5-hectare pond)	Barbecue pits, Bring Your Own Pit (BYOP), children's play equipment, Picnic area, restaurant, cafe, running track, pond
Sunplaza Park	Tampines Avenue 7, Tampines Avenue 9	9.6 hectares	Fantasy Land Playground, Sense Discovery Garden, Sun Plaza (performance venue), beach ball court, Woodball course
Toa Payoh Town Park	Junction of Toa Payoh Lor 2 and Toa Payoh Lor 6	4.8 hectares	Observation Tower, pond, large pavilion
Woodlands Town Garden	Woodlands Centre Road adjacent to Bukit Timah Expressway (BKE)	11 hectares	Playground, pond, amphitheatre

Coastal Parks			
Changi Beach Park	Along Nicoll Drive and Changi Coast Road	28 hectares	Play equipment, barbecue pits, BYOP, camping, water sports
East Coast Park	Along East Coast Parkway	185 hectares	Inline skating, cycling, camping, fishing, water sports, restaurants, a 7.5km sandy beach
Pasir Ris Park	Along Pasir Ris Road, Elias Road, Pasir Ris Green, Pasir Ris Close and Jalan Loyang Besar	71 hectares	Large adventure playground, cycling, restaurants, mangrove forest and boardwalks, horse-riding, inline skating, camping, barbecue pits
Pasir Ris Town Park	Along Pasir Ris Central, opposite Pasir Ris MRT station	14 hectares	Children's playground, large marine pond, cycling, picnicking
Sembawang Park	At the end of Sembawang	15 hectares	Children's playground, barbecue pits, sea sports, fishing, cycling, camping
West Coast Park	Next to West Coast Highway	50 hectares	Large adventure playground, cycling tracks, tent pitching ground, barbecue pit, restaurant, marsh garden

Nature Parks			
Park	**Location**	**Size**	**Key family facilities / activities**
Admiralty Park	Riverside Road, Singapore 730000	27 hectares	Valley, 20-hectare nature area, 2-km nature trail, Boardwalk, mangrove forest, WiFi
Bukit Batok Nature Park	Bukit Batok East Ave 2, Bukit Batok East Ave 6, Lorong Sesuai	36 hectares	Abandoned quarry site, pond, Memorial to Japanese soldiers
Bukit Batok Town Park	Bukit Batok East Ave 5	42 hectares	Little Guilin – granite rock in lake, towering rock cliffs
Dairy Farm Nature Park	100 Dairy Farm Road	63 hectares	Wallace Education Centre, Wallace Trail, Singapore Quarry, nature trails
Labrador Nature Reserve	Labrador Villa Road	16 hectares	Nature Trails, beach, barbecue pit, cycle trails
Yishun Park	Bound by Yishun Ave 4, Yishun Central, Yishun Ave 11 and Yishun Ring Road	14 hectares	SAFRA Clubhouse, Tropical fruit tree plantation, Canopy Challenge Walk (booking through SAFRA Clubhouse: 6852 8200)
Zhenghua Park	Bound by BKE, BKE Slip Road to Kranji Expressway (KJE) & Dairy Farm Road	13.5 hectares	Playground, jogging track, vegetation

HortPark and Southern Ridges			
Park	**Location**	**Size**	**Key family facilities / activities**
HortPark	33 Hyderabad Road, Off Alexandra Road	23 hectares	Herb and Spice Garden, Silver Garden, Garden of Seasons, Floral Walk, HortMart, café
Kent Ridge Park	Vigilante Drive off South Buona Vista Road. Access via Vigilante Drive, Science Park Drive and Pepys	47 hectares	Nature Trails, Turtles and Fish Pond, M114 artillery guns, AMX-13 light tank
Mount Faber Park	Junction of Kampong Bahru Road and Telok Blangah Road	56 hectares	Cable car to Sentosa, Merlion, lookout points, mural wall, Trekking and nature walks, restaurants
Telok Blangah Hill Park	Telok Blangah Green off Henderson Road	34 hectares	Trekking and nature walks, children's playground, terrace garden

The Southern Ridges	Park Connectors spanning 9 km of green, open spaces spanning the hills of Mount Faber Park, Telok Blangah Hill Park and Kent Ridge Park		Henderson Waves, Forest Walk, Canopy Walk

Offshore Islands			
Park	**Location**	**Size**	**Key family facilities / activities**
Pulau Ubin and Chek Jawa	Pulau Ubin	1,020 hectares	Kampongs, Forests, Grassland, Chek Jawa Wetlands, Boardwalk

Riverine Parks			
Bishan Park	Along Ang Mo Kio Ave 1	52 hectares	Skate rental, lakes, bridges, cycling, running tracks, community gardens, restaurants
Bedok Reservoir Park	Along Bedok Reservoir Road	41.7 hectares	Water sports, aerial tree obstacle course, fishing jetty, 4.3-km running track, viewing gallery, bird watching
Kallang Riverside Park	Kallang Road, Stadium Link and Crawford Street	7 hectares	Water sports, butterfly garden, jogging and cycling tracks
Kranji Reservoir Park	Along Kranji way	9 hectares	Birdwatching, fishing, picnicking
Lower Pierce Reservoir Park	Off Upper Thomson Road	6 hectares	Trekking and nature walks
Lower Seletar Reservoir Park	Bound by Yishun Ave 1 and Lentor Avenue	3.3 hectares	Fishing jetty, water sports, *kelong*-style heritage bridge, water fountain playground, performance stage, rain garden
MacRitchie Reservoir Park	Along Lornie Road	12 hectares	Boardwalk, nnature walks and trails, fishing, water sports, bird-watching
Sengkang Riverside Park	Anchorvale Street abutting Sungei Punggol	21 hectares	Kite-flying, wetlands, fruit trees, jogging track
Upper Seletar Reservoir Park	Bound by BKE, SLE and Mandai Road	15 hectares	Watch tower, trekking and nature walks, bird watching, cycling/ jogging track

– Chapter 2 –

ADVENTURE SINGAPURA!

Shopping and eating are often cited as the favourite pastimes of those living in Singapore. Fortunately this is not the whole story. Singapore still has patches of dense tropical forest, wonderful nature reserves and some relatively unspoilt nearby islands. For those who seek something beyond the urban sprawl, manicured parks and man-made activities, there are adventures to be had and discoveries to be made.

ADVENTURE CLUBS

What better way is there to enjoy adventures than by being with like-minded explorers? Even shyer children can benefit from learning new skills and discovering new things in the company of others. After all, facing challenges and conquering obstacles is a sure way of building confidence. Perhaps our kids can't all follow in the footsteps of Steve Irwin but we can still foster in them an enthusiasm for the environment and the skills to enjoy it.

Australian and New Zealand Association (ANZA)

ANZA runs three age-related scout groups that meet on Thursdays at the Australian International School. If you want to join, you must first become a member of ANZA.

Age group: Joeys (6 to 8 years), Cubs (8 to 10 years) and Scouts (10 to 12 years)

Price guide: Family membership fees are $130. Additional registration fees may be incurred for sporting activities.

Location: 69A Boat Quay
Singapore 049857
Tel: 6733 1215 / 6438 4373
Email: info@anza.org.sg
Web: www.anza.org.sg

The Boys' Brigade in Singapore

This charitable Christian organisation is endorsed by the Ministry of Education as one of the Uniformed Youth Organisations in schools. It pursues a programme of educational, physical, social and spiritual pursuits. Adventure activities available include canoeing, mountain biking, rappelling, camps and expeditions.

Age group: Juniors (8 to 11 years),

Seniors (12 to 16 years) and Primers (16 to 19 years)

Price guide: The main cost is the uniform. (The Boys' Brigade runs its own supplies shop.)

Address: 105 Ganges Avenue
Singapore 169695
Tel: 6737 0377
Email: bbhq@bb.org.sg
Web: www.bb.org.sg

Note: Girls are eligible for the Primers Programme.

Girl Guides Singapore

> *To enable girls and young women to develop their potential to the fullest so as to become responsible citizens.*
>
> **–Worldwide Mission Statement of the Girl Guides**

The Guides has a long history and a worldwide membership. It encourages an enjoyment of the outdoors and promotes the skills necessary to develop this appreciation. In addition, it fosters 'service to the community' and girls can pursue programmes based on health and safety, homecare and first aid, to name but a few. Badges awarded at various levels of proficiency prove to be popular incentives.

Established in 1917, the Girl Guides forms part of the youth associations in Singapore. It has its own camp, Camp Christine, on the mainland where camping and various activities can be pursued.

Age group: Brownies (7 to 12 years) and Guides (13 to 16 years)

Price guide: The statutory uniform constitutes the main cost.

Location: 9 Bishan Street,
Singapore 579685
Tel: 6259 9391
Email: queries@girlguides.org.sg
Web: www.girlguides.org.sg

Hash House Horrors–Singapore

> *It's fun following the trails and I make lots of friends.*
>
> **–Neil, age 9**

This offers an adventurous, fun activity for all the family and membership of the club is optional. On every second Sunday of the month at 4.30 p.m. somewhere in Singapore, between 50 and 100 children and their parents follow trails of flour and chalk through Singapore's terrain (from pavements to jungle). The hash is not a race and the emphasis is on fun.

Age group: No age limit

Price guide: $20 per child (no charge for parents). Alternatively, you can take out membership of the HHHorrors Club. Although it is a children's club, parental involvement is vital. The quarterly fees for children in the same family are $50 for the 1st child, $40 for the 2nd child, $30 for the 3rd, 4th, etc., child. There is also a $10 annual insurance charge per child.

Web: http://horrors.hash.org.sg

Outward Bound Singapore (OBS)

An internationally recognised organisation, Outward Bound offers a variety of adventure training programmes. OBS is located on Pulau Ubin and runs its own ferry service from Punggol Point Jetty. It offers a great opportunity for older children to experience firsthand outdoor challenges in a tropical environment that are unlikely to be encountered on mainland Singapore. There is also another campus at the East Coast Park.

Activities: Most Outward Bound courses are catered for on a group basis except for Open Enrolment Programmes. The Open Enrolment courses tend to run during the school holidays, especially at the year-end. Details are available on the website. In the past, Children & Family programmes (8 to 14 years) have featured rock climbing, abseiling and nature trips. The Local Youth programmes target older children and the Overseas Youth programmes offer an exciting alternative in destinations such as India, Sabah and Lumut.

Age group: 15 to 20 years

Price guide: Varies according to programme

Locations: Reception Centre for Pulau Ubin Campus No. 22 Punggol Road Track 19 off 24th Avenue Singapore 828871 / East Coast Campus 1410 East Coast Parkway Singapore 468962

Tel: 6545 9008

Email: PA_Outward_Bound@pa.gov.sg

Web: www.obs.pa.gov.sg

Raleigh International Singapore

Raleigh is a youth development charity that operates internationally. It sends people on 3-month expeditions to primarily developing countries where they participate in challenging, sustainable projects. These projects are community, environmental or adventure-based. Raleigh offers a truly international experience and it also encourage its volunteers to use the skills and experience they gain from their expeditions to identify and develop projects in their own communities.

Adventure projects allow participants to lead a project while, at the same time, find out more about themselves and how teams work. Examples of projects include trekking in the Krau Wildlife Reserve in central Malaysia. Perhaps Raleigh is the ultimate gung-ho experience.

Price guide: Volunteers are encouraged to fundraise to cover the cost of their involvement in any expedition. The target set for applicants varies from project to project but in general is about $650.

Email: admin@raleigh.org.sg
Web: www.raleigh.org.sg

Singapore Adventurers' Club

This 700-member strong club provides outdoor adventure and the acquisition of the necessary skills to support it. Trekking constitutes a major proportion of the club's activities but there are plenty of opportunities to try other activities. Membership is open to all residents of Singapore.

Activities: Includes trekking, camping, rock climbing, sailing, cycling and canoeing
Age group: 14 years and above
Price guide: Provisional membership is $30 to participate in SAC's activities.

Tel: 6749 0557
Email: email@sac.org
Web: www.sac.org

The Singapore Scout Association

The Scouts is an organisation that offers an excellent opportunity for boys to have adventurous fun whilst learning new skills, making friends and finding out more about the environment. Scouting is part of a worldwide movement that promotes outdoor activities such as camping, hiking, canoeing, archery, pioneering, abseiling and rock climbing. It offers a great way to gain confidence through self-development and it promotes team effort.

Over 300 Scout Units are located in different parts of Singapore. There are also Open Scout Units. To find the nearest Scout Unit to you, fill in an application form from the Singapore Scout Association.

Age group: Cub Scouts (7 to 12 years), Scouts (12 to 16 years), Venture Scouts (16 to 18 years) and Rover Scouts (17 to 26 years)
Price guide: A uniform is required which constitutes the main cost.

Location: 1 Bishan Street 12, Singapore 579808
Tel: 6259 2858
Email: hq@scout.org.sg
Web: www.scout.org.sg

Sparkc

The first of its kind in Singapore, SPARKc@Marine Parade is a new children's adventure training centre that has facilities and training programmes specially customised to meet the needs of young children. It is the result of a joint project between the People's Association and the South East Community Development Council and is developed and managed by Outward Bound Singapore.

The project seeks to encourage independence and a can-do attitude. Its emphasis on safety is reflected by the level and standard of instruction and attention to detail. The basic 4-day outdoor explorer course includes activities such as rock climbing, abseiling and rope courses. Other programmes include a 5-day young leadership course, a 7-day outdoor challenge course and family programmes.

Age group: 10 to 14 years

Price guide: Contact SPARKc@Marine Parade direct

Coordinator: SPARKc@Marine Parade, 1410 East Coast Parkway, Singapore 468962

Tel: 6445 0510

Email: SPARKc@pa.gov.sg

Note: Courses require a minimum of 24 children. Residential and non-residential programmes are usually available.

ADVENTURE SPORTS

see also Sports, pp. 79 – 127

Sporting activities are a good way to prepare children for adventure as well as develop adventurous skills and an open mindset. Included here are just a few of the more demanding sports that come to mind. These won't suit all children and you really must check that they want to do it and that they know in advance what is involved. My son rapidly changed his mind when he saw a paintball session in progress!

Cable Skiing

Cable Skiing @ SKI360°

Also known as cable wakeboarding, participants are pulled by an overhead cable instead of a boat. For the more ambitious, you can slalom, trick ski, kneeboard or even surf without the wave!

Age guide: 7 years and above and able to swim (adult supervision is required)

Price guide: Ski passes are available from $32 for 1 hour on weekdays / $42 weekends and public holidays. Students get a $5-discount for 1-hour passes (until 7.00 p.m.) upon presentation of their student pass.

Location: 1206A East Coast Parkway, Singapore 449891

Tel: 6442 7318

Email: enquiry@ski360degree.com

Web: www.ski360degree.com

Note: There is also a restaurant and bistro on site.

Go-Karting

Go-karting is great fun for most children. It offers the chance to imitate heroes of the racing track as well as foster Grand Prix ambitions. Suitable for girls as much as for boys, go-karting is also an ideal family pastime.

Escape Theme Park

For a gentle introduction to go-karting, you can try the Daytona Go-Kart Beginner's Track (with 2-seater karts) or if you are more confident, there are 1-seater karts available.

Age group: The 2-seater Daytona go-karts will accommodate children 1 to 1.47 metres in height, provided that an adult above 1.47 metres drives. Children above 1.47 metres in height can try out the 1-seater karts.

Price guide: Park entry is $8.90 for children (3 to 12 years) / $17.70 for adults / $42.80 for a family ticket (2 adults and 2 children)

Location: Downtown East, 1 Pasir Close, Singapore 519599
Tel: 6581 9112
Web: www.escapethemepark.com.sg

Paintball

For the uninitiated, paintball can be described as a more sophisticated combination of tag and hide-and-seek. It is a team game during which opponents seek to mark each other with non-toxic paint pellets shot from toy guns. Those marked with paint are then eliminated from the game. Okay, so it may not sound like everyone's ideal pastime (mine included!) but it does have tremendous appeal for those so inclined. It is not random mayhem — strict rules apply, proper clothing must be worn (usually camouflage gear) and whilst physically challenging, it necessitates quick thinking and has been described as a character-building sport.

Age group: 14 years and above (Parents of 14- to 17-year-old participants must sign a waiver.)

Price guide: Entrance fee: $15 (9.00 a.m. to 5.00 p.m.) / $20 (5.00 p.m. to midnight). 1,000 paintballs cost $250. There must be six players or more in a group (minimum purchase of 1,000 paintballs). There is a minimum load of 100 paintballs per gun, per player, per game.

Office: Nehsons Building, 24 Peck Seah Street #08-01 Singapore 079314
Playing Field: Turf City, 200 Turf Club Road Singapore 287994
Tel: 6324 0038 / 9636 0038
Email: tag@paintball.com.sg
Web: www.paintball.com.sg

Parkour

For budding spidermen, this discipline is a must! It originated in the Parisian suburbs in the 1980s and has since gained a worldwide following. The aim of the discipline is to attempt to pass obstacles in the fastest and most direct way possible while using the least amount of energy. A participant of the sport is known as a *traceur* (if male) or *traceuse* (if female). Here, *parkour* is practised in urban areas, e.g. HDB estates. It is really only suitable for physically confident teenagers and adults.

Web: www.le-parkour.sg

Rock Climbing

Rock climbing is becoming more

popular in Singapore. It is amenable to children from a relatively young age and can be readily pursued whilst on holiday in the region or further afield. It is an excellent sport for developing strength, endurance and flexibility. There are a number of venues you can choose from:

ACE Adventure

ACE Adventure offers a 1-day, 7-hour course that qualifies anyone above 14 years for the Singapore National Standards (SNCS) Sport Climbing Course Level One certification.

Price guide: $60 per person

Mailing Address: Blk 3027 Ubi Road 1 #03-116 Singapore 408720
Tel: 9790 0281 (Joanne Soo)
Email: info@aceadventure.com.sg
Web: www.aceadventure.com.sg

Climb Asia Climbing Centre

The Climbing Center now is part of the Civil Service Club.

Price guide: Fun Climbing costs $20 per child / Full-day SNCS Sport Climbing Level 1 costs $60 per student.

Location: 60 Tessensohn Road, Civil Service Club, Singapore 217664
Tel: 6292 7701
Email: beta@climb-asia.com
Web: www.climb-asia.com

SAFRA Adventure Sports Centre

The SAFRA Sports Adventure Centre (SASC) offers a wide range of climbing experiences including:

Ice Climbing: Here you can enjoy the first artificial ice-climbing wall in Southeast Asia. Constructed out of an artificial ice-foam material, it is 18 metres high. The ice climbing face even allows you to use ice axes to make the experience as authentic as possible.

Indoor Duplex Bouldering Wall: This air-conditioned bouldering gym has a climbing area of 450 square metres. It is suitable for both novice and expert climbers.

Canopy Challenge Walk: This is open for walk-ins at weekends and during school holidays (9.30 a.m. to 11 a.m. and 2.30 p.m. to 4.00 p.m.). Booking in advance is necessary.

Parachute Jump: The launching point stands at 21 metres high and offers an excellent view of Yishun Park. It is open for walk-ins at weekends and during school holidays (11.30 a.m. to 1.00 p.m. and 5.30 p.m. to 7.00 p.m.). Booking in advance is necessary

Price guide: Prices start at $8 (SAC member) / $15 (guest).

Location: SAFRA Yishun Country Club, 60 Yishun Ave 4, Singapore 769027
Tel: 6852 8200
Email: adventure@safra.sg
Web: www.safra.sg (look under Facilities)

Note: Birthday packages are available.

Border X

This is a rock-climbing wall inside a shoppint centre, Orchard Central. Kids 6 years old and above 1.1 meters can experience basic rock climbing. Kids 12 years old and above can experience advanced rock climbing and abseiling.

Opening Hours: 11.00 a.m. to 9.30 p.m.

Price Guide: Prices start at $23 for an hour of rock-climbing on weekdays.

Location: 181 Orchard Road,
#04-22 Orchard Central,
Singapore 238896
Tel: 6884 4870.
Web: www.borderX.com.sg
Facebook: www.facebook.com/Via Forrata

Tree Climbing

For those so inclined, there is actually a club in Singapore whose prime objective is to scale the trees that the rest of us frequently ignore or use to seek shade under. For any youthful budding tree climbers out there, your first port of call should be...

Sunny Island Tree Climbers Society

This group was founded by a certified tree climber and adopts a professional, instructive approach to tree climbing. It seeks to promote the love of nature and tree climbing among young Singaporeans. Whilst recognising tree climbing as a recreational pursuit, SITC also supports environmental projects and nature research. The club has climbed in various parks around Singapore and also runs a number of courses.

Courses: Basic Course–Getting High, Intermediate 1–Get Knotty, Intermediate 2–Swinging Around and an advanced intensive course

Price guide: Course costs vary from $38 for a student doing the basic course to $350 plus a $140 test fee for the advanced package.

Address: Sunny Island Tree Climbers Society SITC Blk 106 Spottiswoods Park Rd #11-136 Singapore 080106
Email: swingby@treeclimbingasia.org
Web: www.treeclimbingasia.org

OTHER ADVENTURE ACTIVITIES AND VENUES

Combat Skirmish Singapore

Combat Skirmish Singapore provides an opportunity to play combat skirmish, a combat simulation game that can be used for training as well as leisure. It uses infrared technology and leaves no mess. As no projectiles are used, it is suitable for children. The company conducts public shoot-outs (email for details) as well as private events.

Age guide: 7 years and above (children aged 12 and below must be supervised).

Price guide: Student Rates (full-time student with valid student pass): $28

for 2 missions, subsequent mission at $12 (Mondays to Thursdays excluding public holidays) / $30 for 2 missions, subsequent mission at $12 (Fridays to Sundays and public holidays)

Location: Scenarios can be played in forests, parks, schools or gardens
Tel: 67791031
Web: www.combatlasersingapore.com

Note: Great for a party!

Escape Theme Park

see also Where to Go?, pp. 221 – 222

Look out for the Family Roller Coaster and Wet & Wild, Asia's highest flume ride.

Location: Downtown East, 1 Pasir Close, Singapore 519599
Tel: 6581 9112
Email: feedback@leisureguest.com.sg
Web: www.escapethemepark.com.sg

Universal Studios Singapore

Universal Studio is Singapore's latest theme park to open at the Integrated Resort in Sentosa. This park features rides based on movies produced by Universal Studios such as *Shrek*, *Madagascar* and *Jurassic Park*. Look out for the *Battlestar Galatica* Roller Coaster which is guaranteed to leave you breathless and weak-kneed.

Price guide: Adults $72 / Children (4 to 12) $52. Prices do vary, so do check the website for more details.

Contact: 6577 6888
Email: enquiries@rwsentosa.com
Web: www.rwsentosa.com/ (look under attractions)

The Flying Trapeze

The first in Singapore, The Flying Trapeze not only helps develop body coordination but also helps conquer one's fear of heights. Instructors are present.

Age guide: 4 years and above

Opening hours: 4.00 p.m. to 6.00 p.m. (Tuesdays to Fridays) / 4.00 p.m. to 7.00 p.m. (Saturdays, Sundays and public holidays)

Price guide: $10 per swing / $20 for 3 swings.

Location: Siloso Beach, Sentosa. Get the blue or red line internal bus service or the Sentosa Express to Beach Station and then the Siloso Beach Tram.
Tel: 1800-SENTOSA (736 8672) from 9.00 a.m. to 6.30 p.m. daily
Web: www.sentosa.com.sg (look under Attractions)

G-Max Reverse Bungy Jump

Experience G-forces similar to those felt by astronauts in a rocket launch! You are strapped into an open-air capsule between two 36-metre high towers and catapulted 60 metres into the air.

Opening hours: 2.00 p.m. to 1.00 a.m. (Mondays to Thursdays) / 2.00 p.m. to 1.00 a.m. (Fridays) / 1.00 p.m. to 3.00 a.m. (Saturdays) / 1.00 p.m. to 1.00 a.m. (Sundays)

Age guide: 12 years and above, with a minimum height of 1.20 metres. Children must be accompanied by an adult.

Price guide: A single ride costs $45 for adults / $30 for students.

Location: Clarke Quay
Tel: 6338 1766
Email: simon@marketingworld.co.nz
Web: www.gmax.com.sg

HSBC TreeTop Walk

see also Back to Nature, pp. 37 – 38

The HSBC TreeTop Walk consists of a free-standing suspension bridge that connects the two highest points in MacRitchie. The first of its kind in Singapore and in the region, it offers a spectacular view of the plants and animals that live in the forest canopy. The total length of the walkway is about 250 metres.

A book titled *TreeTop Trail @ MacRitchie* is available upon donation from Bukit Timah Nature Reserve and the TreeTop Walk ranger post. It features a map showing the various routes you can take and brief descriptions of the flora and fauna of the tropical rainforest at the Central Catchment Nature Reserve.

Web: www.nparks.gov.sg (search TreeTop Walk)

Flying Fox, Flying simulator

Sentosa Luge & Skyride

Part-go-kart and part-toboggan, the Luge gives you a fun-filled gravity ride down concrete-sealed tracks through a scenic area of Sentosa. And if you want more, you can always get the Skyride (a chairlift) back up and take another ride!

Opening hours: 10.00 a.m. to 9.30 p.m. daily

Age guide: Children need to be at least 1.10 metres in height to ride on their own (or they can pair up with an adult).

Price guide: One Luge and Skyride costs $12 per person (2 rides are $17). A family ticket is $29 for 4 rides / $49 for 8 rides.

Location: Imbiah Lookout, Sentosa. All the Sentosa bus lines go there and it is near the Beach and Imbiah station.
Tel: 1800-SENTOSA (1800-736 8672) from 9.00 a.m. to 6.30 p.m. daily
Web: www.sentosa.com.sg (look under Attractions)

Singapore Flyer

see also Where to Go?, pp. 206 – 207

The Singapore Flyer is the world's largest observation wheel. Standing at a stunning 165 metres from the ground, the Flyer offers breathtaking, panoramic views of the Marina Bay and the Central Business District. One can also see Malaysia and Indonesia on a clear day.

Opening hours: 8.30 a.m. to 10.00 p.m. daily. (Last admission at 10.15 p.m.)

Prices: Tickets are $29.50 for an adult and $20.65 for a child.

Location: Marina Bay
Tel: 6734 8829 (for sales, marketing and tickets)
Web: www.singaporeflyer.com.sg

Wild Wild Wet

see also Where to Go?, p. 224.
Highlights include the Ular-Lah, the first raft slide in Southeast Asia, and the Slide Up, which allows you to plunge down a 4-storey ramp.
Ticket Prices: Adult: $15.50 / Child: $10.50 / Family (2 adults and 2 children): $42

Location: Downtown East, 1 Pasir Close, #01-08, Singapore 519599
Tel: 6581 9112 / 6581 9128
Email: feedback@leisurequest.com.sg
Web: www.wildwildwet.com

BUKIT TIMAH NATURE RESERVE

see also Back to Nature, p. 29
Singapore has a wonderful selection of nature reserves but for those seeking a more adventurous expedition, Bukit Timah Nature Reserve has to be the first choice. Many factors support this. It retains the only substantial area of primary rainforest left in Singapore, contains the island's highest hill and has one of the richest, most diverse ecological systems in the world. Trekking, nature walks and cycling (take your own bike) are popular activities, with the reserve having an official biking trail. Hindhede Nature Park, which is located within the reserve, has an adventure playground that is better suited to children aged 6 and above. Facilities include a Visitor Centre that contains an exhibit giving information about the flora and fauna of the reserve.

Web: www.nparks.gov.sg (look under Nature Reserves)

CAMPING

At its best, camping is a novel, cheap and exciting way to experience the great outdoors. At its worst, well, preparation is the key to survival! For those who are used to camping overseas, it should be noted that camping Singaporean-style may have a twist. Of course, there is the universal pleasure taken from sleeping under the stars and spending time outside, but many campers here highlight the convenience of being so near home. In addition, a plot near a McDonald's outlet is often sought after. As a result, popular mainland sites can become very crowded during peak periods. That said, there is something for everyone and a little research into your preferred destination should ensure that you get your choice of location.

Mainland

Permits are required for camping at the following five coastal parks: Changi Beach, East Coast, Pasir Ris, Sembawang and West Coast. Camping is also restricted to designated areas within the five parks. Campers can apply for camping permits on the NParks website. It is expected that those who apply for a camping permit clean up after themselves or face a hefty $300 fine.

Web: www.nparks.gov.sg (look under Activities)

Park facilities are summarised as follows:

Changi Beach

Barbecue pits and toilets are available. The park is lit from 7.00 p.m. to 7.00 a.m.

Note: It is located near the airport so noise may be a consideration.

East Coast

Here, you'll find barbecue pits, toilets and a number of restaurants for those who fancy a break from self-catering. The park is fronted by a 7.5-km stretch of sandy beach on which children will enjoy playing.

Pasir Ris

This park contains a 4-hectare children's playground, a Mangrove Boardwalk, toilets and changing rooms. There are also several seafood outlets here. The park is lit from 7.00 p.m. to 7.00 a.m.

Sembawang

Barbecue pits, a foot reflexology path, a children's playground and toilet and shower facilities are all available. There is also a seafood restaurant in the grounds of Beaulieu House. The park is lit from 7.00 p.m. to 7.00 a.m.

West Coast

This park has several children's playgrounds including an adventure-style one, bicycles to rent, a fitness corner, foot reflexology facilities, nature zones, barbecue pits and toilets. The park is lit from 7.00 p.m. to 7.00 a.m.

Offshore

For the more intrepid adventurer, you can camp on one of several of Singapore's islands.

Pulau Ubin

Camping on Pulau Ubin is a more strenuous and challenging affair than a day visit and, without doubt, a more ulu, or 'rustic', destination than Sentosa. You need to provide your own tent and food and refreshment arrangements should be well planned. That said, it really does offer a unique experience within Singapore and provides an ideal get-away-from-it-all venue for more experienced campers with older children. Camping permits are required here as well.

Sentosa

Although overnight camping is no longer allowed on Sentosa, you can still pitch tents for day use on any of its beaches from 7.00 a.m. to 7.00 p.m. daily.

Singapore's Southern Islands

For more information about these islands, refer to the section on Island Hopping (pp.74 – 76)

For overnight camping on Pulau Hantu and Sisters' Islands, you need to obtain a free permit first from the Sentosa Development Corporation. Write to the Executive (Southern Islands Management), Sentosa, or email administrator@sentosa.com.sg with the following details: your name, contact number, number of campers, camping date and choice of island. Alternatively, fax 6275 0161.

Kusu: Overnight stays are not allowed here.

Pulau Hantu: Choose from pitching a tent or using one of the shelters by the beach.

Sisters': Again, you can take cover under your tent or use one of the shelters near the beach.

St John's: Overnight stays are only allowed for those staying at the Holiday Bungalow or for organised groups staying at the holiday camps.

DIVING WITH MARINE ANIMALS

I thought snorkelling with brightly coloured fish around me was amazing, so I can only assume that diving with sharks must be a wonderful experience. Underwater World on Sentosa has taken its marine encounter one step further and now offers scuba diving inside its tanks. Friends and family can view this fishy experience from inside the aquarium.

Activities:

Marine Discovery: For anyone over 6 years old who can swim and/or is confident in the water, this offers a chance to interact with shovelnose rays, blue-spotted stingrays and other marine creature. A 60-minute programme for $45 per person.

Tel: 6275 0030

Email: uwspl@underwaterworld.com.sg

Web: www.underwaterworld.com.sg

Note: Parental consent is required for participants under 21.

DOLPHIN ENCOUNTERS

Dolphin Lodge

Activity: The Dolphin Lodge is located on a small island situated between Batam and Bintan in the Riau Straits. Both children and adults can interact and play with the pod of dolphins.

Age group: Participants must be

a minimum height of 1.35 metres and aged 10 and above to enjoy full interaction with the dolphins. Partial interaction is permitted if these requirements are not met.

Price guide: $120 per person including lunch (excludes ferry tickets)

Contact: Dolphin Lodge offers a 1-day package through Fascinating Holidays (Tel: 6735 5511) and Panda Travel (Tel: 6337 1616).

Email: enquiry@dolphinslodge.com

Web: www.dolphinslodge.com

Underwater World

Activity: *Swim with the Dolphins* offers an exciting 60-minute encounter with pink Indo-Pacific humpbacked dolphins. A trainer will show you how to give simple hand cues and you can also feed the dolphins.

Age group: 6 years old and above (must be able to swim and confident in the water and a minimum of 0.9 metres)

Price guide: $150 per person (includes admission to Underwater World and Dolphin Lagoon)

Tel: 6275 0030

Email: uwspl@underwaterworld.com.sg

Web: www.underwaterworld.com.sg

Note: Parental consent is required for participants under 21.

ISLAND HOPPING

There are many islands off Singapore's mainland that have something to offer everyone. For sheer peace and relaxation, Sisters' Island is difficult to beat; for cycling and nature spotting, Pulau Ubin is to be recommended; and for pure fun and entertainment, Sentosa is your place (*see* Where to Go?, pp. 215 – 221). Listed here are the best venues for those seeking a bit of adventure. All are perfectly feasible for day visits or for camping, and a little preparation should ensure a successful outing. Again there is no harm in taking a small first aid kit and some extra refreshments. Needless to say, sunblock is essential and so are sun hats for all the family. Don't forget to pack costumes if you are planning to swim and I'd recommend closed-toe sandals or trainers when cycling on Pulau Ubin.

Pulau Ubin

Pulau Ubin makes sense if you want to explore the local environment more and see something different. It is easy to get to and is a great day trip. My kids love it but it can be very hot and tiring and I wouldn't recommend it to parents with toddlers or babies in tow.

–Andrew

An expedition to the mangrove island of Pulau Ubin is well worth making.

This can be comfortably done within a day, giving plenty of time to walk or cycle around, enjoy a tasty seafood lunch or just relax. Children's bicycles and baby seats are available for hire although the heat and bumboat crossing are probably not suitable for younger children.

Once on the island, there is much to see in the way of flora and fauna and it is not unknown to encounter a snake (we spotted a krait along a dry track) or even a monitor lizard. Sights to see include a Thai temple, prawn farms, *kelong* huts and limestone quarries. The beaches are not that clean so cycling is probably the predominant attraction. Nature enthusiasts will be drawn towards Chek Jawa beach which marks the southeast coast of the island.

Directions: Take the MRT to Tanah Merah and then a bus or taxi to Changi Point. At the jetty, you can get a bumboat across to the island.

Price guide: Bumboat is $2.50 one way ($4.50 with bike) / Cycle hire ranges from $3 to $7 an hour.

Tel: 6542 4109 (Pulau Ubin Information Kiosk)

Web: www.nparks.gov.sg

Note: For more information on Pulau Ubin and Chek Jawa, *see* Back to Nature, pp. 29 – 30 & pp. 41 – 42..

Singapore's Southern Islands

There are a number of islands constituting Singapore's Southern Islands but only Kusu, St John's, Sisters' and Pulau Hantu are open to the public. While a regular ferry service operates from Marina South Pier (31 Marina Coastal Drive) to Kusu and St John's, the other islands are only accessible by hired boats. The islands can be visited at any time but it is best to avoid them during the rainy season from November to January.

Kusu and St John's

Of the many small islands off Singapore's mainland, the most popular are Kusu and St John's. They are good venues for family trips, with picnicking and swimming the favourite activities on both the islands. The swimming lagoons at Kusu and St John's are among the cleanest beaches in Singapore. There are shelters, changing facilities and a washroom on each island.

Kusu attracts both sightseers and devotees because of its religious shrines, especially the Da Bo Gong (God of Prosperity) Chinese Temple and *kramat* (holy shrines of Malay saints). In October/November, many people flock to the island during the annual Kusu Pilgrimage. The island also has a tortoise sanctuary.

Directions: Take the ferry from Marina South Pier. There is limited capacity, so a first come, first served basis operates. The ferry departs from the Pier at 10.00 a.m. and 2.00 p.m. on Mondays to

Saturdays and 9.00 a.m., 11.00 a.m., 1.00 p.m., 3.00 p.m., 5.00 p.m. on Sundays and public holidays. It goes to Kusu first and then St John's.

Amenities:

Kusu: There are no accommodation facilities but toilet facilities are available.

St John's: The island has a Holiday Bungalow that sleeps up to 10 people as well as holiday camps with dormitories that sleep up to 60 people and basic cooking facilities. Rates for the bungalow vary from $53.50 to $214 while rates for the holiday camps are from $64.20 to $107 per day. Overnight stays are only allowed for those staying at the Holiday Bungalow and the holiday camps.

Price guide: $12 for children (3 to 12 years / $15 for adults. Tickets are sold at Marina South Pier (6265 3520).

Tel: 1800-736 8672 from 9.00 a.m. to 6.30 p.m. daily

Pulau Hantu

If you are interested in diving, the Hantu bloggers (a non-profit, environmental awareness initiative) regularly dive here (http://habitatnews.nus.edu.sg/news/pulauhantu/).

Directions: There are no regular ferries to Pulau Hantu. You can hire a boat from West Coast Pier.

Price guide: Rates will have to be negotiated with the operator but expect to pay $120 upwards for a two-way trip.

Tel: 6275 0388 / 1800-SENTOSA (736 8672) from 9.00 a.m. to 6.30 p.m. daily

Sisters' Islands

As the islands' beaches are sandy and the waters clean, you can swim and snorkel here as well as have a picnic. For those seeking a quiet spot away from the hustle and bustle of city life, this is a suitable destination.

Directions: There are no regular ferries to Pulau Hantu. You can hire a boat from Marina South Pier.

Amenities: The island does not have any accommodation but you can camp. There are 19 wooden shelters by the beach, toilets with showers and picnic tables.

Price guide: Rates will have to be negotiated with the operator but expect to pay around $180 upwards for a return trip.

SINGAPORE DUCKTOURS

This highly enjoyable, 1-hour sea and land tour is certainly great fun for children. Starting at Suntec City, you are driven through the civic district of Singapore in a specially converted, US army amphibious vehicle.

The highlight of the trip is, of course, when the Duck lives

up to its name, driving through the undergrowth and splashing straight into Singapore Harbour! Once in Marina Bay, you enjoy the sweeping view of the water-spouting Merlion, the Grand Fullerton Hotel and Clifford Pier. But the most picturesque sight is the memorable, durian-shaped Esplanade complex, which looks most spectacular when viewed from the water.

All the Ducktours' staff are very welcoming, and our guide was hospitable and humorous. Over all, we got some of the most kid-friendly customer service in Singapore on this tour. The expedition can even become a hands-on activity for kids because the guide invited all the children to take turns driving the Duck around the harbour, which most of them were really keen to do.

–Andrew Leng, an enthusiastic father!

The appeal of travelling on something that turns from being a bus on land one minute to being a boat in the water the next holds an obvious fascination for children of all ages. Ducktours have proven popular in the United States, Europe and Australia and are now available in Singapore. The Duck is an authentic American Vietnam War vehicle, now used to conduct city and harbour tours that cover Singapore's Civic District and Clifford Pier Harbour. Special ducktainers provide a commentary and entertainment on board, with a captain in charge of the amphibious vehicle. Head down to Suntec City to book a place on one of these 60-minute trips that depart hourly from 10.00 a.m. to 6.00 p.m. (night tours may be available).

Age group: 2 years and above

Price guide: $2 for children below 3 years / $17 for children between 3 to 12 years / $33 for adults. Special membership deals are available for Singaporeans and PR holders.

Tel: 6333 3825

Email: sales@ducktours.com.sg

Web: www.ducktours.com.sg

Note:

- Book at least a week in advance for weekend tours and other peak times.
- It does get hot so bring some drinks. Although the whole deck of the Duck is covered with canvas, sunblock and hats would not go amiss.
- Afterwards you can cool off and enjoy inexpensive snacks in the basement area of Suntec City.

GHOULISH TRAILS

Singapore Paranormal Investigators (SPI) visits haunted sights with stories based on history, folklore and memories. Listen to intriguing accounts of paranormal sightings, legends, mysteries and gruesome crime stories. SPI promises a night of 'fun, spooks, chills and thrills for everyone'!

Age group: Tours are not recommended for children under 12 years (stories can be macabre, scary and distressing).

Price guide: Upon application

Locations: Numerous tours are available (see website)

Email: ghoulish@spi.com.sg

Web: www.spi.com.sg

Note: Take a jumper and a torch.

– Chapter 3 –

SPORTS

As there are many opportunities in Singapore for those who like sport or wish to develop new skills, there is bound to be something that your child will enjoy. A good starting point is to examine the Extra Curricular Activities/Co-Curricular Activities (ECAs/CCAs) offered by your child's school and those available through your local Community Centre. It is also worth noting that sporting ECAs run by International Schools may be open to non attending students.

FAST FACTS

Singapore Sports Council

As the service provider of public sporting facilities in Singapore, this should be your first port of call when seeking information about sporting activities and venues.

Tel: 6500 5000

Web: www.ssc.gov.sg

Let's Play

This website is a lifestyle portal which lists useful information about sporting events. You will need to register to exchange information with other people on the website and to obtain the membership card which has various shopping and dinning benefits.

Tel: 6345 7111 (Singapore Sports Council)

Web: www.singaporesports.sg

Sportsguide.sg

This comprehensive guide to Singapore's sport industry is an online version of 'Let's Play Sports Guide'. It features supporting services and sport facilities and advice about where to go for coaching.

Email: bizinfo@sg.marshallcavendish.com
Web: www.sportsguide.sg

UWCSEA Community Education Programme

United World College of South East Asia hosts recreational activities under their Community Education Programme (C.E.P.) that are open to everyone. A wide range of activities are available to children from the age of 5 upwards, including swimming, cricket, football, martial arts and rock climbing. Courses are all fee-paying and pre-registration is required

Tel: 6775 5344
Email: info@uwcsea.edu.sg
Web: www.uwcsea.edu.sg

Water-Venture

The People's Association Water-Venture (PAWV) has various outlets throughout Singapore that offer facilities and courses for a number of water sports. Abseiling, dragon boating, kayaking, power boating, wind surfing, sailing and sport climbing are just some of the adventure and water sports available. Course fees and rates are reduced for members of PAWV (you need to be over the age of 12).

Price guide: $30 to $42 for a 5-year membership and $20 to $290 for course fees (member rates)

Email: PA_Online@pa.gov.sg (help desk). You can sign up online.
Web: www.water-venture.org.sg

Metropolitan YMCA

Metro-Y programmes for children include an introduction to gymnastics, swimming, basketball and soccer. Classes are open to both members and non-members.

Price guide: $3210 entrance fee and annual subscription fee for Associate Youth membership (below 21 years) (thereafter $20 + GST a year) / $128.40 (thereafter $40 + GST for Youth Ordinary membership. Note: Fees for sports programmes are extra.

Tel: 6839 8333
Email: programmes@mymca.org.sg
Web: www.mymca.org.sg

Community Centres

Contact your nearest Centre to check out its sports programmes.

Web: www.pa.gov.sg

Australian and New Zealand Association (ANZA)

ANZA offers a range of sporting activities for children, including netball, athletics, cycling and soccer.

Price guide: $130 for full family membership ($80 for 6 months).

Tel: 6733 1215

Email: info@anza.org.sg

Web: www.anza.org.sg

The Singapore American Community Action Council (SACAC)

The SACAC offers an extensive sports programme that anyone can join. Activities include swimming, gymnastics, basketball, baseball, girl's softball, tennis, soccer, football, flag football, golf, fencing and cheerleading.

Price guide: $160.50 for annual family membership.

Note: Fees for sports programmes are extra.

Tel: 6363 6454

Email: sacac@sas.edu.sg

Web: www.sacac.com (new website to be announced)

SPORTS FOR ALL

Singapore Sports Council

The Singapore Sports Council (SSC) is the service provider of public sporting facilities for all Singaporean residents. The SSC's Sportsweb website provides an excellent online sports and fitness guide. Through this portal, you can find out about up-and-coming events, where you can play the sport of your choice, how to book facilities and how to find a registered coach Children and adults can pursue water sports, racket sports and martial arts, to name but a few.

Tel: 6500 5000

Web: www.ssc.gov.sg

Note: The SSC hosts a broad range of Learn-To-Play (LTP) programmes which offer an incredible variety of affordable sports and fitness classes such a Bhangra aerobics, inline skating, badminton, dance, pilates and wushu. Follow the appropriate link for you area on the website.

Jurong West Sports and Recreation Centre (JWSRC)

At Singapore's largest integrated sports complex, you can enjoy a variety of facilities including the Aquatic Centre, which has a sheltered competition pool, rooftop tennis courts and dance studios.

Location: 20 Jurong West Street 93, Singapore 648965
Tel: 6515 5259
Email: SSC_Jurongwestsrc@ssc.gov.sg
Web: www.ssc.gov.sg

Singapore Sports School

If your child show signs of excelling at a particular sport and has a true passion for it, then it may be time to take things a step further...

The Singapore Sports School is a specialised independent school that provides an academic and training environment for talented youth athletes. To enrol, children must apply to take part in selection trials that are usually held in July every year.

Courses: The Sports School focuses on a variety of sports, including: track and field events, golf, swimming, badminton, bowling, soccer, netball and table tennis.

Age group: The school usually admits students between the ages of 12 and 15 years.

Location: 1 Champions Way, Singapore 737913
Tel: 6766 0100
Email: enquire@sportsschool.edu.sg
Web: www.sportsschool.edu.sg

Special Needs

Singapore Disability Sports Council (SDSC)

The SDSC is the national sports body for the disabled in Singapore. It promotes a Learn-To-Play Sports Programme which encourages people with disabilities to enjoy sports as both a life style choice and as a means of recreation. Basic introduction programmes are available for a variety of sports e.g. sailing, swimming, equestrian, football, boccia and handcycling. It also supports a Fun-to-Play programme that seeks to introduce sports to the disabled community, especially the young, in a fun manner. In addition, it operates a School Outreach Programme that supports various projects, e.g. raising awareness of disability sports and hosting disability sports programmes.

Location: 230 Stadium Boulevard, Singapore 5397799
Tel: 6342 0961
Email: sdsc@sdsc.org.sg
Web: www.sdsc.org.sg

Special Olympics

This charitable welfare organisation offers a number of sport training programmes, including aquatics, athletics, bowling and table tennis.

There is also the opportunity for athletes of all abilities to take part in competitions. Athletes must at least 8 years old to be eligible to take part in Special Olympics.

Location: Block 2 Saint Georges's Road, #01-65, Singapore 322002
Tel: 6293 3182
Email: admin@specialolympics.org.sg
Web: www.specialolympics.org.sg

Gymnastics and Physical Education

Above & Beyond Gymnastics and Sport

Above and Beyond provide gymnastic classes for children of all ages. They also offer a series of gym and sport camps during the school holidays.

Locations: Bishan Sports Hall, 5 Bishan Street, Singapore 579783 / Katong Community Centre, 51 Kampong Arang Road, Singapore 438178 / Pasir Ris East Community Centre, 1 Pasir Ris Drive 4, #01-08, Singapore 519457 / Singapore Sports School, 1 Champions Way, Singapore 737913
Tel: 9762 2175
Email: email@abgymsport.com
Web: www.abgymsport.com

Royce Kids Gym

This facility provides programmes and physical education for children with learning differences. It hosts a marvellous indoor, sensory playground. The gym class aims to improve children's gross motor skills coordination and sensory issues.

Age group: 10 months to 10 years

Location: Liang Court, 177 River Valley Road, #02-20/21, Singapore 179030
Tel: 6720 1111
Email: lovebabyroyce@yahoo.co.uk
Web: www.roycekidsgym.com

Horse Riding

Riding for the Disabled Association of Singapore

This organisation offers free therapeutic horse riding to the disabled in Singapore. Volunteers over the age of 16 are welcomed.

Location: RDA Centre, 5 Jalan Mashhor, Singapore 299174
Tel: 6250 0176
Email: mail@rdasingapore.org.sg
Web: www.rdasingapore.org

Sailing

Sailability Singapore

Run by the Singapore Disability Sports Council, the Sailability Singapore programme takes place every Sunday morning. It is suitable for all disability groups.

Location: Changi Sailing Club, 32 Netheravon Road, Singapore 508508 (assistance with transport to the club can be arranged)
Tel: 6342 3501
Email: sdsc@sdsc.org.sg
Web: www.sailability.org/sg/singapore

Swimming

Marsden Swim School

This popular swim school offers individual aquatic classes, squads for adults and children and instruction for those with disabilities.

Location: 113 Holland Road, Singapore 278566
Tel: 6473 8353
Email: swim@marsdenswimschool.com
Web: www.marsdenswimschool.com

SPORTS INSTRUCTION

see also Adventure Sports in Adventure Singapura!, pp. 65 – 68

Acrobatics

Acrobatics as an activity for children has become increasingly popular in recent years. Research has shown that it helps improve coordination and motor control. Acrobatics can also develop patience by virtue of the concentration required.

Jazz Cats

Age group: 5 years and above
Price guide: Upon application

Location: 491 River Valley Road, #01-09 Valley Point Shopping Centre, Singapore 248371
Tel: 6732 4078
Email: lissy@pacific.net.sg

Archery

It is claimed that archery develops hand-eye coordination and balance. And it goes without saying that self-discipline and concentration are necessary to ensure that the target is struck. The prime attraction to most children, however, is probably the sheer fun of using and controlling a weapon. No doubt, visions of the famous outlaw Robin Hood may reinforce the thrill of archery.

Archery Association of Singapore

This body organises and promotes archery in Singapore and it is a useful first point of contact.

Postal address: 77 Jalan Chengam, Singapore 578630
Tel: 9304 4473
Email: via website link
Web: www.archerysingapore.com

Archery Club of Singapore

This non-profit organisation is affiliated to the Archery Association of Singapore. Group archery courses are available.

Age group: 8 years and above (Participants can sometimes be younger depending on their height and physique.)
Price guide: $80 per annum for Ordinary Membership

Range location: Punggol South Archery Range at the junction of Hougang Ave 8/6
(Open field next to Blk 543)
Tel: 9455 1809

Email: simonho@
archeryclubsingapore.com
Web: www.archeryclubspore.com

Dm Archery

Age group: Parents of children under the age of 10 must be present.

Price guide: $125 per person for a beginner's group course of 4 lessons / $80 for a private beginner's lesson. Shooting rates vary between $6 to $24 according to the number of arrows, length of session and location.

Outdoor location: 173A Hougang Avenue 1, Singapore
Indoor range: Suntec City, 3 Temasek Boulevard Tower 3, #03-040 Singapore 083938
Tel: 6346 4788
Email: dmarchery@hotmail.com

Note: This is a party venue.

Athletics

Australian and New Zealand Association (ANZA)

ANZA hosts a very popular athletics programme.

Course components: The track events offered are 70 m, 100 m, 200 m, 400 m, 800 m, 1100 m, 1500 m and hurdles. The field events are long, triple and high jump, shot put and discus.

Age group: 5 to 16 years

Price guide: $270 per season per child

Location: Serangoon Stadium, 35 Yio Chu Kang Road, Singapore 545552
Tel: 6438 4373
Email: info@anza.org.sg
Web: www.anza.org.sg
Contact details: see ANZA, FAST FACTS, p. 81

Aussie Rules Football

Singapore Wombats

The Singapore Australian Football Club runs a popular junior programme.

Age group: Under 8's, Under 10's and Under 12's

Price guide: Upon application

Location: Australian International School Singapore (AISS), 1 Lorong Chuan, Singapore 556818
Tel: 6883 5155 (AISS)
Email: info@singaporewombats.com
Web: www.singaporewombats.com

Badminton

Singapore Badminton Association (SBA)

This Association is the governing body for badminton in Singapore and its website should be the first port of call for anyone interested in the sport.

Courses: The SBA's badminton satellite centre offers instruction from qualified coaches for both beginner and intermediate players.

Age group: 6 to 16 years

Price guide: $192.60 for once a week for 12 weeks (Badminton Satellite Centre)

Location: 3 Champions Way, Singapore Sports School #03-50,

Singapore 737912 (SBA HQ) / North Vista Primary School – Indoor Sports Hall, 20 Compass Link, Singapore 544974 (Satellite Centre)
Tel: 6767 2868 (SBA HQ)
Email: secretariat@singaporebadminton.org.sg
Web: www.singaporebadminton.org.sg

Baseball

Singapore American Community (SACAC)

The SACAC run eight separate baseball leagues from PeeWee (for both girls and boys) to High School Teams (boys only). Games are played on Saturdays with practice sessions held once a week.

Age group: 4 to 19 years

Price guide: A prerequisite is membership of the SACAC ($160.50 for annual family membership and $160 and extra for programme fees).

Location: SACAC Sports Office, Singapore American School, 40 Woodlands Street 41, Singapore 738547
Tel: 6363 6454
Email: sacac@sas.edu.sg
Web: www.sacac.com
Note: SACAC also runs girls' softball and basketball programmes.

Little League Baseball (Singapore)

Established in 2007, Little League Baseball is exclusively for younger children. Training, teams and tournaments are all on offer.

Age group: Under 12's (Majors) and Under 14's (Juniors)

Price guide: $350 registration fee

Location: Training is held at various venues including Turf City Baseball fields
Tel: 9732 1135
Email: registration@littleleaguesingapore.org
Web: www.littleleaguesingapore.org

Basketball

Basketball Association of Singapore (BAS)

Basketball in Singapore has a long history, and it remains a popular sport. Contact the BAS to find out more about events, facilities and the Junior Basketball League (Under-12's, U-14's, U-16's and U-20's).

Location: 601 Aljunied Crescent #01-04, Singapore 389862 (Beside Geylang Swimming Complex)
Tel: 6743 8425
Web: www.bas.org.sg

Note: If you like basketball, look out for the Singapore Slingers (www.singaporeslingers.com).

Bowling

Bowling is a very popular pastime in Singapore and is suitable for all the family. There are over 200 centres across the island but the following companies are the major operators.

Cathay Bowl

All centres are open to the public and feature flat screen scorers, 36-inch colour overhead displays and bumper bowling for children. The bumper facility means that no matter how inexperienced children are, they will definitely strike some pins.

Price guide: Upon application

Locations: Raintree Cove #02-01, 1018 East Coast Parkway, Singapore 449877 / The Chevrons, 48 Boon Lay Way, #04-01, Singapore 609961 / The Grassroots' Club, 190 Ang Mo Kio Avenue 8, Singapore 568046
Tel: 6444 0118 (Raintree Cove) / 6759 9737 (SAFRA Yishun) / 6795 5900 (The Chevrons) / 6458 0353 (The Grassroots' Club)

Note: The bumper bowling facility at these centres creates a novel party activity. Party packages are available but there must be a minimum of 15 children. As the balls are heavy for little ones (even the lighter balls), I'd recommend it for children of 8 years and above.

Orchid Bowl@Tampines

This bowling centre is open to both the general public and members of SAFRA.

Price guide: $2.70 to $4.10 per session

Location: SAFRA Tampines, 1A Tampines Street 92 #03-01, Singapore 528882
Tel: 6783 60001
Web: www.safra.sg follow the clubhouse link)

SuperBowl

The SuperBowl group manages entertainment services and facilities islandwide for family recreation. It offers the option of annual membership for frequent players.

Price guide: $2 and above per game for students. Charges vary according to location, time of day and whether it's a weekday, weekend or public holiday. An option is membership at $200 per annum ($20 renewal).

Locations: Hougang, 50 Hougang Ave 1 Tampines Road, Singapore 538885 / Jurong, 1 Yuan Ching Road, Jurong Town, Singapore 618640 / SAFRA Mount Faber, 2 Telok Blangah Way #02-06, Singapore 098803
Tel: 6286 1333 (Hougang) / 6226 1000 (Jurong) / 6276 5225 (SAFRA Mount Faber)
Email: superbowl@superbowl.com.sg
Web: www.superbowl.com.sg

Canoeing/Kayaking

People's Association Water-Venture (PAWV)

This club runs a STAR qualification programme that is accredited by the Singapore Canoe Federation and the National Sport Association. It also runs a 1-day Orientation Programme during which participants are introduced to the sport. Kayaking is conducted at all of the clubs except East Coast Sea Sports Club (which specialises in windsurfing).

Age group: 10 years and above

Price guide: $30 to $42 for a 5-year membership. The kayaking Orientation Programme is $20.

Locations: Pasir Ris Sea Sports Club, 125 Elias Road / Kallang Sea Sports Club, 4876 Beach Road / Changi Sea Sports Club, 285 Nicoll Drive / Bedok Reservoir Park / Sembawang, 57 Jalan Mempurong / Jurong Lake, Taman Jurong / Lower Seletar Reservoir

Tel: 6582 4796 (Pasir Ris) / 6296 6683 (Kallang) / 6545 1140 (Changi) / 9710 1697 (Bedok) / 6755 0225 (Sembawang) / 6266 4648 (Jurong) / 9710 1826 (Seletar)

Email: pa_seasports@pa.gov.sg

Web: www.water-venture.org.sg

Note: You must be able to swim 50 metres with the use of a permissible buoyancy aid before enrolling on a course.

Singapore Canoe Federation

For canoe enthusiasts (or those who aspire to be so), the Singapore Canoe Federation is a useful contact that runs programmes for children. The Junior Power programme offers three courses, which starts with an introduction course that focuses upon water safety and then moves onto Canoe Polo and Sprint Kayaking.

Age group: 10 years and above

Tel: 6344 3915

Email: JrProgram@scf.org.sg / info@scf.org.sg

Web: www.scf.org.sg

If you want to canoe on an ad hoc basis, various private operators at Pasir Ris and Changi Beach parks rent out canoes. Currently only Rasa Sentosa Resort (Tel: 6275 0100) hires out kayaks on Sentosa. A popular venue is the Kayak Sports n Beach Pub (Tel: 9620 5672) at East Coast Park.

Cricket

Ceylon Sports Club

This club runs sessions on Tuesdays and Saturdays.

Age group: 12 years and below for junior membership

Price guide: Upon application

Location: 101 Balestier Road, Singapore 329678

Tel: 6297 1009

Email: cscsingapore.org.sg

Web: www.cscsingapore.org.sg

Singapore Cricket Association (SCA)

The SCA have strong school cricket programme in place and an active coaching/training programme. They recently launched a special assistance programme which offers personalized coaching sessions by professional coaches. This helps develop the skills of participants with regular feedback given to parents. The SCA are also looking into a national development programme for Under 15's, 13's and 10's.

Courses: The SCA have held a weekend cricket clinic for children in the past and they are worth approaching to find out if this has been reinstated.

Location: 31 Stadium Crescent Road, Singapore 397630 (opposite the Kallang McDonald's and KFC drive-thru)
Tel: 6348 6566
Email: dharmichand@singaporecricket.org
Web: www.cricket.org.sg

Cycling

The popularity of cycling and mountain biking has steadily increased in Singapore. Whether you and your child wish to enjoy a quiet ride or scale the slopes of Singapore's wilderness and jungle, there is a venue for everyone. The main attractions of recreational cycling are the control and freedom you have as well as it being something that the whole family can enjoy. A useful website providing information about cycling in Singapore and where to rent a bike can be located at:

Web: www.bicyclekingdom.com/rental/Singapore.htm

Having sourced your bicycle, the following tried and tested cycling venues are worth a visit:

Bukit Timah Nature Reserve

This is a popular spot for mountain biking, especially at weekends, as there is a gruelling 7.5-kilometre trail that will tax the leg muscles of most cyclists! The major attraction here is the diverse animal and insect life and it is also a botanist's dream. In fact, the reserve houses one of the most diverse ecological systems in the world so you may want to do some specimen hunting whilst out cycling! The terrain here is challenging and it would be unrealistic to expect a young child to cycle far. However, a visit can be combined with general exploration of the park and a trip to the Visitor Centre.

Pulau Ubin

This is a good place for those who like to get back to nature or simply spend time in an environment different to that of mainland Singapore. The terrain, however, is generally better suited to the more serious cyclist. Bikes can be rented from kiosks near the jetty for between \$5 and \$12 or you can take your own bike across to the island. Whilst Pulau Ubin is a feasible venue for older children, parents with babies may want to think twice before going as it can get very hot and facilities are minimal.

Reservoirs

Some of Singapore's reservoirs offer pleasant cycling venues away from the traffic and activity of the city. Ulu Pandan, Lower Seletar and MacRitchie are all attractive venues but watch out for the monkeys at MacRitchie!

Sentosa

Cycling is an ideal and enjoyable way of exploring this recreational playground. You can take your own bike or rent one from kiosks at Siloso Beach (Tel: 6272 8738 SDK Recreation). You can also rent regular bi-pedal bikes and hybrid electrical bikes at Go Green Cycle and Island Explorer from $12 to $28 an hour (Web: www.gogreencycle.sg / Tel: 6271 1057). Seats for toddlers and bikes for younger children are also available upon request.

Singapore Botanic Gardens

An early morning cycle around the Singapore Botanic Gardens is a blissful affair. The terrain is suitable for all the family and should be enjoyed at leisure. This can be combined with breakfast at one of the Gardens' food outlets — for a special treat try Halia Restaurant near the Ginger Garden for a la carte brunch (Tel: 6476 6711). As the Gardens get busy at weekends, cyclists should avoid the narrower walkways around the park.

Tampines BMX Track

There is a 7-km mountain biking trail and a 300-m long BMX track at the junction of Tampines Avenue 7 and Avenue 9, opposite Sun Plaza Mall. Here, children can practise their freestyle stunts. The trail is currently being upgraded to make it technically even more challenging.

National Parks

Singapore's national parks are safe, green environments in which to cycle. Snack kiosks are at hand as are other distractions such as children's playgrounds. For those who don't own a bike, rental is a practical option.

Popular parks for cycling include East Coast and Pasir Ris in the east, Jurong Central and West Coast Parks in the west and Admiralty and Sembawang Parks in the north.

For the more adventurous at heart there are also four mountain bike trails in Singapore. You can find these at Bukit Timah Nature Reserve, Kent Ridge Bike Trail (downhill), Ketam Bike Trail (Pulau Ubin) and Tampines Bike Trail (as above).

Web: www.nparks.gov.sg (look under Activities)

Bishan Park: Skateline at Bishan Park II (Tel: 6453 3959) rents out small bikes from $4 per hour / medium-sized bikes for $6 per hour / large bikes (mountain bikes) for $8 per hour. Located next to the skating rink, Parks Resort Enterprise (Tel: 6451 5905) rents children's bikes for $2 per hour.

East Coast Park: Beach Cabana (Tel: 6344 4773) at Park Area C (5-minute walk from McDonald's) rents out bikes for all the family. Children's bike rental costs from $1.50 to $4 per hour and mountain bikes cost $4 to $7 per hour. Alternatively, you can go to Our Family Corner (Bicycle Station) (Tel: 6443 3489) at Car Park E2. Here, children's bike rental is $2 to $4 per hour and a 26" bike with baby seat can also be rented for $6 per hour.

Pasir Ris Park: At Rent-a-Bike Kiosk (Tel: 9151 1296 / 9622 1042) at Car Park C, children's bikes are $2 per hour and mountain bikes are $5 per hour.

Park Connector Network (PCN)

Currently there are over 100 km of park connectors that link up major parks, nature sites and housing estates in Singapore. The East Coastal PCN is particularly popular while the Western Adventure PCN is near completion. You can rent a bike from a PCN Pitstop and return it at another without the need to back track. eGuides for the connector routes and pitstops can be obtained online:

Tel: 1800 4717300 (helpline)
Web: www.nparks.gov.sg (follow the Park Connectors link)

Note: In some instances, you may need to cross roads when following the connector links so children should be supervised.

Diving

Living in Southeast Asia affords access to some fabulous diving sites. Pulau Hantu is a popular spot in Singapore, but the best dives can be found further afield in locations like Pulau Sipadan in Sabah. Before diving in open waters, beginners should consider an introductory course (primarily Discover Scuba) in a standard swimming pool. Make sure that the course is conducted by a PADI professional.

Gill Divers

Courses: PADI Discover Scuba, PADI Junior Open Water Diver, PADI Open Water Diver and further advanced courses

Course components: Discover Scuba is an introductory session that teaches basic skills and is conducted in a swimming pool. Open Water Diver teaches safe diving skills through theory, pool practice and open water classes.

Age group: 10 years and above (Discover Scuba) / 12 years and above (Open Water Diver)

Price guide: $80 for Discover Scuba

Location (training pool): Outram Secondary School, 3 York Hill, Singapore 168622

Tel: 6734 9373
Email: gillmen@gilldivers.com
Web: www.gilldivers.com

Note: Marsden Brothers also conducts PADI diving courses (*see* Swimming, p. 118)

Waikiki Dive Centre

Courses: Discover Scuba (a number of open water and advanced courses are also available)

Course components: Discover Scuba introduces participants to scuba diving under the close supervision of a PADI professional. The pool session is held at Outram Secondary School.

Age group: 10 years and above

Price guide: $80

Location: Block 462 Crawford Lande #01-45, Singapore 5190462
Tel: 6291 1290
Email: john.lee@waikikidive.com
Web: www.waikikidive.com

Fencing

This interactive sport develops physical fitness, quick reflexes, speed, agility and hand and body coordination.

Fencing Masters

Age group: 6 years and above

Price guide: Upon application

Location: 177 Ubi Avenue 4, #02-00 Pan Malayan Warehouse, Singapore 408792
Tel: 6841 7671
Email: enquirires@fencingmasters.com
Web: www.fencingmasters.com

Note: Look out for holiday programmes.

Fencing Singapore

Age group: 6 years and above

Price guide: Upon application

Location: 518 Clementi Avenue 3, Clementi Sports Hall, Singapore 129907
Tel: 6778 9918
Email: info@fencingsingapore.org.sg
Web: www.fencingsingapore.org.sg

Z Fencing

Age group: Zketeers programme for children aged 4 to 12 and Zyouth for those aged 13 to 20

Price guide: $192.60 per month for weekday lessons / $224.70 per month for weekend lessons

Locations: 101 Thomson Road, #01-41/42 United Square Shopping Mall, Singapore 307591 / 1 Jalan Anak Bukit, #02-23 Bukit Timah Plaza, Singapore 588996 / 1 Kim Seng Promenade, #03-01 Great World City, Singapore 237994
Tel: 6352 1010 (Main Salle) / 6352 6010 (United Square) / 6295 1432 (Bukit Timah Plaza) / 6325 1084 (Great World City)
Email: fence@zfencing.com
Web: www.zfencing.com

Fishing

Children aged 4 to 12 can enjoy fun fishing at Farmart's Fishing Village in Sungei Tengah Road (Tel: 6767 0070 / Email: enquiry@farmart.com.sg) or at the Kid's Kampong at Pasir Ris Farmway. Catch Sea Water Fish at Kidz Channel in the Fisherman's Village (Pasir Ris Park) also offers recreational fishing for young people.

Kid's Kampong

This is a good fishing venue for young children. Here they can catch fish in the longkang (drains) or feed the ducks and koi fish in the pond. They can also enjoy rod fishing, which is a fishing game that uses a rod to hook up a fish.

Opening hours: 9.00 a.m. to 6.00 p.m. (weekdays) / 10.00 a.m. to 7.00 p.m. (weekends and public holidays)

Price guide: Upon application

Location: 11 Pasir Ris Farmway 1, Singapore 519355 (enter by Aqua Fauna)

Tel: 6583 9030

Email: kidskpg@singnet.com.sg

Web: www.prkidskampong.com

Note: Special packages for birthday parties are available.

For older children or more serious aficionados, freshwater recreational fishing is available at Bishan Park or the following venues:

Pasir Ris Fishing Pond

Opening hours: Open 24 hours daily

Price guide: $32 weekdays / $36 for weekends and public holidays. There is also a catch-and-release pond, which costs $20 per hour to use (suitable for those who have fished before). Children may enjoy the prawn fishing, which costs $14.50 per hour, or pole fishing at $21 per hour (both activities frequently offer a promotion of book 3 hours and get 1 hour free). The sure-catch pond (which is packed with fish) costs $10 per fish caught. The daily time for fish releasing is noon and 10.00 p.m.

Location: 92 Pasir Ris Central, Pasir Ris Town Park

Tel: 6785 5327

* For more about fishing within Singapore's National Parks, *see* Back to Nature, pp. 24 – 28

Flying

Singapore Youth Flying Club

Established in 1971, the YFC promotes aviation among Singaporean youths. It has a Co-Curricular Activity programme in secondary schools, which should be your first point of contact. To qualify for membership, you need to be both a Singaporean citizen and a student. To qualify for the programmes, you must meet various height, eyesight, education and health specifications. The club also runs aeromodelling courses.

Courses: A 3-month course of basic flying with more advanced training available if selected

Age group: 16 to 23 years

Price guide: $10 annual membership (Flying is free of charge for students who meet the stated prerequisites.)

Location: Singapore Youth Flying Club, 515 West Camp Road, Singapore 797695
Tel: 6483 6236/7
Email: info@syfc.org
Web: www.syfc.sg

Go Karting

see Adventure Sports under Adventure Singapura!, pp. 65 – 66

Golf

If your child already has a basic understanding of golf or if you are able to do the coaching yourself, you can try the following venues:

Bukit Batok Golf Range

This driving range is open to the general public and there are golf professionals at hand for those who want coaching.

Opening hours: 7.00 a.m. to 12.00 a.m. daily

Price guide: $6 for 100 balls (4.00 p.m. to 6.00 p.m. weekdays) / $8 for 100 balls (peak for non-members)

Location: 2 Bukit Batok West Ave 7, #01-08 CDANS Bukit Batok Golf Range, Singapore 659003
Tel: 6567 4800
Web: www.mygolfrange.com

Green Fairways

This is a 1,887-m, 9-hole public course.

Opening hours: 6.45 a.m. to 5.35 p.m. daily

Price guide: $40 for 9 holes weekdays / $50 for 9 holes weekends and public holidays

Location: 60 Fairways Drive (off Eng Neo Avenue), Singapore 286966
Tel: 6468 7233/ 6468 7043

* There are other public courses at Upper Seletar Rersevoir, Mandai Road, Track 7, Singapore 779384 (Tel: 6486 0808) / Marina Bay Golf Course, 80 Rhu Cross, Singapore 437437 (Tel: 6342 5730) / Seletar Base (Tel: 6481 4745) / Tanglin Golf Course, 130 Minden Road, Singapore 249543 (Tel: 6473 7236)

Instruction

KinderGolf

KinderGolf specialises in golf instruction for children, using child-specific teaching methods and instructional aids.

Courses: Introduction/Foundation programmes are available leading to more advanced, development programmes. The TeeONE is a unique golf performance course specialising in grooming junior golfers (8 to 15 years) using the latest techniques and training aids.

Age group: 2 to 7 years (8 to 15 years for TeeONE)

Price guide: $180 to $220 per month. A one-time registration fee is also applicable. Trial classes are available for a chargeable fee.

Locations: Ang Mo Kio Hub #03-04, 53 Ang Mo Kio Ave 3, Singapore 56993 / United Square #02-07, 101 Thomson Road, Singapore 307591 / 10A Maju Avenue, Singapore 556688 / Orchid Country Club 10 Orchid Club Road, Social Club House #02-33A, Singapore 769162 / 100 Turf Club Road, #01-02T Horsecity, Singapore 287992 / 9 Science Road, Singapore 609078 / Laguna National Golf and Country Club, 11 Laguna Golf Green, Singapore 488047 / National Service Resort & Country Club, 1 Changi Coast Walk, Singapore 437764 / Great World City Shopping Mall #03-17, 1 Kim Seng Road, Singapore 237994
Tel: 6441 3383
Email: wecare@kindergolf.com
Web: www.kindergolf.com/ www.teeonelab.com (for information about TeeONE)

Note: Golf holiday camps are available

Mini-Golf

LilliPutt

Here you can try out your skills at indoor mini-golf in air-conditioned comfort! No experience is necessary.

Age group: 5 years and above

Price guide: Child (5 to 12 years): $12.80 / Student: $16 / Family (2 adults and 2 children): $57.80

Location: 902 East Coast Parkway, Block B #03-05, Playground@ BigSplash, Singapore 449874
Tel: 6348 9606
Email: info@lilliputt.com
Web: www.lilliputt.com

Gymnastics and Fitness

The trampoline is the best thing in the gym. At first, I was a bit frightened of falling off but now I don't worry at all. At the moment, I'm learning to do twists which I really enjoy!

–Carmen, age 8

There a number of organisations that offer gymnastic and physical education classes. Some of them focus on younger children and usually feature a large, colourful air-conditioned playground. Others are ideal for older children and those seeking coaching and advancement opportunities. Of the latter, Prime Gym and Sporty Joes are ideal venues.

Above & Beyond Gymnastics and Sport

Above & Beyond provides gymnastics classes and fitness activities for children, as well as sets up programmes for schools and clubs. It also conducts a number of gymnastics and sports camps during school holidays.

Age group: 18 months and above

Price guide: Varies according to location

Locations: Venues islandwide including Bishan Sports Hall, 5 Bishan Street 14, Singapore 579783 / Katong Community Centre, 51 Kampong Arang Road, Singapore 438178 / Pasir Ris East Community Club, 1 Pasir Ris Drive 4 #01-08, Singapore 519457 / Singapore Sports School, 1 Champions Way, Singapore 737913
Tel: 9762 2175
Email: email@abgymsport.com
Web: www.abgymsport.com

Note: Above & Beyond also conducts Special Needs classes, currently at Bishan Sports Hall, which are free of charge.

Alpha Gymnastics

Here you will find a variety of recreational and competitive gymnastic programmes, including parent-accompanied sessions for those just starting to develop their gross and fine motor skills.

Courses: Rompers (walking to 3 years old) / Jumpers (3 to 5 years old) / GymStars (5 years and above). More progressive achievement programmes are also available upon selection.

Age group: All ages including adults

Price guide: Upon application

Location: Block B, Unit #02-07, Playground@Big Splash, 902 East Coast Parkway, Singapore 449874
Tel: 9380 3033
Email: info@alphagym.com.sg
Web: www.alphagym.com.sg

Note: A party venue

Busy Buddies

This is a play centre for younger children where they can enjoy a wide range of hand-on activities. Although the emphasis is upon learning skills and socialising, this is conducted in a relaxed environment that encourages exploration and physical activity. Art, cooking, story-telling, sand and water play and puppet work are featured.

Courses: There are a selection of age-grouped classes that focus on physical games and activities. Music, art, drama and crafts and some learning activities are also featured. On Fridays a family playgroup for children of mixed ages is held.

Age group: 6 months to 6 years

Price guide: Upon application

Location: #03-06/08 Great World City, 1 Kim Seng Promenade, Singapore 2397994
Tel: 6733 4140
Email: enquiry@gracekids.com.sg
Web: wwwgracekids.com.sg

Note: A party venue

GIM Sports

GIM Sports is housed in a 5,000 square foot facility and it is equipped with state-of-the-art equipment for gymnastics and fitness classes.

Courses: As well as recreational and competitive gymnastic classes there are trampoline, aerobic and stunt performer's programmes. Ad-hoc Playgym sessions are also available at $10 per session (an adult must accompany the child).

Age group: 18 months to adult

Price guide: $350 per term (10 sessions) for 1 hour of gymnastic instruction per week plus a one-time registration fee of $100. Discounts are available for siblings. Trial classes are $35.

Location: 200 Turf Club Road, #02-10 Turf City, Singapore 287994
Tal: 6468 1103
Email: admin@gimsports.com
Web: www.gimsports.com

Note: Holiday camps are available

Gymboree

While Gymboree is not strictly a gym, it does develop young children's motor skills using fun equipment and fitness activities with music and song. Music, art and social skills are also available.

Courses: Play and Learn Courses (Level 1 to 7) to give children the opportunity to explore play environments and participate in movement games and parachute activities.

Age group: Level 1 (0 to 6 months) to Level 7 (3 to 5 years)

Price guide: Various term packages are available. 12 sessions once a week costs $450. Annual family membership is $50. Trial classes are $34.

Locations: Tanglin Mall #03-21, 163 Tanglin Road, Singapore 247933 / HarbourFront Centre, #03-09/10 1 Maritime Square, Singapore 099253
Tel: 6735 5290 (Tanglin Mall) / 6271 1545 (HarbourFront)
Email: harbourfront@gymboree.com.sg/ Gymboree@singet.com.sg
Web: www.gymboree.com.sg

JWT Kids Gym

Here you'll find fun programmes to foster self-confidence and agility in young children.

Courses: JWT offer a number of courses which seek to develop several skills rather than focusing on one specific area. However, Baby Gymnastic (a fun-led foundation course) and Gymnastic Kids (a real gymnastic programme) concentrate more on gym work. A number of speciality classes are also available including hip-hop, soccer, circus and even personal training!

Age group: 2.5 to 3 years Baby Gymnastics (parent participation classes) / 3 to 9 years Gymnastic Kids (non-parent participation)

Price guide: Upon application. $60 one-time participation fee

Locations: #02-12, 81 Clemenceau Avenue, Singapore 239917 / 46 East Coast Road, Singapore

428766 / Kallang Leisure Park
5 Stadium Walk, #02-03,
Singapore 397693
Tel: 6333 8511 (Clemenceau Avenue) / 6348 1889 (East Coast Road)/ 6344 2320 (Leisure Park)
Email: funnergym@jwtkids-singapore.com
Web: www.jwtkids-singapore.com

Note: Look out for the fun-packed Kids' Night Out happenings! JWT Kids Gym can also host birthday parties.

The Little Gym

Programmes feature movement, music, gymnastics, sports, exercise, games, listening and cooperation.

Courses: A motor skills development programme (Beasties) for young children and a recreational, non-competitive gymnastics curriculum (Flips) for older children.

Age group: Parent and child motor development classes 19 months to 2.5 years / Gymnastics 2.5 years to 12 years

Price guide: $438 per 10-lesson term (Developmental Gymnastics). The membership fee is $55. Trial lessons are $42.50.

Location: Forum – The Shopping Mall, #B1-24, 583 Orchard Road, Singapore 238884/ Marina Square, #03/164, 6 Raffles Boulevard, Singapore 039594
Tel: 6238 6331 (The Forum)/ 6336 9734 (Marina Square)
Email: info@thelittlegym.com.sg
Web: www.thelittlegym.com.sg

Note:
- The Little Gym also offers classes for children with special needs.
- A possible party venue.

My Gym

My Gym at Great World City is located within a one-stop family outlet featuring a children's fitness centre, a shop and a café — all under one roof. Busy Buddies and Rhythm In Me are also located at this site.

Courses: A wide variety of courses are available.

Age group: 7 months to 13 years

Price guide: $375 for 10 sessions once a week (45-minute classes) / $425 for 1-hour classes. There is a one-time membership fee of $55.

Locations: Great World City, #03-06/08, 1 Kim Seng Promenade, Singapore 237994
Tel: 6733 4140
Email: enquiry@gracekids.com.sg
Web: www.gracekids.com.sg

Note: This is a party venue.

Prime Gymnastics Club

This parent-run club has a large, non-air-conditioned gym (which is surprisingly breezy) and a very strong membership. The gym has a separate floor area dedicated to Gymtots and Kindergym and a spacious viewing gallery for parents. For beginners and competition squads, a full range of gymnastic equipment is available.

Courses: Ranges from recreational classes to competitive programmes for all age groups. There is a select advanced class for the most promising gymnasts.

Age group: 3 years and upwards (very young children must be accompanied)

Price guide: Fees vary according to the class and the number of weeks per term. There is also an annual membership fee of $20 per family and a one-time registration fee of $50. Trial classes are $30.

Location: #01-109, Block 17A, Lorong 7 Toa Payoh, Singapore 311017
Tel: 6773 2901
Email: admin@primgym.com
Web: www.primegym.com

Sky Gym

Here you will find standard Olympic sized apparatus including 2 big rectangular trampolines and one that is 12 m long. There is also a slide which leads to a ball pit, a flying fox and many different games.

Courses: Gymtots (1 to 3½ years) / Kindergym (3 to 6 years) / Recreational (5 years and above) / Advanced (by invitation) / Trampoline (7 years and above)

Age group: 8 months and above

Price guide: Upon application

Location: Turf City, 200 Turf Club Road, #02-07, Singapore 287644
Tel: 6466 4656
Email: contact@skygym.com.sg
Web: www.skygym.com.sg

Note: A birthday party venue

Tumble Tots

Each 45-minute session is designed to develop children's physical skills of agility, balance, coordination and climbing using brightly coloured equipment. Programmes also incorporate music and language skills through the use of action songs and rhymes.

Courses: Gymbabes (6 months to walking) / Tumble Tots (walking to 2 years old) / Canopy Preschoolers (3 to 5 years) / Gymbobs (5 to 7 years)

Age group: 6 months to 7 years

Price guide: Upon application

Location: Tampines Sports Hall, 495 Tampines Avenue 5, #02-27/28, Singapore 529649 / Block 134 Jurong East Street 13, #04-309E, Singapore 600134/ CCK Sports Complex, 1 Chua Chu Kang Street 53, #02-10 Singapore 689236
Tel: 6784 0241 (Tampines) / 6897 0413 (Jurong) / 6760 6306 (CCK)
Email: enquiry@tumbletotscck.com
Web: www.tumbletots.com.sg

Note: Literacy programmes are also offered.

Private Gym Membership

ClubFITT is run by the Singapore Sports Council and has a minimum membership age of 12. Members of California Fitness must be 14 and above. For most other privately run gyms the minimum age to use the equipment is about 16 years, but this may be subject to whether a minor is accompanied by an adult or not. Personal trainers operate both privately and within gyms. (Costs vary from $60 to $120 an hour.)

* *see* also Metropolitan YMCA and SACAC under FAST FACTS on pp. 80 – 81 for more information on gymnastic classes

Horse Riding

There are a couple of options for those wishing to extend their child's experience of horses beyond a pony ride at the Zoo. However, horse riding can be a costly business and it is advisable to start with a few ad hoc lessons before committing to anything. That aside, horse riding can quickly become addictive and is an excellent way to improve posture.

The Bukit Timah Saddle Club

The BTSC aims to make horse riding and equestrian sports accessible and affordable to all residents of Singapore (citizens, permanent residents and expatriates) through a non-profit-making philosophy. The beginner's course for non-members is popular as it allows you to try out horse riding to see if the sport is for you before making a commitment.

Activities: Includes school riding, leisure riding, dressage, horse livery and amateur racing

Age group: 5 years and above (Beginner's course)

Price guide: $520 (eight 45-minute lessons) for the beginner's course / $35 per session for Tiny Tots (Under 5's) which is a lead-rein walk on the heath track

Location: 51 Fairways Drive,
Singapore 286965
Tel: 6466 2264
Email: ridingschool@btsc.org.sg
Web: www.btsc.org.sg

Horse City

Here you can participate in riding lessons or simply enjoy trail rides or carriage rides. You can even lease a horse if you are unsure about the commitment involved in owing one. There is a shop onsite and a restaurant.

Age group: 7 and above for lessons (younger children can enjoy a pony ride)

Price guide: There is a wide variety of packages available at various prices. A 45-minute weekday session is $90 / $100 at weekends. A package of five half-hour private Junior lessons (7 years and above) is $400 weekdays / $450 weekends. $275 for five 20-minute pony sessions with a handler (3 to 5 years old).

Location: 100 Turf Club Road,
Singapore 287992

Tel: 6463 6012
Email: enquiry@horsecity.com.sg
Web: www.horsecity.com.sg

Note: A birthday party venue

Singapore Polo Club

As a rule, I have not listed activities specific to privately run clubs. However, as horse riding is an expensive sport, you might consider becoming a member of this equestrian club to consolidate the costs involved and guarantee regular rides.

Activities: At the age of 5, children can join Trail Rides, which teaches them how to handle a horse. Formal riding lessons begin at 7 years and above.

Price guide: Membership packages are available or you can pay for private lessons.

Location: 80 Mount Pleasant Road, Singapore 298334
Tel: 6256 6715
Email: enquiry@singaporepoloclub.org
Web: www.singaporepoloclub.org

Ice Hockey

Canadian Association of Singapore (CAS)

The Ice Hockey Club is known as the Singapore Ice Dragons.

Age group: Mites (5 to 7 years) / Squirts (8 to 9 years) / Pee Wee (10 to 11 years) / Bantams (12 to 13 years) / Midgets (14 years and above)

Price guide: To be eligible to play, you must be a member of the Canadian Assocation (open to everyone). Annual family membership costs $90.

Location: Contact for details
Tel: 6734 5954
Email: singaporekidshockey@yahoo.com
Web: www.canadians.org.sg

Ice Skating

Kallang Ice World

This is Singapore's largest ice-skating rink, which was constructed to meet competition standards. A comprehensive range of ice-skating courses are also offered. The rink can be booked for private functions and parties.

Price guide: $15 to $17.50 skate rental for 2 hours

Opening hours: 10.00 a.m. to 10.00 p.m. (Sunday to Thursday) / 10.00 a.m. to 12.00 a.m. (Fridays, Saturdays and Eve of public holidays)

Location: Kallang Leisure Park, 5 Stadium Walk, #03-06/07 Singapore 397693
Tel: 6348 1123
Email: kallangiceworld@jackinv.com.sg /enquirykallangiceworld@jackinv.com.sg
Web: www.superbowl.com.sg/promotion5.htm

Inline Skating/Rollerblading

In recent years, inline skating has enjoyed a boom. It is relatively easy to pick up, a fun way to exercise and the equipment is portable. It's also a great way to get around the cycling tracks of Singapore's various parks! That said, it is important that anyone rollerblading takes safety precaution and wears protective gear.

National Parks

Inline skating is welcome in a number of the National Parks: Bedok Reservoir park, Bedok Town Park, Bishan Park, Pasir Ris Town Park, Sun Plaza Park, Punggol Park, East Coast Park, Jurong Central Park, Sembawang Park and Pasir Ris Park. Blades can be rented at various outlets In Bishan Park, East Coast Park and Pasir Ris Park. Rental of equipment varies from about $10 an hour upwards.

Inline Culture

Courses: Fun 2 Skate offers classes from beginner level (level 1) to more advanced sessions (level 5). Private lessons can also be arranged.

Price guide: $95 for a 30-day pass (lessons on Saturdays and Sundays) for the Fun 2 Skate programme.

Locations: East Coast Park C3 (skate rink) / East Coast Park E2 (F1 Learner's Track) / Pasir Ris Park (carpark C)/ West Coast Park (McDonalds) / Sengkang Riverside Park (Visitor's Centre)
Tel: 6244 5522
Email: info@inlineculture.com.sg
Web: wwwinlineculture.comsg

Singapore Inline Skating Training Centre

This centre is run by former regional figure-skating champion Mr Law Kum Seng who has more than 20 years' coaching experience.

Courses: Beginner's rollerblading course as well as intermediate and advanced courses

Price guide: $120 for group beginner lessons (4 sessions) and $220 for individual lessons / $250 for individual intermediate lessons. Rental of skates and protective gear is free.

Location: #02-149, Block 3 Queen's Road, Singapore 260003 (and also at East Coast Park on Saturdays and Sundays). The centre also has two fully stocked trucks and will come to any suitable venue, provided that there are more than 10 students.
Tel: 6474 5139 / 9853 1239
Email: Singaporeinline@singaporeinline.com.sg
Web: www.singaporeinline.com.sg

Skateline

Courses: Ranges from Level 1 (beginners) to Level 6 (accomplished/aggressive skaters). Pay-Per-Lesson classes are also available, whereby you register online, buy a lesson pass and then select a time from the lesson timetable.

Price guide: $89 for four weekend Pay-Per-Lesson classes ($25 for one lesson pass). $80 for first Private

Beginner lesson applicant and $25 for any additional learners within a private group. Rental of skates and protective gear is included in the price of lessons.

Locations: Bishan Park I, 25 Ang Mo Kio Avenue 1 / Learner's Track, East Coast Park, Car Park F1. Alternative venues can be agreed with students taking private lessons.
Tel: 6289 0021 (General enquiries) / 6289 4378 (skate lessons)
Email: info@skateline.com.sg
Web: www.skateline.com.sg

SkateSports

Courses: Learn 2 Skate provides an opportunity to learn to inline blade as well as develop better blading techniques. Private classes are also available from beginner to advanced level.
Price guide: $98 for one weekly lesson per month

Shop location: 1 Pasir Ris Close #03-103, E!Hub Downtown East, Singapore 519599
Skate locations: Area C3, East Coast Park / Tampines Neighbourhood Park / Bedok Adventure Park / West Coast Park / Pasir Ris Park (do check website for new locations)
Tel: 6583 0229/ 9182 5447
Email: info@skatesports.com.sg
Web: www.skatesports.com.sg

Martial Arts

The self-discipline and coordination required and developed by martial arts instruction is invaluable to anyone. The added bonus is that you learn self-defence. Many martial arts classes are offered through schools and Community Centres. You may also find ad hoc classes held at weekends in your neighbourhood.

Singapore Taekwondo Federation

Singapore Taekwondo Federation is the national governing body for taekwondo and is a useful contact to find out more information about this activity. Training facilities are available at its National Training Centre.

Location: 260A Tanjong Katon Road, Singapore 437048
Web: www.stf.sg

Aikido Federation (Singapore)

Aikido is a Japanese martial art. It is not a static art but it does place great emphasis upon motion and the dynamics of movement. It involves some throws and joint locks that are derived from ju-jitsu as well as some sword art.
Courses: Classes for all levels
Age group: 6 to 15 years for junior membership
Price guide: Entrance fee is $12 for children / $20 for adults. An annual subscription fee is $24 for children /

$36 for adults. Monthly tuition fees vary from centre to centre.

Locations: Bukit Batok CC, 21 Bukit Batok Central / Bukit Batok East CC, 23 Bukit Batok East Ave. 4 / Buona Vista CC, Block 36, Holland Drive #01-01 / Kampong Glam CC, 385 Beach Road / Raffles Town Aikido Club (only open to Club members) / Siglap CC, Bedok South Avenue 3
Tel: 9669 2851 (main) / 6779 2993(Bukit Batok CC) / 6565 9330 (Bukit Batok East CC) / 6778 5163 (Buona Vista CC) / 6298 4359 (Kampong Glam) / 6323 2323 (Raffles Town) / 6449 8040 (Siglap CC)
Tel: 9669 2851 (general enquiries)
Email: info@aikidofederation.com
Web: www.aikidofederation.com

Aikido Shinju-kai

Aikido Shinju-kai has more than 40 dojos in different locations islandwide and over 2,000 members.
Age group: 5 to 12 years for children's classes.
Price guide: Monthly tuition fees vary from centre to centre. At the HQ at the Poh Leng Building it is $140 for once a week for 3 months / $15 for a single session (member).

Location: Islandwide, especially in Community Centres / Clubs. HQ (and classes) can be found at 3rd Level, Martial Arts Hall, HomeTeam NS-JOM Clubhouse, 31 Ah Hood Road, Singapore 329979
Tel: 6256 0111
Email: hq@aikidoshinjukai.com
Web: www.aikidoshinjukai.com

Chi'Life

Courses: Wushu for Kids, Kickboxing for Teens, Wushu for Teens, Tae Kwan Do for Teens, Wushu Weaponry for Kids, Lion Dance Workshop for Kids and Kids Wire/Stunt Work.
Price guide: $395 for 12 children's sessions. Cost per lesson falls according to frequency of attendance.

Location: Orchard Hotel Shopping Arcade, #02-13, 442 Orchard Road, Singapore 238879
Tel: 6735 8812
Email: kris@chi-life.com
Web: www.chi-life.com

Note: Chi'Life also conducts yoga classes for children. Trial classes for all activities are $40.

Hanmudo Association Singapore

This organisation teaches Korean martial arts instruction.
Age group: 5 years old and above (subject to the student being able to follow the instructions)
Price guide: $75 for 3 months (Tampines Changkat CC)/ $80 for 12 sessions (Paya Lebar Kovan CC). $15 for three months subscription to the Sinagpore Hanmudo Association and $65 for the uniform. The test fee for junior belt is $30.

Locations: Tampines Changkat CC and Paya Lebar Kevan CC
Tel: 9835 3926/ 9623 5493
Email: hbchua@pacific.net.sg
Web: http://pachome1.pacific.net.sg/~hbchua/index

Island Taekwon-Do Centre

This centre is affiliated to the International Taekwon-Do Federation (ITF). Classes are held in a fully air-conditioned gym. You can join regular group classes or have private lessons.
Age group: 4 years and above
Price guide: There are no sign-up fees required to join ITC. Prices for group instruction upon application.

Location: #03-176, 176 Tyrwhitt Road, Singapore 207576 (HQ)
Tel: 6299 8205
Web: www.itf-singapore.com

Note: A free trial lesson is available.

JAG Sport

Although it specialises in children's programmes, JAG Sport offers judo and fitness programmes for all ages. Student-to-trainer ratios are kept low.
Courses: As well as judo, JAG offer chanbara, an art of combat practice that uses special foam-based or air-filled weapons and light protective headgear. Brazilian ju-jitsu classes are also available.
Age group: 4 years and above (age varies according to course)
Price guide: Course fees are payable in advance per term or quarterly and vary according to location. Newcomers are advised to sign up for a two-session trial package at $90.00.

Locations: Budo Academy at 340B King George's Avenue, Singapore 208574 (main facility) / Assumption English School / Canadian International School / The German School / Hollandse Club / Bishan Park Secondary School / Nanyang Junior College / St Gabriel's Secondary School
Tel: 6297 1202
Email: jagsport@singnet.com.sg
Web: www.jagsport.com

Note: JAG Sport also conducts judo camps during some of the school holidays.

J H Kim Taekwondo Institute

The institute is fully air-conditioned with state-of-the-art facilities.
Courses: Taekwondo for Tots/T-KiDs Programme (martial arts/taekwondo programme), Traditional Taekwondo and sport and martial fitness classes for older teens (and adults)
Age group: Below 5 years old for Taekwondo for Tots. Up to 16 years old for the T-KiDs programme
Price guide: Upon application

Locations: #08-00 Lee Kai House, 114 Middle Road, Singapore 188971 / 123A East Coast Road, Singapore 428808 / #01-25 Turf City, 200 Turf Club Road, Singapore

287995 / #01-06 Kovan Centre, 9 Yio Chu Kang Road, Singapore 545523 / #03-11 UE Shopping Centre, 81 Clemenceau Avenue, River Valley Road, Singapore 239917 / Tan Quee Swee Building, 19 Lorong Kilat, Singapore 598120
Tel: 6337 2050 (HQ Middle Road) / 6348 1390 (East Coast Road) / 6348 1390 (East Coast Road) / 6463 0323 (Turf City) / 6288 6993 (Kovan Centre) / 6733 1034 (UE Shopping Centre) / 6467 6728 (Tan Quee Swee)
Email: schoolstaff@tkd-singapore.com (HQ)
Web: www.tkd-singapore.com

Shitoryu Karate Association (SKA)

Formerly known as the Singapore Karate Association, SKA was founded in Singapore in December 1964.
Courses: A junior class is available (5 to 12 years) as well as classes for all other age groups.
Age group: 5 years and above
Price guide: The monthly course fee is $40 for children aged 16 and below/$50 for those above 16 years. There is a $15 registration fee and it costs $40 for the uniform.

Location: 94 McNair Road, Singapore 328561
Tel: 6299 5740
Email: ska94@singnet.com.sg
Web: http://ska.org.sg

Singapore Taekwon-Do Academy

(under Grandmaster B.S. Huan)
This academy is one of the largest taekwondo associations in Singapore.
Age group: 5 years and above
Price guide: Fees according to the training centre.

Locations: Over 17 training centres islandwide
Postal address: Grandmaster B.S. Huan, TaeKwon-Do International, Katong P.O. Box 117, Singapore 914304
Tel: 6241 9098
Email: admin@taekwondo.com.sg
Web: www.taekwondo.com.sg

Tan Zi Gong

Rhythm N'Moves

Tan Zi Gong combines martial arts, dance and gymnastics and it increases flexibility and develop physical strength. Rhythm N'Moves offers a diverse range of dance, music and fitness classes.
Price guide: $100 for a package of 6 sessions (non-member) / $90 member. $20 for membership fee. $20 trial class

Location: 251B Victoria Street, Singapore 188035
Tel: 6221 5315
Web: www.rhythm-n-moves.com

Note: Rhythm N'Moves also conducts dance classes. *See also* p.155

Netball

Netball Singapore

This is the official site of Singapore's netball scene. Here you can find out about the latest developments in the sport, details about the national squad, courses for schools and individuals, as well as a netball forum.

Courses: KidzNet Saturday and Holiday programmes for individual students and KidzNet Primary School Programme. A modular Net4all Novice course is also open to older players (NS arranges the teams, coaches, courts and equipment). NS also has an Under-14 Academy Squad selected from school competitions and open trials. Under-21, Under-19 and Under-17 squads also operate.

Age group: 5 to 10 years for KidzNet Holiday Programme / 7 to 10 years for KidzNet Saturday Programme

Price guide: $160 (about 8 sessions including 2 reserved dates in case of rain) for KidzNet Saturday Programme / $50 (about 2 days) for KidzNet Holiday Programme (about 2 days) / $75 (12 sessions) for Net4all Novice

Location: Kallang Netball Centre,
6 Stadium Boulevard,
Singapore 397797
Tel: 6346 5063 ext. 114
Email: info@netball.org.sg
Web: www.netball.org.sg/
www.sportkulture.com.sg (for online registration to the KidzNet Saturday Programme)

Note: ANZA (Web: www.anza.org.sg) also coordinates netball training and matches

Paintball

see Adventure Sports under Adventure Singapura!, p. 66

Rock Climbing

see Adventure Sports under Adventure Singapura!, pp. 66 – 68

Rugby

Rugby was started by the Singapore Cricket Club as long ago as 1887, although The Singapore Rugby Union was founded in 1948. On the school front, rugby is played by both expatriate and local schools such as Raffles Institution, the Anglo Chinese (Independent) School and St Andrew's School. Rugby in its various forms is also played in primary schools and a few female teams are now appearing on the scene.

Singapore Rugby Union (SRU)

The SRU's primary role is to administer, promote and develop rugby at all levels in Singapore. Therefore, SRU should be the first point of contact for anyone interested in the sport. Its website is comprehensive and provides a good background to the development of rugby in Singapore as well as details of tournaments and events.

Age group: The Standard Chartered

National Rugby Academy (SCNRA) grooms the nation's best age group players from 13 to 18 years old for elite competition. Players from schools and clubs are drafted into five national age group tiers. However, there are opportunities for most children interested in rugby to play the sport, with the existence of various school events for Under-10 Boys and Under-12 Girls upwards.

Tel: 6467 4038
Email: info@singaporerugby.com
Web: www.singaporerugby.com

Blacks Rugby Football Club

The women's wing of the Blacks Rugby Football Club plays both touch and contact rugby. They have a strong programme and are a force to be reckoned with!

Age group: 16 to 35 years

Location: Farrer Park (opposite the APS Swim School)
Email: chongfu@pacific.net.sg
Web: www.brfc.org.sg

Note: BRFC also has a men's section!

Bucks RFC

This amateur sports and social club competes in the SRU's Premier, Division 1, Under-20 and Under-23 leagues. It has a long history in Singapore and organises teams for those under the age of 20.

Activity: One month's rugby training is generally followed by one month's competition.

Price guide: $100 (students) and above per year

Location for training: Yio Chu Kang Stadium, 210 Ang Mo Kio Avenue 9, Singapore 569777
Email: buckrugby@gmail.com
Web: www.brfc.org.sg / www.pitchero.com /clubs/bucksrfc

Note: Bucks RFC also participates in netball.

Dragons Rugby Club

Training is held every Saturday at 4.00 p.m. at Turf City.

Age group: 6 to 16 years

Price guide: Upon application

Location (for training): Behind the driving range at Turf City
Tel: 9663 4342/ 9699 9074
Email: guydicko@gmail.com
Web: www.dragonsrugbyclub.com

Northern Knights Rugby Football Club

Northern Knights is a leading rugby club in Singapore, focusing on youth development as well as social and community rugby programmes.

Location: West Coast Park
Email: edwinkung@yahoo.com
Web: www.knightsrugby.com

Mini Rugby

As the full 15-a-side game of rugby is often too confusing for youngsters, mini rugby is a simplified version designed to introduce them gradually to the game. It lets children use their natural ability to run, chase, throw, catch and score tries.

Centaurs Group

Centaurs Group offers both Rugby Union and Touch Rugby for children. The mini rugby course introduces the skills and technical aspects of Rugby Union in a controlled and graduated programme. There is also an U5s squad that focuses on games and having fun in a rugby environment. The professional coaches are all either current or recently retired experienced rugby players, coupled with over 50 enthusiastic parent coaches, all of whom have experience coaching young children. Other social activities, such as Awards BBQs and Quiz Nights, are also organised.

Courses: Children are taught all the aspects of mini rugby according to a widely adopted Pathway Development Programme that has been endorsed by various International Rugby Unions. Touch rugby follows the Federation of International Touch (FIT) rules.

Age group: Under-5's, Under-6's, Under-7's, Under-8's, Under-9's, Under-10s, Under-11's, Under-12's, Under-13's, Under-14's (Colts) and Under-16's (Colts). Touch Rugby is aimed at girls aged 7 to 18.

Price guide: One time registration fee of $120 (inclusive of player's kit, bag and various discount benefits) / Rugby coaching (for 11 weeks): Minis $275, Colts: $165, U5: $220 / Girls Touch Coaching (for 11 weeks): $55 / Fees for those who start mid-way through a term are pro-rated.

Office Location: Turf City, #02-05, 200 Turf Club Road, Singapore 287994. Pitches are located on parts of the old racetrack.
Tel: 6468 9851
Email: info@centaursgroup.com
Web: www.centaursgroup.com

Sailing

While it is not a prerequisite, most adult sailors began learning to sail when they were young or at least went out regularly on a boat with other family members. Singapore has the climate, environs and facilities to offer all children this opportunity.

Changi Sailing Club

The Sailing Club runs an introductory course that is open to all children. It consists of three sessions of 6-hour instruction.

Course: Optimist Introductory Course. Instruction introducing keelboats and dinghies is also available for older children. Children should be able to swim in order to take the course.

Course components: The course aims to ensure that a child is able to sail one class of dinghy in normal conditions. It involves rigging, launching, all points of sailing and coming ashore.

Age group: 8 to 12 years old.

Price guide: $300 for non-members ($200 for members)

Location: 32 Netheravon Road, Singapore 508508
Tel: 6545 2876
Email: enquiry@csc.org.sg
Web: www.csc.org.sg

SAF Yacht Club

Course: Get Kids Afloat (GKA) programme. (This course runs during the school holidays and gets full quickly, so act fast if you're keen!)
Course components: During this 4-day course, children are taught safety tips and practical skills so that they can sail on a small bathtub boat.
Age group: 7 to 17 years
Price guide: $214 for PR / non-members

Locations: Changi Clubhouse, 110 Tanah Merah Coast Road, Singapore 498800 (HQ) / Sembawang Clubhouse, 43 Admiralty Road West, Singapore 75996. Currently the GKA course is held only at Sembawang.
Tel: 6758 3032 / 6389 3750 (HQ) / 6758 3359 (Sembawang Clubhouse)
Email: ccangel@safyc.org.sg (Changi Clubhouse) / scangel@safyc.org.sg (Sembawang)
Web: www.safyc.org.sg

Note: Your child does not have to be a member to join classes.

Skateboarding

**scape Skate Park*

Run by the National Youth Council, *scape Skate Park forms part of *scape, a 2-hectare youth community space in Orchard Road. This skateboarders' playground has a skating area of over 3,000 square metres, complete with ramps. It is extremely popular with teenagers and noticeable for its colourful graffiti.
Opening hours: 10.30 a.m. to 10.00 p.m. daily

Location: 2 Orchard Link Singapore 237978 (Main Building)
Tel: 6251 6565
Email: enquiries@scape.com.sg
Web: www.scape.com.sg

Skiing and Snowboarding

So you think the slopes of the Blue Mountains in Australia are one of the nearest venues for skiing? Singapore is not a country that readily accepts limitations and this even applies geographically. If it doesn't snow, we'll make it...

Snow City

see Where to Go?, pp. 223 – 224

Soccer/Football

Since coming to Singapore, I've found that mentioning Manchester United is a surefire opening gambit to conversations with any taxi driver I'm seeking assistance from, especially when trying to get a stroller and several bags of shopping into the taxi boot. Contact the following organisations if you want to know more about football or if your children have the urge to get out there and kick a ball.

Since I was young, I have been fascinated by the beauty of football. Since then, my love for the game has never changed. In fact, my passion for the sport grew even stronger when I got the chance to pit my skills against the pros in a competitive professional league — the S-League. The path that I chose to follow was never easy as I have encountered numerous challenges including injuries and coping with the workload of my undergraduate studies. Against such odds, my love for the game never faltered and due to perseverance and sheer determination, it finally paid off when I became a national footballer — the pinnacle of my life. Football has taught me many things. Most important of all, it has shaped my character to make me who I am today. Through my journey as a footballer, I have become more determined, more focused and learnt the strengths of being a teamplayer.

Advice for a young aspiring footballer:

- *Set realistic goals at different stages of your life, i.e., school team, Prime League team, S-League team, national team*
- *Be determined to achieve your goals*
- *Identify your strengths and weaknesses and work on the weaknesses*
- *Learn to accept negative criticism from coaches and prove them wrong*
- *Be down-to-earth when you achieve something*

–Goh Tat Chuan,former midfielder for Woodlands Wellington FC and ex-player for the Singapore National Team (retired from professional football in 2007)

Football Association of Singapore (FAS)

One of the aims of the FAS is to promote the development of the young in the local football scene. To meet this goal, it organises competitions for under-16- and under-18-year-old players. The FAS initiated and helps run the Sunday Mini Football programme for children between the ages of 7 and 12 years. It also assists with the People's Association Children's League, which brings parents and their children (aged 5 to 7) together for fun football activities.

Location: Jalan Besar Stadium, 100 Tyrwhitt Road, Singapore 207542
Tel: 6348 3477
Email: info@fas.org.sg
Web: www.fas.org.sg

National Football Academy

The National Football Academy (NFA) supports the FAS's efforts to promote general interest in football. It aims to take football in Singapore one level higher by providing the framework through which promising players can be identified and nurtured.

It supports this by running regional, feeder training centres called Centres of Excellence (COEs). The academy is housed in its own building with an adjacent training field and swimming pool at Jalan Besar Stadium. Trainees are scouted through a systematic talent identification process and there are teams at every age level from U-14 to U-18. Upon graduation, students are expected to be competent footballers. Professional coaching is given free of charge.

Location: Jalan Besar Stadium, 100 Tyrwhitt Road, Singapore 207542

S-League

The national soccer team (popularly known as the Lions) plays home games at the National Stadium in Kallang. However, it is probably easier to attend S-League matches at the various pitches islandwide. Be it Gombak United, Woodlands Wellington or Geylang United FC, there are a number of teams and venues to choose from. For a nominal fee (cheaper than a movie ticket!), you and your budding footballer can enjoy an excellent night out in a homely crowd. Tickets can be purchased at the entrance to the venue.

Tel: 6348 3477 (FAS)
Email: info@sleague.com
Web: www.sleague.com

Sunday Mini Football League

This league is jointly organised by the People's Association, Singapore Sports Council and the Football Association of Singapore. Qualified coaches appointed by the FAS coach children under 12 years at various football centres every Sunday morning. Parental involvement (e.g., as assistant coaches) on a voluntary basis is encouraged.

Web: www.fas.org.sg (look under FAS programmes and Courses)

Brazilian Soccer Schools

Age group: Under-8's, Under 10's, Under-12's, Under- 14's and Under-16's. 5 to 10 years for girls' sessions only.

Price guide: Upon application

Locations: Turf City, #02-05, 200 Turf Club Road, Singapore 287994 (office address and playing fields are located here) / Farrer Park Fields, 3 Rutland Road, Singapore 218254 / Anglo Chinese School, Tan Chin Tuan Sports Hall 3F, 60 Barker Road, Singapore 309918
Tel: 6468 3802
Email: g.hicks@icdfs.com
Web: www.icdfs.com/singapore

English Soccer School (ESS)

The ESS engages professional English FA and UEFA qualified coaches. The programmes have been developed for Southeast Asia to compliment the English FA's current initiatives for players between the ages of 3 to 17 years old.

Age group: 3 to 5 years (Young Players) / 6 to 10 years (Junior Players) and 10 to 18 years (Senior Players). There are also select teams for Under-14's, Under-16's and Under-18's.

Price guide: $160 for ten sessions. $30 registration fee.

Location: 41 Jalan Pemimpin, #05-04 Hong Beng Building, Singapore 577186 (postal address)
Field location: Next to Kembangan MRT and Community Centre
Tel: 6255 5070
Email: contact@EnglishSoccerSchool.com
Web: www.englishsoccerschool.com

Note: There is also a girls' soccer programme

Global Football Academy

The GFA competes in tournaments and plays friendly games with other schools and academies, besides offering a training programme.

Age group: Under-8's, Under-10's, Under-12's, Under-14's and Under-16's

Price guide: Registration fee is $70 and monthly fees are $50.

Location: Fajar Secondary School Field, 31 Gangsa Road Singapore 678972
Tel: 9488 4126
Email: harman@gfa-sg.com
Web: www.gfa-sg.com/

* An FAS Affiliated Football School

JSSL Arsenal

JSSL was founded in 2002 and is now an official Arsenal Premier League soccer school. Arsenal coaching staff visit regularly during the year to work with both students and coaches.

Age group: 3 to 16 years (Children are grouped according to age in the Under-5's, Under-8's, Under-10's, Under-12's, Under-13's, Under-16's and Under-18's.)

Price guide: Prices vary according to age group. $38 per weekend lesson (you need to register for a minimum number of lessons) / $80 registration fee / $25 per 2-hour weekday session / $20 per lesson for Under-18's and $40 registration fee

Location: Victoria Junior College, 20 Marine Vista, Singapore 449035
Tel: 6348 5780 / 9137 4657
Email: jssl-arsenal@hotmail.com
Web: www.jssl-arsenal.com

* An FAS Affiliated Football School

Note: Each student is allowed one free trial lesson. Parents of Under 5s (only) may pay for just 6 lessons at a time to allow for the child possibly changing his/her mind.

International Soccer Academy (ISA)

Age group: 4 to 16 years (Children are grouped according to age in the Under 5s, Under 6s, Under 8s, Under 10s, Under 12s, Under 14s and Under 16s.)

Price guide: $352 per quarterly term (11 sessions) plus a registration fee of $50

Locations: Turf City (Pitch 4), 720 Dunearn Road, Singapore 289631
Postal address: 39 Arab Street, #02-01, Singapore 199738
Tel: 6291 2337
Email: isasoccer@pacific.net.sg
Web: www.isa.com.sg

Note: Girls' training sessions are available. Holiday camps are conducted in school breaks

Little League Soccer

Little League Soccer hosts football classes in a fun environment and it also organises tournaments so that children can experience competitive football. They currently coach over 1,500 children in Singapore at various locatons, including a number of international schools.

Age group: 4 to 16 years

Price guide: $27 per session at the covered premier Pitch (4 and 5 years old) / $35 per session (8 to 12 years old) / $27 per session at Tanglin Trust School (4 to 6 years old)

Locations: Tanglin Trust School, Portsdown Road, Singapore 139299 / Centre of Excellence (by invitation only), Chatsworth International School, 37 Emerald Hill, Singapore 229313 / The Premier Pitch, 200 Turf Club Road, Singapore 287994
Tel: 6487 5185
Email: info@littleleaguesoccer.com
Web: www.littleleaguesoccer.com

* An FAS Affiliated Football School

Note:

• Trial classes are available.
• It also runs Coaching Clinics during the school breaks.
• Birthday party venue

Nitra United Football Club

Nitra United Football Club actively promotes soccer for young people in liaison with volunteer parents.

Age group: Squads for Under-8's, Under-10's, Under-12's, Under-14's and Under-16's. There is also a squad for girls.

Email: sallehuddin@nitrasoccer.com
Web: www.nitrasoccer.com

Location: Pasir Ris Green Park, Avenue 3 (next to car park C)

Australian and New Zealand Association (ANZA)

Started more than 30 years ago, the soccer activities run by ANZA are extremely popular, with over 1,000 participants. It is a voluntary organisation run by the parents. All nationalities from both local and international schools may participate.
Activities: Training sessions for the Under-5 and Under-6 age groups are held on Thursdays. For the Under-7 to Under-15 age groups, club level technical skills training is also held on Thursdays at Turf City. Technical skills training for all competition team players is held on Tuesday at Turf City. Club level matches are held on Saturdays.
Age group: 3 to 18 years
Price guide: $300 registration fee per season for non-competitive Club Level 'Youth' age groups, Under-5, Under-6, Under-7 and Under-8 ($225 for Under-4) / $380 for Club Level 'Junior' age groups. Fee includes uniform. For competitive teams additional fees may apply. You must also be a member of ANZA, the fee for which is $130 per family per annum.

Location: ANZA Sports City (at Turf City) off Dunearn Road. The Under-4's training is held at the covered Premier Pitch at Turf City.
Tel: 6438 4373
Email: soccer@anza.org.sg
Web: www.anzasoccer.com

Community Development Councils (CDCs)

Some of Singapore's CDCs conduct soccer classes for children, e.g. Central Singapore CDC (Tel: 6370 9901) offers children aged 7 to 15 training every weekend for 2 hours with its Free Kicks programme. Contact your local CDC to find out more (see also Sunday Mini Football League).

Email: feedback@centralsingapore.org.sg
Web: www.cdc.org.sg

Swimming

I love going to the swimming complex at Jurong. My little sister likes the water playground but I like the water slides best. I can only go on the yellow slide because I can't swim but it's good fun. One day when I'm older and can swim, I'll go on the other (blue and green) slides.
–Ying Ying, age 6

Swimming is an essential, life-saving skill. It is also a fun way to exercise and for children who don't like team sports, it is something they can share with others without feeling the stress of competitiveness. Not surprisingly, given the climate and the standard of facilities available, swimming probably ranks as the favourite sport of Singaporeans.

Public Pools

Many excellent public pools have recently been upgraded to feature resort-like amenities such as outdoor jacuzzis, water slides, spa pools, lazy rivers and refreshment and snack kiosks. Particularly outstanding are the facilities at Chua Chu Kang (CCK), Jurong East (JE), Jurong West (JW) and Sengkang (S). Look out for the toddler's pool at Chua Chu Kang and the Kiddy Fun Stations and Bubble Jet Stations at Jurong East, all of which are targeted at younger children. Naturally, they get very busy at weekends.

Opening hours: CCK – 8.00 a.m. to 9.30 p.m. (Tuesdays to Sundays). Closed Monday. / JE – 8.00 a.m. to 9.30 p.m. (Tuesday to Sunday). Closed Monday. / JW – 8.00 a.m. to 9.30 p.m. (Wednesday to Monday). Closed Tuesday. / S – 8.00 a.m. to 9.30 p.m. (Tuesday to Sunday). Closed Monday.

Price guide (for CCK/JE/JW/S) $0.80 for children (weekday) / $1.00 (weekend). $1.50 for adult (weekday) / $2.00 (weekend). Admission fees to other public pools are less.

Locations: Chua Chu Kang, 1 Choa Chu Kang Street 53, Singapore 689236 /Jurong East, #01-01, 21 Jurong East Street 31, Singapore 609517 / Jurong West, 20 Juorng West Street 93, Singapore 648965 / Sengkang, 57 Anchorvale Road, Singapore 544964

Note: For a listing of all public pools, their opening times and facilities, go to www.ssc.gov.sg – the website of the Singapore Sports Council (SSC). Click on the link for Sports Facilities (another useful site is www.swimminglessons.com.sg). Alternatively, all swimming complexes are listed in the Business Guide of Singtel's Yellow Pages under Singapore Sports Council.

SAFRA Mount Faber

This super pool is open to the general public at certain times. In addition to lap swimming facilities, there is a training pool and a wading pool for beginners and kids (adults will enjoy the sunken pool bar!).

Opening hours: (for members of the public) 8.00 a.m. to 9.00 p.m. (Mondays to Fridays, except Tuesdays) / 11 a.m. to 9.00 pm (Tuesdays)

Price guide: $1.60 for children and $3.20 for adults (payment by cash card only)

Location: 2 Telok Blangah Way, Singapore 098803
Tel: 6278 6011
Email: mtfaberclub@safra.sg
Web: www.safra.sg/clubhouse_mf.aspx?pageid=252

For parents seeking swimming instruction for their children in private pools, a few of the better known organisations are listed below. In addition, a number of private instructors will come to your pool or have their own facilities. When appointing an instructor for your child, look for someone who has appropriate accreditation, e.g., from the Singapore Sports Council and/or Austswim.

APS Swim School

Courses: Learn-To-Swim, Endruance Swimming, Cross Training, Competitive Swimming and Stroke Development.

Age group: 3 years upwards

Price guide: Most courses are about $113.40 per month (45 to 120 minutes once a week)

Locations: Anglo-Chinese Junior College Sports Complex, 25 Dover Close East, Singapore 139745 / Anglo-Chinese School (Independent), 121 Dover Road, Singapore 139650 /Farrer Park Aquatic Centre, 2 Rutland Road, Singapore 218253 (opposite KK Hospital)

Postal address: 25 Dover Close East, Singapore 139745

Tel: 6777 5823

Email: admin@apsswim.com

Web: www.apsswim.com

Aquaducks — Swim Centre Vernhoeff

Courses: 6 to 48 months (babies/infants) / 2.5 to 4 years (preschool) / 4 years and above (Learn to Swim) / Development Squad (upon invitation)

Locations: Tanglin Village, 29 Harding Road, Singapore 249537 (next to St James' Church Kindergarten) / The Rutherford, #01-02 Science Hub, Science Park Road, Singapore 118260 / Suntec City, 8 Temasek Boulevard, Singapore 038988 (access to 4th floor through the lift located next to Glamour shots in Tower 2) / Swiss Club, 36 Swiss Club Road, Singapore 288139 / Hollandse Club, 22 Camden Road, Singapore 299814 / Singapore Island Country Club, 180 Island Club Road, Singapore 578774 (babies programme only). Aqua ducks also conduct programmes at various private clubs.

Postal address: 43 Jalan Merah Saga, #02-64 Work Loft@Chip Bee, Singapore 2178115

Tel: 6463 5554

Email: info@aquaducks.com.sg

Web: www.aquaducks.com.sg

Fishlike Aquatic School

FAS specialises in a total immersion training system. This is conceptually similar to the art of Tai Chi.

Courses: All levels from beginner to competitive
Age group: Babies upwards
Price guide: Upon application

Locations: Osim Receation Centre, 65 Ubi Avenue 1, Singapore 408939 / Republic of Singapore Yacht Club, 52 West Coast Ferry Road, Singapore 126887 / Queenstown Swimming Complex, 473 Stirling Road, Singapore 148948
Postal address: 23 Kelantan Lane, #03-016 Kin Hoe Centre, Singapore 208642
Tel: 6583 3031
Email: admin@fishlike.net
Web: www.fishlike.net

Note: Fishlike also conduct a sports academy and offer a triathlon (swimming/cycling/running) programme

LearnSwim Singapore

Why not try your local swimming complex (go to www.ssc.gov.sg) for lessons? LearnSwim teaches at all public pools. Its instructors possess First Aid, CPR and Life-Saving certificates.
Price guide: Group coaching from $50 for 4 lessons (12 years old and below) / Individual coaching from $200 for 4 lessons.

Locations: All public swimming complexes islandwide and private pools
Tel: 6100 7945
Web: www.learnswim.com

Marsden Swim School

This offers friendly, home-based instruction in a private pool run by Austswim-qualified teachers. I found this to be an excellent venue when starting my two-year-old out in the water. The School also conducts swimming lessons for older children at other locations and it runs a number of swimming squads.
Age group: 6 months upwards
Price guide: $28 for a 30-minute group lesson. $28 registration fee. Private lessons are also available.

Locations: 113 Holland Road, Singapore 278556 (Learn to Swim) / Queenstown Swimming Complex, 473 Stirling Road, Singapore 148948 / Australian International School Singapore (AISS), 1 Lorong Chuan, Singapore 556818 and Turf Club Road (enter car park E at Turf City)
Tel: 6473 8353
Email: swim@marsdenswimschool.com
Web: www.marsdenswimschool.com

Note:
- There are qualified swimming instructors for people with disabilities.
- Marsden also conducts diving instruction.

Metropolitan YMCA

Courses: Preschool Progressive Swimming, Youth Progressive Swimming, Swim Club and National Survival Swimming Award (NASSA) tests

Age group: 4 years and above
Price guide: $180 for 10 lessons / $50 monthly for Swim Club / $94.50 upwards for NASSA tests

Location: MYMCA, 60 Stevens Road, Singapore 257854
Tel: 6839 8355
Email: programmes@mymca.org.sg
Web: www.mymca.org.sg

Seal Sports

Seal Sports conducts aquatic courses and activities for individuals, schools and companies.
Courses: The Introduction to Water (Baby Seal) course is for mothers and babies/toddlers. There is also a range of other courses for beginner, intermediate and advanced swimmers (for both children and adults). These include treading water, breaststroke, front crawl, backstroke, butterfly, survival, life saving and competitive swimming. Aqua aerobics, aqua gym, aqua yoga, snorkelling and scuba diving are available for children of 16 years and above.
Age group: Babies upwards
Price guide: Available upon application

Locations: Training centres include numerous swimming complexes, condominiums and swimming pools islandwide.
Postal address: 2 Telok Blangah Way #01-05, Singapore 098803
Tel: 6377 3673
Email: contact@seh.int.com
Web: www.seh-int.com

Singapore Swimming Academy

All swimming instructors are certified by the Singapore Swimming Association.
Age group: 6 years and above for group lessons (private lessons can be arranged)
Price guide: $60 a month for four 1-hour sessions (group)

Location: At public swimming complexes throughout Singapore and private condominiums
Tel: 6680 6530
Web: www.singaporeswimming.com

Swimfast Aquatic School

This school was founded by David Lim, who is well known in Singaporean swimming circles, having won medals at the Olympics and the South East Asian Games.
Courses: There are several courses ranging from Parent / Infant Aquatic Education (5 to 24 months) to Toddler Swimming (2 to 4 years) to more advanced classes (13 years and above).
Price guide: $155.15 (member) for 40 minutes once a week for ten weeks for infant and toddler sessions at SAFRA Yishun / $192.60 (non-member)

Locations: SAFRA Yishun, 60 Yishun Avenue 4, Singapore

769027 / Hwa Chong Swimming Complex, 673 A/D Bukit Timah Road, Singapore 269739 / National Service Resort and Country Club, 10 Changi Coast Walk, Singapore 499739 / Anglo-Chinese School, Shaw Pool, 60 Barker Road, Singapore 309919
Tel: 6472 4288
Email: info@swimfast.com.sg
Web: www.swimfast.com.sg

YMCA

The Swim Safe programme run by the YMCA progresses from water familiarization through play to certification by the Singapore Swimming Association.

Age group: 6 months and above

Price guide: $205 for 10 sessions (member) and $215 (non-member) for Pre-Schoolers / $150 for 10 sessions (member) and $160 (non-member) for older children

Courses: Pre-Schoolers (a parent must accompany each child) is a progressive course covering water safety, water confidence, breathing, balance and locomotion. For older children the course also includes kick and stroke techniques so that they learn to swim breast stroke and freestyle.

Price guide: Upon application

Location: 1 Orchard Road, Singapore 238824
Tel: 6336 6000 (HQ)
Email: members@ymca.org.sg
Web: www.ymca.org.sg (look under Programmes & Facilities)

see also Metropolitan YMCA (for 4- to 6-year-olds) and SACAC under FAST FACTS, pp. 80 – 81, for more information about swimming.

Tennis

Tennis in Singapore does not necessitate a club membership and just about every school offers it within its curriculum or as a CCA. For those seeking coaching outside a school environment, there are a number of establishments to turn to and some of the main ones are listed below. Alternatively, whether you are simply seeking a court to play on or require instruction, try the Singapore Tennis Centre at 1020 East Coast Parkway (Tel: 6442 5966) or The ClayCourts in Alexander Park (Tel: 9636 2007). For a comprehensive listing of public courts, go to Singapore Sports Council's website (www.ssc.gov.sg) and click on the link for Sports Facilities.

Advantage School of Tennis (AST)

AST was the first tennis centre in Singapore to provide an indoor air conditioned mini court (at Turf City) especially for children. It has since opened on the East Coast where the facilities include an indoor Tot Tennis Centre.

Courses: Tennis for all ages and all

levels of ability. Private lessons can be arranged

Age group: Tots Tennis (Pre-School) / Mini Tennis (6 to 10 years) / Junior Programme (8 to 16 years) and adult classes

Price guide: $37.50 weekdays / $37.70 for Tots and Mini Tennis indoor 45-minute lessons (10 lessons per programme) / $25 per outdoor lesson. $60 for a one-time registration fee which includes uniform

Locations: 200 Turf City, #01-63 Singapore 287004 / 902 East Coast parkway, Block B #02-08, Playground@BigSplash, Singapore 449874
Tel: 6466 2643 (Turf City) / 6346 1247 (East Coast)
Email: turfcity@advantageschooloftennis.com
Web: www.advantageschooloftennis.com

The ClayCourts @ Singapore

These are the only true clay courts in Singapore. At present, they are open to everyone and can be booked during the week and at weekends for social purposes. A wide range of lessons and clinics are also available for children and adults.

Courses: Little Aces (4 to 8 years) / Instruction Programme (level 1 to 3) and High Performance Training for older children. Private lessons can be arranged

Age group: 4 years and above

Price guide: Upon application. $15 court booking fee

Location: The ClayCourts, 10A Winchester Road, Alexander Park, Singapore 117784
Tel: 9636 2007 / 8177 9351
Email: art_hobbs@hotmail.com
Web: www.theclaycourts.com

Note: Look out for holiday camps

Savitar

Courses: Savitar's Junior Tennis Programmes cover the entire development cycle, starting with a pre-tennis Skills Builders programme for children aged 3 to 5 years that introduces the basic motor skills and coordination required for any sport. It is conducted in a squash court with specialised equipment and requires parental guidance. Students can then advance to the Parent/Child & Tiny Tots Programme, Junior Introductory Programme, Junior Development Programme and Junior Intermediate/ Advanced Programme. There is also an invitational Tournament Training Team.

Age group: 3 years and above

Price guide: Group programme prices upon application. $75 to $85 for private individual lessons including court hire. A free trial lesson can be arranged.

Locations: Willow Stream Spa Tennis, Fairmount Hotel, 80 Bras Basah Road, Singapore 189560 / Orchid Country Club, Singapore

769162 / United World College, 1207 Dover Road, Singapore 139654 (Savitar also conduct classes at a number of schools and private clubs).
Postal address: Savitar, Bras Basah Post Office, PO Box 302, Singapore 911811
Tel: 6837 3705
Email: tennis@savitargroup.com
Web: www.savitargroup.com/

Note: Savitar also runs holiday programmes.

TFL (Total Fitness Leisure)

Courses: Mini tennis is offered at three levels based upon the LTA's mini-tennis programme. There is also a Beginner Programme for those who have taken up tennis a bit later and who have not followed the mini tennis programme. Children who are more experienced at tennis can join the Intermediate/Advanced Programme and there is an Advanced/Intensive Programme for students showing a great aptitude for the game.
Age guide: 3.5 to 17 years old
Price guide: $110 for four 1-hour sessions per month (except the Advanced/Intensive Programme)

Locations: Shangri-La Hotel, 22 Orange Grove Road, Singapore 258350 /Raffles Town Club, 1 Plymouth Avenue, Singapore 297753 / Australian International School, 1 Lorong Chuan, Singapore 556818 / Chatsworth International School, 37 Emerald Hill, Singapore 229313 / St Regis, 29 Tanglin Road, Singapore 247911 / St Joseph's International Institution, 490/500 Thomson Road, Singapore 2981433 / Avondale Grammar School, 506 Toa Payoh Rise, Singapore 319760 / Canadian International School, 5 Toa Tuck Road, Singapore 5966679
Postal address: TFL Training Consultants, 7 Pine Grove #03-04, Singapore 597592
Tel: 6733 3689
Email: info@tfl-training.com
Web: www.tfl-training.com

Note:

- TFL offer swimming classes for children and personal training for those over the age of 12 years
- (Private lessons can be arranged at an agreed location)

Wakeboarding and Water-Skiing

Singapore is one of Asia's leading wakeboarding and water-skiing nations despite the island's murky waters. Wakeboarding and water-skiing are frequently grouped together but the two do differ. Wakeboarding involves attaching both feet to a board that looks like a water-ski-cum-kneeboard. Part of the fascination with wakeboarding is the many tricks you can do once you have mastered using the board.

Singapore Waterski & Wakeboard Federation (SWWF)

SWWF is a National Sporting Association (NSA) and the National Governing Body for waterskiing and wakeboarding in Singapore. If you want more information about this sport, the SWWF is a useful 'port of call'.

Location: 269A South Bridge Road, Singapore 058818
Tel: 6348 9943
Web: www.swwf.org.sg

Extreme Sports and Marketing

Since 1994, Extreme Sports has provided professional instruction in wakeboarding and water-skiing. It prides itself on using state-of-the-art equipment and facilities. Special equipment is available for children.

The beginner's course is guaranteed i.e. it will be extended until you pass provided you complete it within two weeks. It is recommended that children are 10 years or older and they must be able to swim.

Courses: Beginner's course consists of four lessons on a one-to-one basis. Coaching is available at all levels.

Age group: Although there are skiers aged 3 and above, the beginner's course is only guaranteed for children 10 years and above.

Price guide: Rates from $120 per hour (for instruction) / $30 per slot (about 15 minutes free time with equipment and boat provided) / $150 for beginner's course.

Location: Kallang Riverside Park, 10 Stadium Lane, Singapore 397774
Tel: 6344 8813
Email: cowabung@pacific.net.sg
Web: www.extreme.com.sg

Launch Wakeboard School

Course: The Beginner's course includes a separate driver and instructor and all wakeboarding equipment. If you don't get up on a wakeboard by the 3rd session, you get another session free!

Age guide: 5 years and above

Price guide: $300 for Beginner's Course (3 to 4 sessions) / $400 for Intermediate Course / $450 for Advanced Course

Location: 600 Ponggol 17th Avenue, Marina Country Club, Singapore 829734
Tel: 6581 2202/ 9752 9711
Email: ride@launch2002.com
Web: www.launch2002.com

Maxout Hydrosports Pte Ltd

Maxout Hydrosports runs a 3-hour basic wakeboarding course.

Age group: 5 years upwards

Price guide: Rates for coaching vary from $40 per hour and boat hire from $110 to $120 per hour.

Location: Raffles Marina, 10 Tuas West Drive, Singapore 638404
Tel: 6869 2291
Email: holla@maxouthydrosports.com

Web: www.maxouthydrosports.com

Note: It also offers a basic kayaking course and open banana boat rides and rental.

SKI360° — Cable Ski & Wakeboard Park

For waterskiing with a twist, try here! Participants are pulled by an overhead cable rather than by a boat.

Course: Beginner's Cable Skiing and Wakeboarding course (10 lessons with all the gear included). You must be able to swim 50 metres comfortably to take part.

Age guide: 7 years and above and able to swim (adult supervision is required)

Price guide: $378 for weekday Beginner's Course for a child below the age of 12 years ($478 for weekend). Ski passes are available from $32 for 1 hour at weekdays / $42 weekends and public holidays. Students get a $5-discount for 1-hour passes (until 7.00 p.m.) upon presentation of their student pass.

Location: 1206A East Coast Parkway Singapore 449891

Tel: 6442 7318

Email: enquiry@ski360degree.com

Web: www.ski360degree.com

Wake Dynamics

Age group: 8 years and above

Price guide: $95 per hour weekdays ($85 per hour for students) / $120 per hour weekends. An introduction package is available at $68 for students / $78 for adults (weekdays only, minimum 2 people). Rates are inclusive of equipment and a boat.

Location: 72 Loyang Way@Technics Oil & Gas Docks

Tel: 9760 5084

Email: ride@wakedynamics.com

Web: www.wakedynamics.com

Yoga

Yoga in the West is usually associated with adults but it has a major role to play in the overall well-being of children. Not only is it a means of physical exercise but it also assists in sharpening children's ability to focus. In addition, yoga is an excellent way for children to learn self-control and develop self-discipline as it introduces meditative techniques and, all importantly, correct breathing methods. Boisterous youngsters can particularly benefit from yoga as it has been claimed that the more active the child, the greater the result!

Ananda Marga Yoga Society of Singapore

Course: Yoga for Kids

Age group: 5 to 12 years (there is a 'Workout' programme for 13 to 19 year olds)

Price guide: $170 for 10 sessions. $20 for a trial/drop-in session

Location: #07-01 Parkway Centre,

1 Marine Parade Central, Singapore 449408
Tel: 6344 6519
Email: yoga@anandamarga.org.sg
Web: www.anandamarga.org.sg

KiZroo & MaMaroo (Birth & Beyond)

Course: Yoga for Baby
Age group: Newborns to 1 year
Price guide: Upon application

Location: #05-18 Tanglin Shopping Centre, 19 Tanglin Road, Singapore 247909
Tel: 6736 1636
Email: enquiry@kizroo.com
Web: www.birthandbeyond.com.sg

Shambhala Yoga Centre

Although Shambhala do not currently hold yoga classes for children, they have in the past and it is worth checking them out.

Location: #06-05, Forum – The Shopping Mall, 583 Orchard Road, Singapore 238884
Tel: 6304 3552
Email: singapore@comoshambala.bz
Web: www.singapore.comoshambhala.bz

True Yoga

Lookout for one-hour yoga classes incorporating yogic techniques and basic yoga poses in a playful environment. Currently True Yoga is offering Kid's Combat classes where children can learn self defense moves and improve their concentration and motor skills while having a fun workout.

Course: Kid's Yoga / Kid's Combat
Age group: 4 to 12 years
Price guide: Upon application

Locations: Level 4 Pacific Plaza, 9 Scotts Road, Singapore 228210 / Ocean Towers, Level 27, 20 Raffles Place, Singapore 048620
Tel: 6733 9555 (Pacific Plaza) / 6536 1600(Ocean Towers)
Email: operations@trueyoga.com.sg
Web: www.trueyoga.com.sg

SPORTS AND RECREATION CENTRES			
Centre	**Address**	**Tel.**	**Email**
Bedok	3 Bedok North Street 2, Singapore 469645	6244 5385/6	SSC_BedokSFLC@ssc.gov.sg
Bishan	5 Bishan Street 14, Singapore 579783	6244 5385/6	SSC_BishanSFLC@ssc.gov.sg
Bukit Gombak	810 Bukit Gombak West Avenue 5, Singapore 659081	6896 2193/4	SSC_BtGombakSFLC@ssc.gov.sg
Choa Chu Kang	1 Choa Chu Kang Street 53, Singapore 689236	6767 1735/6	SSC_ChoaCKangSFLC@ssc.gov.sg
Clementi	518 Clementi Avenue 3, Singapore 129907	6872 9180/1	SSC_ClementiSFLC@ssc.gov.sg
Delta	900 Tiong Bahru Road, Singapore 158790	6471 9030/5	SSC_DeltaSFLC@ssc.gov.sg
Geylang	601 Aljunied Crescent, Singapore 389862	6745 7175	SSC_AljuniedSFLC@ssc.gov.sg
Hougang	93 Hougang Avenue 4, Singapore 538832	6315 8670/1	SSC_HougangSFLC@sscgov.sg
Jalan Besar	100 Tyrhitt Road, #01-03 Singapore 207542	6293 9058	
Jurong East	21 Jurong East Street 31, Singapore 609517	6563 5052	SSC_JurongEastSFLC@ssc.gov.sg
Jurong West	20 Jurong West Street 93, Singapore 648965	6515 5259	SSC_Jurongwestsrc@ssc.gov.sg
Kallang Sports and Recreation Centre	15 Stadium Road, Singapore 397718		
Queenstown	473 Stirling Road, Singapore 148948	6473 7269	

Sengkang	57 Anchorvale Road, Singapore 544964	6315 3576	
Serangoon	35-A Yio Chu Kang Road, Singapore 545552	6288 4606	
School of Physical Education **The facilities of this teacher training school are open to the general public after school hours*	21 Evans Road, Singapore 259366	6468 8393	
Tampines	495 Tampines Avenue 5, Singapore 529649	6260 1160/1	SSC_TampinesSFLC@ssc.gov.sg
Toa Payoh	297A Toa Payoh Lor 6, Singapore 319392	6256 7151/2	SSC_ToaPayohSFLC@ssc.govsg
Woodlands	495 Woodlands Centre, No 1 Woodlands Street 13, Singapore 738593	6362 9100	SSC_WoodlandsSFLC@ssc.gov.sg
Yio Chu Kang	200 Ang Mo Kio Ave 9, Singapore 569770	6483 9370/1	SSC_YioCKangSFLC@ssc.gov.sg
Yishun 101	Yishun Avenue 1, Singapore 769130	6851 8600/1	SSC_YishunSFLC@ssc.gov.sg

Note about facilities: In most instances, badminton courts are available, which can be converted into other sports courts, such as basketball, volleyball or netball.

– Chapter 4 –

THE PERFORMING ARTS

It is no exaggeration to say that the performing arts in Singapore have undergone a Renaissance in the 21st century! In the last decade, there has been a spectacular growth in the quality and quantity of events produced specifically for children, with companies such as Act3 International leading the way.

The performing arts education scene has blossomed concurrently in local schools. This has been due mainly to the National Arts Council Arts Education Programme (NAC-AEP), which offers a wide range of quality arts education programmes for students that cover the literary, performing and visual arts. In 2006, the NAC-AEP programme comprised 623 activities! In addition to arts education flourishing in schools, there are now also a number of excellent courses available to the public.

Because this chapter is so large, I've divided it into **drama** (including cinema) and **music and movement** (including dance). In these two categories, you'll find information about children's classes, arts venues and performing arts organisations.

WHAT'S ON?

The following suggestions are a number of ways of finding out and being kept up-to-date on what is on in town to entertain the whole family.

Websites

National Arts Council Singapore

Check out the sections on dance, literary arts, music, theatre and visual arts as well as its comprehensive directory that lists arts groups and arts locations.

Web: www.nac.gov.sg/

The Flying Inkpot

Look here for a comprehensive guide to theatre and dance productions. As well as reviews, there is also information about auditions and workshops.

Web: http://inkpot.com

singaporetheatre.com

This is a useful portal for information about local and international productions.

Web: www.singaporetheatre.com

SISTIC

This site features up-and-coming events and you can also book online.

Web: www.sistic.com.sg

TicketCharge

Find out about TicketCharge's events. You can also book online.

Web: www.ticketcharge.com.sg

Your Singapore

The Singapore Tourist Board website is invaluable as it lists what to do and what to see in Singapore.

Web: www.yoursingapore.com

Publications

(*All available from your local newsstand or *free publications*)

see also Introduction, pp.14 – 15

Expat

Refer to its What's On section towards the back of the magazine.

see also www.theexpat.com

*The Finder**

Check out the section called What's On.

www.thefinder.com.sg – check out Diary of Events

IS Magazine*

Refer to the sections on music, onstage and stuff.

Web: http://is.asia-city.com/

Lianhe Zaobao

This newspaper offers good coverage of arts events in Mandarin.

Web: www.zaobao.com

The New Paper

Various events are advertised throughout, with TV listings and sports towards the back of the paper.

Web: www.tnp.sg

*SISTIC Entertainment Guide**

This is a good guide for finding out about upcoming events.

The Straits Times

Look under What's On in the Life! section of this newspaper. Every Friday in the Life section there is also a very comprehensive page on Events in the upcoming week.

Mailing Lists

Act3 International

Act3 International has both mailing and Email lists. The company puts on some excellent events for children, with its Prudential Children First! festival being the annual highlight. This festival showcases performances for children by artists from around the globe. Just sign up on their website at www.act3international.com.sg/

SISTIC

For information about the latest event, show or promotion, subscribe to SISTIC Buzz. Just go to their website at www.sistic.com.sg and sign up for free newsletter.

WHERE?

Where and how do you get tickets? Where are performances held? Look below for a quick listing of some ticketing agencies and the main venues that feature children's shows from time to time.

Ticketing Agencies

There are 3 major ticketing agencies in Singapore that have outlets in many locations (look in most of the central shopping centres):

GATECRASH

Opening hours: 9.00 a.m. to 8.00 p.m. Mondays to Fridays/ 10.00 a.m. to 8.00 p.m. weekends and public holidays

Tel: 6100 2005 (Hotline)

Web: www.gatecrash.com.sg

SISTIC

Opening hours: 10.00 a.m. to 10.00 p.m. Mondays to Saturdays/ Noon to 8.00 p.m. Sundays and Public Holidays

Tel: 6348 5555 (Hotline)

Web: www.sistic.com.sg

TicketCharge

Opening hours: 9.00 a.m. to 9.00 p.m. Mondays to Saturdays/ Noon to 6.00 p.m. Sundays and public holidays (Hotline only)

Tel: 6296 2929 (Hotline)

Email: booking@ticketcharge.com.sg Web: www.ticketcharge.com.sg

Major Venues

Below is a listing of some of the main venues that feature children's shows:

The Arts House

Location: 1 Old Parliament Lane, Singapore 179429

Tel: 6332 6919 (Ticketing Hotline)

Email: tickets@toph.com.sg Web: www.theartshouse.com.sg

DBS Arts Centre

This is home to The Singapore Repertory Theatre.

Location: 20 Merbau Road, Robertson Quay, Singapore 239035

Tel: 62215585

Web: www.srt.com.sg

Esplanade – Theatres on the Bay

This state-of-the-art performing arts complex houses a 2,000-seat theatre, a 1,600-seat concert hall, a 250-seat recital studio and a 200-seat theatre studio. Here you can enjoy international musicals such as *The Sound of Music* as well as local theatre and concerts by the Singapore Symphony Orchestra (SSO).

Location: 1 Esplanade Drive, Singapore 038981
Tel: 6828 8377 (General Enquiries)
Web: www.esplanade.com

ONE-TWO-SIX Cairnhill Arts Centre

This venue regularly holds children's programmes and houses performing companies such as Act3 International and the Society of Mime Unlimited.

Location: 126 Cairnhill Road, Singapore 229707

Singapore Indoor Stadium

The indoor stadium is the venue of the popular Disney on Ice productions that are usually held annually in March.

2 Stadium Walk, Singapore 397691
Tel: 6344 2660
Web: www.sportshub.com.sg

The Substation

This arts centre hosts an assortment of events throughout the year, mainly aimed at older children and adults. Nevertheless, look out for events such as its Children's Mozart Festival.

Location: 45 Armenian Street, Singapore 179936
Tel: 6337 7535
Web: www.substation.org

University Cultural Centre

This performing arts venue houses a museum, a café and a theatre. Children's events include Babies Proms (SSO) and special kids' events during the annual NUS Arts Festival (in March).

Location: 10 Kent Ridge Crescent, Singapore 119260
Web: www.nus.edu.sg/cfa/venues/overview.php

The Victoria Concert Hall and Theatre

This is a traditional-style theatre venue. Look out for the Stage Club's Christmas Pantomime, musical concerts and other children's productions.

Location: 9 Empress Place, Singapore 179556

Tel: 6338 4401

Web: www.vch.org.sg/

SPECIAL NEEDS

Very Special Arts Singapore acknowledges that access to the performing arts should not be restricted. Therefore, I've chosen to highlight its activities in recognition of its role as a coordinating agency for arts aimed at people with disabilities.

VSA Singapore is a partially funded affiliate of the National Council of Social Service. It is also a non-funded affiliate of Very Special Arts International (USA) and its network of organisations in more than 80 countries.

VSA Singapore runs visual and performing arts courses for children, youths and adults with disabilities. These courses include craft classes, dance and art therapy workshops, exhibitions, public performances, arts camps, overseas exchanges and international festivals. The company enhances the training and rehabilitation of people with disabilities and showcases their talents. Integration into the local arts scene is also actively encouraged.

Postal address: #01-138,
133 Bedok North Avenue 3,
Singapore 460133
Tel: 6448 6275
Web: www.vsa.org.sg

Note: VSA Singapore is also listed in Classes under Arts, Crafts and Cooking (pp. 185 – 186) and under Long School Break Activities (pp. 312)

MEMBERSHIPS

Singapore Chinese Orchestra (SCO)

To receive notification of various events and performances, priority booking and select discounts, you can also become a Friend of the Singapore Chinese Orchestra. *See* SCO under Orchestras, pp. 169.

Web: http://sco.com.sg/

Singapore Symphony Orchestra (SSO)

To receive priority booking for all events and discounts on SSO subscription concerts, it is worth considering becoming a Friend of the Singapore Symphony Orchestra. This can be done online at www.sso.org.sg. You can also download the free and informative Young Friends Newsletter, which lists forthcoming SSO Educational and Outreach Events, from this website. See SSO under Orchestras (pp. 170 – 171) You can also find them on Facebook at www.facebook.com/singapore.symphony.orchestra.

DRAMA

Drama/Theatre helps develop a child's ability to think creatively in terms of the quick reflexes and improvisational skills required. It also fosters the capacity for teamwork in a child since theatre is very much a collaborative endeavour that emphasises the importance of camaraderie. The vocal aspect of theatre means that the child is trained in elocution, learns to project his or her voice and ends up as a more articulate speaker with clearer enunciation.

I often tell the students in my Theatre Studies Programme that apart from learning about theories of performance and honing their stagecraft, they will be equipped with both a sound grasp of the principles of rhetoric and effective presentational skills at the end of the course. And that is a bonus not offered by other disciplines. In our society where first impressions leave an indelible mark and where image is increasingly paramount, to be able to project oneself with poise and confidence is a great asset.

Instead of the old adage 'Don't put your daughter on the stage, Mrs Worthington', I would urge all parents to send their children to speech and drama classes early in life. In the worst scenario, even if your child discovers he or she has no innate talent for the craft, he or she will still grow up to become an astute, discerning member of the next generation of theatre audience.

—Dr K K Seet, founder of the NUS Theatre Studies Programme

Singapore can offer the budding thespian many opportunities and venues in which to foster and develop star qualities. Various companies also put on numerous productions throughout the year that are catered specifically for children.

Many drama schools and companies offer trial classes or run open days. These occasions provide opportunities to see if your child is happy to participate in formal drama training and/or comfortable in the environment in which this will take place. For some children, acting classes will build self-confidence. For others, it develops the skills of self-expression and effective communication. For many, though, drama is simply fun and exciting. One point to note is that some courses/classes may stress language skills rather than focus on acting techniques. While this may suit some parents and their children, emphasis on language may require you to sacrifice the creative side of drama.

Drama Classes

> *The very active teaching/learning method helps a 'loud' kid like Margaux express herself.*
>
> **—Mrs Abigail Levy, mother of 3-year-old Margaux**

Act3 International

Act3 International puts on some super children's productions and has also hosted award-winning short films for children within its Animation for the Young programme. The company was founded in 1984 and has since made a notable commitment to the children's arts scene in Singapore. It conducts drama enrichment courses for children aged 18 months and above. One-hour classes are held over 10-week terms and there is the option of external examinations certified by The London Academy of Music and Dramatic Art.

Courses: Includes prose, poetry, music, puppetry and masks

Age group: 18 months to 15 years

Price guide: $250 standard rate per term or under $210 per term for a module package over 4 terms.

Location: ONE-TWO-SIX Cairnhill Arts Centre, 126 Cairnhill Road, Singapore 229707
Tel: 6735 9986
Email: act3int@act3international.com.sg
Web: www.act3international.com.sg

Note:

• Act3 International hosts the very popular Prudential Children First! festival every March (see pp. 172 – 173).

• Act3 also runs holiday courses during the May/June break and in September and December.

• Act3 also presents the very popular NTUC Income Kite Festival during the September break at Marina Bay where 20 thousand kites soar into the air.

Centre Stage School of the Arts

Centre Stage School of the Arts was founded in 1999 to create an environment in which children can use drama to explore both the imaginative and the concrete world.

Courses: Baby Stage (6 to 18 months) and Play Stage (18 months to 3½ years). There are also classes for children and teenagers that feature acting, speech and drama, voice, music and movement and dance as well as holiday workshops.

Course components: Play Stage includes drama, music and movement, word play and puppets in a fun environment. Drama classes follow a steady progression of acting skills and stagecraft, culminating in acting coaching, audition preparation, television and film acting, improvisation and theatre history in the Upper Stages class (for aged 16 and above). The Theatre Workshop gives students an overall experience of performing arts and theatrical methods. Training includes drama and acting skills, singing and musical presentation and backstage support.

Age group: 1½ years to adult (There is a registration fee of $40.)

Location: Block 15 Woking Road
Singapore 138694
Tel: 6732 7211
Email: info@centre-stage.com
Web: www.centre-stage.com

Note:

- Play Stage classes require an adult to be in attendance.
- Drama and Movement Therapy is also available for children with learning difficulties, special needs or behavioural difficulties.

Community Centres

For convenience, value for money and established programmes, it is worth considering what is on offer at your neighbourhood Community Centre. An additional attraction may be that your child can attend classes with friends, which may encourage shyer youngsters to participate. As both English and Mandarin drama courses are available, it is worthwhile looking on the People's Association website to find out whether your local Community Centre conducts these classes.

Age group: 5 years and above

Locations: A listing of Community Centres can be found on the website given below. Alternatively look in telephone listings.
Web: Go to one.pa.gov.sg and search under PA Kiddies for courses for children between ages 5 and 12.

Crestar Learning Centre

Established in 1977, Crestar Learning Centre has 16 branches throughout Singapore and has taught over 50,000 students. Each of the centres has Chinese, English, dance, music and art departments as well as a playgroup.

Courses: Ballet, speech and drama, arts and languages, music, Chinese, English

Age group: 3 years and above

Price guide: Chinese lessons are $247.15 for 11 lessons over 3 months.

There is a registration fee of $32.10 and a deposit of $100.

Locations: Islandwide
Tel: 6553 6450 (Thomson Plaza) / 6287 6385 (Hougang) / 6560 9997 (Jurong East) / 6344 4588 (Marine Parade) / 6858 9624 (Serangoon) / 6782 8822 (SAFRA Tampines) / 6365 0010 (Woodlands Mart) / 6892 8892 (Woodlands Civic Centre)
Email: enquiry@crestar.com.sg
Web: www.crestar.com.sg

Helen O'Grady Children's Drama Academy

This drama academy pursues a curriculum and teaching method devised under the Helen O'Grady Drama System which coordinates branches worldwide.

Courses: 8 years and below, Pre-teens (9 to 12 years) and Youth Theatre (13 to 18 years)

Course components: Includes speech, creative movement, dance, drama, language development, improvisation, scene starters and parent and end-of-year productions

Age group: 5 to 18 years

Price guide: $40 registration fee with a refundable $100 deposit. $240 per 10-week term

Locations: Main headquarters in Upper Thomson.
Helen O'Grady Headquarters
215/215A Upper Thomson Road
Singapore 574349
Branches in Jurong East, Marine Parade and Woodlands.
Tel: 9223 8443
Email: enquiries@helenogrady.sg
Web: www.helenogrady.sg

Julia Gabriel Centre for Learning

> *I love the BookRoom. It is difficult to choose because there are lots of books! My teacher, Andy, is great fun too. We play games and share our news with everyone but sometimes I can't remember what I've done.*
>
> **—Rohan, age 4**

This centre runs a number of programmes including speech and drama courses. When children reach the age of 5, they can embark upon the Speech Communication Arts Achievement Award Scheme, which goes from Level 1 to Gold Award. The scheme seeks to reward, encourage and motivate learning. For very young children, there is PlayClub which consists of stimulating sessions structured around age-appropriate activities, including drama, song and music.

Courses: EduDrama (Speech and Drama) (2 to 18 years), Mandarin Speech and Drama (4½ to 18 years) and Chinese Cultural Arts (3 years and above)

Course components: EduDrama (Speech and Drama) involves speech training, mime, choral speaking, drama, public speaking and sound appreciation. Mandarin Speech and Drama is aimed at those learning Mandarin as a second language. The course includes voice training, speech and pronunciation, conversational skills, story making and drama. Chinese Cultural Arts teaches Mandarin (and later the Chinese script) through drama, visual arts, dance and music.

Age group: 6 months and above

Price guide: From nursery to kindergarten is $320 for a term of 10 weeks. Beyond that it's $480 for a term of 10 weeks up to secondary school. There is a refundable deposit of $200 for PlayClub and $300 for Play Nursery. For all other programmes, there is a refundable deposit of $50.

Location: #04-00, Forum – The Shopping Mall, 583 Orchard Road, Singapore 238884 / 26 Evans Road #01-08Singapore 259367
Tel: 6733 4322 (Forum branch) / 6737 5348 (Evans Road branch)
Email: enquiries@juliagabriel.com
Web: www.juliagabriel.com

Little School of Big Dreamers

The Little School of Big Dreamers is part of MediaCorp's Singapore Media Academy. The Little School offers a media-based programme designed to help children learn different ways of expressing themselves using Mandarin, body language and performing arts. The programme features a fun curriculum that incorporates singing, acting, movement and speech training to facilitate Mandarin learning.

Courses: Mandarin / English Nurturing Course from 4 to 12 years

Price guide: Registration Fee of $20. $375 for one term of 10 lessons of the Mandarin Nurturing Course, 1 ½ hours per session

Postal Address: Singapore Media Academy, 30 Merchant Road, Riverside Point, #01-13, Singapore 058282
Tel: 6435 6000
Email: kids@eSMA.sg
Web: www.eSMA.sg

Lorna Whiston Speech & Drama Centre

Courses: Early Bird Programmes (3 to 4 year olds), Speech and Drama Programmes (Elementary Speech and Drama, 5 to 6 year olds, Intermediate Speech and Drama (7 to 8 year olds, Advanced Speech and Drama, (9 to 12 year olds), Kids Drama Club (8 to 10 years old, Kids Theatre Club (11 to 13 years old), Trinity Speech and Drama (Grade 4-5 examination), GCE 'O' Level Equivalent Speech and Drama Programme

Course components: Students make presentations, develop good speech habits and act as a means of building up their confidence, character and verbal communication skills.
Age group: 3 to 17 year olds
Price guide: $235.40 (weekdays) / $258.94 (weekends) for a 10-week programme. There is an enrolment fee of $26.25 and a deposit fee of $50.

Location: United Square #04-23, 101 Thomson Road, Singapore 307591
Tel: 6251 7662
Email: enquiry@lornawhiston.com.sg
Web: www.lornawhiston.com.sg

Practice Performing Arts School (PPAS)

The PPAS was founded in 1965 by two Cultural Medallion recipients: choreographer/dancer Goh Lay Kuan and dramatist Kuo Pao Kun. The school teaches theatre and dance in English and Chinese and has an impressive alumni of local talents, including Alvin Tan of The Necessary Stage and Ivan Heng of W!ld Rice. The school was also the founding force behind the Substation Arts Centre in Armenian Street. PPAS is also an important contributor to the development of national arts by virtue of those it has trained and the initiatives it has inspired. It runs a large number of courses for children and teenagers.

Courses: The Story Banq course centres around story building and seeks to nurture language articulation (5 to 6 years and 7 to 9 years).
Age group: 5 to 18 years
Price guide: Stay Banq: $255 (10 sessions) / Drama class: $255 (10 sessions) / Play in Arts: $200 (10 sessions) / Chinese Aerobics: $196 (11 sessions). Do check the website for further details and other courses.

Location: #02-08 Stamford Arts Centre, 155 Waterloo Street, Singapore 187962
Tel: 6337 2525
Email: ppas@practice.org.sg
Web: http://en.practice.org.sg

The Substation

This cutting-edge performing arts centre largely targets teenagers and adults. However, it is worth checking its schedule from time to time for events for younger children, e.g. the Children's Mozart Festival. It also conducts a number of course and workshops.

Location: 45 Armenian Street, Singapore 179936
Tel: 6337 7535
Email: info@substation.org
Web: www.substation.org

The Young Company

The Young Company is a two-year educational platform for 17 to 25 year-olds, and Singapore Repetory Theatre's investment in future stage talents. Members are selected from open auditions held annually. An outstanding few will also work on stage with celebrated actors from all over the world. The Young Co.'s new two-tier model of training aims to help students build vital theatre skills enabling them to establish themselves in the local theatre scene with a thorough, holistic training by dynamic theatre trainers who are themselves specialist teachers, jobbing practitioners and employers.

Age group: 17 to 25 years

Price guide: Free

Location: DBS Arts Centre, 20 Merbau Road, Robertson Quay, Singapore 239035
Tel: 62215585
Web: www.srt.com.sg

Young People's Performing Arts Ensemble

The origin of this ensemble goes back to Singapore Broadcasting Corporation's Radio 3 Children's Workshop but it acquired its current status and title in 1999. The prime aim of the ensemble is to enable children to speak Standard Mandarin with greater confidence and poise and to foster this in conjunction with acting and singing talents.

Courses: Standard Mandarin Speech and Drama: Beginners: 4 to 5 years old / Elementary: 6 years old / Junior 1: 7 to 9 years old / Junior 1: 10 to 12 years old / Junior 2: 8 to 13 years old

Age group: 4 to 13 years

Price guide: $520 for a class of 12 students and $480 for a class of 20 students.

Location: Block 261, Waterloo Street, #03-28, Singapore 180261
Tel: 6336 6776
Email: hotline@yppae.org
Web: www.yppae.org

Theatre Companies

My early exposure to drama and performance work was when I was at primary school. I remember having to crouch behind a very low rostrum backstage during an open-air performance to make a quick costume change! To this day, that moment of being 'invisible' and appearing on stage with a totally different persona remains vivid in my memory.

I believe it was those early opportunities for acting and being on stage before an audience that spurred me on to make theatre my livelihood. I thoroughly enjoy acting and although I am not doing that as my job, I think about it all the time. It gives me the greatest of pleasure to watch my colleagues and the other actors we employ work at the pieces we have conceived and have them help us materialise our ideas.

Having been introduced to performance and performing so early in life, I realise that this is the driving force that makes me produce theatre for children. I therefore wholeheartedly support the ideology of providing opportunities early in a child's life and development. These opportunities feed the imagination and give the child a totally different dimension of learning about the world around him/her. They also enable self-realisation through thought and feeling.

Theatre is magic because it can engage children at different levels: intellectual, sensory and emotional. Good theatre reaches children when it tells a good story and tells it well. Having children participate either in performance work or in a class using drama as a learning tool develops their minds and stretches their imaginations by encouraging a suspension of disbelief, the confidence to test out ideas and the need to seek answers in different ways. A child is never afraid to try and venture; what we need to do is to provide the safe environment for him or her to do just that.

I believe 'Children First' when it comes to the arts. We need to collectively continue to engage our children and young people in the arts so that they do not become like us – predictable, compliant and unadventurous. The arts will pave the way for our children to explore, express and project themselves without fear of embarrassment or shame. Only then can they trust their own thoughts, ideas and feelings. A greater sense of self-awareness can only be good for the next generation. By having confidence in themselves, they will realise their potential for learning and living in communities and societies that demand a deeper understanding of others.

—Ruby Lim-Yang, Artistic Director of Act3 International

As you would expect from the number of drama classes available, there are also many theatre companies. In fact, theatre is the most popular performing art in Singapore. Listed here are some of the companies worth contacting when considering more child friendly, or younger people-orientated, productions.

Arts Theatre of Singapore

Founded in 1955, this company recently shifted direction and now focuses on Chinese-language theatre programmes for children. Past productions (in Mandarin) include fairy tales, such as *Pinocchio* and *Snow White*, and children's musicals.

Course: The Speech and Drama course develops Mandarin speech skills. Activities for 4- to 7-year-olds include acting, singing and song composition, devising tongue twisters, prop making, and adapting children stories. There is also a 4-day Creative Chinese Drama workshop for kids.

Price Guide: $160 for Creative Chinese Drama course. (Runs from 9.00 a.m. to 5.00 p.m. for 5 to 10 year olds. Inclusive of two tea breaks and one lunch break.)

Location: #02-00/04 TAPAC, 182 Cecil Street, Singapore 069547
Tel: 6221 5684
Email: artst@artstheatre.com.sg
Web: www.artstheatre.com.sg

Note: Check the website for further details on other courses and performances.

The Finger Players

Set up under the Theatre Practice in 1996, this puppetry company stages works for children that fuse theatre, human actors and puppetry. It conducts an extensive Arts Education Programme in schools and is also active within a number of schools for children with learning disabilities.

Location: #03-01/02, ONE-TWO-SIX Cairnhill Arts Centre, 126 Cairnhill Road, Singapore 229707
Tel: 6738 6061
Email: tfplayer@singnet.com.sg
Web: www.fingerplayers.com

I Theatre

This company focuses on theatre for children, youths and families and seeks to promote all its works within an educational context. Productions include *Rainbow Fish*, *The Nightingale* and *The Little Red Hen*. I Theatre also conducts educational drama courses and projects in schools.

Location: 27 Kerbau Road Singapore 219163
Tel: 6341 5960
Email: team@itheatre.org
Web: www.itheatre.org

Imaginarts

Imaginarts is a company that focuses on children's and young people's educational drama and theatre. In addition to its touring shows, Imaginarts conducts an extensive Arts Education Programme in schools.

Its current school workshops include First Stages (a creative drama skills course), Showtime (the final outcome of this course is an exciting production), Theatrecraft (applicable to students with some experience of drama and theatre) and WordPlay (involves exposure to a specific text).

Tel: 9742 9286 / 6341 5960
Email: team@imaginarts.org

Web: www.imaginarts.org

The Little Company

This is a division of The Singapore Repertory Theatre that produces quality plays for children featuring professional actors. The plays are staged for two age groups: under-5's and 6- to 12-year-olds. Past productions include *The Selfish Giant, The Ugly Duckling* and *The Gingerbread Man.*

Location: DBS Arts Centre, 20 Merbau Road, Singapore 239035
Tel: 6733 8166 (SRT)
Email: venue@srt.com.sg / youth@srt.com.sg
Web: www.srt.com.sg (SRT)

MIME Unlimited

Past performances for children include *Cinderella Dreams.*

Location: #03-01 Cairnhill Arts Centre, 126 Cairnhill Road, Singapore 229707
Tel: 6235 1325
Email: mimeunlimited@pacific.net.sg

The Necessary Stage

Founded in 1987, The Necessary Stage is known for its challenging and innovative productions. Its Theatre for Youth and Community develops and conducts programmes for schools and other organisations. The Necessary Stage also presents the annual M1 Singapore Fringe Festival, a festival of contemporary theatre (and other arts).

Location: #B1-02, Marine Parade Community Centre, 278 Marine Parade Road, Singapore 449282 (office)
Tel: 6440 8115
Email: admin@necessary.org
Web: www.necessary.org

The Stage Club

Founded in 1945, The Stage Club holds the honour of being Singapore's oldest theatre company. It is an amateur theatre company that is open to Singaporeans and expatriates and provides people with opportunities to participate both on and off stage. It holds regular social evenings in its new clubhouse and plans to offer workshops. The club has put on productions at various venues, including The Victoria Concert Hall and Theatre, The Drama Centre and Raffle's Jubilee Hall. Past performances include *Alice in Wonderland, Ali Baba and the Forty Thieves* and *The Miracle Plays.* A unique feature of its programme is the annual pantomime or Christmas production targeted at children of all ages.

Price guide: Annual subscription for a family is $60 / individual subscription is $40. There is a joining fee of $10.

Location: 24 Whitchurch Road, Singapore 138830
Tel: 6251 1380
Email: admin@stageclub.com
Web: www.stageclub.com

Cinema

Watching movies is immensely popular in Singapore and, in the last decade, there has been a spectacular upgrading of cinemas into cineplexes with digital technology and luxurious seats, and the momentous decision to allow food and drink bought on the premises into auditoriums! It's no wonder that Singapore is said to have the highest movie-going rate in the world!

In some cinemas, 'booster' seats are available for younger children but as availability is on a first come first served basis, inquire in advance and get there early if necessary. Alternatively, I find that an inflatable air pillow — the type you use on planes — is adequate.

Blockbuster films are often sold out at weekends so book your tickets online to prevent your kids from being disapointed (and to avoid long queues

CINEMA VENUES

Central cinema venues include:

Cinema management: Shaw Organisation

Booking hotline: 6738 0555

Online booking: www.shaw.sg

Bugis Cineplex

#04-02 Parco Bugis Junction

Shaw Theatres Nex

23, Serangoon Central #04-64 Singapore 556083

Shaw Theatres Balestier

360 Balestier Road Shaw Plaza #04-04 Singapore 329783

Shaw Theatres Choa Chu Kang

Lot 1 Shoppers' Mall Choa Chu Kang Ave 4,
Level 5 and 6, Singapore 689812

Shaw Theatres Century

2, Tampines Central 5, #05-00, Century Square, Singapore 529509

Cinema management: Golden Village

Ticket hotline: 1900 912 1234 (30 cents a call, $1 booking fee)

Email: customersvc@goldenvillage.com.sg

Online booking: www.gv.com.sg

GV Gold Class

(at GV Grand and GV VivoCity)

For extra leg room, a huge recliner armchair and a waiter in attendance, this is your venue. Be prepared to pay $25 a ticket.

GV VivoCity

(Levels 2 and 3, VivoCity, HarbourFront Precinct)

GV VivoCity is the new flagship of Golden Village Multiplex. It is the biggest and the most luxurious cinema in Singapore comprising 15 screens, all with extra leg room and stadium or electronic recliner seats. GV Max houses one of the widest screens in Asia. There are also 3 Gold Class Cinemas.

GV Plaza Singapura

Plaza Singapura (Level 7)

68 Orchard Road Singapore 238839

GV Marina

Marine Cineplex (Level 3) 5A Raffles Avenue Singapore 039801

GV Tampines

4 Tampines Central 5 #04-17/18, Tampines Mall Singapore 529510

GV Grand

1 Kim Seng Promenade #03-39/40, Great World City Singapore 237994

GV Jurong Point

1 Jurong West Central #03-25B/26 Jurong Point Singapore 649846

GV Yishun : Asia's First Green Cinema with 3D Digital Screen

51 Yishun Central 1 Singapore 768794

GV Tiong Bahru
302 Tiong Bahru Road #04-03/04 Tiong Bahru Plaza Singapore 168732

GV Bishan
9 Bishan Place #04-03 Junction 8 Singapore 579837

Cinema management: Cathay
Email: corporate_services@cathay.com.sg
Online booking: www.cathay.com.sg

The Cathay Cineplex
The Cathay
2 Handy Road (Levels 5 and 6)
Singapore 229223

Cineleisure Orchard
Cathay Cineleisure Orchard
8 Grange Road, Levels 4, 5, 6 and 9
Singapore 239695

Causeway Point
1 Woodlands Square Level 7
Singapore 738099

AMK Hub
53 Ang Mo Kio Ave 3 AMK Hub Level 4
Singapore 569933

Downtown East
1 Pasir Ris Close Level 4, Ehub
Singapore 519599

On weekdays, all children below 7 years of age will enjoy free movie admission with every ticket purchase by an accompanying adult (valid for shows before 2.00 p.m.)

Cinema management: Eng Wah Cinemas
Online booking: www.ewcinemas.com.sg
Email: mail@engwah.com.sg

Suntec Cineplex
Suntec City Mall Tower 3 (above Carrefour)
3 Temasek Boulevard Singapore 038983

Eng Wah West Mall
West Mall Complex
1 Bukit Batok Central Link #05-01Singapore 658713
Booking Hotline for this Cineplex: 6898 9230

**see also* the Omni-Theatre at the Science Centre under Where to Go?, pp.201 – 202

MUSIC AND MOVEMENT

At some stage, most children will participate in music or dance classes. As there are many programmes in Singapore that offer various forms of music and dance, it is advisable to request trial lessons, or at least view a class, before deciding what is right for your child.

It is important to note that many instrumental classes do not accept children below the age of 6 or so, as some teachers believe that younger ones cannot concentrate and do not have the motor skills to play an instrument competently at this age. Of course, everyone knows stories to the contrary but do proceed cautiously as the drop-out rate for instrumental instruction is often very high. You should also consider renting an instrument in the initial stages, if possible.

Dancing is a creative form of exercise and, like music, is an intelligent pastime that requires concentration and self-discipline. Ballet — that perennial favourite of most girls — is said to help develop coordination, improve posture and flexibility and assist in building self-confidence. All these benefits are very attractive but don't forget that some children may not be ready (physically or developmentally) for such classes, .

As a precursor to any class, do expose your child to live performances. These can fuel an ambition or extinguish a whim!

FAST FACTS

National Arts Council

The local directory in the Dance section of the National Arts Council's website is an indispensable reference guide.

Web: www.nac.gov.sg/dan/dan04.asp

Community Centres

Your local Community Centre is always a good starting point when considering most courses, including dance. Ballet, Chinese classical dance, Indian classical dance, Malay dance and other forms of dance may be available. Courses are generally aimed at children over 5.

Web: www.pa.gov.sg

Royal Academy of Dance Singapore

This UK-accredited academy is the focal point for most ballet schools worldwide in terms of curriculum and examinations. It is the largest examining and teacher education organisation for classical ballet in the world and many Singaporean ballet schools follow its syllabus. Contact the website below to find out more or locate a teacher.

Tel: 6762 8993

Email: rad.org@pacific.net.sg

Web: www.rad.sg

Dance Teachers On-Line (DTOL)

DTOL is a membership organisation for dance teachers. It also provides a useful registry of dance teachers, their areas of specialization and contact details.

Web: www.dtol.ndirect.co.uk/dtolsin.htm

DANCE

Dance Classes

The following are just some of the dance companies operating in Singapore. These groups all offer classes but many of them also conduct public performances.

5678 Dance Studio

Courses: Ballet, Chinese dance, kid's funky jazz and hip-hop

Age group: 3 years and above (varies according to course)

Price guide: On request

Location: Orchard Hotel #02-10, 442 Orchard Road Singapore 238879

Tel: 6738 2668

I like ballet dancing because it is fun. I love everything, the music, the teacher and the friends I've made. I could dance and dance until it was dark! My grandmother was a ballroom dance queen when she was young.

—Isabelle Schymyck-Young, age 6

The ARTS FISSION Company

Initiatives led by this company include performances for children at the Esplande — Theatres on the Bay that combine storytelling and music with dance and theatre. The company also conducts classes run by teachers who are trained professionals. Formal contemporary dance technique is taught, together with classical ballet as a training foundation.

Courses: Creative Dance Play for children 3 to 4 years old, Junior Movers for children 5 to 6, Young Dancers Theatre children 7 to 15.

Price Guide: Registration is $20 and membership is $20 for 2 years. Non-members pay $175 for 8 lessons and members pay $140.

Location: #01-07/09 &
#03-03/04ONE-TWO-SIX Cairnhill Arts Centre, 126 Cairnhill Road, Singapore 229707
Tel: 6238 6469
Email: tafcl@singnet.com.sg
Web: www.artsfission.org

Attitude Performing Arts Studio

This school has flourished since opening in 2000. Classical ballet is its main speciality but other dance courses are offered.

Courses: Ballet, Funky Dance and KBT Moves

Course components: Ballet classes are offered from beginner to advanced levels. Both the Royal Academy of Dance and the Commonwealth Society of Teachers of Dancing programmes are offered. Funky Dance combines jazz and contemporary techniques. KBT Moves is a non-contact martial arts programme that involves karate, boxing and taekwando.

Age group: 4 years and above. Funky Jazz is for 5 years and above.

Price guide: There is a registration fee of $26.75. Ballet is $160.50 for 10 lessons.

Locations: Bukit Timah Plaza, #01-15, 1 Jalan Anak Bukit, Singapore 588996
Tel: 6467 9738 / 9679 2560
Email: apas29@singnet.com.sg
Web: www.attitudearts.com

Note: There is a small café within the school at Bukit Timah Plaza where you can wait during lessons.

Crestar Learning Centre

Crestar has many outlets throughout

Singapore that offer various enrichment courses, including exam-orientated dance programmes.

Courses: Bebe Ballet (3 to 4 years), Classical Ballet (4 years and above), Jazz Ballet (6 years and above) and Tap Dance (3 years and above)

Age group: 3 years upwards

Price guide: There is a $32.20 registration fee and a $100 refundable deposit. Ballet is $192.60 for 11 lessons.

Locations: Islandwide
Tel: Head Office: 6342 5600
Email: enquiry@crestar.com.sg
Web: www.crestar.com.sg

Dance Arts Singapore

Here you can enjoy ballet, tap, hip hop, flamenco, salsa and jazz classes for all ages. Ballet instruction follows the RAD syllabus while tap instruction follows the A1 Gilbert Syllabus.

Courses: Children's ballet, tap, hip hop, flamenco, salsa and jazz (from beginner to advanced levels)

Age group: 3 years and above for ballet / 5 years and above for tap

Price guide: $180 for pre-primary and primary ballet, tap, hip hop and jazz (12 lessons) / $90 for an 8 lesson course for salsa.

Location: #05-39 Funan Digitalife Mall, 109 North Bridge Road, Singapore 179097
Tel: 6338 2124 / 6338 7031
Email: dance@dancearts.com.sg
Web: www.dancearts.com.sg/

Note: Trial lessons are available. Ring to confirm.

ECNAD Project

The ECNAD Education unit comprises classes and workshops for the public and touring Arts Education Programmes (AEP) for schools. It offers a variety of dance-based programmes, arts education programmes and courses, but mainly for adults.

Location: #04-05/06/07 Telok Ayer Performing Arts Centre, 182 Cecil Street, Singapore 069547
Tel: 6226 6772
Email: info@ecnad.org
Web: www.ecnad.org

FORMS Ballet and Dance Centre

This centre teaches the Royal Academy of Dance syllabus.

Courses: Ballet (from 3 to 14 years and above)

Age group: 3 years upwards

Price guide: There is a registration fee of $20 and course fees start from $175.

Location: #02-24A Bukit Timah Plaza, 1 Jalan Anak Bukit, Singapore 588996
Tel: 6467 2589
Email: forms@starhub.net.sg
Web: www.formsballet.com

Note: Trial classes are available at a cost.

Jazz Cats

This centre is very popular for both its dance and acrobatics courses for boys and girls.

Courses: Jazz, ballet and tap

Age group: 3 years and above

Price guide: About $210 per term. Trial classes are available at $30 per session. Each class lasts for 45 mins. (11 sessions)

Location: #01-09 Valley Point Shopping Centre, 491 River Valley Road, Singapore 248371
Tel: 6732 4078

Jitterbugs Swingapore

Jitterbugs Swingapore offers several different classes ranging from tap and ballet to hip hop.

Courses: Dance Babes (2 to 3 years old), Acro Kids (4 to 12 years), Ballet Kids (4 to 12 years), Commonwealth Society of Teachers for Dancing (CSTD) Tap Kids (4 to 12 years), CSTD Jazz Kids (4 to 12 years), Hip-Hop Kids (4 to 12 years). There is also Hip-Hop Teens for teenagers from 13 to 18 years, and CSTD Tap Teens. Also, look out for holiday workshops.

Price guide: From $120 (members) and $160 (non-members) per 8-week term. Annual student membership is $25 and for adults its $50.Trial aerobics and circus classes are available for $25 for members ($35 for non-members), and all other trial classes are available at $15 for members ($20 for non-members).

Location: 2 Handy Road #B1-08
The Cathay Singapore 229233
Tel: 6887 0383
Email: dance@swingapore.com
Web: www.swingapore.com

An Approach to Ballet for Young Children

My first dance steps were taken in my own home. To me, it was a natural expression of the music I heard all around me, played by my sisters on their musical instruments or on the radio. Later on, I started formal ballet classes with an Australian teacher, from whom I learnt not only the technique and discipline but also that dance is fun and creative. These impressions have stayed with me ever since, and I try to impart them to all the teachers and students at The Kavanagh Ballet Centre.

Some of our young students were featured in a radio interview and here is what they think about their ballet classes — in their own words:

'You get to do exercises and lots of fun things in ballet.'

'My favourite teacher is my ballet teacher.'

'I love dancing and listening to the music.'

'I feel happy when I'm dancing.'

'YIPPEE!'

Our school follows the teaching and examination system of the Commonwealth Society of Teachers of Dancing (CSTD) of Australia. This system teaches through Expression, Education, Encouragement and Enjoyment, or as we call them 'The Four Es'. Children learn to express themselves and tell a story through dance, thus helping them develop their personality. They learn what their body is doing, what all the steps are called and the countless ways they can be joined together and performed. We recognise that every child is an individual and encourage each of them to achieve his/her own personal best. We are also aware that the learning starts before the child even enters the studio as well as the importance of the relationship between student and teacher. Lastly, dance is nothing if it is not enjoyed. That is why we want our children to leave class with a sense of achievement and come back the following week ready to achieve more.

Of course in the early stages, the children are not aware of all they're learning. Later on, they will realise the benefits of their training, which will carry them through their school education, instilling confidence, self-motivation and discipline as well as a love of the arts — even if they don't become ballerinas.

—Mrs Ruby Kavanagh, Principal of The Kavanagh Ballet Centre

Kavanagh Dance

Kavanagh Body Principles specialises in various dance forms for children and adults and follows the Commonwealth Society of Teachers and Dancing (Australia) syllabus.

Courses: Ballet for toddlers upwards, jazz (4 years and above) and tap (4 years and above)

Age group: Toddlers upwards

Price guide: $220 per term (11 weeks). A one-time registration fee of $30 applies. Trial lessons are available.

Location: Loewen Gardens
75E Loewen Road Singapore
248845 / Toa Payoh South
Community Club
1999 Lorong 8 Toa Payoh
Singapore 319258

Tel: 9176 5558
Email: kavanaghdance.in.loewen@gmail.com
Web: www.kavanaghdance.com.sg

L.A. Dance Connection

This studio offers a wide range of contemporary dance classes based on popular L.A. dance styles.

Courses: MTV Babies, Jazz Babies, MTV Kids I, II and III, Jazz Ballet I, II, and III, Salsa Kids I, II and III. Teens Hip-Hop

Age group: Babies for 4 to 6 years / Level I for 6 to 9 years / Level II for 9 to 12 years / Level III for those who have completed at least two 6-week courses.

Price guide: $25 for a single class (non-members) / $180 per 12-week course (members). If you join, there is a membership fee of $50 and the cost of classes is discounted.

Location: L.A. Dance Connection currently holds classes at the following locations: Dance Arts – Funan Digitalife Mall #05-39, 109 North Bridge Rd / Jazz Cats – Valley Point #01-19, 491 River Valley Road
Tel: 9077 2607
Email: info@ladanceconnection.com
Web: www.ladanceconnection.com

Metropolitan YMCA

The ballet school's curriculum is based upon that of the Royal Academy of Dance (RAD) and provides for students of all levels.

Courses: Ballet, Jazz and Hip-Hop for students 4 years old and above.

Age group: 4 years and above.

Price guide: Basic ballet is $144.45 for 8 lessons for members. You must pay an entrance fee of $10 and an annual subscription of $20 to join as an Associate Youth Member.

Location: 60 Stevens Road, Singapore 257854
Tel: 6839 8355 (to book a trial session)
Email: programmes@mymca.org.sg
Web: www.mymca.org.sg

Nanyang Academy of Fine Arts (NAFA)

NAFA opened its doors in 1938 and is now one of Singapore's leading arts institutions. It is notable for being the only official organisation in Singapore to jointly organise the Chinese Dance Graded Examination syllabus in collaboration with the Beijing Dance Academy. NAFA's School of Young Talents has junior departments in dance, art, drama and music.

Courses: Classical ballet, Junior Creative Dance classes and Classical Chinese Dance

Age group: Minimum age of 4 to 5 years (depending on course)

Price guide: $288.90 upwards per semester for Ballet and Chinese Dance (18 lessons) / There is a registration fee of $32.10 and an audition fee of $10.70 for students who have previous training.

Location: NAFA Campus 3 (School of Performing Arts & School of Young Talents), 151 Bencoolen Street, Singapore 189656
Tel: 6512 4220
Email: junior_dance@nafa.edu.sg
Web: www.nafa.edu.sg

Nrityalaya Aesthetics Society

(formerly known as Bhaskar's Arts Academy)

Founded in 1952, Nrityalaya Aesthetics Society showcases dance performances. It also has an art gallery, holds various classes (primarily for adults) as well as runs monthly seminars on Indian literature and an annual drama festival. While committed to developing Singaporean-based Indian talent in the arts, the society is open to all and has been involved in cross-cultural and experimental dance performances. It is also an active participant of the National Arts Council's Arts in Education Programme for schools.

Courses: Bharatha Natyam, Kathak and Kathakali

Age group: 5 years and above

Price guide: You must join the society or be the child (below 18 years) of a member in order to join classes. Ordinary membership is $35 per year. Junior membership is $25 per year. Dance course fees are $50 for group classes and $100 upwards per month for individual classes. There is a registration fee of $15.

Locations: #01-01 Stamford Arts Centre, 155 Waterloo Street, Singapore 187962
Tel: 6336 6537 (Stamford Arts Centre)
Email: nas@pacific.net.sg
Web: www.nas.org.sg

Note: The society also holds traditional Indian instrumental classes and teaches classical music and art.

Palais Dance Studio

Founded in 1989, Palais Dance Studio offers a full range of ballet classes for beginners through to advanced (and teacher training level). Pass rates for the studio's RAD Ballet examination candidates are excellent. Pupils also perform in charity and public productions.

Courses: Ballet, modern and tap

Course components: The beginner ballet programme is a 2-year, in-house comprehensive programme that introduces students to the basics of classical ballet, good posture and response to music. Pupils who complete their beginner training may then proceed to follow the RAD syllabus.

Age group: Minimum age of 4 to 5 years (ballet) / 6 years (tap)

Price guide: On request.

Location: #02-16/18 Crown Centre, 557 Bukit Timah Road, Singapore 269694
Tel: 6467 7788
Web: www.palaisdance.com.sg

Rhythm N'Moves

* *see also* Tan Zi Gong, p.106

Rhythm N'Moves offers classes in dance, music and general fitness.

Price guide: $100 for a package of 6 sessions (non-member) / $90 member. $20 for membership fee. $20 trial class

Location: 251B Victoria Street, Singapore 188035
Tel: 6221 5315
Web: www.rhythm-n-moves.com

Singapore Ballet Academy

Established in 1958, the Singapore Ballet Academy is the oldest ballet school in Singapore. It offers a wide range of ballet courses including instruction for young children. Here you can expect quality instruction while commitment and dedication is expected from all would-be ballerinas. Waiting lists are very long for some courses, such as Beginner Ballet.

Age group: 4 years and above

Price guide: There is an assessment fee of $10.70. On acceptance, there is a registration fee of $21.40 and a refundable deposit of $100. Fees are $160 for an 11-week term.

Location: Singapore Ballet Academy 51 Waterloo Street #04-01/02/03 Singapore 187969
Tel: 6337 9125
Email: enquiries@singaporeballetacademy.com.sg
Web: www.singaporeballetacademy.com.sg

Note: The academy assesses children prior to enrolment to determine whether or not they are ready to learn ballet. Boys (usually 7 years and above) can join mixed classes.

Singapore Indian Fine Arts Society (SIFAS)

The Singapore Indian Fine Arts Society was founded in 1949. Its principal activity is training graduates in the performing arts but it also conducts programmes run by visiting performers from overseas and hosts concerts.

Courses: Dance and music (various)

Age group: There is a minimum age of 5 for entry to the academy. Dance students below 8 years must join the preparatory course.

Price guide: There is a $50 membership fee. Fees start from $115 for 4 lessons.

Location: 2A Starlight Road, Singapore 217755 and certain Community Centres
Tel: 6299 5929
Email: admin@sifas.org
Web: www.sifas.org

Tanglin Arts Dance Studio (home of Happy Feet Dance)

something for preschoolers (and above!)

Offering its classes in a pleasant location within Tanglin Village, Tanglin Arts Dance Studio focuses on developing self-esteem and a love of dance.

Courses: Ballet, tap, jazz and hip hop. There are various dance-exercise classes for children aged 5 years and below. Tap and hip hop classes are available specifically for boys. There is even a class for students who are not potty-trained yet — Mommies & Me.
Age group: 2½ years and above. Note that placement of students in classes is based on ability and age.
Price guide: Prices start from $360 for a semester of ½ hour lessons. There is a registration fee of $30 a child. Trial classes are available at $30.

Location: 100 Turf Club Road #01-02 Horsecity Block K Singapore 287992
Tel: 6479 0304
Email: happyfeetsingapore@yahoo.com
Web: www.tanglinartsdancestudio.com/

Note: A great birthday party venue, with an assortment of packages to choose from.

Dance Companies

Odyssey Dance Theatre

This contemporary dance company stages three to four productions a year and also undertakes overseas performances and Artiste-in-School programmes, workshops and master classes. ODT's Arts4yoUths division began in 2003 and offers a number of courses to the public.
Courses: DancEduTRAIN (4 to 13 years) introduces creative dance, movement, dance exercises/activities and basic skills in dance presentations. There are 3 levels: Dance Tots (4 to 6 years), Dance Kids (7 to 10 years) and Dance Teens (11 to 3 years). ODT also offers a 2-week Intensive Dance Programme for beginners to intermediate level that usually runs in the December or June holidays.
Price guide: From a 1-day full programme for $120 to a 2-week full programme for $800.

Location: #04-08, Telok Ayer Performing Arts Centre, 182 Cecil Street, Singapore 069547
Tel: 6221 5516 / 6221 5229
Email: odysseydance@pacific.net.sg
Web: www.odysseydancetheatre.com / www.arts4youths.com

Singapore Dance Theatre

This mixed-repertoire company gives performances in schools as well as publicly. You and your family may well enjoy one of its Ballet under the Stars performances at Fort Canning Park. It also conducts contemporary dance, jazz, ballet and pilates classes for adults, which may interest older children.

Location: 2nd Storey, Fort Canning Centre, Cox Terrace, Singapore 179618
Tel: 6338 0611
Email: ticketing@singaporedancetheatre.com
Web: www.singaporedancetheatre.com

MUSIC

Growing Up with Music

I cannot really remember when I first encountered music. I can however vividly recall my first piano lesson at the age of 4. My music teacher lived in the same neighbourhood and I was walked to her home every week. At the very first lesson, I learnt where middle C was (just above the keyhole!) and played a very simple tune based on the 3 notes around middle C.

She was not worried if I did not take any piano exams; enjoying music was more important. She showed me a piano book with faces of the great composers, read me their names and played some of their pieces. For the first time, I encountered such long and exotic names as Rubinstein and Rachmaninoff and was enchanted by the music even though I could not play it. She also taught me simpler pieces that introduced me to some of classical music's best tunes such as Dvorak's New World Symphony *and Verdi's* Aida. *That marked a turning point. Classical music became accessible and close to my heart rather than some high flown and distant ideal.*

At 6, my mother gave me a beat-up record player that played both 33 and 45 rpm discs and a small collection of old LPs. What treasures these were, opening my ears to more music. I remember arranging the furniture around the player to resemble a mini concert hall, filling the seats with a virtual audience — my collection of teddy bears and stuffed toys. Whenever I hear these pieces today, there is a sense of déjà vu.

As my piano lessons progressed, I was able to play slightly more advanced pieces. One work that caught my attention was Scott Joplin's The Entertainer. *I played that ragtime piece more often and more loudly than any other, leading my parents to wonder what they had started — a spark of interest in music had become a bonfire.*

As a teenager, I had no need for the pop music that my classmates and friends listened to. I did not feel any less hip because I loved classical music. Classical music provided me with all the inspiration and pleasures that formed impressionable minds at that age.

I experienced my first live concert at 14, attending a concert by the Singapore Symphony Orchestra. I was immediately hooked by the wealth of beautiful sounds and the sheer variety of music that was performed. The simple-mindedness and shallowness of pop music soon became apparent. When I had money to spare, I bought tapes of various classical composers' 'Greatest Hits'. In those days, bootleg recordings from Indonesia were legion and cost only $2 a piece.

Although I no longer had piano lessons, I had mustered enough technique to learn the pieces I had heard on tape. How proud I felt each time after playing Beethoven's Moonlight Sonata *or sections of Gershwin's* Rhapsody in Blue*!*

As a student, I was fortunate to have classmates and friends who had similar interests. We organised mini-performances and trips to the orchestra, and some of them later became professional musicians. Lifelong friendships were forged because of a common bond — the love of music.

I cannot over-emphasise the positive impact that music has made on my life. It helped enrich and nurture a growing mind. Most important is a loving and caring family environment that encourages the pursuit and expression of one's passions and dreams.

—Dr Chang Tou Liang, a family physician, is probably Singapore's most prolific writer about classical music. He was the Artistic Director of the Singapore International Piano Festival from 2004 to 2008. He has also been the classical music reviewer of *The Straits Times* (Singapore's national daily) since 1997.

Music Classes

Centre Stage School of the Arts

If your child enjoys creating a noise, perhaps percussion and drum instruction will appeal! Centre Stage offers such a course.

Course: Upbeat!

Course components: Students learn the basics of rhythm and drumming techniques using instruments from all over the world, as well as standard drums. The emphasis is on enjoyment of rhythm, group collaboration and making a noise! In UpBeat! Level 3 the students have the opportunity to be involved in 'Samabassadors', Centre Stage's very own percussion based performance group.

Age group: 6 to 14 years

Price guide: On application. There is a $40 registration fee.

Location: Block 15 Woking Road Singapore 138694
Tel: 6732 7211
Email: info@centre-stage.com
Web: www.centre-stage.com

The Chinese Opera Institute (COI)

The Chinese Opera Institute is active in promoting all facets of Chinese opera, particularly to the young and thus works with schools. It is both a training and research centre and regularly puts on performances, including shadow puppet plays such as *The Monkey King* and the *White Bone Demoness* and original interpretations of classics such as *Cinderella* and *The Ramayana*.

In 1998, the COI set up the Children's Ensemble. Members of the ensemble are trained in all aspects of Chinese opera including acrobatics. Ranging from 6 to 13 years of age, its members have won overseas acclaim at venues in Japan, Finland and Germany. They have also presented operas at festivals in Singapore including the Asian Storytelling Festival. In addition, the COI organises the annual Youth Opera Showcase (usually held in July/August) to showcase the talents of Singaporean youths in the performance of Chinese opera.

The COI also organises educational programmes like visits to watch street opera for school students as well as children's opera camps during the school holidays.

Location: 182 Cecil Street #02-05 Singapore 069547
Tel: 6222 6551
Email: coisinga@singnet.com.sg
Web: www.chineseoperainstitute.com.sg

Note: For those interested in Chinese opera, the Chinese Opera Society is worth contacting. It also runs a Chinese Opera Resource Centre.

Coronation Music School

Courses: Classical singing, guitar, violin, clarinet, flute, piano, saxophone and cello

Age group: 5 years and above

Price guide: On application.

Location: #03-10 Coronation Shopping Plaza, 587 Bukit Timah Road, Singapore 269707
Tel: 6467 3883

Crestar Learning Centre

Crestar's music department offers both Suzuki and classical approaches to music instruction. The Suzuki approach, also known as the mother-tongue method, differs from traditional methods of teaching instrumental music because it involves students at a very young age. It is based upon the philosophy of late master Professor Shinichi Suzuki.

Courses: Suzuki violin course (3 years and above) and classical violin course (5 years and above). Piano lessons are also available at some branches.

Age group: 3 years and above

Price guide: Fees start from $272.85 for group lessons per term or $390.55 for individual lessons per term.

Locations: Islandwide
Tel: 6342 5600 (Head Office at Marine Parade)
Email: enquiry@crestar.com.sg
Web: www.crestar.com.sg

Cristofori Music School

Courses: Music for Baby Mozarts is for children below 3 years 6 months of age and its aim is for them to enjoy the fun of music. Music for Little Mozarts (3 ½ years to 5 years), violin, guitar, electric organ, music theory and both classical and pop piano

Course components: Music for Little Mozarts is a formal music foundation course. It involves singing, music theory, note reading, keyboard playing, movement and rhythmic skills. Parents need not accompany their child during the lesson. The violin course combines traditional and Suzuki methods while the music theory course follows the ABRSM music syllabus. The classical piano course is a one-to-one course (with one group interactive lesson per month) and follows the ABRSM music syllabus.

Age group: Music for Little Mozart is for 3 years 10 months to 5 years / Classical Piano is for 5 to 15 years / Classical Violin is for 6 years and above

Price guide: Music for Baby Mozarts is $200+ for an 11-week course, 45 mins per lesson / Music for Little Mozarts starts off at Level 1, $192.60 for 8 lessons of one hour each and ends off at Level 4, $240.75 for 10 lessons of one hour each.

Locations: Islandwide
Tel: 6338 0009
Email: cmmusic@pacific.net.sg
Web: www.cms.edu.sg

Curtis Music School

This school also offers concert performing opportunities and holiday camps.

Courses: Musikgarten (24 months to 6 years), Prep Course for the Young Beginner (4 years and above), Suzuki Cello (3 years and above) and instrumental classes for piano, violin, guitar and vocal training

Course components: Musikgarten is an introduction to music using song, stories and dance. The Prep course develops keyboard skills and music literacy. Instrumental classes range from beginner to diploma level and follow the ABRSM, Trinity and AMEB music board syllabuses.

Price guide: On request

Location: King's Arcade,
#02-02A 559 Bukit Timah Road,
Singapore 269695
Tel: 6465 4998
Email: info@curtismusicschool.com.sg
Web: www.curtismusicschool.com.sg

eZoo

Located in a beautiful environment, eZoo teaches a range of arts courses.

Courses: Music Appreciation, classical and pop piano, classical and electric guitar and violin (Group sessions with four to six children or individual sessions are available.)

Course components: Music Appreciation involves using percussion instruments, performing body movements to music as well as exposure to a variety of other musical instruments.

Age group: 4 years and above

Price guide: $120 per month for individual piano lessons (four 30-minute lessons) for the basic grade to $300 a month for 4 lessons for Grade 8.

Location: #01-01, 2 Swiss View,
Singapore 288008
Tel: 6469 4660
A second branch is opening up at 2 Hindhehe Road Singapore 589239, opposite Bukit Timah Courts.
Email: enquiry@ezoomusic.com
Web: www.ezoomusic.com

Gramercy Music School

This music school also has a small showroom, with instruments and sheet music for sale.

Courses: Instrumental classes include classical piano, pop piano, guitar, recorder, flute, clarinet, violin, saxophone, trumpet and French horn. There is also a Children's Music Course.

Age group: 3 years and above

Price guide: On request.

Location: Chip Bee Gardens,
#01 –72, 43 Jalan Merah Saga,
Singapore 278115
Tel: 6474 9598

Gymboree

something for preschoolers!

Gymboree's programme offers a year-long rotation of musical styles ranging from classical to Cajun Zydeco. It emphasises exploration, enjoyment and foundational experience in music rather than achievement or performance as the goal.

Courses: Music I (6 to 16 months), Music II (16 to 28 months), Music III (28 months to 5 years), Family Music (6 months to 5 years)

Course components: Music I is to discover melody, pitch and rhythm. Music II introduces a new music style each month including Latin, Rock 'n' Roll and Classical. Music III is where children express their your singing voice and emerging musical knowledge through rhythm, pitch, tempo and musical forms. Family music is for the whole family to get musical through instruments, song, dance, games and more, while building a solid foundation of musical skills for everyone.

Price guide: Membership is $50 for one year. Classes start from $320 for 12 lessons.

Locations: Tanglin Mall, #03-21, 163 Tanglin Road, Singapore 247933 / #02-02/03 Marine Parade Central, Parkway Centre, Singapore 449408 / #03-60/61/62 HarbourFront Centre, 1 Maritime Square, Singapore 099253
Tel: 6735 5290 (Tanglin Mall) / 6440 6306 (Marine Parade Central) / 6271 1545 (HarbourFront)
Email: gymboree@singnet.com.sg
Web: www.gymboreeclasses.com/ (Click under International and click under Singapore)

Note:
- An adult must accompany every child except for Music III lessons, where family participation is optional.
- Gymboree runs regular play sessions for children below 5.
- It is also a party venue.

Kawai Music School

This busy music school offers examinations with the Trinity Board.

Courses: Toddlers Inc classes offers courses for toddlers from 18 months to 5 years of age. There are leisure courses for piano and guitar, and classical courses for piano, violin, guitar, voice and flute.

Age group: 18 months and above

Price guide: There is a $37.45 registration fee. Course fees start from $107 for 4 weekday lessons of ½ hour each or $117.70 for weekend lessons.

Locations:
Millenia Walk: 9 Raffles Boulevard, #02-33/36A, Singapore 039596 / Parkway Parade: 80 Marine Parade Road, #03-07/08, Singapore 449269 / Paragon: 290 Orchard Road, #05-49/51, Singapore 238859
Tel: 6333 9495 (Millenia Walk) / 6344 1903 (Parkway Parade) / 6732 0031 (Paragon)
Email: info@robertpiano.com
Web: www.robertpiano.com

Kindermusik

something for preschoolers (& others)!

Kindermusik runs an early childhood music and movement programme based upon the belief that every child is musical.

Courses: Kindermusik Village (newborn to 18 months), Our Time (18 months to 3 years), Imagine That! (3 to 5 years), Young Child (5 to 7 years) and Family Time (newborn to 7 years)

Age group: Newborn to 7 years

Price guide: All courses require a one-time registration fee of $53.50. Trial classes are available from $30 to $38 per session. Kindermusik

Village is $307.43 per semester (comprising 8 sessions), Kindermusik Our Time is $545.27 per semester, Kindermusik Imagine That is $565.60 per semester, Kindermusik for the Young Child is from $669.29 to $708.88 per semester, depending on the level the child is in, and Kindermusik Family Time is $427.79 per semester.

Locations: #03-11B Tanglin Mall, 163 Tanglin Road, Singapore 247933 (main studio) / 30 centres in preschools, childcare and enrichment centres islandwide
Tel: 6467 1789
Email: enquiries@kindermusik.com.sg
Web: www.kindermusik.com.sg

Note:

- An adult must sit in with children below the age of 3.
- Kindermusik also conducts birthday parties.

Klassique Musik

something for preschoolers!

Courses: Music Appreciation (from 18 months), Baby Paganini Violin (2-year-olds), theory (various courses are offered, including Grade 1 to 8) and Junior Excellence (consisting of a variety of instrumental courses such as Suzuki violin and piano, cello, flute, clarinet, classical piano and gospel music)
Price guide: There is a registration fee of $35. Classes are $420 for 11 lessons of ½ hour each.

Location: #02-19 Balmoral Plaza, 271 Bukit Timah Road, Singapore 259708
Tel: 6333 6486
Email: klmusik@singnet.com.sg

Learning Horizon

something for preschoolers!

Learning Horizon is a leading provider of quality enrichment programmes with more than 20 locations islandwide. It provides a holistic music education through play, ensemble and innovative games.
Course: Music for the Intelligent Mind which is split into 4 components: Jump Start program prepares and primes the child's mind for more advanced musical studies. MIM Playtime is for children from 24 to 35 months and provides a holistic approach to introduce formal music training at an early age. MIM in me is for children from 36 to 47 months and seeks to nurture the child's creativity through music dictation, improvisation, music mapping and composition.
Age group: 18 months and above
Price guide: On request.

Location: The Grassroots Club, 190 Ang Mo Kio Ave 8, #03-02, Singapore 568046
Tel: 6552 4142
Email: grassroots@learninghorizon.com.sg
Web: www.learninghorizon.com.sg

Note:

- Learning Horizon also conducts

Young Shakespeare Speech and Drama (in English, Mandarin and Malay), Little Einsteins' Junior Science Programme, Art Appreciation, an Adventure Programme and holiday camps.

Mandeville Music and Drama

Mandeville offers lessons for both children and adults on an individual or group basis.

Courses: Violin, piano, cello, harp, drums, guitar, flute, saxophone, clarinet, trumpet and Suzuki Baby Violin instrumental classes as well as voice training. Preschool Music Exploration and Baby Music courses are also available.

Course components: In Baby Music, musical concepts are taught through the use of audio and visual props, flashcards, puppets, percussion instruments and singing games.

Through interactive music play, Preschool Music Exploration seeks to develop aural skills, coordination, imagination and creativity via action songs, games, percussion playing, movement, rhythm and pitch vocabulary.

Age group: 2 to 3 years (Baby Music and Suzuki Baby Violin), 3 to 4 years (Preschool Music Exploration)

Price guide: There is a registration fee of $58.85 and a materials fee of $29.45. Fees start from $123.05 for 11 lessons of Baby Music to $369.45 for 11 lessons for the top grade in violin.

Location: #03-21/#03-01 United Square, 101 Thomson Road, Singapore 307591
Tel: 6250 1911
Email: mandeville@pacific.net.sg
Web: www.mandevillemusic.com

Note: The Suzuki Baby Violin course requires parental involvement. A term lasts three months and lessons are 45 minutes.

Methodist School of Music

Founded in 1997, this large music school is registered with the Ministry of Education. It has seven music studios as well as many other facilities.

Courses: Seraphim (4 to 5 years) is a broad-based introductory course to music. There is also the MSM Children's Choir (7 to 15 years) and a Young Organist course (6 to 12 years). In addition, musical instrument instruction is offered for the piano, organ, violin, flute, harp, clarinet, trumpet, French horn, guitar (electric/acoustic/bass), keyboard and drums as well as voice instruction. Music theory and aural training courses are also offered.

Course components: Seraphim introduces music, rhythm and basic keyboard skills through games, songs, dances and other fun-filled activities. It is designed to stimulate active listening and help children sing creatively. The MSM Children's Choir meets weekly for music appreciation, music theory, sight reading, ensemble singing and performance instruction. The Young Organist offers an alternative to the pop organ and features an introduction to the family of stops, the basics of music theory and keyboard performance skills.

Price guide: There is a registration fee of $30. Seraphimm is $272.85 for 11 lessons of an hour each.

Location: John Wesley Centre, #03-20, 496 Upper Bukit Timah Road, Singapore 678099
Tel: 6767 5258
Email: msm@msmusic.edu.sg
Web: www.msmusic.edu.sg

Nanyang Academy of Fine Arts (NAFA)

NAFA's School of Young Talents has junior departments in dance, art, drama and music. The school offers an extensive range of certificates and ongoing courses in junior music. Students are expected to be committed as one of the aims of the programme is to talent spot future musicians. Older students are expected to participate in competitions and recitals.

Courses: Gifted Young Pianists, Gifted Young Violinists, Gifted Young Cellists and Gifted Young Chinese Instrumentalists. Courses are taught at elementary, preparatory, intermediate, diploma and advanced levels.

Age group: 3 to 16 years

Price guide: The Gifted Young Pianist Course is charged at $1844.70 for 20 practical and 20 theory lessons for Grade 1 and $2509.65 for 20 practical and 20 theory lessons for Grade 8. The Gifted Young Chinese Instrumentalist Course is charged at $1249.00 for 18 lessons of 45 minutes each for the preparatory grade and $1326.30 for the higher grades. There is a registration fee of $32.10 and an audition fee of $21.40 (for the basic grades).

Location: NAFA Campus 3 (School of Performing Arts & School of Young Talents), 151 Bencoolen Street, Singapore 189656
Tel: 6512 4168 (Junior Music & Drama)
Email: junior_music@nafa.edu.sg
Web: www.nafa.edu.sg

Nrityalaya Aesthetics Society

As well as numerous dance courses for children and adults, this highly reputable society offers music instruction, including traditional Indian instrumental classes.

Courses: Vocal, violin, flute, mridangam, tabla, veena, sitar, piano, keyboard and guitar

Age group: 5 years and above

Price guide: You must join the society or be the child (below 18 years) of a member in order to join classes. Ordinary membership is $35 per year. Junior Membership is $25 per year. Music course fees are between $50

and $90 for group classes and $100 upwards per month for individual classes. There is a registration fee of $15.

Locations: Stamford Arts Centre, #01-01, 155 Waterloo Street, Singapore 187962
Tel: 6336 6537 (Stamford Arts Centre)
Email: nas@pacific.net.sg
Web: www.nas.org.sg

Playhouse Music

Children move and listen to music in an informal setting, with songs, chants and instruments. Tailored programmes and music lessons for both children and adults available.

Courses: Piano (Pop/Classical) / Violin / Guitar (Electric/Classical) / Double Bass / Cello/ Singing / Flute
Age group: Above 4 ½ years
Price guide: There is a one-time registration fee of $20. Fees start from $40 for a ½ hour session.
Opening hours: 12.00 p.m. to 7.00 p.m. (Mondays to Fridays), 9.00 a.m. to 4.00 p.m. (Saturdays)

Location: 5A Greendale Avenue, Singapore 289502
Tel: 6467 9508
Web: www.phmusicschool.com
Email: enquiries@phmusicschool.com

Grace Kids

something for preschoolers!

Grace Kids runs the Rhythm in Me programme. Set up by a music specialist, this studio has developed a successful creative music and dance programme that is particularly popular with younger children.

Courses: Mini Mover (6 to 24 months), Walkie Talkie (2 to 5 years), Scallywags (5 to 7 years) and Family Make Music (1 to 6 years)
Age group: 6 months to 7 years
Price guide: On request.

Location: Great World City, 1 Kim Seng Promenade, #03-06/08, Singapore 237994
Tel: 6733 4140
Email: gracekids@hotmail.com
Web: http://gracekids.com.sg

Note: A birthday party venue

Singapore Lyric Opera (SLO)

Formed in 1990, Singapore Lyric Opera provides entertainment for the family and budding opera buffs alike. Past performances have included *The Wind in the Willows, The Reluctant Dragon* and *I Can Give You the Starlight* (by SLO's Children's Choir) as well as open-air concerts such as Opera Bites (held in the Singapore Botanic Gardens).

The SLO's Children's Choir offers young singers aged 7 to 18 years with comprehensive vocal training and performance skills. Dance and drama lessons and choral workshops and clinics are also provided. Members of the choir are given the opportunity to perform in the company's opera productions, concerts and other activities. Junior group members are aged 7 to 11 years and senior group members are aged 12 to 18 years.

Age group: 7 to 18 years (Children's Choir)

Price guide: $125 per month for SLO's Children's Choir. There is a non-refundable audition fee of $20. Voice lessons vary from $240 to $400 per month depending on the level of ability and length of the lesson.

Location: Stamford Arts Centre, #03-06, 155 Waterloo Street Singapore 187962
Tel: 6336 5945 (general enquiries) / 6336 1929 (auditions)
Email: mail@singaporeopera.com.sg
Web: www.singaporeopera.com.sg

Tanglewood Music School

Tanglewood was the first music school in Singapore to specialise in teaching the cello. Both Suzuki teaching methods and materials as well as traditional methods are incorporated to teach the cello to both children and adults. The school has enjoyed increasing popularity since its inauguration in 2000 and now offers classes for other stringed instruments and the piano.

Courses: Cello, violin, viola, double pass, piano, pop guitar and orchestra

Age group: 3 years and above

Price guide: Fees start from $50 per ½ hour session on weekdays and $60 per ½ hour session on weekends.

Location: 01 Fusionopolis Way #02-24, Connexis Singapore 138632
Tel: 6733 1730
Email: admin@tanglewood-music.com
Web: www.tanglewood-music.com

Victor Doggett Music Studios

This government-registered school was established in 1950.

Courses: Preparatory Piano Course (PPC) (4 to 6 years) and piano lessons (7 years and above). Music theory, music appreciation and aural training are also available.

Age group: 4 years and above

Price guide: Fees start from $200 per term of 1-hour lessons.

Location: #01-05 Eastern Mansions, 1 Jalan Kechil, Singapore 438468
Tel: 6344 8324

Yamaha Music School

Yamaha offers courses for children and teens and also runs Contempo Pop Music School.

Courses: Music Wonderland (3 years to 3 years and 11 months), Yamaha Junior Music (4 years to 5 years and 6 months), Piano School for Children (6 to 8 years), guitar, electone, electronic organ and individual piano lessons. A range of music enrichment courses (primarily for those aged 13 and above) is offered by Contempo Pop Music School (contact details in next column). At Contempo, you can join classes offering instruction for cool electric guitars, bass guitars, drums and keyboard.

Course components: Yamaha Junior Music includes singing with lyrics, music appreciation and keyboard work. It also introduces the solfege, or *do-re-mi*, method of learning to enable very young children to learn basic notes.

Age group: 3 years and above

Price guide: Yamaha: $288.90 per term for Music Wonderland, $90.95 a month for the Junior Electone Course, $69.95 a month for the Junior Guitar Course / Contempo: $85.60 a month for the Lead Guitar Course, $171.20 for the acoustic guitar course, $90.95 a month for the Drums Course, $224.70 for 3 months for the portable keyboard course, $90.95 a month for the pop piano course. Free trial lessons are available at Yamaha.

Locations: Islandwide
Address: Plaza Singapura, #06-01, 68 Orchard Road, Singapore 238839
Email: sales@gmx.yamaha.com
Web: sg.yamaha.com
Tel: 6339 1171
Web: http://sg.yamaha.com/en/music_education/yamaha_music_school/

Note: Parents must accompany their children to Little Notes, Music Wonderland and the first 2 years of Yamaha Junior Music classes.

Young Musicians' Society (YMS)

Since its inauguration in 1969, the YMS has carved a niche in the arts community as an organisation dedicated to the promotion and support of local musical arts. The society plays a central role in raising the standard of musicianship in Singapore through its numerous concerts and competitions organised for schools and the public. It also provides music education through lectures, seminars and workshops.

However, under advice from the Singapore Land Authority, they cannot commit to any bookings for 2011 as they will be undergoing remodeling works for an indefinite duration.

Location: 54 Waterloo Street, Singapore 187953
Tel: 6332 5813
Email: makemusic@yms.org.sg
Web: www.yms.org.sg

Singing Companies

Chinese Opera Institute

see under Music Classes, p. 159

Chinese Theatre Circle

Established in 1981, the Chinese Theatre Circle has staged numerous performances both locally and internationally. It is noted for its pioneering efforts to create awareness of Chinese opera, which is epitomised in its staging of the Singapore International Cantonese Opera Festival. As well as public performances, it is active within the Arts Education Programme in schools.

Location: 5 Smith Street, Singapore 058919
Tel: 6323 4862
Email: ctcopera@yahoo.com
Web: www.ctcopera.com.sg

Singapore Lyric Opera

see under Music Classes, pp. 166 – 167

Singapore Youth Choir Ensemble Singers

The SYC Ensemble Singers places emphasis on contemporary works (written within the last 50 years) and the work of Asian composers. It has toured extensively worldwide and has won many awards. To become a member, you need to attend one of its public auditions.

Location: YMS Arts Centre, 54 Waterloo Street, Singapore 187953
Tel: 6332 5815
Email: enquiries@syc.org.sg
Web: www.syc.org.sg

* If your child enjoys singing, also look out for the **Philharmonic Choral Society** and the **International Festival Chorus**. The latter can be enjoyed at Chijmes during the traditional Christmas by Candlelight in December.

Orchestras

Singapore Chinese Orchestra (SCO)

The SCO comprises a mixture of local and foreign talents, from China and other regional countries. During performances, traditional Chinese musical instruments are played, including the *dizi, sheng, zheng* and *pipa*. The orchestra performs to children and their families in programmes such as the Young Children's Concert series.

Price guide: Starts from $15 for a full-time student. (The SCO runs a Friends programme that has benefits such as priority bookings, discounts for various events and placement on the mailing list. This costs $30 for full-time students / $50 for adults.)

Location: Singapore Conference Hall, 7 Shenton Way, Singapore 068810
Tel: 6557 4034
Email: sco@sco.com.sg
Web: www.sco.com.sg / www.sistic.com.sg (for ticketing)

Singapore National Youth Orchestra (SNYO)

The SNYO aims to be Singapore's premier national orchestra for young musicians. The main orchestra gives at least three major public performances a year, in April, July and December. The SNYO conducts three auditions a year to recruit members. (There is no minimum age but the maximum age is 25.) The SNYO also promotes the appreciation of orchestral music in schools.

Contact address: The Secretariat, Singapore National Youth Orchestra,

CCA Branch, MOE, 21 Evans Road, Singapore 259366
Contact: Mr Hoo Cher Liek, CCA Officer (Music) Tel: 6460 9806
Email: HOO_Cher_Liek@moe.gov.sg / Miss Sharon Cheong, CCA Officer (Music) Tel: 6460 9804 Email: Sharon_CHEONG@moe.gov.sg
Web: www.moe.gov.sg/ccab/musicdance/snyo.htm

Singapore Symphony Orchestra (SSO)

The SSO was founded in 1979 and has since gone from strength to strength. It accommodates and encourages children with creative initiatives such as its Babies' Proms, the SSO Open Rehearsals and its Concerts for Children and Storytelling for Children.

Mainstream performances may not appeal to children under the age of 10 or those with little classical music exposure. A much better way to introduce your child to classical music is to attend the specialist performances and programmes for children. I'd also recommend the SSO in the Park concerts, which are held at the Shaw Foundation Symphony Stage in the Singapore Botanic Gardens, and the annual Christmas Concert for all the family during which you can participate vocally and join in the fun! Tickets are excellent value for money. Expatriate audiences in particular will appreciate this as concert tickets in Europe or the United States cost two to three times as much.

An SSO Children's Choir was started in June 2006 and they give annual performances at the SSO Christmas Concerts. For more information regarding the Singapore Symphony Children's Choir, please contact:

Ms Regina Lee, Programme Executive (Choral)
Tel: 6602 4215
Email: choral@sso.org.sg

Price guide: $12 and above for full-time students but prices vary according to the performance. (Concessions are available for full-time students and remember to bring along proof of status.)

Location: Singapore Symphonia Company Limited
4 Battery Road #20-01, Bank of China Building Singapore 049908
Tel: 6602 4200
Email: ssonet@singnet.com (general enquiries)
Web: www.sso.org.sg / www.sistic.com.sg (for ticketing)

Note:

• Children under 4 cannot attend concerts unless otherwise indicated.
• You can download the free and informative *Young Friends* Newsletter, which includes concert guides and lists forthcoming SSO Education and Outreach Events, from the SSO website. Go to Community Outreach ® SSO Kids.

Look out for their casual concerts programme with Performances in the Park and the Heartlands, which are free. They also have regular Baby Prom concerts (for children 6 years of age and below, children below 2 are admitted for free) and regular concerts for children at Victoria Concert Hall for children from 5 to 12 years old.

Yong Siew Toh Conservatory of Music

The Yong Siew Toh Conservatory of Music is situated in state-of-the-art premises behind the National University of Singapore's University Cultural Centre. It is Singapore's first conservatory of music. It offers numerous performances in its Concert Hall, Recital Studio and Rehearsal Studio including concerts by the Conservatory Orchestra, student recitals (Thursday Noon Recital series), solo piano concerts (Primarily Piano series) and a number of special events featuring both students and guest artists.

Price guide: Tickets are available from all SISTIC outlets and many concerts are free. Check their website for details.

Postal address: National University of Singapore, 3 Estate Office Drive, Singapore 117485
Tel: 6516 1167
Email: musgeneral@nus.edu.sg
Web: www.music.nus.edu.sg

SPECIAL EVENTS

There are a number of special events worth watching out for as they offer entertainment for all the family. I've listed some of the most popular ones below.

Ballet Under the Stars

For a few days each year, the Singapore Dance Theatre (*see under* Dance Companies) hosts an open-air performance of contemporary dance and ballet. This comprises a BYO picnic followed by a performance.

Price guide: $25 / $15 for students and full-time NS men

Location: Fort Canning Green
Tel: 6338 0611
Email: ticketing@singaporedancetheatre.com
Web: www.sistic.com.sg (ticket sales)

Note: The picnic generally starts at 5.00 p.m., with the performance beginning at 7.30 p.m.

Chingay

see Special Events under Annual Events, p. 241

Disney on Ice

This annual production features world-class skaters in Disney performances such as *Princess Classic*, *Finding Nemo* and *The Lion King*. A very popular event, it is very colourful thanks to the marvellous costumes that the performers wear.

When? March (during the school break)
Age group: 3 years and above
Price guide: $15.50 to $85.50 (tickets are available through SISTIC)

Location: Singapore Indoor Stadium, 2 Stadium Walk, Singapore 397691
Tel: 6319 3299 (telephone operator), 6348 5555 (ticketing hotline)
Web: www.disneyonice.com.sg

M1 Singapore Fringe Festival

This annual festival is presented by The Necessary Stage. Presented by international and local artists, it features contemporary visual arts, theatre, film, dance and cinema. The festival has a different theme each year. It is more likely to be of interest to teenagers and adults.
When? Usually held in February/ March
Price guide: Some activities are free while ticket prices for other performances can be obtained through SISTIC.

Locations: The Esplanade and various other venues
Tel: 6440 8115 (The Necessary Stage)
Email: info@singaporefringe.com
Web: www.singaporefringe.com

Mosaic Music Festival

This spectacular 10-day festival is held at venues throughout the Esplanade and features top acts from Singapore, the region and around the world. Music ranges from jazz to folk rock to electronica. Highlights have included jazz piano legend Chick Corea, the Duke Ellington Orchestra and Senegalese legend Youssou N'Dour. Although this event is not targeted at young children, special performances such as Jazz 123, which featured children's songs like the theme from Sesame Street performed by a jazz guitarist, bassist and drummer in session, are worth looking out for.
When? March
Price guide: $38 to $148 (a number of outdoor theatre performances are free)

Location: Esplanade – Theatres On The Bay, 1 Esplanade Drive, Singapore 038981
Tickets: www.sistic.com.sg
Web: www.mosaicmusicfestival.com

Prudential Children First! by Act3 International

> The Magic of the Sea *was very different from anything else I've ever seen. First of all, the actors came around and talked to us before the show and then they used special lanterns and slides to tell the stories. We had to take part too and join in the singing!*
>
> **–Lena, age 8**

A highlight in any child's arts schedule should be the annual Prudential Children First! festival. Launched in 2000, this festival is presented every March by Act3 International in conjunction with Prudential. Performances from both here and overseas are held for children of all ages at various venues throughout Singapore. Whether it is puppetry from the Philippines or circus theatre from Switzerland, mime, music or digital animation, there is bound to be something to delight and entertain most children.

My children and I have enjoyed a number of these performances and my only comment would be that the shows for very young children (3 years and below) should come with an obligatory request that parents have snacks and picture books at hand — keeping a 2-year-old sitting still on the floor for 45 minutes can be an impossible challenge!

Age group: 3 to 12 years

Price guide: Some events are free but most cost about $20 and above per person. Family packages are available as well as various discounts. Tickets are available through SISTIC.

Locations: Various venues are used, including Act3 Theatre (Cairnhill Arts Centre), Jubilee Hall (Raffles Hotel), Ngee Ann Auditorium at the Asian Civilisations Museum and the Arts House.

Tel: 6735 9986 (Act3 International) / 6348 5555 (SISTIC hotline)

Email: act3int@act3international.com.sg

Web: www.childrenfirst.com.sg / www.sistic.com.sg (for ticketing)

Singapore Arts Festival

> *The Arts Festival gets better every year. As a family, we all enjoy the performances at Fort Canning and this year we had a picnic. It was great! My kids are all teenagers and they probably enjoyed the atmosphere there as much as the music. I guess it can get a bit noisy and crowded for younger kids, especially over the weekends.*
>
> **–Eva B.**

Held annually over three weeks, this festival aims to be an international arts event with a distinctive Asian identity. The event showcases some of the world's best dance, theatre and music companies, with local and international artists giving performances. A Festival Village that hosts music, dance and food stalls is erected at Fort Canning Hill and many free arts events for all the family is conducted throughout the island.

In 2011, the first ever Kids Arts Village was launched. Art shows, craft workshops, and a children's art gallery are part of its programme. Check the website for details.

Web: www.singaporeartsfest.com

Singapore River Buskers' Festival

To see the performing arts in a street context and the variety of skills and displays this involves, you can do no better than visit the buskers who arrive annually from all over the world to entertain along Singapore River and at other venues. During this festival, you can see theatre, comedy, juggling, sword swallowing, acrobatic and magic acts.

When? A week-long extravaganza in November

Price guide: Free

Location: Singapore Riverbank, Marina Bay and Orchard Road

SSO Christmas Concerts

For Christmas songs, carols and music, the SSO Christmas Concerts are a highlight in the music calendar. Tickets for these concerts sell out quickly so do book early. This is an opportunity for all the family to celebrate and join in with the singing!

When? Mid-December (Friday, Saturday and Sunday evenings)

Location: Victoria Concert Hall, 11 Empress Place, Singapore 179558

Email: ssonet@singnet.com.sg (for general enquiries)

Web: www.sso.org.sg /www.sistic.com.sg (for tickets)

WOMAD (World of Music, Art and Dance)

The WOMAD Singapore Festival is a feast of music and dance from all over the world. As a venue for families, the Global Village, which is set up especially for WOMAD in Fort Canning Park, is a great attraction, with its numerous indigenous arts and crafts vendors and cosmopolitan food and beverage outlets. In addition, there are workshops and storytelling for children and DJs spinning grooves for teenagers and the young at heart!

When? Usually the last weekend in August

Price guide: Free for children below 7 years/tickets from $35 for an adult 1-day pass bought in advance. A family pass (2 adults and 2 children aged 7 to 12 years) costs $82 (advance purchase).

Location: Fort Canning Park

Tel: 6220 2676 (WOMAD Projects Singapore) / 6348 5555 (SISTIC Hotline)

Web: www.sistic.com.sg

Note: Gates usually open at 5.30 p.m. and performances start from 7.00 p.m. onwards.

Tip: While it is easy to buy food on-site, this is a good place to enjoy a picnic.

OTHER THINGS TO DO

Chinese Opera Teahouse (Chinese Theatre Circle)

This is an excellent venue to view a performance of the sights and sounds of Chinese opera in a restored shophouse. There are two shows that both have English subtitles.

Opening hours: Noon to 5.00 p.m. Tuesdays to Sundays (Sights and Sounds takes place from 7.00 p.m. to 9.00 p.m./8.00 p.m. to 9.00 p.m. Fridays and Saturdays.)

Price guide: $20 / $35 (includes food and beverages)

Location: 5 Smith Street,
Singapore 058919
Tel: 9630 2886
Email: ctcopera@yahoo.com
Web: www.ctcopera.com.sg/ctc.html

library@esplanade

If your children are budding arts aficionados, this state-of-the-art venue, which is Singapore's first performing arts library, is well worth a visit. The library's strategic location on the 3rd level of The Esplanade makes it one of the few libraries in the world to be housed in a performing arts complex. The collections in this uniquely themed library are arranged into four performing arts 'villages': Music Village, Dance Village, Theatre Village and Film Village. Not only can you borrow books and materials in electronic formats but there are also DVDs to view, performances to see and even a piano to play for a nominal fee.

Opening hours: 11.00 a.m. to 9.00 p.m. daily (closed on public holidays)

Price guide: National Library membership: Free for Singaporeans / $10.50 for Permanent Residents / $10.50 registration fee and a subsequent annual fee of $10.50 for non-citizens. (Children below the age of 7 are issued a free membership card while adults are encouraged to use their NRIC card.)

Location: Esplanade—Theatres on the Bay, #03-01, 8 Raffles Avenue,
Singapore 039802
Tel: 6332 3255
Email: ASK@nlb.gov.sg
Web: www.nlb.gov.sg

– Chapter 5 –

ARTS, CRAFTS AND COOKING

When encouraging children to develop an interest in arts and crafts, why not take them to art galleries and exhibitions and, if possible, let them see an artist in action? Doing this may also foster an existing interest. The saying 'lead by example' also applies and a home with pictures on the walls (especially those of your children), photographs on display and visible craftwork is an important starting point.

The other important thing to note is that children develop at different rates and while being able to colour in pictures without going over the lines may look good, it doesn't necessarily have a bearing upon artistic expression and creativity. Ultimately, art should be fun, stimulating and make your child want to go back for more!

CLASSES

Arts and Crafts

Angkatan Pelukis Aneka Daya (APAD) (Association of Artists of Various Resources)

The APAD organises various annual activities such as art exhibitions, art classes, Artist-in Residence schemes, art courses and seminars. In 1990, it introduced the ACTION series of art exhibitions to provide an opportunity for its younger members (especially those aged between 16 and 40) to present their latest and best works. It also conducts a children's art exhibition under the title of TUNAS, which serves as a valuable means of encouraging the artistic talents of the young.

Courses: Art sessions for children (5 to 12 years), secondary students and adults. Batik printing and graphic design classes are also held occasionally.

Price guide: There is a registration fee of $30 per month for children's art classes /$40 per month for Intermediate / Advanced / Batik Painting courses. Call Mr Saiman Ismail at 9832 3324.

Location: Telok Ayer Performing Arts Centre (TAPAC), #03-07, 182 Cecil Street, Singapore 069547
Tel: 62210904

Email: enquiry@apad.org.sg

Web: www.apad.org.sg

Note: APAD also has an annual Art Outing and Family Day that promotes public awareness of its programmes.

The ARTS FISSION Company

As well as being known for its dance programmes, The ARTS FISSION Company runs creative art workshops. These are conducted on

FAST FACTS

National Arts Council (NAC)

The NAC is the Statutory Board appointed to spearhead the development of the arts in Singapore. As well as the performing arts, its website features a section on the visual arts, which highlights festivals and events, arts venues and other useful links.

Tel: 6746 4622

Web: www.nac.gov.sg

The National Arts Council now has an Arts Education Programme specially for the young in Singapore. Go to the National Arts Council website and click under Arts Education Programme.

Location: The Arts Education Programme Centre

Goodman Arts Centre, 90 Goodman Road,

Blk A #01-01, Singapore 439053

The contact person would be Ms Jumirah (Senior Arts Education Officer)

Tel: 6346 9400

Email: Jumirah_N@nac.gov.sg

Singapore Art

This website has good links to sections on museums, artists, art organisations and galleries in Singapore. It is useful for older children interested in local art and for those studying it at school. You can also access a forum for the arts community in Singapore via this site.

Web: www.singaporeart.org/

Community Centres

When looking for classes, a useful first port of call is your local Community Centre. Most offer children's art classes which are extremely popular.

Web: www.pa.gov.sg

a project basis and provide training in creative ideas as well as technical art skills.

Courses: Preschooler Workshop (3 to 6 years old), Junior Workshop (7 to 12 years old))

Course components: Includes drawing, painting, printmaking, collage, assemblage and construction in a wide range of media and materials

Age group: 3 to 12 years

Price guide: $180 for non-members (8 sessions), $160 for members. Membership is $30 for 2 years and there is a $20 registration fee.

Location: ONE-TWO-SIX Cairnhill Arts Centre, #01-7/09, 126 Cairnhill Road, Singapore 229707 /Mountbatten Community Centre, 35 Jalan Satu, Singapore 399479 (site for art workshops)
Tel: 6238 6469
Email: tafcl@singnet.com.sg
Web: www.artsfission.org

Centre Stage School of the Arts

Centre Stage offers a variety of performing and visual arts courses.

Course: Fun Factory is the art and craft class from 3 ½ years to 6 years. Various elements are taught including drawing, sculpture, collage, printing and puppet making. Each term has a special theme.

Age group: 3 ½ years to 6 years

Price guide: On application. There is a registration fee of $40.

Location: Block 15 Woking Road Singapore 138694
Tel: 6732 7211
Email: info@centre-stage.com
Web: www.centre-stage.com

The Chinese Calligraphy Society of Singapore

Founded in 1968, the Chinese Calligraphy Society of Singapore operates within the Singapore Calligraphy Centre. It offers courses for adults and children and holds a number of events throughout the year.

Courses: Chinese calligraphy for children and Chinese painting for children. (Classes are held in Mandarin.)

Age group: 7 years and above

Price guide: Course fees are $125 for 9 lessons of 1 ½ hours each.

Location: 48 Waterloo Street, Singapore 187952
Tel: 6337 7753
Email: ccss@ccss.org.sg
Web: www.ccss.org.sg

Note:

- As these classes are popular, long waiting lists to join classes are not uncommon.
- The society also conducts holiday classes for children.

Clay Cove

Clay Cove specialises in pottery making as a creative activity for children. Figurine modelling is

emphasised which is excellent for developing 3-D visualisation.
Courses: Pottery for Toddlers, Basic (pinching and figurine methods), Intermediate (coiling, slab-building and hollowing methods) and Advanced (combination methods)
Course components: In the Basic class, children start by making pinch pots and figurines. In the Intermediate class, they make cups, bowls, pencil holders and boxes and in the Advanced class, they undertake their own small projects.
Age group: 3 years and above (including teenagers and adults)
Price guide: $100 (4 sessions) for Pottery for Toddlers / $130 (4 sessions) for the Basic course / $180 (6 sessions) for the Intermediate and Advanced courses

Location: #05-38 Funan DigitaLife Mall, 109 North Bridge Road, Singapore 179097
Tel: 6338 7769 / 9109 2701
Email: mag@claycove.com
Web: www.claycove.com
Email: info@claycove.com

Note:
- Clay Cove runs school holiday programmes.
- It is also a party venue.

Crestar Learning Centre

Established in 1977, this company runs enrichment courses worldwide.
Courses: Kinder Art (4 to 5 years) and Junior Picasso (5 years and above)
Age group: 4 years and above
Price guide: There is a $32.10 registration fee. Art courses for children are $133.75 for 11 lessons of 1 hour each.

Locations: Islandwide
Tel: 6342 5600 (Head Office – Marine Parade)
Email: enquiry@crestar.com.sg
Web: www.crestar.com.sg

eZoo

Courses: Art and Craft, Ceramic and Fine Arts (water and oil painting)
Course components: The Art and Craft course introduces colour concepts, basic drawing techniques, different painting media, printmaking and making models and cartooning. The Ceramic course features drawing, shaping, painting and firing. Currently, lessons are conducted every Wednesday from 4.00 p.m.
Age group: 4 years and above
Price guide: There is a registration fee of $30. Trial lessons are $25 for 1 hour.

Location: eZoo School of Music and Fine Arts 2 Swiss View La Suisse 2, #01-01 Singapore 288008
Tel: 6469 4660
Email: enquiry@ezoomusic.com
Web: www.ezoomusic.com

Genius R Us

This centre runs fun cooking courses for kids regularly where kids get to make fun food such as cupcakes and sushi. These cooking workshops are

largely available during the school holidays but do check the schedule.
Courses: Tots Can Bake (2 ½ to 5 years) / Kidz Can Bake! (5 to 12 years old)
Price guide: Kidz Can Bake: $135 for 4 sessions / Tots can Bake: $225 for 4 sessions

Location: 75B Tanjong Pagar Road, Singapore 088496
Tel: 6221 4561 / 8183 0563 (SMS)
Branch: City Square Mall
180 Kitchener Road #07-08
Singapore 208539
Email: info@geniusrus.com
Web: www.geniusrus.com

Note: Birthday party packages can be arranged.

Isadora's Workshop

Courses: Drawing classes are available for beginner, intermediate and advanced levels. The content varies from basic drawing skills to learning about perspective and exploring different art styles. On the last Saturday of every month, there is also a 2-hour art and craft session, where your child (and you!) can learn a new technique. These sessions vary from month to month, ranging from printmaking, paper decorating, T-shirt printing to bookmaking.
Age group: 4 years and above
Price guide: From $65 for a stand-alone workshop on printmaking books and $200 for a series of classes on printmaking.

Location: 102 Gardenia Road
Singapore 578873
Tel: 9273 4991
Web: www.isadoraworkshop.com

Note: The studio conducts workshops during the school holidays and it also hosts themed birthday parties.

Junior De Artist

Activities: This shop has one-offrubber stamping classes, masking making, 3-D Card making, and water-colouring classes.
Age group: 4 to 12 years
Price guide: $64.20 a class for members. Membership is $120 a year with discounts on products as well. Non-members have to pay $5 extra a class.

Location: #03-22 Novena Square, 238 Thomson Road, Singapore 307683
Tel: 6255 7860
Email: enquiry@juniordeartist.com.sg
Web: www.juniordeartist.com.sg

Note: This is also a party venue.

Kinderart

Following the US National Standard for Visual Art Education, Kinderart conducts a wide range of art programmes for children.
Courses: Baby Art (2 to 3 years) / Play Art (3 to 6 years) / Crayons and Paints (3 to 6 years and 7 to 11 years) / Little Artist (5 to 11 years) / 100 Artists (6 to 12 years).
Course components: The drawing

course teaches children to draw simple animals, human forms, landscapes and objects. 100 Artists introduces children to various artists and their artwork, a range of styles and techniques. Complimentary trial art classes are available at some centres. Check the website for further details.

Age group: 3 years and above

Price guide: Upon application

Locations: Kinderart SG Pte Ltd, 10 Ubi Crescent, #03-52 Ubi Techpark (Lobby C), Singapore 408564 (Main Office) / Centres islandwide

Tel: 6327 4200

Email: kinderartasia@gmail.com

Web: www.kinderart.com.sg

Note:

• Holiday programmes and birthday packages are available.

Little Art Bug Workshop

This art education programme is targeted at younger children.

Courses: Very Young@Art (4 to 6 years) / Young@Art (7 to 12 years) / Art Pass (7 to 12 years)

Course components: Very Young@ Art looks at lines, shapes and colours using interactive play and hands-on activities. Young@Art is the workshop's signature programme for children who want to learn to draw and colour. Split into 3 modules, it focuses on both the creative process and the physical artistic products. Art Pass aims to give a foundation of art and drawing programmes to all Primary School students.

Age group: 4 to 12 years

Price guide: $300 for 3 weeks of Clay Making Holiday Programme. There is a registration fee of $20.

Location: 51 Waterloo Street, #02-04/05, Singapore 187969

Tel: 6338 1920

Email: info@littleartbug.com

Web: www.littleartbug.com

Note: Look out for its holiday art workshops (for 7 to 12 years).

Little Artists

Set up in 1997, this reputable private homeschool is run by a professional artist. Emphasis is placed on free expression, creativity, skills and techniques within small groups.

Courses: Little Blossoms (2.5 to 8 years), Junior Picasso (6 to 8 years), Budding Artists Programme (8 to 17 years), My Favourite Medium (8 to 17 years). There is also a course for Special Needs Children.

Course components: Little Blossoms introduces children to the world of art through fun and play activities. Junior Picasso Artists covers techniques such as fundamental sketching, cartoons, still life, colour sense and botanical art. These techniques are taught in a variety of mediums including oil pastels, watercolour, acrylic, charcoal and pencils.

Age group: 2½ to 15 years

Price guide: Junior Blossoms: $90 per hour, $130 for 2 hours / Junior Picasso: $155 for 2 hours / Budding Artists: $120 for 1 ½ hours or $155 for 2 hours / My Favourite Medium: $155 for 2 hours / Art for Special Needs Children: $145 for 2 hours (includes assessment.)

Location: Mandarin Gardens, #01-07 No 15 Siglap Road Singapore 448904
Tel: 6449 0960
Email: shalini@little-artists.com
Web: www.little-artists.com

Note: Look out for holiday programmes in June and November. This is also a birthday party venue.

Nanyang Academy of Fine Arts (NAFA)

NAFA has a flourishing Junior Art Department (under the School of Young Talents), which offers a variety of programmes, including part-time certificate courses.

Courses: Kinder Art, Children's Art, Lower Secondary Art and Integrated O-Level Art

Course components: Kinder Art features drawing, painting and simple craft formation. The Children's Art syllabus covers lessons in drawing with different media, Chinese painting, 3-D crafts and art appreciation. Lower Secondary Art includes still life drawing, painting techniques, figure sketching, Chinese painting, 3-D and mixed media and art appreciation.

Age group: 5 to 6 years for Kinder Art / 7 to 12 years for Children's Art / 13 to 14 years for Lower Secondary Art

Price guide: There is a registration fee of $32.10. Kinder Art and Children's Art: $380 per semester of 20 weeks / Art for Lower Secondary: $240 per 10 week term / Art for GCE "O" Levels: $360 per 10 week term.

Location: NAFA Campus 1, HQ and School of Visual Arts Building (Level 3), 80 Bencoolen Street, Singapore 189655
Tel: 6512 4159 (Junior Art) / 6512 4209
Email: Junior_art@nafa.edu.sg
Web: www.nafa.edu.sg

Nrityalaya Aesthetics Society

Courses: Oil Painting is available here.

Age group: 5 years and above

Price guide: You must join the society or be the child (below 18 years) of a member in order to join classes. Ordinary membership is $35 per year / $25 for junior members (students over 18 years). Course fees are $180 per month for oil painting. There is a registration fee of $15.

Locations: #01-01 Stamford Arts Centre, 155 Waterloo Street, Singapore 187962
Tel: 6336 6537 (Stamford Arts Centre)
Email: nas@pacific.net.sg
Web: www.nas.org.sg

PaintWorks

Experienced lecturers conduct art classes for all levels at this relaxing studio.

Courses: Fundamentals in Art (6 years and above), Juniors in Art (4 to 5 years)

Fundamentals in Art develops basic concepts, e.g. colour, shape, texture, drawing and styles, using a variety of media. Juniors in Art uses stimuli to encourage children to experience, explore and experiment. Working with a variety of media and tools, children will learn about fundamental aspects of art such as colours and shapes — through drawing, painting and 3-D work.

Age group: Above 6 years (Fundamentals in Art) 4 to 5 years (Juniors in Art)

Price guide: Fundamentals in Art is $200 for 6 lessons of 1 ½ hours each, and Juniors in Art is $256 for 6 lessons of 1 hour each.

Location: Watten Estate,
Watten Hill Condominium
Tel: 9637 4438
Email: info@artatpaintworks.com
Web: www.artatpaintworks.com

Note: PaintWorks hosts school holiday workshops and can also help you with your birthday plans.

Sculpture Square

Situated in a disused church, this gallery exhibits various works and also conducts classes and workshops. Celebrate Art at Sculpture Square is held one day in August and is a very popular carnival.

Courses: Various workshops are held during the annual carnival. Previous workshops include fun with boxes, ostrich egg painting, clay and puppet-making.

Price guide: There is a charge of $16 per child for the carnival with two workshops free. All other workshops are charged at $5 each.

Location: 155 Middle Road,
Singapore 188977
Tel: 6333 1055
Email: arts@sculptures.com.sg
Web: www.sculpturesq.com.sg

Studio Haroobee

This studio allows flexible scheduling of art classes.

Courses: Young Artists (3 to 12 years),

Course components: Various media are used, e.g. poster colours, crayons, watercolours and acrylic pencil. Different subject matters are explored and children are taught how to use art tools properly.

Age group: 3 to 12 years

Price guide: $140 for 4 weekday lessons / $155 for 4 weekend lessons / Trial lessons are $36. There is also a flexible 18 lessons package for $594 (for the basic grade) and a flexible 36 lessons package for $1070 (for the basic grade).

Location: Esplanade Mall, #02-20, 8 Raffles Avenue, Singapore 039802

Tel: 6336 9611

Email: admin@studioharooclub.com

Web: www.studioharoobeeclub.com

Note:

• School Holiday Art Workshops are available.

• The teacher-student ratio is 1:4. There are ad-hoc workshops during the school holidays and long weekends

Studio Miu

Courses: Children's Regular Art Class A (4 years old and above) / Children's Regular Art Class B (7 years old and above) / Children's Regular Art Class C (11 years old and above) / Fun Toddler Art (2 ½ to 4 years old) / Manga Drawing / Chiho's Illustration Class / Fun with Chinese Ink.

Course components: Although the curriculum for kindergarten and primary classes may be similar, the art and craft materials used vary according to the age group.

Age group: 2½ years and above

Price guide: There is a one-time registration fee of $50 / Children's Art Class: $78 for materials, $420 for a 10-week term.) / The Fun Toddler Art: $35 a session for members, $50 for non-members or $120 for 4 sessions / Chinese Ink: $40 a session for non-members, and $30 a session for members / Japanese Manga Drawing: $55 a session for non-members, and $43 for members / Membership is $50, a one-time off payment. (If you cannot make it for a class, you need to give them 24 hours notice and they will replace it with another class.)

Locations: Ngee Ann City, #04-20V, 391 Orchard Road, Singapore 238872

Tel: 6733 0917 / 6735 4228

Email: studiomiu_art@pacific.net.sg

Web: www.studiomiu.com.sg/

Note:

• Reservation is requested for Sunday Painting.

• Studio Miu can help with your birthday party requirements

UniqArts and Technologies

Established in 1995 by a Singaporean artist, UniqArts focuses on art education for the young and offers a wide range of programmes. Courses are conducted by experienced and qualified art teachers, artists or instructors.

Courses: Programmes include basic drawing and colouring, Chinese calligraphy, fine arts, sculpture, manga art and comic and cartoon techniques. There is a class for Special Needs Children — Arts Connect.

Age group: 4 years and above

Price guide: Starts from $205 per 10-session course fee. Add-ons include materials: $75, registration fee: $30, non-refundable deposit: $50.

Locations: Roxy Square 1, #02-32, 50 East Coast Road Singapore 428769

Tel: 6344 1670
Email: uniqArts@yahoo.com
Web: www.uniqarts.com.sg

Note:

• UniqArts also runs an e-Learning site that offers art courses on the Internet. It can be found at www.onlineartclass.com

• Courses are also run during the school holidays in November/December and June.

Fresh Art Studios

This studio in the basement of Orchard Central features clay workshops for children at $20 per workshop. There are workshops for adults as well at $40 per workshop.

Location: Orchard Central, B2
181 Orchard Road Singapore 238896
Tel: 9273 7373 (Angela)

Abrakadoodle Art Studio for Kids

This is a leading children's art education franchise from the US, which hosts art classes, camps and parties. The curriculum imparted surpasses the US National Standards for Visual Arts Education.

Price Guide: Twoosy Doodlers (20 months to 36 months): $275 per term of 10 lessons, 45 minutes each / Mini Doodlers (3 to 6 years): $295 per term of 10 lessons, 1 hour each / Doodlers (7 to 12 years): $315 per term of 10 lessons, 1 hour 15 min each. All courses include a materials fee of $85 and a registration fee of $50

Locations: Cluny Court, #02-13/15, 501 Bukit Timah Road Singapore 259760 / Playground @ Big Splash Blk B #02-05B, 902 East Coast Parkway Singapore 449874
Tel: 6763 9219 (Bukit Timah) / 6247 7288 (Playground)

LPN Art School

This school specialises in art programmes for children from 3 years old and up, where they learn to unleash their imagination through a variety of hands-on activities.

Price Guide: $264 per term of 12 lessons / Evaluation Test: $10 / Art Materials / $38 / Registration Fee: $38

Location: Suntec City Mall, #03-013C, Tower 2, 9 Temasek Boulevard Singapore 038989
Tel: 6238 0317/9622 7586

Very Special Arts Singapore

VSA Singapore runs visual and performing arts programmes for children, youths and adults with disabilities, as well as special education teachers, trainers, volunteers and parents.

Courses: Programmes range from handicraft workshops, Saori hand weaving, art seminars, arts camps, art and handicraft exhibitions, public performances to overseas arts exchanges and artist attachments.

Postal address: 133 Bedok North Avenue 3, #01-138, Singapore 460133
Tel: 6448 6275
Email: general@vsa.org.sg
Web: www.vsa.org.sg

Note:

• The Annual Art Exhibition is an excellent showcase of the artistic talents of children and adult artists with disabilities. It is held at a public venue.

• VSA Singapore also runs camps during the school holidays in June and November (*see* Long School Break Activities, pp. 312 – 313).

Cooking

You can't be in Singapore for long before realising that eating truly is the national pastime! It's not surprising, then, that cooking workshops are very popular, and no less so for the young. Besides regular classes, look out for one-off events that are run for children by various hotels and restaurants. I'd particularly recommend those conducted by the Shangri-La Hotel (check out its Mother's Day Cooking Workshop) and the Annual Little Chef in the Making held by Lawry's The Prime Rib (usually in September/October).

Location: Shangri-La Hotel, 22 Orange Grove Road, Singapore 258350
Tel: 6737 3644
Web: www.shangri-la.com/en/property/singapore/shangrila

Location: Lawry's The Prime Rib, 333A Orchard Road #04-01/31 Mandarin Gallery, Meritus Mandarin Hotel Singapore 238897
Tel: 6836 3333
Web: www.lawrys.com.sg

academy at-sunrice

Cooking courses at academy at-sunrice are open to groups only, with a minimum of 20 participants required for any course.

Courses: Kindergarten to primary and secondary level culinary skills

Course components: Kindergarten workshops follow a specific theme, e.g. bananas. Workshops for older children look at herbs and spices, food art and flower arranging as well as baking and cooking.

Age group: Kindergarten and above

Price guide: $40 upwards per child per workshop

Location: At-Sunrice Global Chef Academy 28 Tai Seng Street Level 5 Singapore 534106
Tel: 6416 6631 / 32 / 33 / 35 / 36
Email: academy@at-sunrice.com
Web: www.at-sunrice.com

Note: A birthday party venue

Cookery Magic

Ruqxana is known for her culinary skills and popular home-style classes. A hands-on learning approach is used for meal and snack preparation while basic nutrition information is reinforced. She has also been featured in *Lonely Planet Singapore*.

Courses: Ruqxana will conduct a children's cooking party where the children will bake and then decorate pre-made cookies or cupcakes with colourful icing. Ingredients and tools will be provided.

Age group: 4 to 12 years (excellent classes for adults too!)

Price guide: $400 for the children's party, $25 per child and $80 onwards for the birthday cake (depending on size and design).

Location: 117 Fidelio Street,
Singapore 458492
Tel: 6348 9667 / 9665 6831
Email: info@cookerymagic.com,
ruqxana@cookerymagic .com
Web: www.cookerymagic.com

Genius R Us

Kidz Can Bake! workshops are held throughout the year, particularly during the school holidays. Parental involvement is encouraged.

Courses: Themes vary, e.g. Christmas and Chinese New Year dishes, baking and decorating cupcakes, making doughnuts, creating sushi and making ice cream

Age group: 3 to 12 years

Price guide: $58.80 per parent-child workshop, $48.80 for the second workshop in the same month.

Location: 75B Tanjong Pagar Road,
Singapore 088496 / City Square
Mall 180 Kitchener Road #07-08
Singapore 208539
Tel: 6221 4561 (Tanjong Pagar
Branch) / 6634 6020 (City Square
Mall Branch) / 81830563 (sms)
Email: info@geniusrus.com
Web: www.geniusrus.com

Note: Birthday party packages can be arranged.

Kooky Art

Kooky Art specialises in food decorating art for children, using techniques developed especially for them.

Courses: Regular classes and workshops are not offered in Singapore anymore. Special events can be arranged on request.

Tel: 9815 2711
Email: enquiry@kookyart.com.sg
Web: www.kookyart.com.sg

Note:

- Birthday party packages are available.
- Holiday workshops are conducted at various locations.

SoEZ Cooking Studio

Courses: SoEZ Cooking Playground at United Square specializes in cooking courses for kids from 4 to 12 years old and does birthday parties as well. Participants can select online the dish they would like to make, and once there are three participants, a class will proceed. There are dishes that kids will love, such as doggie cookies and panda cakes.

Age Group: 4 to 12 years

Price Guide: Workshops start from $48 a kid. Their brochure is available on request from their store.

Location: SoEZ Cooking Playground United Square 101 Thomson Road #B1-02 Singapore 307591
Tel: 6259 0606
Web: www.soez-cooking.com
Facebook: www.facebook.com/pages/SoEZ-Cooking/182979638770

Asian Food Channel Cooking Studio

Courses: This lovely studio hosts ad-hoc workshops for parents and kids
Age Group: 4 to 12 years
Price Guide: Workshops start from $65 a parent-and-child pair. Visit their website for details.

Location: Orchard Central, #07-02, `181 Orchard Road, Singapore 238896
Tel: 6834 4829
Web: www.theafcstudio.com

Lifeskills & Lifestyle @ People's Association

Check with your local Community Centre for any children's cooking workshops. The workshops are reasonably priced and usually held during the long school breaks. They are open to both members and non-members.

Courses: Includes sushi, cookies and muffins, doughnuts and gingerbread men.
Age group: 5 years and above

Location: Islandwide
Web: www.pa.gov.sg (look under Lifeskills & Lifestyle/Courses for Children)

VENUES AND EXHIBITIONS

Where do you go to see visual art in Singapore? Although there are many private galleries and shops selling artwork, I'd suggest taking your children to the following venues for an initial foray into the visual arts scene.

The Arts House

see also Performing Arts, p. 131

In this heritage building, you can enjoy a diverse mix of contemporary visual and performing arts (music, film, theatre and dance and visual art and fashion design are all part of this multidisciplinary art centre). This venue will probably appeal more to older children but do check out what is on. Previous exhibitions have featured artwork inspired by Hello Kitty, children's photographs from Vietnam and Japanese dolls. There is also an excellent coffee shop/café on site, with books and magazines to browse and for sale.

Opening hours: 10.00 a.m. to 8.00 p.m. (weekdays) / 11.00 a.m. to 8.00 p.m. (Saturdays) /Closed Sundays
Price guide: Free admission. Charges vary for exhibitions and performances.

Location: 1 Old Parliament Lane,
Singapore 179429
Tel: 6332 6900
Email: enquiries@toph.com.sg
Web: www.theartshouse.com.sg

Note: Combine a trip here with a walk along the river or a visit to the Asian Civilisations Museum, which is opposite the Arts House.

Asian Civilisations Museum

This museum houses arts and crafts from China, Southeast Asia, India and West Asia. Past exhibitions include Chinese paintings, photographic displays, Islamic calligraphy and jewellery exhibits. Look out for some excellent children's workshops that are held periodically. These are usually chargeable and places need to be reserved. The museum also conducts Sunday Family Fun! events that offer free drop-in activities, e.g. storytelling, tours of exhibits and art and craft sessions. Check the website for further information.

Opening hours: 1.00 p.m. to 7.00 p.m. (Mondays) / 9.00 a.m. to 7.00 p.m. (Tuesdays to Sundays)

Price guide: $8 for adults / Free to children aged 6 and below / Free admission for all Singaporean / PR students and teachers / Free Admission for all Singaporeans and PRs 60 and above everyday. / 50 per cent discount for foreigners aged 60 and above every day. / Family admission for a family of 5 pax for $20 is available during special exhibitions. (Admission is discounted between 7.00 p.m. and 9.00 p.m. on Fridays.)

Location: 1 Empress Place,
Singapore 179555
Tel: 6332 7798 / 6332 2982
Web: www.acm.org.sg
nhb_acm_vs@nhb.gov.sg

Note: Admission charges may vary during special exhibitions.

NUS Museum

This is an excellent venue to view Asian art pieces. Here you see ceramics, paintings, calligraphy, jade and bronze spanning 7,000 years of Chinese history. Also on display are South and Southeast Asian art pieces and a collection of works by Singapore's leading sculptor, Ng Eng Teng.

Opening hours: 10.00 a.m. to 7.30 p.m. (Tuesdays to Saturdays) / 10.00 a.m. to 6.00 p.m. (Sundays) / Closed on Mondays

Price guide: Free

Location: University Cultural Centre
Annex, 50 Kent Ridge Crescent,
National University of Singapore,
Singapore 119279
Tel: 6516 4616 / 6516 4617
Email: museum@nus.edu.sg
Web: www.nus.edu.sg/cfa/museum/index.php

Raffles Square and the Riverfront sculptures

I've included this area because it is home to some excellent, world-class sculptures that are talking points for any child interested in art. Here you can see works by Salvador Dali (*Homage to Newton* at the atrium of UOB Plaza), Fernando Botero (the curvaceous, giant *Bird* by the river appeals to everyone!), Henry Moore (*Reclining Figure* at the front of the OCBC Centre) as well as sculptures by Aw Tee Hong and Yang Ying-Feng immediately within Raffles Square. The nearby Pidemco Centre is also home to Chern Lian Shan's *Rainbow*.

Combined with a walk along the riverfront and a light meal at one of the many food outlets in the area, this makes for a good family afternoon activity. In fact, the river itself is the site of a series of life-size bronze sculptures collectively called People of the River that provides a fascinating foray into Singapore's past. These include Chong Fah Cheong's *First Generation* in front of the Fullerton Hotel. This delightful representation of children playing by and jumping into the river is an eye-catcher for all generations.

red dot design museum

Located in the red dot Traffic, a colonial building that was formerly the Singapore Traffic Police Headquarters, the red dot design museum was opened in November 2005. Older children will enjoy viewing the latest in product and brand design. Red dot designs are awarded globally to quality, cutting edge innovations. You'll also find various food and beverage outlets here.

Opening hours: 11.00 a.m. to 6.00 p.m. (Monday, Tuesday and Friday) / 11.00 a.m. to 8.00 p.m. (Saturday and Sunday)

Price guide: Adults: $8 / Students: $4 / Children (under 12): $4 / Seniors: $4

Location: red dot Traffic, 28 Maxwell Road Singapore 069120
Tel: 6327 8027
Email: museum@red-dot.sg
Web: www.red-dot.sg/concept/museum/main_page.htm

Note: Mums might enjoy the market,(Market for Artists and Designers) which is held every 1st Saturday and Sunday of the month from 11.00 a.m. to 8.00 p.m. (www.maad.sg)! It features original creative fashion, art and craft works.

Singapore Art Museum

see also Where to Go?, pp. 197

Opening hours: 10.00 a.m. to 7.00 p.m., except Fridays: 10 a.m. to 9 p.m. Last admission to the museum at 6.15 p.m. There is free admission on Friday night from 6.00 p.m. to 9.00 p.m.

Price guide: Admission is free for visitors aged 6 years and below. Singaporean and PR senior citizens all full-time National Service men (NSFs) students and teachers from local schools EXCEPT when special exhibitions are on. During special exhibitions: Adult: $10 / Student: $5 / Senior Citizens: $5. Free admission to SAM every Friday from 6.00 p.m. to 9.00 p.m. and on Open House days.

Location: 71 Bras Basah Road,
Singapore 189555
Tel: 6332 3222
Web: www.singaporeartmuseum.sg

Note:

• Free guided tours in English, Mandarin and Japanese are available. Ring for the latest schedule.

• A good way to introduce this art venue to young children is to combine about 30 minutes' art appreciation with one of the workshops that are conducted for younger ones from time to time. Past activities include balloon sculpting, face and henna painting and a sculpture workshop called Moving Statues.

Singapore Tyler Print Institute (STPI)

This organisation is situated within a restored 19th-century warehouse. It focuses on the creation of outstanding printworks by international Asian and Western artists and its facilities include a state-of-the-art printmaking workshop, paper mill and international art gallery. Here you can see lithography, intaglio, woodblock, relief printing, screen printing, papermaking and unique experimental print and paper forms.

Opening hours: 10.00 a.m. to 6.00 p.m. (Tuesdays to Saturdays) / Closed Sundays / Mondays by appointment only

Price guide: Free

Location: 41 Robertson Quay,
Singapore 238236
Tel: 6336 3663 ext 112
Email: stpi@stpi.com.sg
Web: www.stpi.com.sg

Note: There are free guided tours from time to time. Please check the website.

– Chapter 6 –

WHERE TO GO?

Having to keep your children, particularly younger ones, occupied is par for the course and venturing out of the home necessitates careful planning and organisation. At times this can represent a real challenge – one child wants to stay at home and watch television, the other wants to go to the BirdPark while you're already too tired from trekking around Bukit Timah Nature Reserve the day before! Fortunately, there are a variety of places to visit, from tried-and-tested venues such as the Singapore Zoological Gardens to less obvious sites such as the Live Turtle and Tortoise Museum at the Chinese Garden. In this chapter, I have included something for everyone. Hopefully some of these venues may inspire you and your child to try something new or simply revisit old haunts with a fresh approach.

For places that involve the great outdoors, please refer to *Back to Nature* (pp. 23 – 60). Happy sightseeing!

MUSEUMS AND INFOTAINMENT VENUES

There are many museums in Singapore but I've chosen to concentrate on the ones I believe will be of most interest to children.

Air Force Museum

Most children are interested in the activities of the armed forces and this museum provides an excellent opportunity to view the past and present of Singapore's air force. An outdoor gallery houses numerous aircraft that are displayed both on the ground and suspended from the roof. These planes can be seen from a viewing deck. Aircraft armaments and air defence artillery are also on display. Several galleries (including a History of Aviation Gallery) and a theatrette can be found indoors. Soundscapes, videos and animation are used throughout the exhibitions to enhance viewing and promote an interactive experience. The overall theme for the entire display is Men, Machine and Method.

Opening hours: 8.30 a.m. to 5.00 p.m. (Tuesdays to Sundays). Closed Mondays and public holidays)

FAST FACTS

www.sg – Your Official Gateway to Singapore

Singapore's national website, gives an up-to-date and quick guide on where to go and what is on.

Web: www.sg (look under Where To Go and What To Do)

Singapore Tourist Board

You don't need to be a tourist to access these sites. Look here for the latest events, places to go and things to do.

Tel: 1800 736 2000

Web: www.yoursingapore.com

Heritage trails

This is a great website, giving details of numerous heritage trails around Singapore. You can view NHB listed trails or register to view those created by other people.

Web: http://heritagetrails.sg

National Heritage Board

The National Heritage Board seeks to cultivate awareness and appreciation of Singapore's cultural heritage through a programme of exhibitions, educational events and fringe activities. Singaporean and Permanent Resident (PR) students can now enjoy free access to all NHB museums (special exhibitions will incur extra charges).

Tel: 1800 2255 642 (NHB HQ)

Web: www.nhb.gov.sg / www.museums.com.sg

Urban Redevelopment Authority

I'd recommend looking at this website, which has a number of super walking guides available to download. Some of these focus upon areas/place that are not so well known and are really worth looking at – the Rediscover Singapore guides are particularly interesting. A limited number of the guides are also available at URA's Singapore City Gallery, STB's Visitor Centres and NHB's museums.

Location: 45 Maxwell Road, Singapore 069118

(open 9.00 a.m. to 5.00 p.m.)

Tel: 6321 8321

Web: www.ura.gov.sg/rediscover

Price guide: Free

Location: 400 Airport Road,
Singapore 534234
Tel: 6461 8504 / 6461 8506
Web: www.mindef.gov.sg (search for air force museum)

Note:

• There is a cafeteria on site.

• The Singapore Navy Museum is also open to the public but you'll need to produce a passport or identity card to get in. The museum is housed in a pre-World War II building renovated to resemble the interior of a ship. It is situated within Endurance Block, Levels 1 to 3 at Sembawang Camp, 36 Admiralty Road West, Singapore 759960 (Tel: 6750 5585). Admission is free. Opening hours are 8.30 a.m. to 4.30 p.m. (weekdays) / 8.30 a.m. to 12 noon (Saturdays.) Do ring before you go as the museum was closed at the time of printing.

Army Museum of Singapore (ARMS)

This museum intends to preserve the heritage of the Singapore Army as well as honour the contributions of its soldiers. A free guided tour of the museum is available on the hour every hour during museum opening hours.

Opening hours: 10.00 a.m. to 6.00 p.m. (except Mondays). Open every public holiday (including Mondays).

Price guide: $3 for children (6 to 12 years old) / $5 for adults / $12 for a family ticket Free admission for SAF and Home Team NSF and NSmen and SAF servicemen/women (they are allowed up to four guests each on weekends and public holidays).

Location: SAFTI Military Institute,
520 Upper Jurong Road (near the Singapore Discovery Centre),
Singapore 638367
Web: www.armymuseum.sg

Note: A café is located on site

ArtScience Museum

This museum embraces a spectrum of influences from art and sciences to media and technology to architecture and design. A series of blockbuster exhibitions from around the world are planned for this beautiful lotus-design inspired building.

Opening hours: 10.00 a.m. to 10.00 p.m. daily (last entry at 9.00 p.m.)

Price guide: $17 for children (2 to 12 years old) / $30 for adults

Location: 10 Bayfront Avenue,
Singapore 018956
Tel: 6688 8868
Email: MuseumEnquiries@MarinaBaySands.com
Web: www.marinabaysands.com/ArtScienceMuseum

Asian Civilisations Museum (ACM)

The Asian Civilisations Museum is one of Singapore's largest and most impressive museums. The ACM at Empress Place traces and presents the ancestral cultures of Singaporeans. Thus, the main interest areas of this museum encompass China, Southeast Asia, India and West Asia.

The ACM has 11 exhibition galleries, two dining outlets, a museum shop, a fully equipped auditorium and a function room with a spectacular view of the Singapore River.

Look out for weekend activities specially designed to appeal to children. Children's workshops and Family Fun Days present an opportunity for parents and children to explore the galleries together, listen to stories, join a tour or even create a piece of artwork. Activities are usually free. The museum also hosts a number of Celebration Days that will appeal to the whole family. Free Children's Activity Booklets are also available from the Front Desk.

Opening hours: 1.00 p.m. to 7.00 p.m. (Mondays) / 9.00 a.m. to 7.00 p.m. (Tuesdays, Wednesdays, Thursdays, weekends) / 9.00 a.m. to 9.00 p.m. (Fridays)

Price guide: Free to children aged 6 and below/Free to all Singaporean and Permanent Resident students / $8 for adults. Admission is discounted between 7.00 p.m. and 9.00 p.m. on Fridays. (Admission charges may vary during special exhibitions.)

Location: 1 Empress Place,
Singapore 179555
Tel: 6332 7798 / 6332 2982
Email: NHB_ACM@nhb.gov.sg
Web: www.acm.org.sg

Tip: There are two adjoining food outlets next to the ACM at Empress Place. I'd recommend Siem Reap (which is accessed from Level 1). Here, you can eat outdoors or inside and there is a limited but well-priced children's menu available as well as high chairs. Alternatively, a visit to the museum can be complemented by a stroll along the Riverfront and a meal at one of the food outlets in Boat Quay or Clarke Quay. Most of the food outlets in this location (including Siem Reap) open after 11.00 a.m.

Peranakan Museum

Here you will find one of the most comprehensive collections of Peranakan artefacts in the world. There are 10 galleries, children's interactives and special merchandising in two shops. Temporary exhibitions are also regularly held.

Opening hours: 1.00 p.m. to 7.00 p.m. (Mondays) / 9.00 a.m. to .7.00 p.m. (Tuesdays to Sundays) / Late closing on Fridays at 9.00 p.m.

Price guide: Free to children aged 6 and below / $3 for full time students / $6 for adults. Admission is discounted between 7.00 p.m. and 9.00 p.m on Fridays.

Location: 39 Armenian Street,
Singapore 179941
Tel: 6332 7591/ 6332 2982
Email: nhb_pm_vs@nhb.gov.sg
Web: www.peranakanmuseum.sg

Chinatown Heritage Centre

see Chinatown under A Cultural Investigation pp. 209 – 212

Images of Singapore

Inside Images of Singapore, you will learn more about Singapore's heritage and view exhibits depicting the nation's diverse cultural practices and traditions. Popular exhibits include Singapore Celebrates, which gives a pictorial explanation of the main cultural festivals, and Singapore Adventure, an informative display of Singapore's history. There is also a well-stocked shop on site with some interesting souvenirs. Free guided tours are available on Fridays Saturdays, Sundays and public holidays at 11.00 a.m. and 2.00 p.m.

Opening hours: 9.00 a.m. to 7.00 p.m. (last entry 6.30 p.m.)

Price guide: $7 for children / $10 for adults. (Admission cost to the island is extra.)

Location: Imbiah Lookout, Sentosa. Get the blue or red line internal bus service from Sentosa or the Sentosa Express and alight at Imbiah Station.
Tel: 1800 736 8672 (9.00 a.m. to 6.30 p.m. Monday to Sunday)
Web: www.sentosa.com.sg (look under Attractions)

Tip: Sentosa usually gets very busy at weekends but a morning visit should avoid the crowds.

Malay Heritage Centre

The centre is currently undergoing re-development works. It is due to re-open in June 2012.

Nine galleries trace the history of the Malay community in Singapore, with exhibits featuring the regalia of Malay royalty and artefacts. Workshops (e.g. batik-making) and cultural shows are held from time to time. There is a fine-dining restaurant on site.

Location: 85 Sultan Gate, Singapore 198501
Tel: 6391 0450
Web: www.malayheritage.org.sg

The Mint Museum of Toys

The Mint Museum of Toys is the world's first purpose-built museum for toys with over 5,000 toys from more than 25 countries. The museum showcases an extensive collection of vintage toys, including rare and unique one-of-a-kind toys spanning the mid-1800s to the mid-1900s. Highlights include rare collections of cartoon and comic characters, e.g. Popeye the Sailor and Batman, which are worth thousands of dollars. There is a shop and restaurant on site.

Opening hours: 9.30 a.m. to 6.30 p.m. daily.

Price guide: Child (2 to 12 years): $5 / Adult: $10 / Family ticket (2 adults and 2 children): $24

Location: 26 Seah Street, Singapore 188382

Tel: 6339 0660
Email: info@emint.com
Web: www.emint.com

Memories at Old Ford Factory

This museum gives a fascinating insight to life in Singapore during Japanese occupation in the Second World War. The location was the site of the first Ford vehicle assembly plant in Southeast Asia and the place where the formal surrender of Malaya to the Japanese in 1942 took place.

Opening hours: 9.00 a.m. to 5.30 p.m. (Mondays to Saturdays) / 12 noon to 5.30 p.m. (Sundays)

Price guide: Free to children aged 6 and below / Free to Singaporean and PR students / $3 Foreign Student Pass / $8 for a family

Location: 351 upper Bukit Timah Road, Singapore 588192
Tel: 6562 6724
Email: NHB_NASReg@nhb.gov.sg
Web: www.s1942.org.sg/s1942/moff/index.htm

Singapore Art Museum (SAM)

This beautifully restored building has 18 galleries, an auditorium, a multi-purpose hall, a museum shop, a café, restaurants and a tiled court yard. On the Second Level are the artLAb and artPLAY areas where child-orientated activities are frequently available. The museum also conducts activities for children from time to time, including Children's Day celebrations, performances, storytelling and workshops.

Opening hours: 10.00 a.m. to 7.00 p.m. (Mondays to Sundays) /10.00 a.m. to 9.00 p.m. (Fridays)

Price guide: Free for children below 6 years / Free for Singaporean and PR students / $5 for students / $10 for adults. The museum is free from 6.00 p.m. to 9.00 p.m. on Fridays.

Location: 71 Bras Basah Road, Singapore 189555
Tel: 6332 3222
Email: NHB_SAM@nhb.gov.sg
Web: www.singaporeartmuseum.org.sg

Note:

- There are diaper changing areas in the toilets
- Admission is free on International Museum Day and certain public holidays (check website for more details).

Tip: Hungry? Try the Dome restaurant which is adjacent to the museum. It offers special lunch and tea sets. A cheaper eating venue is the nearby Kopitiam, which has a typical food court layout.

Singapore Discovery Centre

Singapore Discovery Centre describes itself as a 'hands on, minds on' place where you can explore what keeps Singapore going. Here you can learn about Singapore's technological endeavours and achievements in an entertaining (there are lots of hands-on activities) and educational setting.

Facilities: There are a number of permanent exhibits including Visionarium, where you can build the Singapore of the future, and the Digital Dance Studio where you can learn some of the traditional Asian dances. Children may also enjoy the opportunity to become an On Location Reporter and be projected onto a screen. Older children will be thrilled by the 4-D Stimulator ride in the XD theatre which has hair raising state-of-the-art technology. A SAFTI bus tour is also available, which takes guests around the army training ground, which is just next door.

The iWERKS Theatre shows 2-D and 3-D giant screen movies (check out the schedule on the website). It has a 5-storey-high screen and an excellent sound system.

Older children may enjoy the Shooting Gallery with its four-lane computerised simulated shooting range. And for those who are 18 years and above, there is a Crossfire Paintball facility (www.crossfire.com.sg)

There is a shop, cafeteria and small food court on site. A nappy changing facility is located in the ladies' toilets.

Opening hours: 9.00 a.m. to 6.00 p.m. (Tuesdays to Sundays) /Closed Mondays except public holidays

Price guide: Child (3 to 12 years): $6 / Adult: $10 / Family (2 adults and 2 children): $28 / Ravine Racer simulator ride: $8 (child), $10 (adult) / Shooting Gallery: $6 (child/adult). Entry into the iWERKS Theatre is extra and depends on the performance being screened.

Location: 510 Upper Jurong Road, Singapore 638365
Tel: 6792 6188
Web: www.sdc.com.sg

Tip: Sometimes it is difficult to get a taxi unless you call for one. The bus journey to Boon Lay interchange takes about 20 minutes and you can continue your journey more easily from there.

Singapore Mint Coin Gallery

The main attraction for children is the opportunity to mint their own souvenir coin at the gallery's coin press. For the more money-minded, learning about the production of coins, their history and the variety available (the Chinese Zodiac coins will appeal to many children because of their personal relevance) will ensure that this is a spot worth visiting. You can also purchase coins here.

Opening hours: 8.30 a.m. to 4.30 p.m. weekdays

Price guide: Free (you have to pay a small fee if you wish to join a short, guided tour)

Location: 20 Teban Gardens Crescent, Singapore 608925

Tel: 6566 2626

Email: salesadmin@singaporemint.com.sg

Web: www.singaporemint.com

Singapore Coins and Notes Museum

This is the first and only museum in Singapore dedicated to displaying currency. There are innovative and educational displays that include an interesting section on the peculiar ways in which coins and notes are used for weddings, ornamentation and other purposes in different culture. You can also make your own coin rubbings to take home as souvenirs.

Opening hours: 10.00 a.m. to 8.00 p.m. daily

Price guide: $6 for a child (3 to 12 years) / $10 for adults / $25 for a family ticket (2 adults and 2 children)

Location: 2 Trengganu Street (entrance at Pagoda Street), Singapore 058456

Tel: 6222 2486

Email: enquiries@scnm.com.sg

Web: wwwscnm.com.sg

Singapore National Museum

Singapore's largest museum comprises two main galleries: the Singapore History Gallery, which goes back to the 14th century, and the Singapore Living Galleries, which focus on the following four lifestyle themes — food, fashion, film & wayang and photography.

Facilities: The History Gallery features various historical characters who 'talk' to their audience and relate something of their past. In the Living Galleries, highlights include the Food Gallery, which explores the origins of street food culture in Singapore, and the shopping experience within the Fashion Gallery. In addition, special exhibitions are held throughout the year. There are food outlets and a shop on the ground floor.

From time to time, there are special programmes for children, such as mosaic art workshops, interactive tours, storytelling, performances and school holiday programmes.

Opening hours: Singapore History Gallery is open 10.00 a.m. to 6.00 p.m. daily. Singapore Living Galleries is open 10.00 a.m. to 8.00 p.m.

Price guide: Admission into the museum building is free. Admission to both galleries is free for children under 6, $5 for children under 18, free for Singaporean and PR students and $10 for adults. Admission to Singapore Living Galleries from 6.00 p.m. to 8.00 p.m. daily is free.

Location: 93 Stamford Road, Singapore 178897

Tel: 6332 3659/ 63332 5642

Email: nhb_nm_corpcomms@nhb.gov.sg

Web: www.nationalmuseum.sg

Singapore Philatelic Museum

Stamp collecting as a children's hobby does not enjoy the popularity it did 20 years ago. However, these pictorial miniatures still fascinate some children and, by virtue of their variety and the stories they tell, a trip to the philatelic museum is still a worthwhile venture. Who knows? It may even spark a new pastime that is inexpensive and easy to pursue. The museum has a Purple Room that houses a permanent exhibition showing how stamps are made from their conceptualisation to their circulation through the mail. Look out for the museum's open house when admission is free (and usually special activities are available) as well as workshops and school holiday programmes.

Opening hours: 1.00 p.m. to 7.00 p.m. (Mondays) / 9.00 a.m. to 7.00 p.m. (Tuesdays to Sundays)

Price guide: Singaporean and PR students (3 to 12 years): Free / Child (3 to 12 years): $4 / Adults: $5

Location: 23B Coleman Street, Singapore 179807
Tel: 6337 3888
Email: nhb_spm_adm@nhb.gov.sg
Web: www.spm.org.sg

Note: Birthday parties can be held here!

Singapore Science Centre

This is an excellent venue for children of all ages, and one I'd strongly recommend. There are 12 galleries featuring static and interactive science-related exhibits.

The Discovery Zone is targeted at 4- to 12-year-olds and is a hands-on exhibition featuring water play, a hatchery, a sensory section and even small animals! 'Where kids play to learn' is the philosophy of this section and it truly is a fun experience.

The Kinetic Garden is in open grounds between the Science Centre and the Omni-Theatre. This is an outdoor interactive science park, to which admission is free. It shows how different forms of energy are interrelated in the form of exhibits like the lithophone (a musical instrument made of rock or stone), a Magic Swing and a Sundial.

Another super attraction is Waterworks, which is a large, interactive space based on the theme of water. Children (and adults!) can have great fun playing with the 11 hands-on exhibits. Be prepared to get wet!

You might want to avoid weekend afternoons when the throngs of visitors may deter those with preschoolers.

Facilities and exhibits: Includes Discovery Zone, Ecogarden, The Mind's Eye (which reveals some of the secrets behind illusions), iSpace, a great interactive Sound exhibition, Waterworks (don't forget to pack the swimsuits!) and an exciting schedule of temporary exhibitions. There is also a shop, a café and a McDonald's at the entrance.

Opening hours: 10.00 a.m. to 6.00 p.m. (Tuesdays to Sundays) / Closed Mondays/ Open all school and public holidays (including Mondays)

Price guide: Child (3 to 16 years): $5 / Adults: $9 / Family Membership per year (unlimited visits to the Science Centre only) start from $50 / Individual membership per year: $28. Also look out for promotions and discounts and combo-packages with IMAX movies and Snow City.

Location: 15 Science Centre Road, Singapore 609081
Tel: 6425 2500
Email: enquiry@science.edu.sg
Web: www.science.edu.sg

Note: Strollers/buggies are available from the Visitors' Services Centre. If your child is a keen scientist, the Primary Science Club and Questa Club (for Secondary School pupils) may appeal. These schemes issue badges upon completion of set activities.

Omni-Theatre

This complex is part of the Science Centre and you'll find it immediately adjacent to the main building. The theatre is equipped with state-of-the-art IMAX technology which delivers the world's most immersive experience. Sitting inside the dome-shaped theatre, you'll become engulfed in whatever you are viewing, so be prepared for rapid journeys, sheer drops and heady heights! Within this complex, there are also exhibition galleries, a souvenir shop and a restaurant.

Next door is an Observatory, which is one of the few observatories situated so near to the equator (and thus on a clear evening stargazing can be particularly rewarding).

Opening hours: 10.00 a.m. to 6.00 p.m. daily. Some shows may have additional screenings on weekends. The Observatory is open to the public for stargazing sessions every Friday night from 7.50 p.m. to 10.00 p.m.

Price guide: 3-D movies vary in price from $8 upwards for a child/adult. Check website for schedule and cost.

Web: www.omnitheatre.com.sg

Tip: It is within easy walking distance to Snow City.

ON YOUR DOORSTEP

Civil Defence Heritage Gallery

Located within Singapore's oldest fire station, this gallery showcases the island's civil defence developments from the 19th century to the present day. You can view antique fire engines as well as ascend the Hose Tower, which was Singapore's highest viewpoint in the 1920s (children must be higher than 1.2 metres for the this). There is a souvenir shop on site.

Opening hours: 10.00 a.m. to 5.00 p.m. (Tuesdays to Sundays) / 7.00 p.m. to 8.00 p.m. for the Lookout Tower Tour (Tuesdays and Fridays)

Location: Central Fire Station, 62 Hill Street, Singapore 179367
Tel: 6332 2996
Web: www.scdf.gov.sg (look under CD Heritage Gallery)

Fire Stations

All Singapore Civil Defence Force's fire stations, except Jurong Island Fire Station, offer an open house every Saturday morning. The tour of the fire station generally takes about an hour. Tours may vary from station to station, but children generally get to view and go inside a fire engine, see a fire fighting demonstration and possibly try on a uniform, use a hose or even ride on a crane. These tours are a sure win with any child!

Opening hours: 9.00 a.m. to 11.00 a.m. (Saturdays only)
Price guide: Free

- Alexandra Fire Station: 6471 7481
- Ang Mo Kio Fire Station: 6484 3101
- Bishan Fire Station: 6355 5032
- Bukit Batok Fire Station: 6314 6906
- Changi Fire Station: 6543 3900 (N.B. Due to renovation, there will be no visits until after September 2011)
- Central Fire Station: 6332 3000
- Clementi Fire Station: 6341 1100
- Jurong Fire Station: 6267 4700
Geylang Fire Station: 6743 1500
- Paya Lebar Fire Station: 6849 1850
- Sengkang Fire Station: 6312 7002
- Sembawang Fire Station: 6257 1221
- Tampines Fire Station: 6587 8344
- Tuas Fire Station: 6865 4180
- Woodlands Fire Station: 6884 1350
- Yishun Fire Station: 6852 7995

Web: www.scdf.gov.sg (look under Community & Volunteers and Fire Station Open House)

OUT AND ABOUT

Changi Airport

Why not go to the airport as a destination in itself? Plane spotting can be combined with the fun of getting there and even having breakfast or a light meal while in transit.

Getting there: One way to get there is by MRT (which arrives in Terminals 2 and 3). You will have to transfer trains at Tanah Merah MRT Station (EW4). For under $2 for adults and even less for children (according to age/height), you can travel in air-conditioned comfort between Changi and Orchard Road. An alternative way back to the city centre is to take the public bus. The No. 36 bus goes from the basement bus bays of Terminals 1, 2 and 3 to Orchard Road for $2 (adult single fare, child fares are lower. The journey takes about an hour and you will need the exact change.

Terminal 1

Facilities: Restaurants and fast food outlets are in both the arrival and departure lounges. The Viewing Mall is on the second level and is clearly signposted. There are plenty of seats in the vicinity and toilets nearby.

Terminal 2

Facilities: As per Terminal 1. The Viewing Mall has the added attraction of having Swensen's restaurant immediately adjacent and a playground area with slides in it.

Terminal 3

Facilities: As well as a 24-hour food gallery, children will enjoy the Hard Rock Café, McDonald's or Burger King, to name but a few of the dining options available. The Viewing Mall is situated on Level 3.

Tel: Terminal 1: 6542 9727 /
Terminal 2: 6542 9792 /
Terminal 3: 6307 8555
Web: www.changiairport.com

Special Attractions

Changi Aviation Gallery

This is located at Terminals 2 and 3. It is a multi-sensory zone with hands-on interactive displays that will appeal to everyone.

Playgrounds

There are playgrounds suitable for children between the ages of 1 to 12 years old located in all terminal departure lounges. However, at Terminal 3 there is one located in the public area next to the water fountain at B2 Mall.

The Slide@T3

The tallest indoor slide in Singapore is located at Terminal 3, Arrival Hall (level 1) in the public area. For every $10 spent in a single receipt, members of the public can redeem one token to ride the 12 m slide.

Zone X

Located at Terminal 3, #B2-23 this arcade features redemption games, toy and sweet catcher machines and many other amusement games.

Note:

- You can travel between the three terminals for free on the Skytrain.
- If you are travelling by public bus, have the exact fare ready if you don't possess an ez-link card.

Tips:

- The MRT stops at Expo Station just before Changi Airport, so you could also visit any ongoing exhibitions.
- If you travel by bus, you could also stop off at East Coast Park for a stroll along the seafront or to go cycling.

If you are flying, the facilities for children inside both of the transit terminals are excellent and will keep your child entertained for the day if need be! Terminal 1 has an Explorer's Lounge (Level 3) that has a children's playground and screens the National Geographic and Discovery channels. There is also a small movie lounge on this level. Parents' Rooms with a hot water dispenser are situated near Gates C24 and D36 (Level 2) as well as in the public area next to Délifrance in Arrival Hall West (Level 1). There are three Parents' Rooms with diaper changing stations and other facilities including hot water dispensers.

Terminal 2 has an Entertainment Deck (Level 3) which is a one-stop integrated, multi-media entertainment centre. Here you can enjoy access to game consoles Xbox 360 or PlayStation 3, watch music videos, see the latest movie screening on Star Movies cable TV or enjoy free LAN gaming. There is a children's playground next to the Family Zone at the Departure Lounge on Level 2. Parents' Rooms are situated near Gate E1 (Level 2), behind Sunglasses Hut in Transit Hall South (Level 2) and in the public area near Check-in Row 7, Departure Hall Central (on Level 2).

Terminal 3 also has a movie theatre (on Level 3) and two playgrounds located near to the Departure Lounges (Central and South) on Level 2. There are a number of Parents' Rooms.

Fort Canning Park and The Battle Box

Situated on Fort Canning Hill, Fort Canning Park is a pleasant venue to walk around and is rich in history. (Artefacts dating to the 14th century have been found here.) At the top of the hill is a 19th-century fort gate, which is all that remains of the fortress that used to be here. You will also find a covered reservoir built by the British in 1926. The park marks the site of the first botanical gardens started by Sir Stamford Raffles. Fort Canning Centre, in the middle of the park, is a restored military barracks that is now a cultural venue.

Activities: Bird watching, history trails and trekking

Opening hours: 24 hours (the park is lit from 7.00 p.m. to 7.00 a.m.)

Price guide: Free

Location: Cox Terrace (adjacent to the Registry of Marriages)
Tel: 6332 1200
Web: www.nparks.gov.sg

Note: The park is a popular venue for events such as Ballet under the Stars, Jazz nights and WOMAD. Look too for regularly organized nature walks.

Tips:

- The park is an ideal setting for a picnic.
- Try the m.i.s. café at The Legends at Fort Canning Park, which was formerly the Far East Command Centre. The Legends Club is just a short walk down a flight of steps from the exit of The Battle Box.

Situated within the park is **The Battle Box**, which was the biggest underground military operations quarters in Singapore during World War II. It is also the site where the British made the decision to surrender to the Japanese in February 1942. Here you can experience events from that time thanks to special audio and visual effects and animatronics. The various key military personnel are very lifelike and being inside this dimly lit, underground centre surrounded by army memorabilia does create a special atmosphere. It is an interesting historical venue for children aged 8 and above.

Opening hours: 10.00 a.m. to 6.00 p.m. (last admission 5.00 p.m.) daily

Price guide: $5 for children (3 to 12 years) / $8 for adults

Tel: 6333 0510

Web: www.legendsfortcanning.com/fortcanning/battlebox.htm

Fountain of Wealth (Suntec City)

Anyone interested in *feng shui* or in need of more cultural awareness will find this site interesting! The aerial view of Suntec City resembles the palm of a hand. The five towers represent the five digits and the fountain (known as the Fountain of Wealth) is the palm. As the design is supposed to bring good luck, you are recommended to walk around the fountain three times, touch the water and make a wish! The fountain is also said to currently be the largest man-made fountain in the world.

Opening hours: The fountain is open daily from 9.00 a.m. to 10.00 p.m. / Touch-water sessions are 9.00 a.m. to noon, 2.00 p.m. to 6.00 p.m., 7.00 p.m. to 7.50 p.m. and 9.30 p.m. to 10.00 p.m. At these times, walk around it and try your luck! There is also a spectacular laser show at 8.00 p.m., 8.30 p.m. and 9 p.m. daily. Song dedications can be made from 7.00 p.m. to 9.30 p.m. (Mondays to Thursdays) / 8.00 p.m. to 9.30 p.m. Fridays to Sundays. Laser message dedications are from 8.00 p.m. to 9.30 p.m. (Fridays to Sundays)

Location: Suntec City Mall 3, Temasek Boulevard (opposite Temasek Avenue)

Tel: 6295 2888

Web: www.suntec.city.com.sg/fountain/indx.htm

Tips:

- If you're hungry, why not try one of the nearby restaurants or stalls in the food court?
- If you have younger children, you can take them to the playground in the Sky Garden on Level 3 of Tower Blocks 1 and 2. Older children may also enjoy this spacious venue, which has excellent views and plenty of shaded seating areas.

HealthZone

I'd be the first to admit that informing my kids they were going to a health exhibition on a Sunday afternoon wouldn't meet with much enthusiasm. However, this initiative by the Health Promotion Board has been carefully planned and structured to entertain as well as inform. The prime aim of HealthZone is to encourage us to cultivate a healthy lifestyle. While a laudable aim, the exhibition is also good fun! There are static and interactive displays, multimedia shows and computer games. Highlights include the Fitness Funhouse and the Exciting Eatery.

Opening hours: 9.00 a.m. to 5.00 p.m. (Tuesdays to Saturdays) / 1.00 p.m. to 5.00 p.m. (Mondays) / Closed Sundays and public holidays

Price guide: $1.50 for children (3 to 18 years) / $3 for adults

Location: Health Promotion Board Building, Level 2, 3 Second Hospital Avenue, Singapore 168937
Tel: 1800 435 3616
Email: hpb_health_zone@hpb.gov.sg
Web: www.hpb.gov.sg (look under Services & Partnership)

The Helix Bridge

This is the world's first double helix pedestrian bridge which opened in 2010. The bridge stretches 280m over Marina Bay and features a computer controlled lighting system which creates an amazing effect. There are five viewing platforms at strategic locations offering stunning views of the Singapore skyline. The bridge also functions as a gallery, where children's paintings and drawings are exhibited for public viewing. I'd recommend a family walk along here at nighttime.

Location: The bridge links Marina Centre with Marina South in the Marina Bay area (it is beside the Benjamin Sheares Bridge)

Istana

see Annual Events, pp. 243 – 244

Singapore Flyer

This 42-storey-high giant observation wheel is the largest of its kind in the world, with panoramic views of Singapore, Malaysia and Indonesia from the top. It looks like a very sophisticated ferris wheel, albeit one that allows passengers to enjoy the spectacular skyline without experiencing lateral movement or vibration. The minimal steel content of the wheel gives the impression that the passenger-seat capsules are actually airborne!

The complex adjacent to the Flyer has various facilities including restaurants, shops and a built-in rainforest occupying the entire central atrium of the main terminal building. A special attraction is the flight simulator on Level 2 featuring a fully enclosed cockpit equipped with fully-functioning avionics and computers.

Opening hours: 8.30 a.m. to 10.30 p.m. daily / Ticket sales: 8.00 a.m. to 10.00 p.m.
Price guide: A basic flight (a 37-minute wheel rotation) is $20.65 for children (3 to 12 years) / $29.50 for adults.

Location: 30 Raffles Avenue, #01-07, Singapore 039803
Tel: 6734 8829
Web: www.singaporeflyer.com.sg/www.flightexperience.com.sg (flight simulator)

Note: Sky dining packages are available

WORLD WAR II — A JOURNEY INTO THE PAST

Evidence of World War II is scattered all over Singapore. Old forts, underground bunkers and war memorials pay tribute to the island's military history and, at times, tumultuous past. Older children who are interested in Singapore's history may find the following places to be of interest:

The Battle Box

see Fort Canning Park and The Battle Box, pp. 204 – 205

Changi Chapel and Museum

This venue commemorates the events of World War II and the impact of the war on Singapore. Because of its subject matter, it is not suitable for younger children.

However, for those who already have some appreciation of the nation's past, it makes for a poignant and informative history lesson. Interesting exhibits include the Changi Murals, Changi Quilts, and Wartime Artists. There is also a gift shop and small café on site.

Opening hours: 9.30 a.m. to 5.00 p.m. daily (last entry at 4.30 p.m.)
Price guide: Free admission. In-house tours are $4 for children and $8 for adults.

Location: 1000 Upper Changi Road North, Singapore 507707
Tel: 6214 2451
Email: changi_museum@pacific.net.sg
Web: www.changimuseum.com

Fort Siloso (Sentosa)

Built in the 19th century, Fort Siloso is one of the 12 coastal batteries that made up Fortress Singapore at the start of World War II. Here you can view a barrack room, laundry room, cookhouse and tailoring shop as well as explore the war tunnels. There is a wide collection of artillery guns on display, dating back to the 17th century and an excellent exhibit about the British surrender in 1942 and the Japanese surrender in 1945.

Opening hours: 10.00 a.m. to 6.00 p.m. daily (last entry at 5.30 p.m.)

Price guide: $5 for children / $8 for adults. There are free guided tours at 12.40 p.m. and 3.40 p.m. every Friday, Saturday, Sunday and public holiday (register at Fort Siloso Tram Station).

Location: Sentosa. Get the blue or red line internal bus service from Sentosa and alight at the stop for Siloso Point. Alternatively, take the Siloso Beach Tram. The distinctive Fort Siloso Tram runs from Imbiah Look on Fridays, Saturday, Sundays and public holidays at 12.30 p.m. and 3.30 p.m.
Web: www.fortsiloso.com / www.sentosa.com.sg

Johore Battery

Here you can see a replica of one of the three 15-inch monster guns used during World War II as well as view the labyrinth of tunnels through a reverse periscope (access into the underground chambers is not possible).
Opening hours: 9.00 a.m. to 5.00 p.m. (Mondays to Fridays)
Price guide: Free

Location: Cosford Road, off Upper Changi Road North
Tel: 6546 9897

Labrador Nature Reserve

Labrador Nature Reserve contains old gun emplacements of the 19th-century fort and an authentically restored 6-inch quick-firing gun. Storyboards give a detailed account of the park's military history. The underground ammunition chambers are currently closed for maintenance but in the past guided tours have been conducted which have provided an interesting insight into the last days of Labrador Battery during World War II.
Opening hours: All day
Price guide: Free Admission

Location: Along Labrador Villa Road, off Pasir Panjang Road
Tel: 1800 4717300 (National Parks Helpline)
Web: www.nparks.gov.sg (look under Nature Reserves)

Reflections at Bukit Chandu

This is an interpretive centre dedicated to the 1st and 2nd Battalion Malay Regiment and its contribution to the Battle for Singapore. There are three galleries and a souvenir corner. Highlights include the 3-D binaural sound effect show titled *Sounds of Battle* and a hologram show depicting the Battle of Pasir Panjang.
Opening hours: 9.00 a.m. to 5.30 p.m. (Tuesdays to Sundays) / Open on public holidays
Price guide: Free for children below the age of 6 years / Free for Singaporean and PR student / $2 for adults / $5 for family ticket (maximum 2 adults) / Free on certain public holidays

Location: 31K Pepys Road, Singapore 118458

Tel: 6332 7939 (weekdays)/
6375 2510 (weekends)
Email: nhb_nasreg@nhb.gov.sg
Web: www.s1942.org.sg (look under Reflections of Bukit Chandu)

Note: Afterwards, if you are feeling adventurous, try the canopy trail that leads to Kent Ridge Park.

Battlefield Tours

A couple of travel companies offer informative tours of the battlefields and war relics of Singapore's past. Currently, these include:

Faber Tours

Tel: 6270 8855
Email: customerservice@mountfaber.com.sg
Web: www.fabertours.com.sg

Journeys Pte Ltd

Recommended!

Tel: 6325 1631
Email: discover@journeys.com.sg / fun@singaporewalks.com
Web: www.singaporewalks.com

Malaysia and Singapore Travel Centre

Tel: 6737 8877
Web: www.mastravel.com

A CULTURAL INVESTIGATION

If you want to explore Singapore's rich variety of cultures and traditions, you can try the following venues and itineraries. Of course, there is a tourist attraction element to these but they are a good introduction to what life in Singapore involves for those from different backgrounds.

Note: I'd recommend the *Yours To Explore* booklets published by the Singapore Tourism Board for self reliant walking tours. These include guides to Chinatown and Little India. Also worth considering are the many walking tours offered by Journeys Pte Ltd (Tel: 6325 1631 / www.singaporewalks.com). Walking trails recommended by the Singapore Tourist Board can also be found online (www.yoursingapore.com) and you can download a wide selection of walking maps and guides for areas throughout Singapore at www.ura.gov.sg/rediscover (URA also publish an Architectural Walking maps for both Chinatown and Little India which are available from their Singapore City Gallery).

Chinatown

Note: It is best to explore Chinatown early in the day, e.g. from 10.30 a.m., or later in the afternoon when it is cooler. During the Lunar New Year festivities, it can get extremely crowded so if you have young children avoid early evening or the few days preceding the celebration.

Look out for fortune-tellers and letter

writers here! Having your name written in Chinese will appeal to most youngsters. Suggested places of interest to children include:

Chinatown Heritage Centre

This centre traces life in pre-modern Chinatown within three beautifully restored shophouses. It houses 13 exhibition galleries and numerous artefacts. The display and exhibit about the cubicles in which many of the early immigrants lived is particularly fascinating. There is a shop and a restaurant which serves fare with a strong Singaporean flavour.
Opening hours: 9.00 a.m. to 8.00 p.m. daily (last admission is at 7.00 p.m.)
Price guide: Child: $6 / Adults: $10

Location: 48 Pagoda Street, Singapore 059207
Tel: 6221 9556
Email: chc@ducktours.com.sg
Web: www.chinatownheritagecentre.sg

Note: Forget about finding any nappy changing facilities in Chinatown!
Tip: Chinatown is spectacular during Chinese New Year when the streets are colourfully decorated and full of stalls selling Chinese New Year goodies (*see* Annual Events, pp. 234 – 235).

Chinese Opera Teahouse

An excellent opportunity to learn more about Chinese opera is offered by the Chinese Theatre Circle. Here you can see a performance on the sights and sounds of Chinese opera in a restored shophouse on Fridays and Saturdays.
Opening hours: Noon to 5.00 p.m. (Tuesdays to Sundays). Performances are held between 7.00 p.m. and 9.00 p.m. on Fridays and Saturdays.
Price guide: $35 for the Sights and Sounds of Chinese Opera performance with dinner / $20 with snacks

Location: 5 Smith Street, Singapore 058919
Tel: 6323 4862
Email: ctopera@yahoo.com
Web: www.ctcopera.com.sg / teahouse.html

Pagoda Street and Temple Street

Once home to the opium dens and coolies of the early days in Chinatown, these streets are now lined with many shops and street markets, which operate from 11.00 a.m. to 11.00 p.m. daily. Look out for the restored shophouses and various unusual items on sale. During Chinese New Year, this area is particularly busy, and it is fun to browse the special festive stalls that retail everything from dried meats (even whole piglets!) to lucky charms and 'orange bags'.

Smith Street

Try out the food on offer here — Cantonese, Peranakan and Teochew cuisine, to name but a few, are available. The Chinatown Market and Food Centre is located at 335 Smith Street and is open daily from 11.00 a.m. to 8.00 p.m. Here you can find exotic fruits, vegetables and meats on sale, including turtles, frogs and even snakes. Fortunately the machine that was used to pluck feathers off live chickens is no longer used!

Sri Mariamman Temple

Brightly and decoratively embellished, this is the oldest and most important Hindu temple in Singapore. The elaborate *gopuram* is a sculptured tower of gods, goddesses and mythological creatures that you can clearly view from the outside. Take off your shoes before entering.

Opening hours: The temple allows all-day visiting, but the best times are from 7.00 a.m. to noon and 6.00 p.m. to 8.30 p.m.

Price guide: Free admission (but you require tickets to use cameras)

Location: 224 South Bridge Road, Singapore 058773

Trishaw Rides

A popular tourist attraction, trishaw rides offer an easy, relatively cool and fun way to explore Chinatown. You'll find the Trishaw Park at Albert Mall located at Queen Street between the Fu Lu Shou Complex and Albert Centre Market and Food Centre. A ride along a fixed route starts from $25 to $36 per person (less for a child). Another alternative is to book a Chinatown Trishaw Tour with Singapore Explorer Pte Ltd (Tel: 6339 6833). You can also book a trishaw tour of Little India with them.

Tip: It is advisable to make a booking through a tour operator at an official kiosk.

Yue Hwa

With a history of more than 45 years, this large Chinese department store is housed in a former Nam Tin Hotel that was built in 1900. It offers a wide range of authentic Chinese products, including tea and foodstuffs, *cheongsams*, handicrafts, Chinese herbs and medicines and antiques. There is plenty to discuss and purchase here!

Opening hours: 11.00 a.m. to 9.00 p.m. (Sundays to Fridays) / 11.00 a.m. to 10.00 p.m. (Saturdays)

Location: 70 Eu Tong Sen Street, Singapore 059805
Tel: 6538 4222
Web: www.yuehwa.com.sg

Unusual Stalls and Shops!

- Try to spot the groundnut seller at 39 Temple Street.
- At 207 and 203 New Bridge Road are outlets selling *bak kwa* (barbecued meat) and *lap cheong* (traditional Chinese sausage).
- Traditional Chinese Medicine Halls can be found at 201 New Bridge Road and 267–271 South Bridge

Road. Try and identify some of the ingredients such as seahorses and bats!

- Located at #01-86, Block 5 on Banda Street is a shop selling paper effigies. As part of Chinese funeral rites, it's not unusual for relatives to burn paper effigies in the form of cars, houses or credit cards.

Little India

For a taste of Indian life, visit Serangoon Road and the surrounding area. Here you will find Bollywood films and flower garlands for sale, smell whiffs of jasmine and spices, have your fortune told by a colourful parakeet and view the riches of the gold and sari shops. Watch Indian delicacies being made on street corners and for those who like curry, why not try one served on banana leaves, as is the custom in the restaurants around here. Avoid Sundays, it's very crowded and don't expect 'pushchair friendly' pavements! Sights your child may enjoy include:

Little India Arcade

This is a complex of restored shophouses where you can shop and eat. Children will be interested in the Indian sweet shop at Ganesan Villas (#01-08), where you can buy various delicacies including *kulfi*, a milk dessert, and *vada*, a savoury lentil doughnut. This is a good place to source handicrafts and trinkets. For girls, the inexpensive costume jewellery and decorated pens and notebooks are sure to appeal!

Location: 48 Serangoon Road, Singapore 217959

Mustafa

This huge shopping complex is often very crowded with both people and produce, so don't venture in there unless you know your child is interested. Piled high with bargains and a vast assortment of goods, this is a shopping grotto.

Opening hours: 24 hours daily

Location: Serangoon Plaza, 320 Serangoon Road, Singapore 218108
Web: www.mustafa.com.sg

Sakya Muni Buddha Gaya Temple (Temple of 1,000 Lights)

In this temple you'll find a huge seated Buddha, some 50 feet high. Light bulbs surround the Buddha which lights up every time someone makes a donation. You can also have your fortune told on a wheel near the prayer hall for a small donation.

Opening hours: 8.00 a.m. to 4.45 p.m.

Location: 366 Race Course Road, Singapore 218636

Sri Veeramakaliamman Temple

Dedicated to the Hindu Goddess Kali, the temple was built in 1881. Its Tower

Gate is richly decorated with gods, goddesses and mythical animals. On Tuesdays and Fridays (both holy days), devotees go to the temple to pray and seek blessings from Kali. You may see devotees breaking coconuts in the aluminium enclosures near the doors to the entrance. This is a symbol of breaking their egos to reveal their pure, inner selves. During the Festival of Thaipusam, a spectacular two-day celebration centres around the temple. Older children may find the sight of devotees in trances with their bodies pierced by heavy spikes fascinating. The temple is closed every day from 12.30 p.m. to 4.00 p.m.

Location: 141 Serangoon Road, Singapore 218042

Web: www.sriveeramakaliamman.com

Note: While I know some mothers who have ventured into Little India with babies, I wouldn't recommend it. I find it very hot and, at times, too busy. However, children aged 5 and above may well enjoy the sights and sounds.

Tekka Market

Tekka means 'the foot of bamboo shoots' in Mandarin and refers to the fact that this was an area where bamboo clumps once grew in abundance. The focus of the original market was primarily cattle trading. This venue now offers an insight into local foods and exotic fruits and vegetables. Try the hawker centre for Chinese, Malay or Indian food (*thosai,* an Indian pancake, is delicious and can be eaten sweet or savoury). Afterwards, go upstairs for clothes, cheap toys and various knick-knacks.

Opening hours: Daily from 7.00 a.m. to 3.30 p.m.

Location: 665 Buffalo Road, Singapore 210665

Unusual Stalls and Shops!

- Look out for the spice grinding shop at 2 Cuff Street. Here you can have spice mixtures ground or flour milled.
- Smell the fresh flowers and garlands of Campbell Lane.
- Get your hands painted with traditional henna designs. Try the Punjab Bazaar on Serangoon Road or the various beauty parlours in Buffalo Road.
- On the corner of Upper Dickson Road, there is usually an Indian fortune-teller with her parrot. You may also find a Chinese fortune-teller along the walkway of Block 663 in Tekka Market.
- Outside a restaurant at 62 Serangoon Road, you may find the last Indian yoghurt street vendor in Singapore. She sells the yoghurt from two red plastic buckets.

Trishaw Rides

A lovely way to explore Little India is by trishaw. As with Chinatown, trips last about 30 to 45 minutes from about $25 per person (less for a child). It is advised that you book the tour through a licensed trishaw operator or go to one of the official kiosks (there are a number at the Trishaw Park just off Albert Mall). You can also consider these companies: Pedicab Tours Pte Ltd (Tel: 6336 0500/1), tour starts fron Albert Mall; Singapore Explorer Pte Ltd (Tel: 6339 6833), tour starts from Liang Court and Bencoolen Link; Trishaw Uncle (Tel: 9767 0648), tour starts from Albert Mall market place; Alphaland Travel Services Pte Ltd (Tel: 6333 0381/2), tour starts from Sungei Road; Trishaw Tours Pte Ltd (Tel: 6545 6311), tour starts from Albert Mall; Triwheel Tours Pte Ltd (Tel: 6336 9025/6), tour starts from Albert Mall.

Geylang Serai

This area is rich in Malay cuisine, costumes and crafts. The best time to visit it is during Hari Raya Puasa (*see* Annual Events, pp. 235 – 236). Highlights around here include:

Geylang Serai NewMarket

This market encompasses a two-storey structure built in a style reminiscent of rustic Malay architecture. On the ground floor is a wet market selling all sorts of fresh produce from live fish to spices and on the second level is a food centre.Try Malay specialities such as *goreng pisang* (fried banana), *nasi pandang* (rice with an assortment of dishes such as spicy mutton or beef), *bandung* (a pink milk drink flavoured with rose syrup) and *keropok* (fish crackers).

Opening hours: Daily from 8.00 a.m. to 10.00 p.m.

Location: 1 Geylang Serai, Geylang Serai Market and Food Centre, Singapore 402001

Malay Heritage Centre

This is currently undergoing renovaton and will re-open in June 2012.

Located at the historic Istana Kampong Gelam, this centre has nine galleries that trace the history of the Malay community in Singapore. It also offers batik-making and pottery workshops and shows from time to time.

Location: 85 Sultan Gate, Singapore 198501
Tel: 6391 0450
Email: nhb_mhc@nhb.gov.sg
Web: www.malayheritage.org.sg

Malay Village

This is due for demolition after the end of 2011.

Here you can learn about traditional kampung life in Singapore during the 1950s and 1960s as well as viewing kite- and batik-making. Supporting this is the Culture Museum that houses an assortment of artefacts on Malay culture. Other attractions within the Malay Village include the Muslim Showcase, Hall of Fame and Geylang Serai Corner which all offer an insight into Malay life in Singapore. There are a couple of food venues on site including an open-air food court as well as some shops.

Opening hours: 10.00 a.m. to 10.00 p.m. daily. (Call to find out dates and times of cultural performances, which are usually held at weekends.)

Price guide: Entry to the village is free. Entry to the Cultural Museum and Kampung Days is $3 for children (below 12) / $5 for adults.

Location: 39 Geylang Serai,
Singapore 409227
Tel: 6748 4700

Arab Street

In and around Muscat and Baghdad streets you can see shops selling sarongs and rugs, beautiful silks, hand-made batik and beads. For a culinary treat, try *murtabak* (a meat crêpe) from the restaurants facing the mosque on North Bridge Road.

Note: Shops are usually closed on Sundays. Some restaurants and shops also close from midday on Friday.

The Sultan Mosque — Masjid Sultan

The most prominent mosque in Singapore, the Sultan Mosque is an excellent example of Muslim architecture, with its notable gold dome and minarets. Look out for the dome base, which features a ring of black bottles, and the scrumptious carpeting, which was donated by a prince of Saudi Arabia and bears his emblem.

Opening hours: 9.00 a.m. to 1.00 p.m. / 2.00 p.m. to 4.00 p.m. (except Fridays). You can visit the mosque between 2.30 p.m. and 4.00 p.m. on Fridays.

Location: 3 Muscat Street,
Singapore 198833
Web: www.sultanmosque.org.sg
Tel: 6293 4405

SENTOSA

People have mixed opinions about Sentosa. Some find it too busy and a tad too developed whereas others really enjoy the opportunity to escape from the mainland and to encounter that sense of being 'on holiday' within minutes. Whatever you think, there is a lot going on at Sentosa and new attractions and features are regularly added. With the opening of Resorts World Sentosa a whole host of new experiences are on offer, some of which are listed below, as well as a number of old favourites.

Tel: 1800-SENTOSA (736 8672)
Web: www.sentosa.com.sg

Imbiah Lookout

This location is a good starting point for a visit to Sentosa. You can easily access many of the attractions from here, including the Butterfly Park and Insect Kingdom, the Cable Car, Images of Singapore, Sentosa 4-D Magix, the Sentosa Luge & Skyride, the Tiger Sky Tower and the Merlion. There are a number of food outlets around here, particularly in the vicinity of the Tiger Sky Tower.

You can reach it by the Sentosa Express, the cable car or by the blue line internal bus service.

Animal and Bird Encounters

Palawan Beach is particularly targeted towards families with young children, with a playground, an aviary and frequent animal shows. Birds, monkeys and reptiles all take part in these daily encounters. As well as a 300-seater amphitheatre, you'll also find food outlets here (including an ice cream parlour) and shower and locker facilities.

Show times: Primate Encounters at 12.30 p.m. / Bird Encounters at 3.30 p.m. / Lorry Feeding at 2.00 p.m. / Multi Animal Encounters at 5.00 p.m. / Close Encounters at noon, 2.00 p.m., 3.00 p.m. and 4.30 p.m.

Price guide: Free

Location: Palawan Ampitheatre. Get there by the Palawan-Tanjong Beach Tram from Beach Station.

Nature Discovery

At Sentosa Nature Discovery you can view interactive nature exhibits within a former monorail station before venturing on the elevated boardwalk into the Imbiah forest reserve. A 1.8-km nature walk will take you through secondary rainforest where you can learn about the insects, wildlife, insects, habitats and plants of Sentosa. Look out for the insectivorous pitcher plants, geckos, long-tailed macaques and over 20 species of birds.

Price guide: Free

Location: Imbiah Lookout. Get the blue or red internal bus lines or the Sentosa Express to Imbiah station.

Butterfly Park and Insect Kingdom

There is a tremendous collection of insects and butterflies to view here, including fireflies which are becoming increasingly rare in Singapore. Of particular interest are the Pupa House, the live insect display in a tunnel (thoughtfully placed at a child's viewing level) and, for the adventurous, the opportunity to be photographed with a live scorpion! This is an excellent scientific exhibit and always appeals to my son.

Opening hours: 9.30 a.m. to 7.00 p.m. daily (last entry 6.30 p.m)

Price guide: $10 for children (3 to 12 years old) / $16 for adults

Location: Imbiah Lookout. Get the blue or red line internal bus service or the Sentosa Express.

Tiger Sky Tower

This is Singapore's tallest observatory tower. An air-conditioned cabin takes you up to 131 metres above sea level, offering spectacular views of the island and beyond.

Opening hours: 9.00 a.m. to 9.00 p.m. daily (last ride at 8.45 p.m.)

Price guide: $10 for children (3 to 12 years old) / $15 for adults

Location: Imbiah Lookout. Get the blue or red line internal bus service or the Sentosa Express.

Note: For a fee, you can have your photo taken at the base of the Sky Tower.

Underwater World Singapore

Here you can enjoy unique encounters with marine animals. Whether its feeding sharks, exploring the Magic T-tank, or even tunneling under the sea to the colourful Reef and Ocean colonies, there is something to delight every member of the family. In addition you can meet the fur seals and pink dolphins, with the opportunity to enjoy live performances.

Opening hours: 9.00 a.m. to 9.00 p.m. daily (last entry 8.30 p.m.). Check the website for Meet-The-Dolphins and Fur-Seals LIVE! Programme Schedule.

Price guide: Children below 3 years: Free / Child (3 to 12 years): $14.60 / Adults: $22.90

Location: Siloso Point. Get the blue or red internal bus service or the Siloso Beach Tram.

Tel: 6275 0030 (for bookings)

Web: www.underwaterworld.com.sg

Note: For the more adventurous, there are Swim with the Dolphins ($120) and Dive with the Sharks ($150-$170) packages available. Advance booking is required.

The Flying Trapeze

see also Adventure Singapura!, p. 69

Learning how to use the trapeze will develop your strength, concentration and co-ordination! Situated next to the beach, this is a great location for a fun an adventurous afternoon!

Opening hours: 2.30 p.m. to 6.00 p.m. (Mondays to Fridays) / 2.30 p.m. to 7.00 p.m. (Saturdays, Sundays and public holidays)

Age guide: 4 years and above

Price guide: $10 per swing / $20 for 3 swings

Location: Siloso Beach: Get the Siloso Beach Tram.

Tip: Enjoy eating alfresco at the Italian Trapizza restaurant just next door

Fort Siloso

see World War II – A Journey into the Past, p. 207

Images of Singapore

see Museums and Infotainment Venues p. 196

Marine Life Park -Due to open-

This houses the world's largest oceanarium and the world's longest man-made rain forest river. You can visit the Maritime Xperiential Museum and climb aboard the world's first 4-D multi-sensory typhoon theatre.

Location: Resorts World at Sentosa

The Merlion

This 12-storey viewing tower stands 37 metres high! From the top you can get panoramic views of Sentosa as well as Singapore's city skyline and harbour. Look out for nearby Indonesian islands on a clear day. If the climb to the top doesn't appeal, don't worry there are lifts. There is a shop and a café on site.

Opening hours: 10.00 a.m. to 8.00 p.m. daily (last entry 7.30 p.m.)

Price guide: $5 for children / $8 for adults

Location: Imbiah Lookout. Get the blue red, or yellow line internal bus services or the Sentosa Express.

Segway Hub and the Gogreen Cycle Hub

Join an organized tour of Sentosa with Gogreen (Cycle and Island Explorer), and visit some fascinating places on the comfort of a hybrid bicycle (eco-friendly electrical bicycle). You can also hire segways nearby. The latter are electrical two-wheeled scooters that effortlessly glide around.

Opening hours: 9.30 a.m. to 8.00 p.m. daily / Segway: 10.00 a.m. to 9.30 pm. daily

Age guide: For use of a segway the minimum height is 90cm (below that you must be accompanied by a trainer) / Maximum weight is 120kg

Price guide: Heritage & Island Explorer (60 minutes): $28 / Regular Bi-pedal Cycle for adult/child (60 minutes: $12) / One Segway run: $12 / Segway Guided Eco Adventure (30 minutes): $38

Location: Go-green Bicycle Hub@ Siloso, #01-01, 51 Siloso Walk, Sentosa, Singapore 099000/ Segway Hub@Beach Station, Siloso Road, Sentosa, Singapore 099001
Tel: 6271 1057 / 9127 0225
Email: reservations@gogreencycle.sg
Web: www.gogreencycle.sg

Sentosa 4-D Magix

At Southeast Asia's largest 4-D theatre, you can enjoy watching films that seem to come out of the screen thanks to a state-of-the-art digital projection system. Expect individually controlled motion seats and special 'live' environmental effects such as wind and water spray!

Opening hours: 10.00 a.m. to 9.00 p.m. daily (last show at 8.45 p.m.)

Age guide: 3 years and above (some young children may not enjoy the simulated rides/seats). The minimum height for a child is 90 cm.

Price guide: Child: $11 / Adults: $18. Various packages are available including Sentosa Cineblast and Desperados

Location: Imbiah Lookout. Get the blue or red line internal bus services or the Sentosa Express.
Web: www.sentosa4dmagix.com.sg

Sentosa Luge & Skyride

see also Adventure Singapura!, p. 70

Described as part go-kart and part-toboggan, it certainly is an exciting ride for all the family to try.

Opening hours: 10.00 a.m. to 9.30 p.m. daily

Age guide: Children need to be at least 6 years old and 1.10 metres in height to ride on their own (or they can pair up with an adult). The minimum height for the Skyride is 135 cm for an unaccompanied child (85 cm with an adult).

Price guide: One Luge and Skyride costs $12 per person (2 rides are $17). A family ticket is $29 for 4 rides / $49 for 8 rides.

Location: Imbiah Lookout. Get the blue, red or yellow line internal bus services or the Sentosa Express.

Songs of the Sea

This stunning evening attraction boasts dramatic water and fire effects and high-tech lasers set on the sea. It also includes a 2,500-seater open-air amphitheatre. Tickets are available online or at Sentosa Station (Vivocity Level 3), Beach Station or Imbiah Lookout Ticketing Counters on the day of show.

Opening hours: 7.40 p.m. and 8.40 p.m. daily (and an additional show at 9.40 p.m. on Saturdays)

Age guide: All ages

Price guide: $10 per person

Location: Siloso Beach. Get the blue or yellow line internal bus service or the Sentosa Express to Beach Station and then the Siloso Beach Tram.
Web: http.//tickets.sentosa.com.sg/Modules/FITReservation/FITReservationIndex.aspx
(You can book your tickets up to 14 days in advance)

Note: Also check out what is on at the Festival Grand theatre at Resorts World at Sentosa.

Universal Studios Singapore

This is the region's first Hollywood movie theme park. It features 24 movie themed rides and attractions. Look out for Jurassic Park Rapids Adventure, Far Far Away Castle (a 4-D adventure with Shrek and his gang) and Revenge of the Mummy which is conducted in scary darkness!

Opening hours: 10.00 a.m. to 700 p.m. (Mondays to Sundays) / 7.00 p.m. to 10.00 p.m. (Fridays and Saturdays for Hollywood After Hours)

Price guide: Adults (13 to 64 years) $72 / Child (4 to 12 years): $52;

Seniors (65 years and above): $36. 2-Day and annual passes are also available (check the website for further details).

Location: Resorts World at Sentosa. Head for Waterfront Station on the Sentosa Express

Other Options

- Enjoy chilling out on Tanjong or Palawan beach, where you can take it easy. Alternatively, head for Siloso Beach for a game of beach volleyball or another activity such as cycling, rollerblading or canoeing.
- Walk across the small suspension bridge at Palawan Beach, which will take you to the southernmost point of continental Asia.
- For an inexpensive, fun day out, why not hop on the Sentosa Express at VivoCity ($3 return) and then enjoy the free attractions such as the beach, the nature trails and the animal shows. Special packages are also available, e.g. Sentosa Choice packages which offer entry into a number attractions at a discount.
- For a treat, try the Sunday Brunch at the Sentosa Resort & Spa (Tel: 6371 1414/ www.thesentosa.com), where you can stay for the afternoon and use the hotel pool.

Getting to Sentosa

Buses: The orange Sentosa bus operates between HarbourFront Bus Interchange and the island from 7.00 a.m. to 10.30 p.m. (Sunday to Thursdays and public holidays) / 7.00 a.m. to 12 midnight (Fridays, Saturdays and eves of public holidays)

There is also an SIA Hop-On Bus which connects with the Sentosa Rider at four connecting stops within the city. This half hourly bus service runs on a loop service from 9.00 a.m. to 7.30 pm daily.

Web: www.singaporeair.com/hop-on

Boardwalk: You can walk to Sentosa from VivoCity's shopping mall on the garden-themed boardwalk which is open all the time. This is an easy stroll with two canopy covered travellators in operation from 7.00 a.m. to 12 midnight daily.

Cable car: The Jewel cable cars feature the best in design, comfort and technology. They leave from HarbourFront Tower 2 or Mount Faber station from 8.30 a.m. to 10.00 p.m. daily.

Web: www.mountfaber.com.sg (look under Jewel Cable Car)

Light railway: The Sentosa Express operates from 7.00 a.m. to midnight daily from Sentosa Station at Lobby 1, Level 3 at VivoCity. It links HarbourFront, VivoCity and St. James' Power Station to Sentosa. Stops on the island include WaterFront Station, Imbiah Station and Beach Station.

Sentosa Rider: This is the official Sentosa attractions' shuttle bus which operates from various stops from Orchard Road and Marina Bay on a loop service with Beach Station its end destination. You have the option to travel directly to Sentosa or to purchase a tour ticket allowing you entry to a number of attractions.

Web: www.sentosarider.com

Price guides: Island admission charges vary: $1 by the Boardwalk / $2 by bus (children above 3 years and adults) from HarbourFront Bus Interchange. Payment is made at HarbourFront Interchange Ticketing Counter. $5 for a one-way pass / $8 for a full-day pass (hop on & hop off) Various inclusive value packages are also available from about $17.90 for a child / $29.90 for an adult.

- Child: $15 / Adults: $26. For a return trip from HarbourFront Tower 2 by cable car (one-way tickets are available).
- $3 by light railway (3 years and above)

A flat gantry admission charge is applicable to each car entering Sentosa. Rates vary from $2 to $7 according to the time of day and whether it is a weekday or weekend. Car parking is available at the Beach, Imbian, Tanjong and Palawan car parks for an additional charge (free between 12 noon and 2.00 p.m. on weekdays).

Tel: 1800-SENTOSA (736 8672)
Monday to Sunday between 9.00 a.m. to 6.30 p.m.
Web: www.sentosa.com.sg

THEME AND AMUSEMENT PARKS

Escape Theme Park

Located within NTUC Lifestyle World Downtown East, this theme park has 16 rides, including a merry-go-round, Choo Choo Train and Ferris wheel for younger children. Older children will enjoy the Family Coaster, Pirate Ship and Wet & Wild rides. The Daytona Go-Kart Beginner's Track with both 1 and 2-seater karts is also great fun. Overall, the park is well maintained and supervised.

Age guide: Basically, the park is not a suitable destination for children aged 3 and below Height restrictions of between 1.1 and 1.52 metres apply, according to your child's choice of ride. For some rides, the minimum height can be waived provided that an adult accompanies the child. However, aggressive motion rides are not really appropriate for little children. The 2-seater Daytona go-karts will accommodate children between the heights of 1 and 1.47 metres provided that an adult above 1.47 metres drives. Children above 1.47 metres can try out the 1-seater carts.

Opening hours: 10.00 a.m. to 8.00 p.m. (weekends, public and school holidays)

Price guide: Child (3 to 12 years): $8.90 / Adults: $17.90 / Family ticket (2 adults and 2 children): $47.80. If this is your scene, annual family (and individual) passes are available. NTUC member rates are also available.

Location: Downtown East, 1 Pasir Close, Singapore 519599
Tel: 6581 9112 / 6581 9128
Email: Submit enquiries via website
Web: www.escapethemepark.com.sg

Note: Strollers and umbrellas are available for rent from the Guest Relations Office.

Tips:

- Food within the park is limited and you cannot bring in any food. However, you can get your hand stamped and venture into NTUC, which has more to offer.
- This is a party venue.

Haw Par Villa (also known as Tiger Balm Gardens)

Originally built in 1937, this Chinese mythological theme park is one of a kind. Despite being rather garish and overpowering in places, it does make mythology come alive and is bound to have an impact on your child. Without doubt, the many colourful and fascinating statues and animal replicas are the main features of the park. I was surprised to find a blue Statue of Liberty here — I can't recall such a presence in Chinese folklore!

Younger children and those of a more sensitive disposition may not take readily to the Crime and Punishment section of the Villa. Ten scenes from the Chinese courts of hell are very graphic and leave little to the imagination. However, many children find these scenes particularly interesting. Entertainers such as acrobats perform in the park from time to time but it is best to ring ahead to check what is on. There are also some snack kiosks and souvenir stalls in the park.

The 'Tiger Car' is a vintage car dressed up to look like a tiger (it is a replica of a car of the founders of the park). Viewing of the Tiger Car at the 'Garage' in Haw Par Villa is free.

There is also small museum on the Villa grounds depicting how Chinese migrants adapted to foreign lands. A more recent is the Jade Collection which displays a wide collection of jades owned by the Aw family. It can be viewed in the Jade House which is a short distance from the main entrance.

The park is rather shabby in parts and some of the descriptions are difficult to read. But don't let this deter you from a visit...it really is something different!

Opening hours: 9.00 a.m. to 7.00 p.m. daily. The museum is open from noon to 7.00 p.m. (Tuesdays to Sundays.)

Price guide: Free (There is a fee for entry into the museum and the Jade House)

Location: 262 Pasir Panjang Road, Singapore 118628
Tel: 6872 2780

Tips:

- The park is set on an incline and can get very hot so wear sunblock and take hats.
- There is a restaurant in the park but you may wish to combine this visit with a trip to Pasir Panjang Village (which you can easily reach by bus) for an assortment of eating places.

Snow City

With temperatures that hover around –5° Celsius, this venue certainly guarantees a cold break from the relentless tropical heat. Upon entry to Snow City, you can go into the Snow Chamber and snow tube, snowboard or ski down the 60-metre long snow slope. Younger children will enjoy the Snow Play Area (for children aged between 2 to 6 years old), a winter playground where snowball fights are possible. There is also a Polar Bear Gallery in the Snow Chamber and for the adults, an Ice Bar.

The centre provides boots and jackets but don't forget to bring along socks, gloves and long trousers! (The latter two items can be rented.) Helmets are provided for children below 6 years when they use the slope and children below 3 years must be accompanied by an adult.

Snowline Snow School within the complex offers a complete package of snow sports services (retail, lessons and tours). It runs a progressive Learn-To-Ski/Snowboard programme. Information can be obtained by calling 6425 0801 or email emeline@sportquest.com.sg

A Hot Chocolate Bar is located on the mezzanine floor and there is the opportunity to take photos in Santa's Cabin, a real log house.

Opening hours: 9.45 a.m. to 5.15 p.m. (Tuesdays to Sundays and all school and public holidays.) There are session times for the Snow Chamber throughout the day. Allow at least 30 minutes to buy tickets and put on your winter gear.

Price guide: Child (3 to 6 years): $14 for a 1-hour single session, $22 for a double session / Glove rental: Child (below 10 years): $1.60, Child (10 years and above): $2.10 / Waterproof trousers rental: $3.20 / Locker rental: $1. Various discounts are available (look under Promotions on the website). Admission prices include entry into the Science Centre and usage of snow tubes.

Location: 21 Jurong Town Hall Road, Singapore 609433
Tel: 6560 2306 (Mondays to Fridays) / 6560 4773 (Saturday, Sunday and public holidays)
Email: contact@snowcity.com.sg
Web: www.snowcity.com.sg

Note:

- While I do know people who have taken toddlers down the slope, I would hesitate – it is fast and you need to be confident that you can keep control. Another factor to consider is how wriggly your little one is!

• Tickets can be booked online.
• This is a party venue.

Tips:

• A soft hat is useful, especially for younger children who lose heat easily.
• Free parking is available next door at the Singapore Science Centre/ Omni-Theatre.

Wild Wild Wet

This water theme park has a number of exciting rides and attractions, including the Ular-Lah, Southeast Asia's first raft slide. The Waterworks is a type of water maze with lots of curves and turns while Professor's Playground will appeal to younger children with its slides, ladders, water cannons and fountains. The park is staffed with qualified lifeguards.

Opening hours: 1.00 p.m. to 7.00 p.m. (Mondays, Wednesdays, Thursdays to Fridays) / 10.00 a.m. to 7.00 p.m. (Saturdays, Sundays and gazetted school and public holidays). See website for details.

Price guide: $10.50 for children (3 to 12 years) / $15.50 for adults.

Location: Downtown East, 1 Pasir Close, #01-08, Singapore 519599
Tel: 6581 9128/ 6581 9112
Web: www.wildwildwet.com

Note:

• Birthday party venue (Tel: 6581 9103)
• Restrictions on height and weight operate for certain rides – these are clearly indicated on site or they can be checked by referring to the website.

CRUISING

A boat ride on the Singapore River or harbour is fun, relatively inexpensive and something the whole family can enjoy (although active toddlers may not be the most receptive companions to have on board). The following venues all offer cruises and rides and can be combined with trips to other nearby sites.

Singapore River

Operator: Singapore River Cruises & Leisure

While a trip on the river is an obvious tourist attraction, it is also a fun thing to do with children. You can add in a bit of local history and geography at the same time. The trip is conducted in a bumboat (look out for its face and eyes) and some of the sights you see along the way include a Merlion (there are several in Singapore), Boat Quay, the landing site of Sir Stamford Raffles and several historical bridges.

The Singapore River Experience tells the story of two quays, focusing upon the area between Boat Quay, Clarke Quay and Marina Bay.

The New River Experience cruise

takes longer, covering Boat Quay, Clarke Quay, Roberston Quay and Marina Bay.

Operating hours: 9.00 a.m. to 11.00 p.m. daily (last departure at 10.30 p.m.)

Price guide: River taxi rides vary from $4 to $12 / Singapore River Experience: $8 (child), $15 (adults) / New River Experience: $10 (child), $20 (adults)

Cruise jetty locations: Raffles' landing site (behind Parliament House), Boat Quay, Robertson Quay, Liang Court Jetty, Grand Copthorne waterfront, Riverside Point Jetty (beside Merchant Court Hotel), The Fullerton, Esplanade and Merlion Park

Tel: 6336 6111/ 6336 6119

Email: enquiry@rivercruise.com.sg

Web: www.rivercruise.com.sg

Tip: Nearby places of interest include Clarke Quay, Raffles Square sculptures and the Merlion.

Harbour and Southern Islands

Operator: Eastwind Organisation

Fairwind, an authentic Chinese junk, takes you away from the harbour, past Sentosa and onto Sisters' Island and St John's Island. However, it is available only for private charter.

Parties (with a minimum of 25 to 30 people) can be held on board the Fairwind V, and there are different set menus that can be selected.

Price guide: Available upon request.

Web: www.fairwind.com.sg

Operator: Watertours

Enjoy sailing on the imperial *Cheng Ho*, a colourful, modern Chinese junk designed to replicate the famous ship *Da Fu* of the Ming Dynasty. Distinctive features include a pagoda-styled roof, ornately carved imperial dragons and a painted tiger's head at the bow.

Your morning or afternoon trip includes a short visit to Kusu Island. Beverages and snacks or meals are included according to the choice of cruise.

Tour departure times and price guide: Morning Glory at 10.30 a.m. ($14 child / $27 adult) / High Tea at 3.00 p.m. ($16 child / $32 adult) / Dragon Cruise at 3.00 p.m. ($14 child / $27 adult) / Imperial Dinner at 6.30 p.m. ($29 child / $55 adult)

Cruise jetty location: Marina South Pier, #01-09 31, Marina Coastal Drive, Singapore 018988

Tel: 6533 9811

Email: Sales@watertours.com.sg

Web: www.watertours.com.sg

Captain Explorer DUKW

see also Adventure Singapura!, pp. 76 – 77

For something completely different, you can cruise the harbour and tour the city without changing vehicle! All this is made possible by riding in a genuine 31-seater Vietnam War machine.

Tour departure times: Hourly from

9.30 a.m. to 5.30 p.m. (daily). A night tour is also available at 6.30 p.m.

Price guide: Child: $20.90 / Adults: $29.90

Departure location: Tourist Hub @ Singapore Flyer #01-05 (with free pickup from major city hotels)

Tel: 6738 3338/ 6738 9897
Email: enquiry@citytours.sg
Web: www.captainexplorer.com

SOMETHING DIFFERENT

Attending a TV Recording!

Undoubtedly we all complain about television and the fact that our children spend too much time watching it and too little time pursuing more constructive activities. The fact is, however, it's easily accessible, available at all times and without Kid's Central TV, Cartoon Network or our personal stocks of videos and DVDs, life would be much more challenging! So why not turn your child's preoccupation with TV into something a bit more dynamic? Instead of watching TV, become part of it! MediaCorp has a 'live' TV recording schedule that is open to the public on a first-come-first-served basis. Most children will leap at the chance to be part of a TV audience and you can attend either Chinese- or English-language programmes.

Email: Promo5@mediacorptv.com
Web: www.mediacorp.com.sg

Note: Don't forget to indicate the programme you wish to attend.

PLAYTIME

see also Childminding, pp. 265 – 267

As well as the playgrounds and play areas I recommend in the FAST FACTS section of Chapter 8 (*see* pp. 246 – 247) and those listed in Shopping Distractions (*see* pp. 247 – 265), the following venues may interest your child.

National Parks

You'll find a playground in most of Singapore's National Parks but special recommendations include:

AMK Park Playground

This is a fairly new playground and it is proving extremely popular.

Key features: Slides, swings and various special play features including the 'turnaround', the 'spider-web', the 'landrover'. The playground is covered in sand so many younger children will enjoy building castles. There is a McDonald's nearby.

Location: Ang Mo Kio West Garden (opposite Ang Mo Kio Town Library and along AMK Avenue 6)

Note:

- The park is not sheltered so try and go there early morning or early evening. If this is not possible, don't forget your sunblock!
- Currently there are no public toilets.

Jacob Ballas Children's Garden

Key features: This playground has an educational purpose, seeking to cultivate an appreciation for plants, nature and the environment through play and exploration. The main attraction is the 'Treehouse' but the Wet Water Playground is also very popular. If you are hungry the prata shop in Evans Road is worth a visit.

Location: 481 Bukit Timah Road, Singapore 259769

Note:

- The Park is closed on Mondays (except public holidays) and last admission is at 6.30 p.m.
- All children must be accompanied by an adult.

Pasir Ris Park

Key features: A large playground with a giant space-net, a two-way cable (flying fox) and plenty of play equipment. Other facilities nearby include a mangrove boardwalk, bicycle and inline blading kiosks, horse riding, and dining outlets. All of these are situated by the seafront.

Location: Along Pasir Ris Road, Elias Road, Pasir Ris Green, Pasir Ris Close and Jalan Loyang Besar

West Coast Park

Key features: Several great playgrounds segregated into age-specific sites. There is a towering rope pyramid (for climbing), several flying fox cableways, slides and lots of other play equipment. A McDonald's is situated on site.

Location: Next to the West Coast Highway

Note: It can get very hot during the day

* Also popular are Tiong Bahru Park (along Tiong Bahru Road), Bishan Park, Labrador Park and Bukit Timah Nature Reserve.

eXplorerkid

This club is open to all children. It features a very large, indoor playground (with 20 play elements) and other facilities, e.g. a toddler area, lighted ball pool, multimedia platform, computer kiosks and a nursing room. You can now also enjoy racing around in the first synthetic ice bumper car rides in Singapore!

Age group: 12 years and below

Opening hours: Noon to 10.00 p.m. Mondays to Thursdays (off-peak) / 10.00 a.m. to 10.00 p.m. Fridays, weekends, public holidays and school holidays (peak)

Price guide: Charges for children vary according to the playtime. The full-day and per hour play rates cover play at the standard play stations (Adventure Highlands, Ball'O'City and The Rink charge separate fees). $20 full day play rate for non-peak periods ($22 peak) / $17 NTUC member ($20 peak periods) / $9 eXplorer Kid members ($11 peak periods). $3 to $6 for the synthetic ice bumper car rides. A membership programme is also available: $10.50 per child (one-time membership fee) / $7.50 for NTUC member.

Location: 3rd Level, E!Hub@ Downtown East, 1 Pasir Ris Close, Singapore 519599
Tel: 6589 1668
Web: www.explorerkid.com

Note:
• A birthday party venue.
• Visitors are encouraged to bring socks or to buy a pair (at $2.50) on site.

Ferris Wheel at E!Hub Downtown East

Enjoy this 25-metre high weather-proof Cadbury Ferris wheel which is situated within the mall. Each ride takes 3 to 4 minutes.

Age group: Suitable for the whole family. Children below 1.3m must be accompanied by an adult aged 18 years and above during the ride.
Opening hours: 12 noon to 10.00 p.m. (weekdays) / 10.00 a.m. to 10.00 p.m. (weekends and public holidays). Last ride at 930 p.m.
Price guide: $6.50 for a single ride / $11.50 for a double ride / $18.50 for a family of four

Location: E!Hub@Downtown East, 1 Pasir Ris Close, Singapore 519599
Web: www.explorerkid.com

Fidgets

This is a large indoor playground with dedicated baby and toddler play areas. It was custom designed and manufactured in Australia by Playtec. There is also a 100-seat café and two party rooms.

Age group: 0 to 10 years old
Opening hours: 9.00 a.m. to 6.00 p.m. daily
Price guide: Free for entry for adults and babies under one year old / $8 under 2 years old / $15 for 2 to 10 years old. Unlimited play per entry.

Location: Turf Club City, 200 Turf Club Road, #04-05, Singapore 287994
Tel: 6469 5069
Email: info@fidgets.com.sg
Web: www.fidgets.com.sg

Go-Go Bambini

This large indoor play centre is based on successful 'pay-for-play' venues in the USA and Europe. Here your children can safely run around and enjoy themselves. The playground has Singapore's tallest indoor slide in an unique playscape that features a flying fox, ball pits, tunnels, two climbing walls, interactive panels and a ball blower. The playscape is 6m high with four levels to explore. There is a café on site and fitness classes are held for mums, with a child care service available.

Opening hours: 10.00 a.m. to 6.00 p.m. (Mondays to Thursdays) / 10.00 a.m. to 8.00 p.m. (Fridays and Saturdays) / 10.00 a.m. to 6.00 p.m. (Sundays)
Age group: 0 to 11 years

Price guide: $17 for 2 hours of play for children between 2 to 11 years (every subsequent 30 minutes or part of is $4.25) / $6 for unlimited play for children under 2 years / Free for adults and babies under 11 months. Being a 'Bambini Buddy' entitles you to reduced admission rates — a $5 non-refundable administration fee applies.

Location: #01-15 Block 8, Dempsey Road, Dempsey Hill, Singapore 249696
Tel: 6474 5492
Email: info@gogobambini.com
Web: www.gogobambini.com

Note:

- A great birthday party venue.
- School holiday programmes are also available.

Gymboree

On top of regular play classes, Gymboree operates a free playtime known as Playgym when your child can enjoy the company's play equipment without joining a structured class.

Age group: 0 to 60 months

Price guide: $12 per hour (member) / $20 (non-member) (additional GST charge at Tanglin Mall only)

Locations: #03-21Tanglin Mall, 163 Tanglin Road, Singapore 247933 / HarbourFront Centre, #03-09/10, 1 Maritime Square, Singapore 099253
Tel: 6735 5290 (Tanglin Mall) / 6271 1545 (HarbourFront)
Email: gymboree@singnet.com.sg
Web: www.gymboree.com (international site / look under Gymboree Play & Music)

Note:

- An adult must accompany children.
- Playgym timings may vary between branches and they are subject to change so do ring in advance. It is advisable to book your slot in advance, especially for peak periods.

Kids Amaze

This 17,000 square feet playground consists of visually stunning and interactive soft play centres. It has a three-storey vertical maze and the latest play technology for both children and adults. There is a fully equipped toddler play area and several party rooms, as well as a number of challenging and fun things for older children to enjoy.

Opening hours: 1.00 p.m. to 7.00 p.m. (Mondays to Fridays) / 10.00 a.m. to 9.00 p.m (Saturdays, Sundays and public holidays) / 10.00 a.m to 7.00 p.m. (school holidays)

Age guide: 0 to 18 years

Price guide: Children (18 months to 18 years old): $11.20 (guest), $9 (SAFRA member), $7.50 (Kids Amaze member)—Mondays to Fridays excluding weekends, public holidays and school holidays / Child (18 months to 18 years old): $16.50 (guest), $12.85 (SAFRA member), $10.70 (Kids Amaze member) — Saturdays, Sundays, public holidays / Accompanying adults: $2.15 / Adults: $5.35 / Family package (2 children, 2 adults): $34.25 (guests), $26.75 (SAFRA member). Kids Amaze membership is available for children at $16.05 for SAFRA members and $42.80 for non-members.

Location: SAFRA Jurong,
333 Boon Lay Way
Tel: 6686 4321
Email: kidsamaze@safra.sg
Web: www.safra.sg (follow the link to Jurong)

Note: Children under 4 years old must be accompanied by an adult.

Little O'Zone

The children's fun maze at Orchid Country Club is open to the general public. Here your child can crawl through the plastic tunnels and chase siblings or friends. There is a toddler area and for older children features include cliff climbers, a teeth bridge and boxing sandbags.

Opening hours: 10.00 a.m. to 8.00 p.m. (Mondays to Thursdays) / 10.00 a.m. to 10.00 p.m. (weekends, school holidays and public holidays)

Age group: Recommended for children aged between 1 and 12 (although older children can use it)

Price guide: $8 for the first hour ($4 for subsequent hour / $3 half an hour) / $6 for members / $7 for NTUC cardholders

Location: #02-36 Social Clubhouse, Orchid Country Club, 1 Orchid Club Road, Singapore 768162
Tel: 6852 2052

Note:

• Children aged 4 and below should be accompanied by an adult.

• It is also available as a party venue for non-members.

Polliwogs

In an area totaling some 6,500 square feet, you will find three party rooms and an outdoor 'Polliwobly', a bouncy pirate ship (which is rotated with a big bouncy castle every month). The indoor play area has a couple of levels of climbing equipment with lots of tunnels and obstacles as well as a toddler area with a ball pit and level area for play. Children will really enjoy the ball guns which shoot little rubber balls. There are two vending machines on site and free flow of coffee and tea, with plenty of room for mums and dads to relax in.

Opening hours: 10.00 a.m. to 7.00 p.m (weekdays) / 10.00 a.m. to 8.00 p.m. (weekends)

Age group: All ages

Price guide: $18 for the first 90 minutes and $8 for each additional half hour on weekends (children above 2 years old) / $6 for the first 90 minutes and $3 for each additional half hour on weekends (children below 2 years old) / $16 for unlimited play on weekdays for children above 2 years old / $6 for unlimited play on weekdays for children below 2 years old. Additional charges for entry into the Polliwobly. A value play pass is available and lookout for promotions.

Location: 1020 East Coast Parkway, #01-02 (nearest car park C3), Singapore 449878
Tel: 6442 2805
Email: contactus@thepollliwogs.com
Web: www.thepolliwogs.com

SAFRA Kids' Adventure

SAFRA Toa Payoh will be closed for redevelopment from July 2011.

A similar facility to the one at Orchid Country Club is run by SAFRA at its Toa Payoh branch. This indoor, air-conditioned two-storey high fun maze is great fun.

Opening hours: 1.00 p.m. to 6.00 p.m. (weekdays, non-peak times) / 9.00 a.m. to 6.00 p.m. (weekends, public holidays and school holidays, peak times)
Age group: 2 to 12 years
Price guide: $4 per hour during non-peak times (non-members) / $7 per hour during peak times (non-members)

Location: SAFRA Toa Payoh, 293 Lorong 6, Toa Payoh, Singapore 319387
Tel: 6355 4536

Note: Birthday packages are available.
Note: Last but not least...A poll of other mothers confirmed all the suggestions above but other popular venues included the playgrounds at the Zoo and Jurong BirdPark (for both the dry and wet areas) and at MacRitchie Reservoir (near the car park).

The Playhouse at Rochester Park

This is an indoor and outdoor playground located in a grand colonial house. There are two floors of play area. The ground floor is for free-play for children up to the ages of 7 years old and it is open to the public the whole of the time. The second floor consists of three rooms and it is targeted to children between the ages of 7 to 12 years old. There is a café next door and a sand pit and water play area outside. Structured classes are also available on weekday afternoons.

Opening hours: 9.00 a.m. to 7.30 p.m. (Sundays to Thursdays) / 9.00 a.m. to 9.30 p.m. (Fridays, Saturdays and eves of public holidays)
Age group: 12 years and below
Price guide: $6 per hour on weekdays / $6 for the first hour and $6 per half hour after that on weekends and public holidays

Location: 7 Rochester Park, Singapore
Email: playhouse@rochesterpark.com.sg
Web: www.rochesterhouse.com.sg

The Toy Rental Club

This is not a play venue but it is a great destination if you want to create or change the play area at home! Here you can choose to rent from a vast selection of educational or creative toys as well as play mats, mobiles and outdoor toys.

Opening hours: 9.30 a.m. to 1.00 p.m. and 2.00 p.m. to 5.00 p.m. (closed on Wednesdays, Sundays and public holidays). Do call to check if open as the premises are closed on occasion for private parties.

Location: #05-04 Pasir Panjang Road, Singapore 118521
Tel: 6276 7602
Email: enquiries@toyrentalclub.com
Web: www.thetoyrentalclub.com

Note: A possible birthday party venue (currently in plan).

– Chapter 7 –

ANNUAL EVENTS

Singapore holds many enjoyable festivals and events throughout the year. You can participate in some of these while others are for you to watch. Some of the main festivals and events are highlighted in this chapter but do keep a lookout for any special events advertised in newspapers and periodicals.

FAST FACTS

Singapore Tourist Board

Visit this site for a useful listing of events and festivals.

Tel: 1800 736 2000

Email: STB_Visitsingapore@stb.gov.sg

Web: www.yoursingapore.com

National Heritage Board (NHB)

The NHB conducts some excellent workshops and activities on the diverse cultures and festivals that are so important to those who live in Singapore. The National Museum of Singapore, Singapore Art Museum, Singapore Philatelic Museum and particularly the Asian Civilisations Museum all run festive programmes.

Tel: 1800 2255 642 (Hotline)

Email: nhb_feedback@nhb.gov.sg

Web: www.nhb.gov.sg

Singapore Zoological Gardens

The Zoo runs festive programmes throughout the year that are particularly catered for children between the ages of 3 and 12. Typically these include the Lantern Festival of Lights, ghoulish Halloween fun and Children's Day celebrations.

Tel: 6269 3411
Email: via web link
Web: www.zoo.com.sg

Jurong BirdPark

Like the Zoo, the BirdPark conducts a host of festive programmes, including Children's Day events, Mother's Day treats and Christmas competitions.
Tel: 6265 0022
Email: via web link
Web: www.birdpark.com.sg

Events Websites

The following websites are excellent sources of information about the latest and up-and-coming events:
www.timeoutsingapore.com
www.sg (look under events)
www.eventful.com/singapore/events

FESTIVE CELEBRATIONS

Chinese New Year

What is it? Celebrating the Lunar New Year is the major event in the Chinese calendar. Festivities are usually centred around two days but they tend to last for two weeks. On the eve of the New Year, families hold celebratory reunion dinners and both families and friends visit each other's homes over the following two days. Children look forward eagerly to receiving their hong bao (red envelopes with money inside).
When is it? In January/February
What is there to do and see?

Chinese Lunar New Year Light-Up

A visit to Chinatown during this period is a must. If you have older children, go at night (it is too busy for little ones) to enjoy the spectacular lights and lanterns. The Annual Light-Up extends along Eu Tong Sen Street, New Bridge Road and South Bridge Road. In addition, Pagoda, Temple, Sago and Trengganu streets are lined with stalls touting festive fare and traditional Chinese crafts. Try New Year goodies such as the special *nian gao* (New Year cakes), pineapple tarts and barbecued sliced meats.

The Lunar New Year Countdown Party is held on the eve of the New Year in Chinatown. This is only suitable for adults and teenagers as it gets very crowded. If you do plan to go, enjoy the dazzling fireworks and look out for the stage performances at Kreta Ayer Square (along Sago Street).

Chingay Parade

Held on the 8th day of the Chinese Lunar New Year, this parade typically marks the end of the two-week celebrations (*see* under Special Events for more details, p. 241).

Open House!

Head down to the Asian Civilisations Museum, Singapore Art Museum or the National Museum of Singapore as these usually celebrate the Lunar New Year with an Open House Day.

Singapore River Hong Bao

This riverside carnival features a variety of performances with regional and local artists in action. There are food kiosks, craft stalls and carnival games to enjoy. The festival features a spectacular display of fireworks both during and immediately after the Lunar New Year.

Look out for special evening Captain Explorer DUKW Ducktour trips (www.captainexplorer.com) or head to the Singapore Flyer as these promise exceptional views of the fireworks.

Location: The Float@Marina Bay (head for the Promenade or City Hall MRT stations)

Web: www.riverhongbao.sg

In recent years, the River Hong Bao has been followed by *Huayi*—Chinese Festival of Arts, which is held at the adjacent Esplanade – Theatres on the Bay. This showcases Chinese artists from various parts of the world in colourful and skilled performances.

Hari Raya Puasa

What is it? Hari Raya Puasa signifies the end of Ramadan, the Muslim fasting month, and the beginning of the holy month of Syawal. During Ramadan, the sound of the Azan Maghrib, or evening prayer call, marks the setting of the sun and the time when fasting Muslims can feast. Hari Raya celebrations last for a month. During this time, Muslims put on their new clothes and an open house policy is practised, with relatives and friends visiting each other. Malay delicacies are served and houses are thoroughly cleaned beforehand.

When is it? Varies according to the sighting of the New Moon

What is there to do and see?

- Don't miss Geylang Serai which is brightly lit up at night from the beginning of Ramadan. Whether you're visiting the Malay Village, shopping at the *pasar malam* or enjoying dinner, there are plenty of sights and sounds to experience. The crowds and heat may not suit younger children but older ones (8 years and above) will enjoy the festive atmosphere. Try the *kuih* and *ketupat* (traditional Malay pressed rice) and admire the *baju kurung* (Malay traditional dress).

- Bussorah Street near Sultan Mosque is lined with food stalls during Ramadan. Here you can enjoy barbecued spiced chicken and fried *lontong* or purchase pineapple tarts and other sweets to take home.
- For younger children, take a look at activities scheduled by the National Heritage Board. Past activities include *ketupat* case-making at the Asian Civilisations Museum.

Thaipusam

What is it? The most important religious festival celebrated by Hindus, Thaipusam is a day of penance and thanksgiving in honour of Lord Murugan. It has to be Singapore's most dramatic festival!

When is it? In the 10th month of the Hindu calendar (January/February)

What is there to do and see?

- Thousands of devotees take part in a ritual journey that starts in the early morning (1.30 a.m.) from Sri Srinivasa Perumal Temple in Serangoon Road to Sri Thandayuthapani Temple in Tank Road. In the early hours, you can see devotees carrying milk pots and wooden *kavadis**. Later in the morning, men begin to carry metal *kavadis* decorated with peacock feathers and offerings. Celebrations continue late into the night. Serangoon Road in Little India is the best place to see this spectacular procession but it does continue along Selegie Road, Princep Stret, Penang Road, Clemenceau Avenue and finally Tank Road.
- Sri Veeramakaliamman Temple in Serangoon Road is the focal point for much of the two-day celebration. Ensure you are suitably dressed (all females should cover their heads) before you enter the temple!.
- You can join a free guided tour at Sri Srinivasa Perumal Temple on the day of Thaipusam or contact City Tours (Tel: 6738 3338/ Web: www.citytours.sg) to join a specially scheduled tour.

Note: Don't take children who are easily frightened to see the ritual. Also be prepared...all those skewers take some explaining.

* A *kavadi* is a semi-circular wooden- or metal-framed structure with long, sharp skewers that are pierced into devotees' bodies.

Vesak Day

What is it? This day celebrates the life of Buddha

When is it? April or May

What is there to do and see?

- You can watch the festivities at venues such as the Buddhist Lodge at River Valley Road, Thai Buddhist Temple at Jalan Bukit Merah and Lian Shan Shuang Lin Temple at Jalan Toa Payoh. Monks chant holy *sutras* and release birds to symbolise the liberation of captive souls. Make sure you are suitably dressed and all females should cover their heads.
- Celebrations are also marked by candlelight processions, in which thousands of devotees chant sutras and pay homage to the Buddha. The highlight of the festival is a mass religious and cultural gathering held either at the Singapore Indoor Stadium or a major public theatre.

Festival of the Hungry Ghosts

What is it? Taoists believe that this is a time when the gates of hell open and the spirits roam the Earth.

When is it? In the 7th month of the Chinese Lunar calendar (August/September)

What is there to do and see?

- Look out for outdoor concerts, *wayang* (Chinese street opera), street banquets and public auctions, all of which are held to appease the spirits. In the streets you may smell joss sticks and see people burning paper money and offerings of cakes and fruits left for the hungry ghosts. All these activities can be observed in many neighbourhoods and, of course, in Chinatown.

Mid-Autumn Festival/ Lantern Festival

What is it? This festival is associated with unity and a cycle completed — traditionally, the end of the farming year and an abundant harvest.

When is it? The Lantern Festival is celebrated on the 15th day of the 8th month of the Chinese lunar calendar, when the moon is at its fullest, typically in September/October.

What is there to do and see?

- An integral part of the Mid-Autumn Festival is the giving and consumption of mooncakes. These delicacies may not suit the palate of young children as they are very rich and very sweet.
- Look out for the Festival Light-Up at the Singapore River. A market, food stalls, Malay dance, Chinese orchestral performances, Chinese opera and dragons are all part of the celebrations that culminate in a grand finale marked by a spectacular firework display and various performances.
- Visit the Chinese Garden to see a spectacular display of lanterns. The garden also has food stalls, lion and dragon dances, cultural

shows and often a mini-funfair for younger children. Celebrations generally follow a theme (e.g., Disney). Tickets are available through SISTIC or at the door.

- Chinatown Point Podium is worth visiting to see its bright and colourful decorations. In previous years, these have included a giant revolving lantern that was 4 metres high and weighed 400 kilogrammes.
- The street light-up in Chinatown (which lasts for a month) is particularly stunning, with the added attraction of a colourful street procession and a fireworks display on the opening night. The festival is usually opened at Kreta Ayer Square in Chinatown and is marked by a multi-racial procession with dancing lions, lantern floats, flag bearers and stilt walkers. Look out for nightly stage shows at Kreta Ayer Square and browse the festive bazaar with over 300 street stalls.
- Many neighbourhoods also conduct family lantern walks (usually combined with dragon dancing), storytelling sessions, calligraphy competitions and classical and folk dance shows. Check what's going on at your local Community Centre.

Deepavali

What is it? Also known as the Festival of Lights, Deepavali is probably the most significant of all the Hindu festivals. The festival celebrates the victory of good over evil. Preparations for Deepavali include cleaning and decorating the home and lighting oil lamps at night to welcome Laksmi, the goddess of prosperity. On Deepavali, Indian families visit each other and their friends and gather in colourfully decorated temples. In homes, *rangolis* or *kolams* are drawn by sprinkling fine powder on the floor.

When is it? Late October/November

What is there to do and see?

- Older children may enjoy visiting the Deepavali Fair in Serangoon Road. It is too hot and crowded for younger children and almost impossible to manoeuvre with a stroller in tow. However, for those over nine years or so, there are delicacies to try, bargains to buy and sights and sounds to enjoy. You will also find a Deepavali village festival around Campbell Lane and Kerbau Road. Little India is brightly lit and you can't miss the vibrant and colourful entrance to Serangoon Road.
- Check out the National Heritage Board activities. Previous events include Indian puppet plays, oil-lamp painting, storytelling and making *rangolis*.
- Look out for the Festival of Lights Procession from Race Course Road to Sri Srinivasa Perumal

Temple in Serangoon Road. This street parade culminates in a splendid finale, with a towering silver chariot and a fireworks display. It is too crowded for young children (who will probably not see much anyway) but, otherwise, it is definitely worth seeing.

Christmas

What is it? This Christian festival marks the birth of Jesus Christ. Homes are decorated with Christmas trees (traditionally pine), advent wreaths and/or strands of tinsel and decorative bowers. Cards are exchanged between friends and presents are given to family members. A special lunch is usually eaten on Christmas Day and many also celebrate by attending church services.

When is it? 25th December

What is there to do and see?

- The Christmas Light Up along Orchard Road and down to Marina Bay lasts for over six weeks, and it really is worth a nighttime trip. You can easily view it by taking a bus or taxi from Tanglin Mall down to Raffles City (or take a HiPPO bus).
- During the Christmas season, many of Singapore's shopping malls are decorated extensively. These become particularly spectacular at night when they are lit up. Highlights include Tanglin Mall, Raffles City, Plaza Singapura, Tampines Mall and Centrepoint. Various malls also conduct special Christmas activities for children. Some of the most comprehensive programmes can be found at Forum — The Shopping Mall, Great World City, Centrepoint, Tanglin Mall, Raffles City and Takashimaya. Typically these activities include carolling, competitions, shows, workshops and meet-Father-Christmas sessions.
- Christmas is a time to party! Most of the expatriates in Singapore run parties for their respective association members. Parties are also held by churches, hotels and various organisations.
- Downtown East usually conducts an extensive programme of festive events. Previous events include Winter Wonderland (with snow!) and Cartoon Network's TinselToon Christmas that featured playzones, competitions, cartoon characters and shows.
- Christmas is a time to feast and culinary temptations are on offer throughout December. Many hotels, restaurants and cafés have festive dining menus while traditional European fare such as gingerbread, mince pies, Christmas fruit cake, *panettone* (Italian Christmas cake) and *Stollen* (German Christmas cake) are available in supermarkets.

- Keep a lookout for the Christmas fairs held by the Danish Seaman's Church (Tel: 6274 6344/ Web: www.dkchurch.com), the Netherlands Charity Association and the German Association. At these fairs, you can buy traditional European decorations, crafts, toys and food.

SPECIAL EVENTS

Singapore Airshow

What is it? This is the largest aerospace and defence event in Asia. Usually the final weekend of the six-day event Is open to the general public.

What is there for children? As well as thrilling aerobatic displays, children will enjoy the fun fairground attractions. There are plenty of food kiosks and retail outlets with unique collectables on sale.

When? This is held every two years with the next one scheduled for February 2012.

Where? Changi Exhibition Centre, 9 Aviation Park Road, Singapore 498760

Web: www.singaporeairshow.com.sg

Asian Children's Festival

What is it? This annual festival is spread over several weeks and it is organised by the National Library Board. The festival promotes learning and Asian culture for children through creative and interesting programmes, performances and workshops that are open to all the family. Ultimately, this is a celebration both of and for children.

What is there for children? The festival generally involves storytelling sessions and other fringe programmes at participating libraries and KidsASIA!. The latter showcases the culture and heritage of Asian communities, with performances from dancers, puppeteers, musicians and other talents.

When? January (it has also been held in November in the past)

Where? Islandwide, largely based in public libraries

Price guide? Many activities are free or individually priced.

Email: ask@nhb.gov.sg

Web: www.asianchildrenfest.com

Children's Day

What is it? This day is a celebration of and for children. There are events held throughout Singapore with a large, national gala organised for younger children. This comprises a number of performances and other activities. Primary school children at local schools do not have to attend school on this day.

When? 1 October annually

Where? Singapore Pavillion (look out for other events at other venues including public libraries and Downtown East)

Chingay Parade

What is it? Chingay comes from the Chinese words *zhuang yi*, which broadly translate as 'the art of costumes and masquerade'. This is a fair description of the parade, which involves more than 3,000 local and foreign performers.

What is there for children? The evening parade offers 90 minutes of colourful cultural performances from all over the world. Special highlights include the lion dance and beautiful float displays. You can either watch the parade live or simply watch it on television in the comfort of your own home.

When? The parade is held over two consecutive evenings at the beginning of the year during the Chinese New Year celebrations. Although the 1st evening is a preview, it is every bit as spectacular. Street parties usually follow the main parade on the 2nd night.

Where? At the Pit Building next to the Singapore Flyer.

Price guide? Free unless you opt for a gallery seat. Seats cost between $24 to $55 and are available through SISTIC.

Web: www.chingay.org.sg (Also watch out for details on TV or in the newspapers)

Tip: Think carefully before taking very young children. It is extremely crowded and public transport afterwards is likely to be packed.

Singapore Grand Prix

What is it? This is an annual racing car event held as part of the worldwide Grand Prix schedule. It features the top names in racing and it is televised internationally.

What is there for children? The highlight is undoubtedly the opportunity to view a world-class event. The organizers recommend that children under the age of 7 years old do not attend the race because of safety and operational reasons (for children under 7 years old parents must sign an indemnity letter obtainable from ticket booths or the website). Any child under the age of 12 years old must be accompanied by an adult who holds a valid ticket.

When? September

Where? Checkout the website for precise details as to how to access the Marina Bay Street Circuit

Price guide? Email tickets@singaporegp.sg for details

Email: info@singaporegp.sg

Web: www.singaporegp.sg

National Day

What is it? Every year since August 1966, Singapore has celebrated its independence with a National Day Parade. As the parade is also an opportunity to mark Singapore's identity as a multi-ethnic nation, many local schools are involved, in the form of choirs, dancing troupes or participants of any of the other colourful performances. The three-hour parade may also be viewed on TV or by live webcast from the NDP website.

What is there for children? This is an opportunity to see Singapore's armed forces on parade and ends with a spectacular firework display.

When? 9th August

Where? The Float@Marina Bay (there are plans to move this to the new National Stadium when it is built)

Price guide? Tickets to view the parade live are free and are obtained by e-balloting (usually in June) on the main NDP website. Only Singaporean citizens and permanent residents above the age of 12 can apply.

Contact: Details of the parade are published in the newspapers and on the official NDP website.

Web: www.ndp.org.sg

Singapore Dragon Boat Festival (*Duan Wu Jie*)

What is it? Dragon boat races are the main feature of this festival. The key event is the prestigious NUS-NTU 1,000-m Dragon Boat Race— Prime Minister Challenge Trophy.

What is there for children? Apart from the dragon boat races, there are cultural and festival activities. Typically, the programme includes a children's colouring contest, children's karaoke competition, dragon boat telematches on land, food and game stalls, dragon kites demonstrations, dragon boat joy rides and other activities and competitions targeted at family participation.

When? Over a weekend towards the end of June/early July

Where? Bedok Reservoir (subject to change)

Price guide? Free to view

Web: www.sdba.org.sg

Singapore Motorshow

At the time of press this show was last held in 2010

What is it? This motorshow is the largest automotive display of revolutionary technology for cars and motorcycles in Asia. The 10-day, biennial motoring event has a varied audience — car buyers, car enthusiasts, motorcycle fans, dealers and, of course, children!

What is there for children? As well as viewing motor vehicles, there is also the opportunity to see exciting stunt-driving performances, buy memorabilia (and copious brochures) as well as enjoy various giveaways.

When? September/ October or November (Note: biennial)

Where? Singapore International Convention and Exhibition Centre, 1 Raffles Boulevard, Singapore 039593

Price guide? Free for children below 3 years / $4 for children / $6 to $8 for adults (Prices are for the most recent show)

Web: www.motorshow.com.sg

Singapore River Regatta

What is it? Here you can see over 100 teams battle in colourful dragon boats and canoes.

What is there for children? Dragon boats to view and land activities to participate in

When? November/December

Where? Singapore River (from Elgin Bridge to Cavenagh Bridge)

Price guide? Free to view

Tel: 6440 9763

Email: admin@sdba.org.sg

Web: www.sdba.org.sg

Singapore Street Festival

What is it? This festival focuses on popular culture by celebrating street culture and youth (it is targeted at teenagers and young adults).

What is there for children? Skateboarding, graffiti and dance competitions, rock bands and fashion displays

When? June

Where? In and around Orchard Road. Key areas include the environs of Plaza Singapura, Orchard Cineleisure, Youth Park and the adjoining skateboard park.

Price guide? Free

Web: www.singaporestreetfestival.com

OPEN DAYS

Various institutions hold open days and listed below are a few that I'd suggest. Some of these take place a couple of times a year rather than annually. Keep a lookout in the entertainment listings of newspapers for dates and times.

Army Open House

Children and teenagers will be interested in the popular Army Open House. This is usually held every three years in September. Activities and facilities available vary but previous open houses have featured equipment and technology exhibits, vehicle parades, combat laser games, military rides and food stalls. There are also inflatable castles and other fun activities specifically for younger children. Details of the Open House are available nearer the time of the event, both in the newspapers and on the army's website.

Price guide: Free admission

Location: Usually Safti Military Institute on Upper Jurong Road but the most recent was held at Pasir Laba Camp at 132 Pasir Laba Road

Web: www.ArmyOpenHouse.com / www.mindef.gov.sg

Istana

The Istana is the official residence of the President of Singapore. The grounds are open to the public in celebration of Chinese New Year, Labour Day, National Day, Deepavali and Hari Raya Puasa. As well as the grounds, there are a variety of performances to enjoy (including music, song and dance) and you may even get the chance to meet the President.

Opening hours: 8.30 a.m. to 6.00 p.m.

Price guide: Singaporeans and Singaporean Permanent Residents: Free. Otherwise, it costs $1 per person. (For $2 you can also view the staterooms.)

Location: Entry is via the main gate on Orchard Road.

Web: www.istana.gov.sg

Note: The Changing of the Guard Ceremony takes place every 1st Sunday of the month (except in July and August) at 6.00 p.m. The display by the Precision Drill Squad of the SAF Military Police Unit is a highlight.

Republic of Singapore Air Force (RSAF) Open House

This is an opportunity to enjoy aerial displays, static displays, performances and aircraft rides. Site visits are also conducted, e.g. to the Flight Simulator Centre, where you can experience how pilots are trained in air combat as well as taught how to handle emergencies in a simulated environment. For younger children, there are kiddy rides and fun activities. This takes place in August or September about every two years.

Price guide: Free admission and a free shuttle bus service between Eunos and Hougang Bus Interchanges and Paya Lebar Air Base

Location: Paya Lebar Air Base, off Airport Road

Web: www.mindef.gov.sg/rsaf/

Singapore Police Force (SPF) — Police Week Carnival

Traditionally, the Police Academy hosts a Police Week at the end of May/beginning of June, although this is not held every year. Part of the celebrations include a Police Week Carnival, during which members of the public learn more about the SPF through fun and enjoyable indoor and outdoor activities. The carnival comprises an assortment of game stalls, kiddy rides and an exhibition that showcases vehicles and equipment used by the police and its home team partners.

Price guide: Free admission. (Tickets for the rides can be bought at the venue and can also be used to purchase food and beverages, police memorabilia and other items on sale.)

Location: The Old Police Academy, 1 Mount Pleasant Road, off Thomson Road, Singapore 298333

Web: www.spf.gov.sg

Note: Information about the carnival can

also be obtained from broadcast media and newspapers nearer the time.

Society for the Prevention of Cruelty to Animals (SPCA)

For all those interested in animals, it is worth visiting the SPCA when it has an open house. This usually takes place on World Animal Day (in September or October) but possibly at other times throughout the year as well. Also look out for other events noted on its website under News & Events.

Location: 31 Mount Vernon Road, Singapore 368054
Tel: 6287 5355
Email: enquiries@spca.org.sg
Web: www.spca.org.sg

– Chapter 8 –

SHOPPING DISTRACTIONS AND CULINARY DELIGHTS

In this chapter, I've chosen to focus on shopping and eating, both of which are commonly cited as the favourite pastimes of Singaporeans! There are plenty of shopping centres, restaurants and hawker centres to choose from and although you may already have favourites of your own, you'll undoubtedly find a few new ideas here as well as all the information needed to ensure that a day out shopping (and eating) with the family is fun.

FAST FACTS

These are purely personal choices but for those seeking quick solutions, I'd recommend the following fixes:

Best Playgrounds

VivoCity (Levels 2 and 3), Forum – The Shopping Mall (if you are a member of the Hip Kids Club on Level 2) and the Sky Garden at Suntec City Mall (Level 3), Nex (4th floor – there is a dry playground and a water playground), IMM (3rd floor, there is a dry playground and a water playground), City Square Mall (outside the front entrance. There is also a maze garden and there is a big open-air area in Basement 1, outside MacDonald's). Marina Square has a lovely indoor playground on Level 3 as well.

Best Family Rooms/Breastfeeding Facilities

Isetan (Level 4, which has several nappy changing stations, private breastfeeding rooms, a sofa, high chairs and hot water), Takashimaya (Level 3), Suntec City Mall (Happy Kidz on Level 3) and Parco Bugis Junction (Seiyu, Level 3). Ion Orchard has lovely family rooms. City Square Mall and Parkway Parade have fairly generous breastfeeding rooms as well. For family rooms, the one at Vivocity on the 2nd floor, just beside the children's playground, is the most generous of all. It reminds me of a changing room in a shopping mall in Europe or Australia. Generous changing stations, sofas, even curtained off breastfeeding areas.

Best Choices for Family Dining

Food court on Level 5 of 313@Somerset, restaurants and food kiosks in the IMM Building and the waterfront at VivoCity (This gets very crowded at weekends but you can also access the food courts on Levels 3 and B2.) The food court at B2 of Takashimaya has a wide variety of food but it is extremely crammed.

Best Location for School Holiday Activities

Forum – The Shopping Mall, Raffles City (for its staged performances) and VivoCity (for trips on the monorail or cable car to Sentosa or even a morning cruise.

SHOPPING DISTRACTIONS

This part of the chapter is mainly aimed at those with younger children but it may come in handy for all parents. As a mother, I know the difficulties involved when doing essential shopping with two young, bored, active children in tow. So hopefully this part of the book will provide some respite in such instances.

Shopping Centres

Note: Kopitiams and food junctions are both forms of food courts, where a variety of inexpensive and predominantly Asian food is available.

The following section focuses on a number of the main shopping centres/malls in Singapore. Do note that facilities, ranging from nappy changing stations to playgrounds to school holiday roadshows, change from time to time but, more often than not, this signals an improvement. Nevertheless, the following observations may assist you in your travels...

The Centrepoint

Main features: Cold Storage supermarket (Level B1), Robinsons department store (Levels 1, 2, 3, 4, 5 and 6), the Gap (Level 2), Marks and Spencer (Levels 1 and 2), Harvey Norman (Level 3) and Times The Bookshop (Level 4). The Customer Service counter is on Level 1 near Mothercare.

Attractions and facilities for children:

- Robinsons' toy department (and children's clothes) can be found on Level 6.
- Mothercare (Level 1) has the mall's only kiddy ride just inside its main entrance. In the new wing, there is a Haagen-Dazs ice-cream parlour.
- There is a PARTY With US store on Level 5. There is also a KinderFun selling desks and chairs for children on the 5th floor as well.
- The foyer area on Level 1 is used to host special events. Activities are usually aimed at young children.

Food: There is an indoor Food Street on Level 1 (go up the stairs near the pharmacy on Level B1) that has several reasonable family restaurants. Look out for the Noodle Place Restaurant, Prima Taste Kitchen (for dishes about $8) and Lerk Thai Restaurant (see Culinary Delights, p. 271). You'll also find a McDonald's on B1. Within Marks and Spencer on Level 2, there is a spacious coffee shop that is quite popular with stroller-pushing mothers. Sanur Indonesian Restaurant is located on Level 4 (see Culinary Delights, p. 273). There is a Kopitiam at Level B1, next to the carpark.

Toilets:

- There is a nursing room on Level 3 (next to #03-25/26 near the 'back' escalators) which has 3 changing stations, seats, a bench and hot water.
- The ladies' toilets on Level 2 of Robinsons (near the shoe department and the escalators) has a separate cubicle for baby changing and a sink. Level 5 has one as well, near the towel department at the corner.
- You'll find nappy changing stations in the main toilet facilities on Levels 1 and 4.

Location: 176 Orchard Road,
Singapore 238843
Tel: 6737 9000
Web: www.centrepoint.com.sg

313@Somerset

Main features: There is a HMV, a Harris Bookstore, a Fish Spa and a Precious Thots novelty shop on the fourth floor. Apart from the restaurants and food, this mall is targeted more at high-end shoppers and there is not too much for kids to do.

Food: There is a spacious Food Republic (food court) on Level 5 and many food outlets in the basement. There is also a Discovery Walk of Restaurants linking to the Orchard Road strip on the first floor. Level 3 features the Blue Mountain Café and the second floor has a Gold Rock Ice Cream Restaurant.

Location: 313 Orchard Road,
Singapore 238895
Web: www.313somerset.com.sg/
Tel: 6496 9300

Orchard Central

This relatively new shopping centre in the Somerset area of Orchard Road also features a number of surprising facilities for kids.

Main features: There is a cool air-conditioned Mediterranean-style market at B2 which features a weekend flea market selling jewellery, clothes and art and crafts. There are restaurants here as well, and a lovely water feature. There is a charming fresco on the wall at the far end that features a Grecian landscape. The Centrepoint is accessible via underpass from here

Attractions and facilities for children:

- Fresh Art Studios at B2 features clay workshops for children at $20 per workshop. There are workshops for adults as well at $40 per workshop.

  Tel: 9273 7373 (Angela)

- On Level 1, there is a HUGE statue spanning five storeys of a lady with shopping bags. Children might find this interesting. Events are regularly held on the first floor as well, i.e. flea markets and exhibitions.
- On Level 4, there is a golf game simulator at MaxSwing Golf Unlimited. They have clubs to accommodate children 8 years old and up, but any potential golfer below that is welcome to bring their own golf clubs. Rental of the simulator is $40 an hour. You could join up as a member and buy a prepaid card for $300. Rental will then be halved and Terence, the friendly manager, will even throw in some free coaching.

  Tel: 6509 0200 / 9661 1128

  Email: terence.woo@maxswing.com.sg

- There is a flight simulator on Level 4 as well, and prices start from $69.50 for 30 minutes. Children should be tall enough to reach the pedals on the simulator to experience flying an AirBus A320.

  Tel: 6634 2797

  Email: info@sgflightsimulation.com.sg.

- There is an indoor rock climbing wall, Border X, on Level 4 as well. Kids above 6 years old and 1.1 meters can experience rock climbing for $23 on weekdays and $28 on weekends. There is also an abseiling program for children 12 years and above for $20 on weekdays and $25 on weekends. There is also an advanced rock-climbing class for children 12 years and above for $33 on weekdays and $38 on weekends for 1 ½ hours. They are open from 11.00 a.m. to 9.30 p.m.

  Tel: 6884 4870

  Web: www.borderX.com.sg

  Facebook: Via Ferrata

- On Level 7, there is an Asian Food Channel Cooking Studio that holds classes on weekends for parents and children.

  Tel: 6834 4829

  Web: www.theafcstudio.com

- There is an exquisite stationery shop on Level 6, Urban Write.

Food:

- On Level 4, there is a Spagheddies Restaurant. On Level 8, there are quite a number of restaurants, among them a Ben and Jerry's.
- Levels 11 and 12 feature a roof garden with interesting sculptures and a spectacular view of Orchard Road. On Level 11 there is a Tung Lok Seafood restaurant and Ochre restaurant serving Italian food. On Level 12, there is a Kuriya Japanese restaurant.

Location: Orchard Central
181 Orchard Road
Tel: 6238 1051
Web: www.orchardcentral.com.sg

Note: There are breastfeeding rooms on Levels 4 and 7. This mall has some of the tallest escalators in Singapore, some inside and some outside the mall. Kids will really enjoy going up and down the escalators, but be mindful of their safety. There are also very interesting bubble lifts in the mall.

Forum – The Shopping Mall

Main features: Julia Gabriel Centre for Learning (Level 4), 24-hour McDonald's (Level B1), Toys "R" Us (Level 3) and lots of branded children's clothing shops. The Customer Service counter is on Level 2 near the children's playground.

Attractions and facilities for children:

- If you use this mall regularly and you have young children, it is worth joining the Hip Kids Club. Membership is $15 for 1 year for children aged 12 years and below. You can then acquire points for purchases made in the mall which entitle you to free gifts upon redemption. You will also be eligible for discount in some of the shops. The main advantage, however, is access to the playground on Level 2, which has soft-fall play apparatus, a ball den and pedal cars. It is ideal for children aged 6 years and below (height limit for entry is 120 cm).
- It is open on weekdays from 11.00 a.m. to 1.00 p.m. and 4.30 p.m. to 8.00 p.m. / 10.30 a.m. to 1.00 p.m. and 2.00 p.m. to 5.00 p.m. and 6.00 p.m to 8.00 p.m. at weekends and on public holidays.
- Bookaburra on Level 2 stocks a good range of quality children's books and also conducts storytelling sessions, which sometimes involve crafts and songs. These sessions are for children aged 2 and above and currently take place every Wednesday and Friday at 4.00 p.m. It is advisable to register beforehand for a nominal fee. Do call to confirm.

  Tel: 6235 9232
- Toys "R" Us on Level 3 is a strong magnet that entices any child to this shopping mall! It is open from 10.00 a.m. to 10.00 p.m. daily.
- There is an Early Learning Centre shop on Level 2.

- On Level B1, you'll find 2 small toy outlets primarily retailing educational toys and a toy model shop for older children (and adult collectors).
- The Little Gym on Level B1 offers recreational gymnastics, karate and sports development classes in a safe and noncompetitive environment.

  Tel: 6238 6331

  FaceBook: www.facebook.com/TheLittleGymsOfSingapore
- There are kiddy rides on Level 2.
- The main concourse on Level B1 is used for children's activities (including special promotions such as the sale of children's books). There is also a small stage here that is used for occasional performances. There is a children's photographer here as well. There is also a NutureCraft shop that sells kids toys.
- The Kidz Station on Level 2 offers classes for preschoolers and a drop-off childminding service. It is extremely popular and most of the morning slots are occupied. It is $50 for 3 hours of walk-in childminding and $60 for 4 hours. There is a playgroup from Monday to Friday from 930 a.m. to 12.30 a.m. and an extension class from 12.30 a.m. to 1.30 p.m. Mandarin classes are also available.

  Tel: 6735 6340
- VitaKids on Level B1 sells health supplements, some organic snacks and toiletries for children.
- There is a baby and kids' clinic and dentist on Level 2.

Food: There are a number of food outlets in the basement.

Toilets: The disabled toilets in the main toilets have nappy changing facilities on Levels B1 and 1. There are nappy changing facilities and a low-level sink in the ladies' toilets on Level 2. There is a Mother's Room on Level 1 with a changing bench and an area in which to breastfeed. Hot water is also available.

Location: 583 Orchard Road, Singapore 238884

Tel: 6732 2479

Web: www.forumtheshoppingmall.com.sg

Note:

• This mall offers some excellent children's entertainment and programmes during most of the school breaks.

• There is a Lorna Whiston Study Centre at #05-04 of the Forum Office Tower (Tel: 6734 0366).

• There is also a "I Can Read" Centre at #07-04.

Great World City

Main features: Cold Storage supermarket (Level B1), Barang Barang (Level 1), Zara (Level 1, the children's clothing is towards the back of the shop), POSBank (Level 2) and a cinema complex (Level 3).

Attractions and facilities for children:

- Timezone (www.timezone.com.sg) is a video games arcade on Level 3. Children below the age of 16 cannot play video games from 7.30 a.m. to 6.30 p.m. on school days and whenever dressed in school uniform.
- On Level 3, there is a Kindergolf.
- My Gym/Grace Kids on Level 3 has a small snack counter inside and Jolly Party, a separate party supplies section.
- The cinema complex is on Level 3.
- Kumon (which offers enrichment classes) is located on Level 2.
- Level 2 has a Ben & Jerry's ice cream bar, a HARRIS bookshop, 2 toyshops and a magic and party supplies shop.

Food: There is a large food court on Level B1, a couple of fast food outlets on Level 1 and some restaurants on Level 3.

Toilets: You'll find some of Singapore's most colourful toilets here! They are decorated according to geographical themes, for example, Dutch bulb fields, the Wild West and Venetian gondolas! There are nappy changing stations in all the toilets and a room for mothers to nurse in can be found on Level 2.

Note:

• There are taxi stands on either side of the mall (along Zion Road and Kim Seng Road) so make sure you know which side you're waiting at if you call a taxi.

• There are free shuttle bus services to and from Orchard MRT, City Hall MRT and Chinatown MRT.

Location: 1 Kim Seng Promenade, Singapore 237994
Tel: 6737 3855
Web: www.greatworldcity.com.sg

United Square Shopping Mall

United Square has positioned itself as a kids learning hub, and mall is fully equipped with kid-friendly features from a luxurious nursing room, colour themed levels, spacious corridor walkways, carpeted grounds, play features right down to animal-shaped bins for your rubbish! There is also a state-of-the art al fresco foodcourt with F&B outlets for the whole family.

Attractions and facilities for children:

- At level B1, there is a Cold Storage supermarket, a Build-A-Bear workshop, a Shooz-4-kids, a Moms R' Us Nursing & Maternity, countless stalls and eateries, and a Vitakids that stocks excellent organic food for children (including fluoride-free toothpaste!) There is also a SOEZ Cooking Playground, where the kids can take up cooking lessons from $48 per session. There are many coin-operated rides for the kids here.
- At Level 1, there is Connectz, a carpeted area with all the kid-friendly stores such as Growing Fun, Growing Up Gifted, KinderGolf and Growing Fun – Toys for Kids to grow

up with. The nursing rooms here are huge, and the area is very child-friendly and comfortable. Petit Bowl (at #01 - 77/78) next to the taxi stand specialises in food for fussy infants, totally organic and addictive-free.

- On Level 2, there is a Ben and Jerry's, a Popular Bookstore, a Challenger and a Toys 'R' Us. This outlet is not as crowded as the other stores and makes shopping here a pleasant experience.
- On Level 3, there is a Hua Language Centre, a Mandeville Music and Drama, and Global Art Singapore (an art school).
- On Level 4, there is a Lorna Whiston Speech and Drama Centre and The Ballet and Music Company.

Location: 1 Goldhill Plaza
Singapore 308899
Tel: 6259 3121
Web: www.unitedsquare.com.sg

ION Orchard

Opening hours: 10.00 a.m. to 10.00 p.m.
This spacious shopping centre to open up at the beginning of Orchard Road has plenty of space for the kids to run around in. Benches and touch-screens are also plentiful, and the management markets ION Orchard as Singapore's first sensory mall. However, the shops are targeted more at high-end shoppers.

Attractions and facilities for children:

- On Level 1, there is a Singapore Visitors Centre.
- On Level 4, there is a Prologue bookshop with a wide selection of books. There is also a spacious café in this bookshop — JAMS. Meatworks restaurant is also here and children will love the spaciousness of the restaurant and its open concept (not to mention the food! Kids portions can be ordered for half-price for pasta).
- On Levels 55 and 56, visitors can enjoy the magnificent view of Orchard Road and its surroundings for a fee. Adults pay $16, children (4 to 12 years) pay $8 and seniors pay $12. There is a family package for 2 adults and 2 kids for $40. Australian restaurant SALT has also opened up here.

Food:

- At Level B4, there is a relatively spacious food court with a wide selection of food. Prices here are a little steeper, but it is worth it as one does not feel claustrophobic like in so many other food courts in Singapore shopping centres. There are plenty of food stalls as well. The Bonchon chicken is excellent and children will love it. The Modern Peking Duck stall in the basement features crispy duck skin wrapped in spring roll paper with a spring onion and duck sauce inside each one – heavenly.
- On level B3, there is a Fish n Co. with numerous other restaurants.

Location: 2 Orchard Rd
Tel: 6238 8228
Web: www.ionorchard.com/en

Holland Village

Main features: Lots and lots of cafés and restaurants! In Holland Road Shopping Centre, you'll find a 24-hour supermarket (Level 1), Lims department store (Level 2) and many smaller shops selling souvenirs, decorative items and home furnishings. There are several banks and a main post office in the vicinity.

Attractions and facilities for children: I only mention this venue because it is very popular with expatriate families and is also a frequent haunt of many mothers with younger children. Despite this, facilities are poor.

There is neither a playground nor a play area in Holland Road Shopping Centre. There are also no kiddy rides.

- Shops that may interest your children in Holland Village Shopping Centre include a small toyshop on Level 2 and a pet shop on Level 3. Girls may like the bead store and a colourful shop featuring sequined items on Level 3. There are also plenty of nail bars where both mums and daughters can enjoy a quick pedicure.
- Nearby, there is a party supplies shop at the shophouse at 27A Holland Avenue.
- Holland Shopping Mall is just around the corner from Holland Village Shopping Centre on Lorong Mambong.

Food:

- Food options are plentiful in Holland Village. Café 211 on Level 4 of Holland Road Shopping Centre has both indoor air-conditioned comfort and an outdoor rooftop dining area. A children's menu is available. A number of restaurants on Lorong Mambong also cater for children.
- There is a food court on the first floor of Holland Shopping Mall (facing Lorong Liput).
- For finer dining (and a heftier bill), head for Jalan Merah Saga, just off Chip Bee Gardens. Here you'll find Italian, French, Indian and fusion food. There is also an excellent organic shop that serves some tasty snacks.

Toilets: In Holland Road Shopping Centre, the toilets (there is a single nappy changing 'tray' in the ladies' toilets on Levels 1 and 2) could do with renovation. The installation of more baby-changing facilities and junior toilets would also make life easier for the many mothers who shop here.

Holland Shopping Mall does not have baby-changing facilities.

Location: Holland Village
255 Holland Avenue,
Singapore 278983
Web: www.hollandvillage.com.sg

Note: Queues for taxis in front of Holland Road Shopping Centre can be very long during peak periods and at weekends.

IMM Building

Main features: Giant Hypermarket (Level 1), Esprit Factory Outlet (Level 1, this has children's clothing), a post office (Level 3) and countless furniture and home improvement shops on Level 2.

Attractions and facilities for children:

- On Level 1 (towards the back of the building), there is as area where staged performances are held at certain times of the year.
- Baby strollers and wheelchairs are available for loan at the Customer Service Counter on Level 2 free of charge.
- On Level 3, there is a good children's craft corner where you can do face painting, woodcraft construction, sand art, stencilling and gift making. There is also a toy and children's shop nearby. There is also a water playground and a 7-metre tall treehouse playground on Level 3, and a huge play area.
- There are automated rides throughout the complex.

Food:

- On Level 1 you'll find fast food, snack kiosks, cafés and restaurants. The Bali Thai Restaurant offers a good buffet at weekends and on public holidays, where you can choose whatever you wish from the menu for a set price (child rates are available).
- On Level 2, there is an inexpensive Kopitiam offering a variety of food.
- There is a Banquet food court on Level 3 adjacent to the escalators offering a variety of food as well.

Toilets: There are separate baby-care rooms adjacent to the toilets on Level 1. These have changing stations and a sink. There is also a baby-care room on Level 2. There isn't a nappy changing station on Level 3

Location: 2 Jurong East Street 21, Singapore 609601
Tel: 6536 1188
Web: www.imm.sg

Note:

• Fuji Ice Palace, Jurong East Library and the Science Centre (on Jurong Town Hall Road) are all a short drive away (walkable with older children).

• If you want to combine shopping with a family outing, the nearby SAFRA at The Chevrons has an excellent bowling alley (you can walk there from IMM).

Marina Bay Sands

This huge Integrated Resort overlooking Marina Bay is the larger of Singapore's two casinos. Apart from enjoying the casino (from which kids are absolutely forbidden) there is plenty for children to see and do.

Attractions and facilities for children:

- The ArtScience Museum (built in the shape of a lotus flower, *see also* Chapter 6: Where to Go! pp. 194) has been called ,"The Welcoming Hand of Singapore" by Mr. Sheldon Adelson, the chairman of Las Vegas Sands Corp. It will host blockbuster international exhibits as well as permanent exhibits on three floors of gallery space across over 4,800 square meters. There are 21 galleries in total. It is also surrounded by a 4,000 square meter lily pond reflecting pool from which water is recycled and used in the museum's bathrooms. A total of 10 "fingers" that make up the building form plus two bay windows with special views of Singapore and Marina Bay Sands. The tallest "finger" stands 60 meters above ground.

- In Basement 2 there is a man-made canal where kids can take rides in a *sampan* (a small wooden boat) for $6 a child and $10 an adult). The *sampan* ride operates from 11.00 a.m. to 8.00 p.m. daily (the last ride leaves at 7.30 p.m.).
- There is a Rasapura Masters Food Court in the basement. Prices here are higher than in other food courts.
- There is a skating rink at B2 which is comparable in size to the legendary ice-rink at Rockefeller Center in New York City. It is open from 10.00 a.m. to 10.00 p.m. The Skating Rink is closed daily from 5.00 to 6.00 p.m. for maintenance. Adults are charged $7 an hour and $5 every subsequent hour. Children (5 to 11 years old) are charged $6 an hour and $3 for every subsequent hour. Skate rental is a $3 one-off fee. Personal skates are not allowed. Purchase of socks is $6 and a pair of gloves is $10.
- The QUBE Kids Club which is going to open up in B2 will occupy a 185 square metre space in the mall. The operating hours are from 10.00 a.m. to 11.00 p.m. and is open to children from ages 6 to 17. It houses computers with internet access and PC games, as well as X-boxes and Play Stations. It will have two large screen TVs playing DVDs throughout the day with bean bags thrown on the floor for the children to sit on. It will also contain two foosball tables and two air hockey tables.
- The theatre at Marina Bay Sands regularly hosts world class productions such as the Lion King. Check the website for details. Tickets are from $65 to $240.
- Sands Skypark: The Sands Skypark, 200 meters in the sky, is an engineering wonder. It stretches longer than the Eiffel Tower laid down or four and a half A380 Jumbo Jets. It offers views of Singapore's CBD and Kusu Island and the future Gardens by the Bay at Marina Barrage. One can even see as far as East Coast Park and

Changi Airport's Control Tower. The Sands SkyPark Public Observation Deck, which is open to members of the public and is a ticketed area, is accessible daily from 10.00 a.m. to 10.00 p.m. Mondays to Thursdays and 10.00 a.m. to 11.00 p.m. on Fridays, Saturdays and Sundays. Tickets are $20 for an adult, $14 for a child (2 to 12 years old) and $17 for a senior citizen (aged 55 years and above).

Location: 10 Bayfront Ave
Singapore 018956
Tel: 6688 8868
Web: www.marinabaysands.com/

Playground@Big Splash

Formerly a water theme park, this complex is now promoted as a 'lifestyle hub' featuring an array of recreational and dining amenities. Gone are the colourful slides and pool and instead your child can indulge in a variety of activities!

Attractions and facilities for children:

- Golf at Lilliputt
  Location: Block B, #03-05
  Web: www.lilliputt.com
- Alpha Gymnastics Club
  Location: Block B, Unit #02-07
  Web: www.alphagymcom.sg
- Advantage School of Tennis
  Location: Block B, #02-08
  Web: www.advantageschooloftennis.com
- For something different, take off down the East Coast on Kangoo Jumps obtainable from the Kangoo Jumps Concept Store (Block C, #01-22). There is a large 'Playtrium' on the ground floor and public shower facilities on Level B2. The beach and barbecue pits are also nearby.

Location: 902 East Coast Parkway,
Singapore 449874
Tel: 6345 6762
Email: event@playground.com.sg
Web: www.playground.com.sg

Resorts World Sentosa

Besides being home to universal studios, Resorts World Sentosa also has a Kids Club for parents to leave their kids (above 3 years old) to be entertained while they take in the sights and sounds of Resorts World. A Marine Life Park (*see* Chapter 6 Where to Go? p. 218) is also due to open after 2010, as is a Maritime Xperiential Museum that will look at the history of the Maritime Silk Route. Festive Walk is a boardwalk that is open 24/7. It has many shops and restaurants and has two free attractions. One is the Crane Dance, a dance between two mechanical cranes, and the other is the Lake of Dreams, a laser and fountain show located close to the casino that plays daily at sunset. As with Marina Bay Sands, there is a series of world class shows at the theatre here. The latest one playing is *Voyage De La Vie*, a circus spectacular.

Location: 39 Artillery Avenue,
Sentosa, Singapore 099958
Tel: 6577 8888
Email: enquiries@rwsentosa.com
Web: www.rwsentosa.com

NEX Mall

Opening hours: 10.00 a.m. to 10.00 p.m.

NEX Mall is Singapore's latest mall to open up in the Serangoon area on the North-East MRT line. It fully opened in January 2011.

Attractions and facilities for children:

- Baby strollers (for children below 3 years old) and wheelchairs are available for loan at no charge.
- There is a SkyGarden on the rooftop with wet and dry play areas for children. There is also a canine park on the rooftop where dog owners can bring their dogs. There are designated lifts and escalators on the exterior of NEX. Pets are not allowed in the mall.
- There are very comfortable Shaw Theatres on Level 4. Discounts of 50 cents a ticket are given to Passioncard members with a purchase of two or more tickets.
- There is a FairPrice Xtra on Level 3 that sells quite a number of high-end groceries. Prices here are cheaper than in Cold Storage. FairPrice Xtra here offers 24-hour shopping.
- Nursing Rooms are located on every level of the mall.

Location: 23 Serangoon Central
Singapore 556083
Tel: 6466 2555
Email: enquiry@nex.com.sg
Website: www.nex.com.sg

Parco Bugis Junction

Main features: Seiyu department store (Levels B1, 1, 2 and 3), Books Kinokuniya (Level 3) and a Cineplex complex (Level 4, with ticketing booth on Level 1). The Customer Service counter and a SISTIC outlet are on Level 2.

Attractions and facilities for children:

- Seiyu's toy and children's clothes departments are on Level 3. Both you and your children may enjoy browsing around Hylam, Malabar and Malay streets, which are located within an air-conditioned dome and lined with small shops, craft kiosks and various food venues. Teenagers in particular may enjoy this venue because of the many small boutique-style shops carrying fashionable and reasonably priced clothing. Younger children may enjoy watching and running in and out of the fountain just outside Seiyu, near Hylam Street. Don't forget to take bathers!
- The Wonderful World of Whimsy is on Level 3 of Seiyu, adjacent to the baby clothing. It has children's rides for the younger ones and various video games for older ones (you'll

need to purchase $0.50 tokens for the video games). Children aged 16 and below cannot play video games between 7.30 a.m. and 6.30 p.m. on school days and no one in school uniform is allowed entry.

- You'll find a small play area for very young children adjacent to the baby-changing facilities in Seiyu (Level 3).

Food: Level B1 has a large food court and various eating venues. There are also family-type restaurants on Level 2 of Parco Bugis.

Toilets: Inside Seiyu, a baby-care room can be found in the corner of Level 3, near the toys. There are six changing stations and an area for breastfeeding. The ladies' toilets on this level and Level 2 also have nappy changing stations.

For the rest of Parco Bugis (Levels B1, 1, 2, and 3), there are separate changing rooms for babies/toddlers on all levels (adjacent to the main toilets). These feature a single nappy changing station with a changing mat and a sink inside. There are similar facilities in Malabar Street on Level 1 (behind The Coffee Connoisseur).

Note: This venue is opposite Albert Street, which is a good place to purchase printed T-shirts, watches, cheap clothing, hawker food and even seasonal festive goodies such as Chinese lanterns.

Location: 200 Victoria Street, Singapore 188021

Tel: 6334 8831

Web: www.bugisjunction-mall.com.sg

Raffles City

Main features: Robinsons department store (Levels 1, 2 and 3), MPH bookstore (Level B1) and Jason's Market Place (Level B1)

Attractions and facilities for children:

- Younger children may enjoy watching the fountain on Level B1. The shows staged at festive times of the year are a big draw for children and are held in the main atrium of Level 1. Other occasional events are also held here.
- Robinsons' children's department is on Level 3.
- There is a Party City shop (party supplies) on Level 3.
- Older children may like the comic shop on Level 3 which features video games and model characters.
- Strollers are available from the concierge.

Food: There are numerous food outlets on Level B1, including fast food. Level 1 has a couple of coffee/snack outlets. Level 3 has a food court.

Toilets: There is a small baby's room on Level 3, near Lift Lobby B and the main toilets. Inside you'll find a nursing room, four changing stations, chairs and a two-seater soft bench.

There are only two other nappy changing stations (and a

breastfeeding room) on Level B1, next to MPH.

Location: 252 North Bridge Road, Singapore 179103
Tel: 6318 0238
Web: www.rafflescity.com

Note:

• City Hall MRT Station is located outside this mall.

• You can continue shopping in CityLink Mall, an air-conditioned underground tunnel, most of the way to Suntec City or take a detour to Esplanade – Theatres on the Bay. Esplande MRT station (on the Circle Line) is also linked to this mall. You can take a walk to Esplande MRT via the linkway which has a number of shops as well.

Suntec City Mall

Suntec City is one of Singapore's largest shopping malls. Rather than try to cover all of it, I've concentrated on the areas that offer the most to children. These are the Tropics Atrium (TA), situated between Towers 1 and 2, and the Entertainment Centre Atrium (ECA), situated between Towers 3 and 4. Most of these features are on Level 3.

Main features: Mothercare (Level 2 of the TA), a cinema complex (between Tower Blocks 4 and 5 on Level 3/ ECA) and Carrefour (Levels 1 and 2/ ECA within the adjacent block). To access the latter, go to Level 2 and walk down the shopping corridor (this avoids having to go outside and cross the road). The Customer Service counters are on Level 1 of TA (access via Lobby T3) as well as at the entrance to the Galleria Atrium on Level 1.

Attractions and facilities for children:

- The Fountain of Wealth (*see* Where to Go, pp. 205 – 206) and the Koi Garden, also on Level B1, within the Fountain Terrace are worth a visit. At the Koi Garden you have the chance to feed the wonderfully coloured fish, as well as view them in their Japanese-landscaped pond.
- Times The Bookshop is on Level 1 of the Galleria Atrium.

Tropics Atrium

- The playground within the Sky Garden on Level 3 is a super facility. Young children will enjoy the opportunity to run around and use the apparatus, older children may just want to hang out while parents can sit in one of the shady areas and take time out! The garden is open daily and has lots of space, various water fountains and water features as well as some good views.
- On Level 3 is Happy Kidz. This mini-mall has shops and services specifically targeted at younger children. Here you'll find a Creative Art Corner (where children can try their hand at crafts), a Junior League (which specialises in children's haircuts

with DVDs and toys at hand), the School of Music Clef (which follows the ABRSM board) and a number of kiddy rides. It also has a spacious baby-care room (*see* Toilets below).

- There is a Toys "R" Us store on Level 3 and an Early Learning Centre.
- Kiddy rides are only situated in and just outside Happy Kidz.
- Shops that may interest your child include Jigsaw Puzzle World (Level 2) and Growing Fun (a toyshop on Level 3).
- There is a post office on Level 3.

Entertainment Centre Atrium

- The cinema complex is on Level 3.
- On Level 3, there are two games centres — Star Factory (video and electronic games for older children) and Virtualand (games and a photographic sticker booth).

Food: At the Fountain Food Terrace on Level B1, there are fast food outlets, cafés and restaurants.

There are several restaurants on Level 3 of the Tropics Atrium.

There is a Kopitiam on Level 3 of the ECA, located near the cinema, which also has a selection of food stalls.

Toilets: Generally, most of the toilets have nappy changing stations and low-level toilets. The baby room facilities at Happy Kidz on Level 3 of the TA are the best in Suntec City. They feature a spacious baby room with several nappy changing stations and a separate breastfeeding room.

Location: Temasek Boulevard, Singapore 038983
Tel: 6337 2888
Web: www.sunteccity.com.sg

Note: The Tropics Atrium at the entrance to Tower Blocks 1 and 2 is used for promotions and staged events.

Takashimaya (TAK)/ Takashimaya Shopping Centre (TSC)

For convenience, I've combined these two venues as they are adjacent to one another. Takashimaya is Singapore's largest single-site department store and retails products aimed at all ages.

Main features: Takashimaya department store (Levels B2, B1, 1, 2, 3 and 4) and Books Kinokuniya (Level 3 of TSC). The Information counter is on Level 1 of TSC and the Customer Service counter is on Level 2 of TAK.

Attractions and facilities for children:

TAK

Located on Level 3 of TAK, the Little Ones club is open to children aged between 3 and 9 for a membership fee of $16.05 for 2 years. The club holds regular events such as art and craft sessions, outdoor trips, parties and games sessions. Members also enjoy various privileges, including discounts at places of interest, e.g., the Singapore Science Centre and selected attractions on Sentosa.

Tel: 6739 9215
Email: littleones@takashimaya.com.sg
Web: www.takashimaya-sin.com/littleones

Children's clothing and toys are on Level 3.

The sports section on Level 4 also has children's swimwear and accessories.

TSC

Kinokuniya (Level 3) has a large children's book collection. You can also find music scores here, including materials for the RSM examinations.

On Level 4, there is Studio Miu (which offers art classes for children), Creative Hands (which stocks art supplies, including a good range of items for children) and The Better Toy Store. There is also The Better Toy Store and Art Friend at Level 4.

On Level 5, you'll find Bricks World, which is a LEGO exclusive shop.

Food: An extensive food court, various food outlets and a supermarket are on Level B2 of TAK. Note that the food court is extremely crowded on weekends and rather crammed.

There are a number of restaurants, including Seoul Garden which has free dining for children on Sundays, on Level 5 of TASC.

Toilets: You'll find nappy changing stations and low-level sinks/toilets in the ladies' toilets throughout Takashimaya. The toilets on B2 of TAK are conveniently located near the food court. There are allocated children's toilets on Level 3 at the back of the store and a nursery room.

The nursery room (on Level 3) is light, spotless and spacious. Children under 12 must be accompanied when entering this room. Baby products are available inside the nursery and there is an in-house consultation facility between 2.00 p.m. and 6.00 p.m. at weekends. You'll find seven changing stations, chairs, magazines as well as boiled water, a sink and a breastfeeding room with a two-seater settee. This is probably the best nursery room within any retail outlet in Singapore.

Location: 391 Orchard Rd
Web: www.takashimaya-sin.com

Note: For those who drive, it is best to note that the parking here is rather pricey.

Tampines Mall

Main features: Isetan (Levels 1 and 2), Popular Bookstore (Level 3) and a cinema (Level 4). The Customer Service counter is on Level 1.

Attractions and facilities for children:

- Isetan's toy and children's clothes departments are on Level 2.
- Yamaha Music School and Crestar are on Level 3.
- Toys "R" Us is on Level 3.
- Level 4 has a TimeZone (arcade games) and Art Serve, a T-shirt printing outlet.

Food:

- Level B1 has a restaurants/cafeterias/stalls and a NTUC supermarket.
- There are restaurants and a Kopitiam on Level 4. Children eat for free at Seoul Garden on Sundays.

Toilets: There are separate changing rooms for babies/toddlers on all levels (Levels B1, 1, 2, 3 and 4 adjacent to the main toilets). These feature a single nappy changing station with a changing mat and a sink inside.

Location: 04 Tampines Central 5, Singapore 529510
Tel: 6788 8370
Web: www.tampinesmall.com.sg

Note:

• This mall is near Tampines MRT Station/bus interchange.

• Adjacent to the mall is Century Square which has Metro department store (children's clothes on Level 2, toys on Level 3), food courts (Levels 3 and 4), games and video machines (Level 5), a photographic sticker shop (Level 5) and a Cineplex cinema (Level 5).

Tampines 1

Tampines 1 is one of the newest malls in the east. This mall features a Japanese Gourmet Town MANPUKU that offers Japanese cuisine direct from traditional establishments in Japan. There is also a Cold Storage, an Urban Write store that features fancy stationery, and a United Kids store featuring Kids and Infant wear.

Location: 10 Tampines Central 1
Singapore 529536
Tel: 6572 5522
Email: contact@tampines1.com.sg
Web: www.tampines1.com.sg

Tanglin Mall

Main features: Tanglin Marketplace (Level B1) and Gymboree (Level 3). The Customer Service counter is on Level 2.

Attractions and facilities for children:

- Kiddy rides are in the foyer of the main entrance (infuriating if you are heading out with bags of groceries and a toddler in tow!).
- Kindermusik and Gymboree are on Level 3. Gymboree has a drop-off programme for children over 3 years for some of its classes.
- Toyshops can be found on Level 2 (Playmobil is available at Fashion 6 to 16) and Level 1 (Gurgles and Kidz Story) and there is a magic supplies and party shop on Level 3.
- The Mother & Child Centre on Level 3 caters for both those with and those expecting a baby.
- If you are looking for organic food and toiletries for your family, look for Brown Rice Paradise on Level 2.

Food: There is a food court on Level B1, restaurants and fast food outlets on Level 1. A Nando's Grilled Chicken just opened up on Level 1.

Toilets: There is a breastfeeding room near the toilets on Level 3. Nappy changing stations are situated within the toilets on Levels B1, 1 and 3.

Location: 163 Tanglin Road,
Singapore 247933
Tel: 6736 4922
Web: www.tanglinmall.com.sg

Note: There is a large post office opposite this mall.

VivoCity

Main features: The waterfront at Singapore's newest and biggest shopping mall is a big attraction. The water theme continues within the centre itself, with prominent water features in the play areas on Levels 2 and 3. Key shops/services include Tangs (Levels 1 and 2), a Cineplex (Level 2), a Hypermarket (Level B2) and the Sentosa Express monorail (Level 3). There is now a pedestrian bridge to Sentosa with restaurants and facilities on the bridge itself. Information counters can be found on Levels 1 and 2.

Attractions and facilities for children:

- Children's clothing can be found at Zara and the Gap, both on Level 1.
- Activities for children can be found at Gymboree on Level 3 or Emiko Arts at the Play Court on Level 2. There is a Build-a-Bear-Workshop on Level 2 (you can purchase a bear here and decorate it or even hold parties at this venue).
- The Play Court on Level 2 is a large outside area where children can run around, climb the apparatus or enjoy the water features. The area is bordered with children's clothes and toyshops, a bookshop and a selection of cafés. You could also rent toy cars/mechanical horses for your children to ride. Prices start from $5 for 5 minutes.
- There is a large Toys "R" Us on Level 2 (a children's hairdressers is situated inside the store), as well as a number of smaller toyshops.
- Mothercare is located on Level 2.
- Movie tickets can be purchased on Level 2. The seats here are particularly comfortable and spacious.
- On Level 3, there is another outside play area for children called the Sky Park. This really is a huge space, featuring wooden walkways as well as soft fall and grassy areas. Although there is not a lot of play equipment, you can paddle here, watch the boats go up and down the harbour and enjoy the water features.
- Older children may enjoy the E-Zone (electronic games) on Level 3. A shop selling video and play station games is located next door.
- For a fun and inexpensive detour, why not hop over to Sentosa? For $3 return, you can take the Sentosa Express monorail from Level 3 to Sentosa's Imbiah or Beach stations (www.sentosa.

com.sg). The journey takes less than 4 minutes. You can also purchase entry tickets to the island's attractions at the VivoCity booth. Alternatively, you can travel by cable car from adjacent HarbourFront Centre or take a shuttle bus from HarbourFront Bus Interchange. You could also just stroll across on the pedestrian bridge to Sentosa. There are restaurants with a view to die for on the bridge itself.

- On the first, second and third floor, there are a number of restaurants with a view across the water of Resorts World Sentosa. Among them is Brazil Churrasco (*see* pp. p. 275).
- If you join the VivoCity Members Club (free of charge), you can redeem your parking charges with every $50 spent. Simply sign up for the Members Club online or go to the Customer Service Counter on the 2nd floor of Vivocity to sign up.

Food: On Level B2, there is a Kopitiam and a Banquet food court, snack kiosks and restaurants. On Levels 1 and 2, you'll find coffee bars, cafés and restaurants, a number of which face the waterfront so you can eat in air-conditioned comfort or enjoy the view outside. On Level 3, there is a Marché Restaurant and Food Republic, an excellent food court with comfortable seating.

Toilets: Although some of the toilets do feature separate rooms with nappy changing stations and a sink (which means dad can take his turn!), these are intermittent so this might prove frustrating when it's busy at the weekends. The toilets that do have facilities can be found at: Level B2 / Level 1: Lobby A / Level 1: Lobby H / Level 1: North Court / Level 2: Lobby A (next to Toys "R" Us) / Level 2: Lobby H/ Level 3: Lobby H / Level 3 (next to the entrance to Food Republic).

Location: 1 Harbourfront Walk, Singapore 098585
Tel: 6377 6860 / 6377 6870
Web: www.vivocity.com.sg

CHILDMINDING

A number of venues offer short-term childminding services that are ideal for those occasions when you need to shop without being distracted. The suggestions below are all established centres that offer guided play programmes (where appropriate).

Kizroo and Mamaroo

Kizroo and Mamaroo provides babysitting services within its centre in a room specially designed for this purpose. It also offers an extensive range of prenatal and postnatal classes as well as home visits and a Well Baby Clinic.

Opening hours: 9.00 a.m. to 9.00 p.m. most days. Evenings are also possible but do arrange at least 2 days in advance.
Age group: Preferably babies, but up to 3 years
Price guide: Rates start from $19 per hour.

Location: #05-18 Tanglin Shopping Centre, 19 Tanglin Road, Singapore 247909
Tel: 6736 1636
Email: ellen.tan@birthandbeyond.com.sg
Web: www.kizroo.com

Note: Babysitting services, at a discounted rate of $5 per hour, are available to parents who attend in-house postnatal exercise classes or talks.

The Garage@Ventures

As well as regular programmes for children between the ages of 15 months and 4 years, this centre of early learning offers a flexible, drop-off child minding service.
Opening hours: 9.30 a.m. to 9.30 p.m. (Mondays to Saturdays). For day minding, give at least 1 day's advance notice. For night minding, 3 days' advance reservation is required.
Activities: Soft fall play area, a life-size mini car and various language, art and craft activities
Age group: 15 months to 7 years old
Price guide: $10 per hour, per child

Location: #05-08/09, 545 Orchard Road, Far East Shopping Centre, Singapore 238882
Tel: 6238 0227
Email: askgarage@yahoo.com

Note: You can hold birthday parties here. Look out too for its holiday workshops.

JWT Kids Gym

This popular children's physical fitness centre holds Kids' Night Out events at least one Friday of every month as well as on special occasions, e.g. Valentine's Day.
Operating hours: Ring to check for child-minding events. (These are usually held in the evening — pyjamas party.)
Activities: 4 hours of arts and crafts, movies and a pizza party. The evening is linked to a particular theme.
Age group: 4 to 9 years
Price guide: There is a membership fee of $60. This is also a birthday party venue — 2 hours for 20 or 25 children.

Locations: #02-12, 81 Clemenceau Avenue, UE Square, Singapore 239917 / 46 East Coast Road, Eastgate Building, Singapore 428766
Tel: 6333 8511 (Clemenceau Ave) / 6348 1889 (East Coast Road)
Email: funnergym@jwtkids-singapore.com
Web: www.jwtkids-singapore.com

The Kidz Station

Programmes: Walk-in play sessions and playgroup programmes
Activities: Music and movement, drama and role playing, language skills, creativity, free and structured play, etc.
Opening hours: The play group programme operates from 9.30 a.m. to 12.30 p.m. on weekdays. There is an extension class from 12.30 p.m. to 1.30 p.m. where required.
Age group: 18 months to 4 years (playgroup programme)
Price guide: It is $50 for 3 hours of walk-in childminding and $60 for 4 hours.

> Location: #02-37 Forum – The Shopping Mall, 583 Orchard Road, Singapore 238884
> Tel: 6735 6340

Note: As this venue is popular, walk-in sessions should be booked in advance.

CULINARY DELIGHTS

Eating, like shopping, is said to be a national pastime. Therefore, it's imperative to make reference to some of the restaurants that cater for children. In this section, I've highlighted venues that clearly accommodate children. However, I would add that most families in Singapore don't hesitate to take their children to most restaurants, other than some of the very expensive, more intimate dining venues. I've not listed the popular fast food outlets but they're everywhere in Singapore and easy to find wherever you are. I've included a few less obvious venues that you may wish to consider when introducing your child to something different as well as places that take into account Singapore's rich culinary inheritance. Try something new with your child by presenting it as a treat rather than something out of the ordinary...you never know, you all may be pleasantly surprised!

Hawker Centres

The cheapest and easiest way to try the food of other cultures is to visit your local hawker centre and sample what is on offer. This can be difficult for parents with young babies and toddlers in strollers as most centres are hot, sometimes only accessible by a steep stairway and often crowded at peak mealtimes. With the aging population in Singapore, most hawker centres now have a ramp located at one end or the other. For those with older children, don't ignore what constitutes the daily, main eating venue for many Singaporeans. In every hawker centre, there is plenty to choose from and some of the must try dishes include Hainanese chicken rice (a good basic dish for children), *roti prata* (a crisp-crusty pancake served with curry gravy), *mee goreng* (fried noodles), fried Hokkien mee (fried seafood noodles), satay, *roti John* (bread dipped in an egg mixture containing onions and minced mutton and then fried) *nasi briyani* (rice cooked with spices), *wanton* noodles (dumpling noodles), *char kway teow* (stir-fried rice noodles) and ice *kachang* (a mound of ice shavings coated in syrup with jelly and beans beneath).

In terms of drinks, there is *bandung, chendol* (green jelly in coconut milk with brown sugar), fresh soya bean milk and the perennial iced milo. Milo Dinosaur is a super-rich Milo drink with Milo powder heaped on the top as well! Children will enjoy watching the process of making *teh tarik* (Malay for 'pulling tea'), an experience you're only likely to see in this part of the world. Tea (a combination of black tea, condensed milk and fresh milk) is poured repeatedly from one cup to another until it cools slightly. This process of cooling tea has turned into an art form, with liquid being poured from a couple of feet into a cup/container without a drop being spilt!

Restaurants

Brewerkz Singapore

Comments: This restaurant is very popular for its burgers and beer and gets particularly busy at weekends. You can sit in air-conditioned comfort or outside by the river. Families are welcome here and sports fans will enjoy watching the action on the big screen. Service is fast and efficient. The buffalo wings here are to die for. If you're feeling adventurous, try the suicide sauce!

Opening hours: 12.00 p.m. to 12.00 a.m. (Mondays to Thursdays and public holidays) / 12.00 p.m. to 1.00 a.m. (Fridays, Saturdays and eve of public holidays) / 11.00 a.m. to 12.00 p.m. (Sundays)

Location: #01-05/06 Riverside Point, 30 Merchant Road, Singapore 058282 / Brewerkz Indoor Stadium
2 Stadium Walk #01-06/07/K1
Singapore Indoor Stadium
Singapore 397691
Tel: 6438 7438 (Riverside Point) / 6345 9905 (Indoor Stadium)
Email: info@brewerkz.com.sg
Web: www.brewerkz.com

Fish & Co.

Comments: Children's dishes include fish and chips and sweet and sour nuggets. It costs $5 to $6 per dish and includes a soft drink and French fries or rice. It starts at $15 for an adult meal.

Opening hours: Hours vary between branches but are generally open from 11.30 a.m. to 10.00 p.m. daily.

Locations and Telephone numbers: The Glass House at Park Mall (Tel: 6334 1858) / #03-34 Jurong Point S.C. (Tel: 6898 4248) / / #B1-48/49 Suntec City Mall (Tel: 6835 0180) / #B1-02 Tampines

Mall (Tel: 6787 3437) / The Heeren Shops (Tel: 67327255) / Paragon (Premium) (Tel: 67330938) / AMK Hub, #02-03 (Tel: 6555 6298) / Novena Square #03-11/12 (Tel: 6255 7001) / Waterfall@Parkway, #01-18B, Parkway Parade (Tel: 6348 9727) / Great World City #01-22 (6235 1993) / Changi Airport Terminal 2, Level 3, Viewing Mall South #036-058 (Tel: 6546 4485) / West Coast Plaza #B1-06/07 (Tel: 6777 8861) / Ion Orchard, #B3-20 (Tel: 6509 8259) / IMM Building #01-111 (Tel: 6565 9268) / Sembawang Shopping Centre #01-02 (Tel: 6481 9192)

Note: The fish and chips is recommended for adults too!

Globetrotters

Comments: This fun travel-themed restaurant is very popular. There is a play area for younger children and puzzles, colouring activities and table toys for older children. Children have their own milkshake bar and they can make their own pizza and watch it cook. Babies even have their own menu! Birthday party packages and cooking workshops for children are also available. Weekday set lunches start from $11.90

Opening hours: 8.00 a.m. to 10.00 p.m. (weekdays) / 9.00 a.m. to 10.00 p.m. (weekends and public holidays)

Location: United Square, #02-02
101 Thomson Road,
Singapore 307591
Tel: 6356 5285
Email: enquiry@globetrotters.com.sg
Web: www.globetrotters.com.sg

Hard Rock Café

Comments: There are two outlets — one at Resorts World Sentosa (RWS) and the other at Cuscaden Road. Service is good, fast, friendly and efficient. If your children like rock and roll (in fact, pop music in general), this is an ideal venue, although the music can get a bit loud. A children's set meal (you can choose from a cheeseburger, quesadillas, a hot dog or pasta) is $7.50+, including a soft drink. Younger kids are plied with balloons, crayons and paper and they have their own menu. Adult portions are large. Expect a cheerful, up-beat environment.

Features: Rock memorabilia and a souvenir shop

Opening hours: Cuscaden Road: 11.00 a.m. to 2.00 a.m. (Sundays to Thursdays), 11.00 a.m. to 3.00 a.m. (Fridays, Saturdays and eve of public holidays) / Resorts World Sentosa: 11.00 a.m. to midnight (Mondays to Thursdays), 11.00 a.m. to 1.00 a.m. (Fridays to Saturdays)

Location: #05-01 HPL House, 50 Cuscaden Road, Singapore 249724 / Resorts World Sentosa #01-209 The Forum, 8 Sentosa Gateway
Tel: 6235 5232 (Cuscaden) / 6795 7455 (RWS)

Email: sgp-anpasst@hardrock.com.sg
Web: www.hardrock.com.sg

Note: This is a party venue.

IKEA

Why not combine shopping and eating within the same venue?! IKEA is very popular with families and is often used as a place for browsing as much as for buying. Children whose height is between 0.98 to 1.2 metres can play in the ball room or watch videos at the entrance to the store while you shop. Do note that neither of these areas is supervised. Child-sized shopping carts are also available.

Comments: The restaurant is counter service, with special trays for children, and the cooked meals are reasonably priced. In both IKEA branches, baby food can be bought in the restaurant and you can warm milk and food up in the microwaves provided. There is an area for young children with children's chairs and tables and videos for entertainment. Special children's dishes are available at $2.90 each. There are baby-changing rooms (including a nursing room) opposite the restaurant.

Opening hours: 10.00 a.m. to 10.00 p.m. daily

Locations: 317 Alexandra Road, Singapore 159965 / 60 Tampines North Drive 2, Singapore 528764
Tel: 6786 6868
Web: www.ikea.com.sg

Note:

• If you have toddlers/preschoolers, avoid IKEA on public holidays and weekend afternoons as it can get extremely busy.
• There is a shuttle bus from Tampines MRT, Bedok, Pasir Ris and Sengkang MRT Station to IKEA Tampines. There is a shuttle bus from Bukit Batok, Choa Chu Kang, Boon Lay and Jurong East MRT to IKEA Alexandra.
• Anchorpoint shopping centre can be reached from IKEA by walking across the covered bridge.

Jerry's BBQ & Grill

Comments: Jerry's specialises in American food and it is known for its steaks. It features a terrace bar and terrace dining area that are both air-conditioned. It also does a delivery service that includes a children's menu. Prices range from $10.95 for deep-fried mushrooms to $49.95 for an order of Australian Wagyu Steak.

- There is a set lunch from $15.95 to $19.95 Monday to Friday, and there is a set dinner from $21.95 to $25.95 from Monday to Thursday at the Jalan Kayu outlet.
- For every adult main course above $19 ordered on Sunday, a kid's meal valued at $6.95 will be served for free.
- A gift voucher for $15 will be given for every $100 spent from Monday to Thursday.

- A gift voucher for $10 will be given for every $100 spent from Friday to Sunday.
- For both outlets: You can print a voucher from their website for a 15 per cent discount from Monday to Thursday, and a 10 per cent discount from Friday to Sunday.

Opening hours: Food is served from noon to 11.00 p.m. daily.

Locations: 277 Jalan Kayu, Singapore 799505 / 92 Club Street, Singapore 069460
Tel: 6484 0151(Jalan Kayu) / 6323 4550 (Club Street)
Web: http://jerrybbq.com

Note:
• Do check their website for promotions at their different outlets.
• Takeaway, deliver and catering services are also available. More information is available on their webiste.

Noodle Place Restaurant

This Hong Kong-style restaurant is famous for its delicious noodles. From an extensive menu, you can choose from 18 types of noodles and 21 kinds of *congee* (rice porridge) as well as an assortment of Chinese desserts.

Comments: Service is quick and efficient and the quality of the noodles makes it well worth visiting. This is a very popular restaurant so you can expect to queue during peak dining hours. High chairs are available.

Opening hours: 10.00 a.m. to 10.00 p.m. daily

Location: #01-53/56 Centrepoint, 176 Orchard Road, Singapore 238843
Tel: 6733 3171
Web: www.pfs.com.sg/restaurants/noodle_place/

Parkway Thai Restaurant

Comments: Just opposite the Noodle Palace Restaurant is another excellent family dining venue. The wonderful selection includes traditional favourites such as pineapple rice, honey chicken, tom yam soup, *kuehs* and green curry chicken. It's a good way to try out Thai food!

Opening hours: 11.00 a.m. to 10.00 p.m. daily

Locations: #01/59-62 Centrepoint Shopping Centre, 176 Orchard Road, Singapore 238843
Tel: 6737 8080 (Centrepoint)

Pasta Fresca Da Salvatore

This Italian restaurant chain is popular with many families because of its laid-back style and generally warm attitude towards children.

Comments: There is a kid's set menu and also children's à la carte dishes. A kid's set costs $17.20 and comes with a choice of pizza, pasta or fish fingers, garlic bread, dessert and a drink.

Opening hours: Hours vary slightly between branches but, in general, they are open 11.30 a.m. to 3.00 p.m. and then 5.30 p.m. to 11.00 p.m. On

Sundays and public holidays, most branches are open from 11.30 a.m. to 11.00 p.m.

Locations: 30 Boat Quay / #01-02/03 Royalville, Block 833, Bukit Timah Road / #01-01/02, 77 Upper East Coast Road, Siglap / 43 Cuppage Terrace / 306 Tanjong Katong Road

Tel: 6778 0401 (Head Office) / 6532 6283 (Boat Quay) / 6469 4920 (Bukit Timah) / 6241 5560 (Siglap) / 6836 0739 (Cuppage Terrace) / 6346 6575 (Tanjong Katong)

Email: enquiries@pastafresca.com

Web: www.pastafresca.com

Peach Garden

Comments: This restaurant is popular with local families and an excellent venue for dim sum. It is run in the traditional manner with 'aunties' pushing around trolleys laden with goodies such as siew mai (pork dumplings), fried carrot cake and char siew pau (barbecued pork buns). High chairs are available. While there are no nappy changing facilities, the toilets are clean and spacious.

Opening hours: 11.30 a.m. to 2.30 p.m. and 6.30 p.m. to 10.00 p.m. (weekdays) / 11.00 a.m. to 2.30 p.m. and 6.30 p.m. to 10.00 p.m. (weekends and public holidays)

Locations: #01-88 Thomson Plaza, 301 Upper Thomson Road, Singapore 574408/01-06 Novena Gardens, 273 Thomson Road, Singapore 307644 / Peach Garden @ 33, 65 Chulia Street, #33-01, OCBC Centre, Singapore 049513 / 1 Orchid Club Road #02-35 Social Club House Singapore 769162 / 1 Orchid Club Road #01-04 Driving Range Singapore 769162 / 401 Havelock Road Hotel Miramar Level 3 Singapore 169631

Tel: 6451 3233 (Thomson Plaza) / 6254 3383 (Novena Gardens) / 65357833 (OCBC Centre) / 67593833 (Orchid Country Club) / 67363833 (Hotel Miramar)

Web: www.peachgarden.com.sg

Note: If you are visiting the Thomson Plaza outlet, why not combine with a trip to MacRitchie Reservoir or nearby Joan Road to see the many garden centres?

Prego

Comments: This restaurant is very popular with mums and dads too! Located within the Raffles City shopping complex, it can get very busy at weekends. High chairs, crayons and colouring paper are all available. Children have their own menu which features pizza, lasagne, chicken and fish nuggets and home-made ice cream.

Opening hours: 11.30 a.m. to 2.30 p.m. (lunch) / 6.30 p.m. to 10.30 p.m. (dinner) (There is also a pizzeria which is open 11.30 a.m. to 12.30 p.m. daily, and a deli which is open from 11.30 a.m. to 10.30 p.m. daily.

Location: Level 1, Swissotel the Stamford, 80 Bras Basah Road, Singapore 189560
Tel: 6431 6156
Web: www.swissotel.com (look under Restaurants and Bars Details)
Email: dining.singapore@fairmont.com

Sakae Sushi

Comments: Lots of children enjoy watching the sushi going round on the conveyor belt. What's even better is that they can order from a selection of special sets that include a Yakult drink, priced from $8 to $9. Your child also has an option of getting his meal served in a colourful aeroplane or a fire engine! (for children aged 12 years and below). The interactive ordering is also likely to appeal to children. You can preview menu items and place orders by clicking the mouse attached to a computer screen at your table. Just keep an eye on those hungry children!

Opening hours: 11.30 a.m. to 10.00 p.m. (Call to confirm)

Locations: Over 30 branches islandwide
Tel: 6438 6281 (OUB Centre) / 3349276 (Suntec City Tower 3 – near Carrefour) / 6334 9015 (Parco Bugis Junction)
They also have a delivery menu – check their website. Their delivery hotline number is 6388 8383
Web: www.sakaesushi.com.sg

Sanur Indonesian Restaurant

Comments: Indonesian fare can be a bit spicy for young palates but this popular chain of restaurants offers a selection of dishes that are all reasonably priced. The atmosphere within Sanur is casual and families are welcome. Children may enjoy *tahu telor* (fried bean curd and eggs topped with sweet sauce), *nasi kuning* (rice with saffron and coconut milk) and the fresh lime juice. High chairs are usually available.

Opening hours: 11.45 a.m. to 2.30 p.m. and 6.00 p.m. to 9.30 p.m. (Causeway Point)

Locations: Centrepoint #04-17/18 / Ngee Ann City #04-16 / Suntec City B1-10 /#02-47/48
Tel: 6734 2192 (Centrepoint) / 6734 3434 (Ngee Ann City) / 6338 6768 (Suntec City)

Seoul Garden

Here you can cook your food in a pot of boiling stock at your table or concoct your own sundae or ice *kachang*.

Comments: The main attraction here is free eating for children on Sundays. Children may enjoy the brightly coloured interiors or have fun making their desserts.

Opening hours: 11.30 a.m. to 10.30 p.m. (for most branches)

Locations: Islandwide
Tel: 6836 1339 (#05-10/11 Ngee Ann City) / 63391339 (#02-08/09 Marina Square)

Spageddies Italian Kitchen

Spageddies is a popular, casual-dining, full-service restaurant.

Comments: Children's meals cost $6.50+ and include a choice of main dish (e.g., spaghetti, macaroni and cheese or kiddy pizza) and a soft drink. Children are given fun game sheets to complete.

Opening hours: 11.00 a.m. to 9.30 p.m. (last order) (weekdays) / 11.00 a.m. to 10.00 p.m. (last order) (weekends)

Location: Orchard Central 181 Orchard Road #04-01 Singapore 238896
Tel: 67387798
Web: www.spageddies.com.sg

Swensen's

This chain of family restaurants offers an American casual-dining concept.

Comments: There is a special children's menu with the usual fare of French fries, burgers, spaghetti, chicken wings and special feature sundaes. Younger children are also given complimentary crayons and colouring paper.

Opening hours: Generally 10.30 a.m. to 10.30 p.m.

Locations: Islandwide
Tel: 6786 2866
Web: www.swensens.com.sg

Note:
- This is a party venue.
- Swensen's is also a supplier of special occasion ice-cream cakes.
- This chain runs a kids' club (for 4- to 12-year-olds), membership of which entitles you to various discounts and special offers. To apply one must just spend $30 in a single receipt and send in the receipt with the application form.

Tung Lok Seafood

Comments: The Tung Lok group has restaurants throughout Singapore and the region. The restaurants are well known for their delicious Chinese cuisine, which is consistently of a high standard. I've chosen to focus on its seafood outlet, which has an excellent choice of fresh fish and assorted sashimi.

This is a popular family restaurant and high chairs are available. You can combine a trip here with a visit to the adjacent East Coast Park.

Opening hours: 11.30 a.m. to 3.00 p.m., 6.30 p.m. to 11.00 p.m. (weekdays) / 10.00 a.m. to 3.00 p.m., 6.00 p.m. to 11.00 p.m. (weekends and public holidays)

Location: East Coast Recreation Centre, Building B, 1000 East Coast Parkway, Singapore 449876
Tel: 6246 0555
Web: www.tunglok.com

La Braceria Pizza and Grill

The ambience is warm and cozy with the pizza oven adding a nice glow to the place. The decor is generally simple but tasteful. The service is impeccable and the staff are very responsive, always attentive to clearing of plates, providing new plates, refilling of water, etc. The price is very decent and they welcome families with children here. Fabio is the friendly owner ever ready to welcome diners. **Opening hours:** Lunch: 12.30 p.m. to 2.30 p.m. / Dinner: 6.30 p.m. to 10.30 p.m.

Location: 5 Greendale Avenue
Tel: 6465 5918

Bella Pizza

This friendly restaurant absorbs all GST and service charges. It does a lovely set lunch for $18 on weekdays from 11.30 a.m. to 2.30 p.m. and the food is authentic genuine Italian. It is a cozy restaurant that seats 30 indoors and 22 outdoors, and it is very popular with families on weekends, so reservations are highly recommended! You can seem the handsome chef Antonio preparing food in his open kitchen, and he is always available for a little chitchat. **Opening Hours:** 11:30 a.m. to 2:30 p.m., 6.00 p.m. to 11.00 p.m., (Tuesdays to Fridays) / 11:30 a.m. to 11:30 p.m. (Saturday, Sunday and Public Holidays). Closed on Mondays except for public holidays

Location: 30 Robertson Quay,
#01-14 Riverside View,
Singapore 238251
Tel: 6734 0139
Web: www.bellapizza.com.sg/
Email: antoniobellapizza@gmail.com

Brazil Churrasco Sixth Avenue

If your children are meat-lovers, they will adore this restaurant! Waiters come to the table with huge skewer of meat. For a set price, you can order as much as you want. Kids pay less than adults, and the quality of the meat is sublime. There is also a branch on the first floor of Vivocity.

Location: 16 Sixth Avenue,
Singapore 276476
Tel: 6463 1923 (restaurant) /
6467 8175 (office)
Web: www.brazilchurrasco.com
Email: singapore-6thavenue@
brazilchurrasco.com

Old School Delights

This lovely café located in a stretch of eateries along Upper Thomson Road has toys that can be purchased along with your food as well—old-fashioned toys such as paper aeroplanes and tops It is really spacious and it has items such as Little Chicken Nibbles (which kids will love). Everything here is prepared from scratch, from the *mee siam* gravy to the lime juice (genuine limes and not from a syrup mix). The cakes are mouthwateringly addictive and moist, and are as good as the bigger, more established dessert chains cakes. Olivia and Aaron are the brother and sister team that own the store, and they are always ready for a friendly chit-chat. They also do catering and takeaways.

Opening Hours: 12.00 p.m. to 11.00 p.m.

215m Upper Thomson Road
Singapore 574408
Tel: 6458 4518 / 8117 9407 (Olivia)
Email: Info@oldschooldelights.com
(For bulk orders / Events - Olivia@oldschooldelights.com)

Brunches

Some of the hotels have super family brunches on Sundays that cater for everyone. These usually include a children's area with activities to keep the little ones occupied and the sort of food that most adults balk at! These brunches generally cost from $68 to $120 per adult, with a reduced price for children (children aged 3 and below usually eat for free but do check with individual hotels). I've listed some particularly popular venues below. Details will change from time to time and you should ring in advance to book a table.

Four Seasons Hotel

One-Ninety

Children have their own supervised playroom upstairs, with a kid's buffet and lots of games and activities.

Opening hours: 12.00 p.m. to 3.00 p.m..

Tel: 68317250

Jiang-Nan Chun

At weekends, you can also enjoy an amazing choice of dim sum and Cantonese dishes at this restaurant. Soft drinks are included in the price and there is a good selection of fresh fruit juices for children.

Opening hours: 11.30 a.m. to 2.30 p.m. (Saturdays) / 10.30 a.m. to 12.30 p.m. and 1.00 p.m. to 2.30 p.m. (Sundays)

Location: Four Seasons Hotel
190 Orchard Boulevard,
Singapore 248646
Tel: 6831 7220

Fullerton Hotel — The Town Restaurant

Set in a beautiful historic building, this features a huge spread. A children's room is available.

Opening hours: 12.00 p.m. to 3.30 p.m.
Price guide: $118 per adult / $42 for 5 to 12 years / Free for children below 5 years

Location: 1 Fullerton Square
Singapore 049178
Tel: 6877 8128
Web: www.fullertonhotel.com

Grand Copthorne Waterfront — Café Brio's

Café Brio showcases a distinctive range of cuisine of both Western and Asian sensibilities. Currently a Sunday *dim sum* brunch is available. Check their website for more details.

Opening hours: Noon to 3.00 p.m.

Price guide: The Sunday *Dim Sum* Brunch is $48 per adult and $24 per child (5 to 12 years old).

Location: 392 Havelock Road Singapore 169663
Tel: 6233 1100
Email: enquiry@grandcopthorne.com.sg
Web: www.millenniumhotels.com.sg/grandcopthornewaterfront/

Grand Hyatt — mezza9

Also known as the mezzamunch, Sunday bunch at the mezza9 boasts a selection of international cuisine ranging from Thai, Japanese, Chinese and Western.

Opening hours: 11.30 a.m. to 3.00 p.m.

Price guide: Adult: $138++, $288++, $108++ (free flow aof various alcoholic beverages) / Child (13 to 17 years): $108++/ Child (7 to 12 years): $69++ / Free for children below 5 years

Location: 10 Scotts Road, Singapore 228211
Tel: 6732 1234
Web: www.singapore.grand.hyatt.com/hyatt/hotels/

The Ritz-Carlton — The Greenhouse

Currently diners can enjoy a Sunday Vintage Champagne Brunch.

Opening hours: 11.30 a.m. to 3.30 p.m.

Price guide: Adult: $158++ / Child (6 to 12 years): $79++ / Child (3 to 5 years): $39.50

Location: 7 Raffles Avenue, Singapore 039799
Tel: 6337 8888
Web: www.ritzcarlton.com/

The Sentosa Resort & Spa — The Terrace

Head here for a lovely, lazy afternoon and some great food. Children can play chef and take part in activities such as making their own pizza toppings.

Opening hours: Noon to 3.00 p.m.

Price guide: $146++ per person

Location: 2 Bukit Manis Road, Sentosa, Singapore 099891
Tel: 6371 1414
Email: theterrace@thesentosa.com
Web: www.thesentosa.com/en/hotel/beaufort/singapore/sentosa/resortandspa/

Hilton
Checkers Brasserie

There is a dedicated play area for kids here filled with fun entertainment. The champagne brunch includes fresh seafood, succulent meats and foie gras.

Opening hours: Noon to 3.00pm

Price Guide: Adult: $85, $105 (3 glasses of wine), $110 (3 glasses of champagne or free flow of wine), $160 (free flow of champagne) / Child (6 to 12 years) $25

Location: Hilton Singapore Hotel
581 Orchard Road,
Tel: 6730 3390
Web: www1.hilton.com/en_US/hi/hotel/SINHITW-Hilton-Singapore/index.do (see under dining)

For non-hotel buffet venues that are a must, try:

Halia Restaurant

The breakfast brunch here is perfect combined with an early morning stroll around the Botanic Gardens. You can sit indoors or dine alfresco. Do note that no reservations are taken for this Weekend a-la-carté brunch.

Opening hours: 9.00 a.m. to 3.30 p.m. (weekends and public holidays)

Location: Ginger Garden, Singapore Botanic Gardens, 1 Cluny Road, Singapore, 259569
Tel: 6476 6711
Web: www.halia.com.sg/

Paulaner Bräuhaus

This buffet focuses on beer rather than champagne. Nevertheless, it is popular with families because of the relatively low cost and the hearty fare on offer (German specialties). There is a children's corner with activities.

Opening hours: 11.30 a.m. to 2.30 p.m. (Sundays)

Price guide: Adult: $45++ (without alcohol), $55++ (with alcohol) / Child (6 to 11 years): $12++ / Children of 5 years and below are free.

Location: 9 Raffles Boulevard, Time2 @ Millenia Walk, Singapore 039596
Tel: 6883 2572
Web: www.paulaner-brauhaus.com/singapore
Email: singapore@paulaner-brauhaus.com

Sakura

This extensive buffet features a variety of Japanese, Italian, Western and Chinese food. It gets very busy (especially in the evenings), so book beforehand.

Opening hours: Noon to 2.30 p.m./ 6.00 p.m. to 9.30 p.m. daily

Price guide: $21 per adult (lunch) / $25 per adult (dinner) / $11.90 for children below 12 years (lunch or dinner). There is an additional charge of $2 for adults on Friday nights and at weekends and on public holidays.

Locations: Admiralty Park 31 Riverside Road Singapore 739087 / Cairnhill Place 15 Cairnhill Road #02-01 Singapore 229650 / Clementi Woods Park 93A Clementi Road Singapore129781 / Dhoby Ghaut Green 10 Penang Road #01-02 Singapore 238469 / Downtown East 1Pasir Ris Close #02-02 Singapore 519599 / Jurong West Sports and Recreation Centre 20 Jurong West St 93 #02-06/07, Singapore 648965 / Keat Hong Shopping Centre 253 Choa Chu Kang Ave 1, #01-11, Singapore

680253 / Omni-Theatre 21 Jurong Town Hall Road, Singapore 609433 / SAFRA Tampines, 1A Tampines St 92, #01-00, Singapore 528882 / Shaw Plaza – Twin Heights, 360 Balestier Road, #04-01, Singapore 329783 / Yio Chu Kang Stadium 210 Ang Mo Kio Ave 9, #01-28, Singapore 569777

Tel: 6368 8197 (Admiralty) / 6735 8197 (Cairnhill Place) / 6474 8197 (Clementi Woods Park) / 6334 8197 (Dhoby Ghaut Green) / 6755 8197 (Downtown East) / 6899 8197 (Jurong West Sports and Recreation Centre) / 6760 8197 (Keat Hong Shopping Centre) / 6566 8197 (Omni Theatre) / 6784 8197 (SAFRA Tampines) / 6736 8197 (Shaw Plaza) / 6754 8197 (Yio Chu Kang Stadium)

Senso Ristorante & Bar

This is one of my favourites – for the quality of the food, the ambience and the excellent serving staff. My children really like it too. As the food has an Italian emphasis, the pasta is particularly good here. There is a corner set aside for children, with activities at hand.

Opening hours: 11.30 a.m. to 3.30 p.m. (Sundays)

Price guide: $88++ (including free flow of prosecco, fruit juices, coffee and tea)

Location: 21 Club Street, Singapore 069410

Tel: 6224 3534

Web: www.senso.sg/

Email: senso@singet.com.sg

Note: Prices do not include GST and service taxes.

– Chapter 9 –

READING AND RESOURCES

This chapter concentrates on reading as a form of edutainment, a hobby and as part of an enrichment activity.

FAST FACTS

National Library Board (NLB)

This is the coordinating body for all public libraries in Singapore.

Email: ref@nlb.gov.sg

Web: www.nlb.gov.sg

National Book Development Council of Singapore

This site provides useful information about reading events islandwide as well as links to events in specific bookshops.

Web: www.bookcouncil.sg

The Society for Reading and Literacy (Singapore) (SRL)

Through its public education programmes and publications, the SRL seeks to promote reading and literacy within the community. It organises activities for parents and teachers throughout the year, some of which are for the public while others are only for SRL members. For a small annual fee, you can join the SRL and receive a regular newsletter, notification of events and the opportunity to join a storytelling group.

Address: 33 Sembawang Hills Drive

Singapore 575909

Tel: 6455 1218

Email: secretariat@srl.org.sg

Web: www.srl.org.sg

Storytelling Association (Singapore)

This association encourages storytelling in English, Mandarin, Malay, Tamil and sign language. It runs courses and hosts events and you can even book a professional storyteller for a special occasion, such as a birthday party. Check out its website to find out about storytelling sessions for children.

Address: 126 Hillcrest Road, Singapore 288995

Email: secretary@storytellingsingapore.com

Web: www.storytellingsingapore.com

LIBRARIES

In addition to the school library, your child can enjoy access to the extensive public library network in Singapore. The National Library Board (NLB) operates one national library, three regional, 19 public libraries and one community children's libraries. For an extensive guide to using Singapore's libraries, just go to www.pl.sg and click on Library Guide.

The NLB has three language-library services. The Chinese library service is located at Tampines Regional Library (the Chinese collection at Woodlands Regional Library is also one of the most comprehensive collections available), the Malay library service operates at Bedok Community Library and the Indian library service can be found at Ang Mo Kio's Community Library. These libraries also feature English-language, non-fiction books relating to the respective cultures.

Specialist Services for Children

As well as library orientation tours for new members, the NLB offers various services specifically for children, including the following:

Children's Resource Centre

There are Children's Resource Centres (CRCs) at Jurong and Woodlands Regional Libraries. Here you can find selected reference collections on children's literature and reading as well as storytelling resources such as large-size picture books, story cards and props. The resources can be viewed upon request at the Children's Advisory Counter.

Kids ASK!

This is a Children's Advisory Service that provides sources of information and advice on recommended reading for children, resources for school projects, resources for parents and resources for child development. There are Children's Advisory

Counters at Jurong Regional Library, Tampines Regional Library and Woodlands Regional Library. Services are available daily from 1.00 p.m. to 9.00 p.m.

Kids Discover!

Kids Discover! offers experiential learning in science, based on three themes: water, Earth and sound. For example, children can touch, feel and hear the effects of a volcanic eruption or the movement of the solar system. Programmes are conducted once a month and are available at Marine Parade Public Library. The interactive exhibits are especially suited to children between the ages of 6 and 12 years.

Reading Programme

Stories, Songs & Craft

The children's librarians at all libraries conduct regular storytelling sessions and other related activities for children up to the age of 12 years. This includes storytelling for children between 4 and 8 years, special programmes for children aged 1 to 3 years (Fun With Tots) and stories with craft activities. These sessions vary from library to library so you will need to ring to find out more. Alternatively, look under the Latest Events section on the NLB webpage for each respective library. Also look out for special holiday programmes.

Verging All Teens

a library for teens!

Jurong Regional Library has a library service that's been created by teens and is dedicated to teens called Verging All Teens (V.A.T.). Features include various genres of comics and graphic novels (mainly in English and Chinese) as well as works by mainstream writers. In addition, there is a special music CD reference collection that features works of popular artistes/producers of MTV Pop Music. There are various programmes and activities linked to V.A.T., including a book club, performances and lifestyle-based activities. There are also sections for teens in the Bishan Public Library, Toa Payoh Public Library and Woodlands Regional Library as well.

Volunteering (Community Involvement Programme)

Upper Primary School children (aged 10 to 12 years) can volunteer to assist at their public library through their school's Community Involvement Programme (C.I.P). Activities include buddy reading to younger children, writing book reviews about books in the library's children's collection, constructing book displays and shelving library materials. Email ask@nlb.gov.sg for further information or to register your interest.

Regional and Community Libraries with Children's Facilities

Apart from the library@esplanade, all of Singapore's community libraries have children's sections. They also conduct workshops, activities and storytelling sessions from time to time as well as provide special programmes during the school holidays. Some of these activities may be conducted in Mandarin and many are free or charge a nominal fee.

Particularly outstanding children's sections are housed in Jurong Regional Library, Woodlands Regional Library and Marine Parade Community Library. At Jurong, there is a large area for teenagers (4th level) as well as a Children's Advisory and Information Desk and a Children's Resource Centre (basement). An extensive collection of children's books and an activity area is also located in the basement. At Woodlands, the focal point is the reading park (Level 5) which has a life-size tree with overhanging branches. There are also listening posts that play nursery rhymes and instrumental songs. The children's section is further enhanced by its five distinctive areas that make it very user friendly. A Children's Resource Centre and a Children's Advisory and Information Counter are also available for educators and researchers. At Marine Parade, the children's section (2nd level) has a prototype museum-library concept that is based on the theme of Kids Discover! You will also find a preschoolers' corner and an activity room in the children's section.

Locations and Opening Hours

Nearly all libraries are open from 10.00 a.m. to 9.00 p.m. daily. They close at 5.00 p.m. on the eve of Christmas, New Year and Chinese New Year and are closed on public holidays. The exceptions to this are libraries situated in shopping centres (indicated with an asterisk), which open at 11.00 a.m.

Contact: For further information, ring the central library line at 6332 3255.

Community Libraries

- Ang Mo Kio
  4300 Ang Mo Kio Avenue 6, Singapore 569842
- Bedok
  21 Bedok North Street 1, Singapore 469659
- Bishan
  #01-01, 5 Bishan Place, Singapore 579841
- Bukit Batok*
  West Mall, #03-01, 1 Bukit Batok Central Link, Singapore 658713
- Bukit Merah
  3779 Jalan Bukit Merah, Singapore 159462

- Bukit Panjang*
  Bukit Panjang Plaza, #04-16/17,
  1 Jelebu Road,
  Singapore 677743
- Central Lending Library
  National Library Board, 100 Victoria Street, Singapore 188064 (Basement)
- Cheng San*
  NTUC Hougang Mall, #03-11,
  90 Hougang Avenue 10,
  Singapore 538766
- Choa Chu Kang*
  #03-01 Lot 1 Shoppers' Mall,
  21 Choa Chu Kang Avenue 4,
  Singapore 689812
- Geylang East
  50 Geylang East Avenue 1,
  Singapore 389777
- Jurong West
  #01-03, 60 Jurong West Central 3,
  Singapore 648346
- Marine Parade
  Marine Parade Community Building,
  #01-02, 278 Marine Parade Road,
  Singapore 449282
- Pasir Ris*
  White Sands, #04-01/06,
  1 Pasir Ris Central Street 3,
  Singapore 518457
- Queenstown
  53 Margaret Drive, Singapore 149297
- Sembawang*
  Sun Plaza, #03-01, 30 Sembawang Drive, Singapore 757713
- Sengkang*
  Compass Point, #04-26 / 27,
  1 Sengkang Square, Singapore 545078
- Serangoon*
  NEX, 23 Serangoon Central, #04-82/83, Singapore 556083
- Toa Payoh
  6 Toa Payoh Central,
  Singapore 319191
- Yishun *
  Northpoint Shopping Centre,
  930 Yishun Ave 2, #04-01,
  Singapore 769098

Regional Libraries:

- Jurong
  21 Jurong East Central 1,
  Singapore 609732
- Tampines
  31 Tampines Avenue 7,
  Singapore 529620
- Woodlands
  Woodlands Civic Centre, #01-03, 900 South Woodlands Drive,
  Singapore 730900

National Library:

- Lee Kong Chian Reference Library
  National Library Board,
  #14-01, 100 Victoria Street,
  Singapore 188064

Price guide: Free for Singaporeans. A one-time non-refundable registration fee of $10.50 for Permanent Residents. $10.50 registration fee and a subsequent 6-monthly fee of $10.50 for non-citizens. Children below 7 get a free membership card while adults are encouraged to use their NRIC card. Children (Singaporeans and PRs) aged 7 to 14 years can pay $1 and those aged 15 years and above can pay $5 to get their own membership card.

Otherwise children aged 7 to 14 years can use their MOE School Smart Card and those above 15 years can use their NRIC/NTUC Link Card/ SAF11B/MOE School Smart Card/ Singapore Mint Personalised ez-link card/Personal CashCard to borrow from the library.

There is also a Premium Service that allows you to borrow four additional items (on top of the standard four loans). You can borrow books, magazines, CD-ROMS, videos, VCDs and DVDs. The annual subscription fee is $21.

The Premium Plus membership enables you to borrow 16 library items. The annual membership fee is $42.

Tel: 6332 3255 (NLB)
Email: helpdesk@nlb.gov.sg
Web: www.lib.gov.sg

Community Children's Libraries (CCLs)

The only Community Children's Library left in Singapore is located in Clementi.

Opening times: 4.00 p.m. to 9.00 p.m. (weekdays) / 1.00 p.m. to 6.00 p.m. (weekends). Closed on public holidays.

Price guide: Membership of the Clementi Community Children's Library is linked to the NLB membership policy and procedure (*see* pp. 284 – 285).

Location: Clementi Community Children's Library
Block 332, Clementi Avenue 5.
Tel: 6776 1887 / 6332 3255
Email: helpdesk@nlb.gov.sg
Web: www.nlb.gov.sg (look under Visit Us/Community Children's Libraries)

Annual Book Sale

Look out for the NLB's annual book sale. The sale is usually held over a weekend at the beginning of the year at a venue such as Singapore Expo. Books are sold for $1 each!

BOOKSHOPS

Why is Reading Important for Children?

Reading is a fundamental survival requirement in society today because one needs to function as an informed and productive citizen in this world. Reading is essential for making informed decisions, developing one's potential in one's chosen career and, above all, for personal fulfilment as an individual. Reading not only initiates children to language acquisition in an unintimidating way, it also provides a basis for discussion of their feelings, personal experiences and thoughts. Research has shown that children who read do better at school and beyond.

Reading starts with initiating the element of pleasure in the activity of reading. Selection of simple and enjoyable books that the child will enjoy is important. Educators and caregivers must understand that it is not necessary to stick too strictly to books for the recommended age level. Some children may want more advanced reading while some simply do not outgrow their level and that is fine. Pushing a child to a more advanced level of reading in an effort to improve reading skills will only counteract the positive intentions. Children read best when they are allowed to read at their own pace and time. At the end of the day, positive attitudes regarding books will cultivate a life-long love of reading.

—Zubaidah Mohsen, Senior Librarian, Children's Services

Bookaburra Books

Bookaburra's focus is solely on children and most of the materials available are of Australian or English origin. Bookaburra has an excellent selection of books as well as audio tapes, videos, clothes for dressing up and other learning resources.

It holds popular weekly storytelling sessions for children aged 2 and above, which often include crafts and songs. These sessions need to be booked in advance at a cost of $5 per child. The sessions are currently held at 4.00 p.m. every Wednesday and Friday. Do ring to check times.

Opening hours: 9.30 a.m. to 8.00 p.m. daily

Location: #02-05 Forum – The Shopping Mall, 583 Orchard Road, Singapore 238884
Tel: 6235 9232
Email: bookaburra@pacific.net.sg
Web: www.bookaburra.com

The Little Bookshop

This quaint bookshop holds storytelling sessions once every week on Saturdays and Sundays at 1.00 p.m. and 4.00 p.m., along with props and souvenirs for the kids. They also serve gourmet coffees, teas and gelato. To seal the deal, there are comfy armchairs for parents to sit in and savour a cuppa while waiting for their children. Sessions have to be booked at $5 a session. Art classes are also held here on weekends. A trial lesson costs $25.

Location: 687A East Coast Road
Tel: 6677 3083

Email: inquiry@thelittlebookshop.com.sg
Web: http://thelittlebookshop.com.sg/

Books Kinokuniya

These stores offer an international selection of books and the main store in particular has an excellent selection of children's literature. Look out for the audio cassette selection too.

Facilities:

- A Privilege Card is available for $21 per year. This entitles you to 10 per cent off the original retail price for purchases at Books Kinokuniya stores islandwide
- The main store hosts talks and special events and has a cafeteria.
- There is also an online book ordering service, Bookweb Singapore.

Opening hours:
Takashimaya: 10.00 a.m. to 9.30 p.m. Sundays to Fridays / 10.00 a.m. to 10.00 p.m. Saturdays / **Liang Court:** 10.30 a.m. to 9.30 p.m. daily / **Parco Bugis Junction:** 10.30 a.m. to 10.00 p.m. daily

Locations: Takashimaya Shopping Centre, #03-10/15, 391 Orchard Road (main store) / Liang Court, #03-50, 177C River Valley Road / Parco Bugis Junction, #03-09/12, 200 Victoria Street
Tel: 6737 5021 (Takashimaya) / 6337 1300 (Liang Court) / 6339 1790 (Parco)
Web: www.kinokuniya.com.sg

Borders

This American bookstore has a prime location in the centre of Orchard Road and in Parkway Parade shopping centre in the heart of Marine Parade. It has a comprehensive book collection for children and usually showcases Caldecott Medal winners and seasonal books. You can browse in comfort here, although the store does tend to get very crowded at weekends. It has awesome children's sections where both children and parents can sit and browse children's books comfortably.

Facilities: Special events and workshops are conducted fairly regularly for both adults and children. Join its mailing list to keep updated. There is also a cafeteria and restaurant on site.

Opening hours: 9.00 a.m. to 11.00 p.m. (Sunday to Thursdays) /9.00 a.m. to 12.00 a.m. (Fridays and Saturdays, Wheelock Place) / 10.00 a.m. to 10.00 p.m. (Parkway Parade)

Location: Wheelock Place: #01-00 Wheelock Place, 501 Orchard Road, Singapore 238880 / Parkway Parade: 80 Marine Parade Road Unit #B-155 Parkway Parade Singapore 449269
Tel: 6235 7146 (Wheelock Place) / 6345 9796 (Parkway Parade)
Web: www.borders.com.sg/

Harris

Facilities: Harris stocks a good

selection of quality children's books, especially paperbacks for children above 9 years. The range isn't extensive but it is carefully selected. As Harris is now owned by Popular bookstore, Popular cardholders can get a 10 per cent discount at all Harris bookshops in Singapore and Malaysia as well.

Opening hours: Great World City: 10.30 a.m. to 9.30 p.m (Mondays to Thurdays & Sundays), 10.30 a.m. to 10 p.m. (Fridays & Saturdays) / 313@ Somerset: 10.30 a.m. to 9.30 p.m. (Mondays, Thurdays & Sundays), 10.30 a.m. to 10 p.m.(Fridays & Saturdays) / Jurong Point 10.30 a.m. to 10 p.m.(Mondays to Sundays and public holidays)

Tel: 6732 3679 (Great World City), / 6514 6755 (313@Somerset) / 6514 6398 (Jurong Point)
Locations: Great World City #02-22/24, 1 Kim Seng Promenade / 313@Somerset 313 Orchard Road #04-25/28 / Jurong Point Shopping Centre 63 Jurong West Central 3 #B1-92/93
Email: gwccustsvs@harrisbook.com (Great World City) / 313custsvs@harrisbook.com (313@Somerset) / jpcustsvs@harrisbook.com (Jurong Point)
Web: www.harrisbook.com/

MPH

Facilities: The Raffles City branch stocks children's books (towards the back of the store) as well as a small section of stationery.

Opening hours: 10.30 a.m. to 10.00 p.m. daily (Raffles City)

Locations: Raffles City Shopping Centre #B1-21, 252 North Bridge Road / #01-01/02, 63 Robinson Road / #02-25/28 Novena Square, 238 Thomson Road / MPH Parco Millenia, #P3-08/09/10 PARCO,9 Raffles Boulevard, Millenia Walk
Tel: 6336 4232 (Raffles City) / 6222 6423 (Robinson Road) / 6353 7133 (Novena Square) / 6338 5845 (Parco Millenia)
Web: www.mph.com.sg

Page One

Facilities: At its flagship store in VivoCity, you'll find English and Chinese books (including children's books), periodicals, stationery, music and movie DVDs and even a small selection of Asian artefacts and handicrafts.

Opening hours: 10.00 a.m. to 10.00 p.m. daily (VivoCity)

Locations: #02-41/42 VivoCity, 1 HarbourFront Walk
Tel: 6272 0822 (VivoCity)
Web: www.pageonegroup.com/1/singapore.html

Popular

This budget bookshop offers a wide range of books in English and Mandarin as well as stationery. The latter in particular is well priced, with children's sketchpads and pens a fraction of the price you'd expect to pay in Europe and generally cheaper than other Singaporean outlets. Other value-for-money children's items are the Ladybird series of books and Puffin books. This bookstore is also popular for its range of assessment books and revision guides. Their range of DVDs and CDs is very wide, particularly the educational section, and they have also expanded into e-learning. This is the place to buy cheap stationery for your children. You can subscribe to their e-newsletter on their website.

Facilities: You can become a member to receive discounts and notification of special events and promotions. Membership is $12 for one year or $30 for 3 years. As Popular also owns Harris bookshops, {prologue} bookstore at ION Orchard and the upper-crust UrbanWrite stationery stores at Orchard Central and Tampines 1, you can get discounts at these shops as well. Popular also has an online ordering facility.

Opening hours: 11.00 a.m. to 9.00 p.m. (Mondays to Thursdays and Sundays). Call individual branches to confirm.

Locations: Islandwide
Tel: 6462 9555 (Hotline)
Web: www.popular.com.sg

Select Books

This specialist bookshop should be the first stop for those seeking literature on Southeast Asia. It also has a good online listing of children's fiction and non-fiction.

Opening hours: 9.30 a.m. to 6.30 p.m. (Mondays to Saturdays) / 10.00 a.m. to 4.00 p.m. (Sundays and public holidays)

Location: Tanglin Shopping Centre, #03-15, 19 Tanglin Road, Singapore 247909
Tel: 6732 1515
Email: info@selectbooks.com.sg
Web: www.selectbooks.com.sg

Times bookstores

Facilities: As well as books, Times stocks some children's magazines and comics (including perennial favourites like *Beano*). A Times Privilege Card is available for $10 and lasts for 1 year / $15 for 2 years. Card holders enjoy a 10 percent discount on books and a 5 percent discount off select magazines.

Times (its business name is now Marshall Cavendish) actively encourages young local writers. Look out for its annual writing competition Budding Writers Projects, which is targeted at young writers below the age of 16 years.

Opening hours: 10.30 a.m. to 9.30 p.m. daily (Centrepoint)

Locations: #04-08/16 Centrepoint, 176 Orchard Road / #02-17 Jelita Cold Storage, 293 Holland Road / #04-18 Plaza Singapura, 68 Orchard Road / #03-142/143/144/145 6 Raffles Boulevard (Marina Square)

/ #03-26 Tampines 1, 10 Tampines Central 1, #03-07 / Suntec City Mall, 3 Temasek Boulevard, #01-21 / Paragon, 290 Orchard Road, #04-41
Tel: 6734 9022 (Centrepoint) / 6466 5702 (Jelita) / 6837 0552 (Plaza Singapura) / 6334 4650 (Marina Square) / 67827017 (Tampines 1) / Suntec City (63389730) / Paragon (68366182) / Customer Enquiry: 6734 9022
Email: timesbookstores@tpl.com.sg
Web: www.timesbookstores.com.sg/ (for online orders)

Others

Apart from the online ordering facilities mentioned above, you can also visit AcmaMall books section. Established in 2000, this online portal for shopping features children's fiction and non-fiction at discount prices as well as seasonal selections and promotions. The site is easy to use and you can pay online, via credit card over the phone, by cheque or by eNETS debit. You'll need to register to use this site but membership is free.

Tel: 6492 3510
Web: www.acmamall.com/books.html

Asiapac Books

This online portal specialises in books about Asia and is fairly affordable.

Web: www.asiapacbooks.com

CHILDREN'S BOOKS ABOUT SINGAPORE

The following recommendations focus on books relating to Singapore. These books are specifically targeted at children and can be read alone or with the assistance of an adult.
*(*indicates the favourites of my children and those I've enjoyed reading with them)*

Attack of the Swordfish and Other Singapore Tales

by Charlotte Lim (National Heritage Board, 2005)
Content: This book features 6 illustrated tales based on Singaporean legends or traditions and is targeted at early Primary schoolchildren. A glossary and suggestions for activities or visits accompanies each story.
Price guide: $15

*BP Guide to Nature series

For those interested in nature, a number of guides are available on Bukit Timah Nature Reserve, the amphibians and reptiles of Singapore, the threatened animals of Singapore and common spiders in Singapore, among others. In fact, there are 39 titles in the series. These guides are best suited to older children (14 years up) who have good reading skills but they can be a useful addition

to any family nature trip. My son particularly enjoys the one on butterflies of Singapore.
Publisher: Singapore Science Centre
Price guide: Below $10

Come to the Party! Malay Muslim Festivals
by Susan Lauridsen (Educational Publishing House, 2001)
Content: This book is about two friends and how they take part in the celebrations of the Malay Muslim community. With some activities to try out, this book will interest those between 8 and 10 years especially.
Price guide: Below $5.50
Note: Guides to Chinese and Indian Hindu festivals are also available in this series.

Welcome to Singapore (Welcome to My Country)
by James and Junia Baker, Yong Jui Lin (Gareth Stevens Publishing, December 2002)
Content: Part of a series, this factual book covers various topics relating to Singapore including its geography, history, government, economy, literature, festivals and food. Children between the ages of 9 to 12 will find this book informative.
Price guide: Below $30

Discover Nature
By Grace Leng and Tat Small (Small Books, 2005)
Content: This colourful book examines nature in the home and around the island. Containing lots of facts, drawings and suggestions for activities, it will appeal to children under 13 years.
Price guide: Below $15

**Explore Singapore*
by Tat Small (2008)
Content: This activity guidebook for children aged 7 to 14 years focuses on places to visit in Singapore. Fun, colourful and interestingly illustrated, it includes facts and questions to be answered.
Price guide: Below $15

**Feasts and Festivals of Singapore*
by Vivian Lee, illustrations by Patrick Yee (Educational Publishing House, 1999)
Content: This attractively illustrated book describes and explains the major festivals in Singapore. An informative book, it can be read by all ages but may be most suitable for children aged 8 to 13.
Price guide: Below $10

**Let's Celebrate!: Singapore Festivals*
by Tat Small (Small Books, 1999)
Content: This book is full of information and activities about the eight main public holiday festivals in Singapore. It is a colourful, fun

book that entertains and keeps children occupied.
Price guide: Below $15

A Picture History of Singapore
by Amy Chua (Federal, 1997)
Content: This pictorial history book is a good introduction to Singapore's history for any child aged 9 and above.
Price guide: Below $10

Samsui Girl
by Ho Lee-Ling (Candid Creation, 2006)
Content: This delightful book is an excellent way to explore a unique part of Singapore's social history. It is easy to read and the story it tells will interest most children aged 9 and above.
Price guide: Below $10

Sasha in Singapore
by Shamini Flint (Sunbear, 2005/2006)
Content: To date there are five books in this series about a young girl visiting various places in Singapore. Suitable for readers between 2 and 6 years (the words are simple and there are plenty of illustrations). These colourful books are fun and educational. There is also a Sasha in Asia series, which includes Sasha Visits Singapore.
Price guide: Below $15 or below $70 for all 5 books.

**Sights and Scenes of Singapore*
By Vivian Lee, illustrations by Patrick Yee (Educational Publishing House, 1999)
Content: This book gives an overview of the historical sights and places of interest in Singapore. Again, the illustrations in the book bring the information to life.
Price guide: Below $10 (gift pack below $20). This is also available for download for free from the International Children's Library at http://en.childrenslibrary.org/.
Note: Both of Yee's books are sold as a combined gift pack with six postcards, six bookmarks and a notebook.

Singapore Children's Favourite Stories
By Di Taylor (Periplus Editions, 2003)
Content: These 11 stories originate from the age-old myths and legends of distant times. They are illustrated with imaginative pastel drawings and will appeal to children aged 5 to 10.
Price guide: About $30

Stamford Raffles: Founder of Modern Singapore
Translated by Geraldine Goh and illustrated by Zhou Yimin (Asiapac Books)
Content: A lovely comic book on Sir Stamford Raffles, the founder of modern Singapore
Price Guide: About $8.50

SINGAPOREAN WEBSITES FOR CHILDREN

A Family Friendly Internet

To address concerns about the Internet's use and young people's exposure to it, the Media Development Authority (MDA) (mda.gov.sg) has worked with the three Internet Service Providers in Singapore to provide optional family access networks. These networks filter out undesirable sites and provide an optional network solution to parents who are unfamiliar with the use of stand-alone filtering software, such as CyberPatrol and NetNanny. Singnet offers the Family Online service, Pacific Internet has its Cyber Guard Family Access Plans and Starhub Internet provides the Infinity Family Access Plan.

okto.sg

Look here for TV updates, games, contests and freebies. Preschoolers can also join Club Magic (click on the banner on top of the okto website or go to http://www1.mediacorp.sg/clubmagic/). M.A.G.I.C is an acronym for Music, Adventure, Games, Ideas and Creativity with fun activities such as Song of the Day', 'Letter of the Day' and 'Adventure Quest'. It also has advice for parents under the "Positively Yours" section and parents can email their questions.

www.nlb.com.sg

Sign up for the digital library to have free access to childrens' books (and adults' books and resources as well!) There are read-a-long ebooks that children can read on their own online with an audio recording and epuzzles that children can do after they have read the books. There is even language learning where parents can select from French, Spanish, Chinese, Italian and Russian ebooks! This service is free for Singaporeans and PRs (one just needs to register online). However, foreigners can only access this service from any public library.

Web: www.singaporeforkids.com

This one-stop portal has everything that busy parents in Singapore need to know for their children, from events that are happening to getting a birthday organised. There are even online games for kids (click under Kids' Corner® Fun Stuff® Playtime.) Check out the list of Speech and Drama, Arts and Crafts and Music Programmes offered here. One can even send epostcards of Singapore!

SPECIAL EVENTS

Asian Children's Festival

see also Special Events under Annual Events, p. 240

This festival is headlined as 'celebrating childhood' but it is also an opportunity for children to celebrate. Despite the name of the festival, it does not preclude non-Asian children as it offers them the opportunity to be exposed to and learn about the various cultures of Singaporean nationals.

The event is supported by two major conferences, the Asian Congress of Storytellers and the Asian Children's Writers and Illustrators Conference. These conferences are of interest not only to writers and storytellers but also to teachers, librarians and parents. The major organiser of this event is the National Library Board of Singapore.

An annual festival incepted in the year 2000, Asian Children's Festival aspires to connect people and institutions related to children in the literary, publishing, library, book information and creative world of arts. This is done in the hope that the professionals will network, share, learn, research, write and develop Asian contents, products and services that meet children's educational, creative and emotional needs. This range of services and products would subtly promote a deeper understanding of the Asian way of life.

—ACF Organisers

Location: Programmes are held at all public libraries in Singapore. Log on to the Asian Children's Festival website for more details and programme schedules. There is also storytelling at public libraries in Singapore in line with the Asian Children's Festival theme.

Web: www.asianchildrenfest.com

Features of the festival may vary from year to year but those of particular interest to children include:

KidsASIA!

This family event showcases the rich culture, heritage, traditions and flavours of Asian communities. Cultural performances, traditional games, Asian storytelling sessions and activity zones ensure that this is a fun-filled event. Log on to the Asian Children's Festival website for programme schedules.

Budding Writers' Awards

This annual project is organised by Marshall Cavendish Education for children below the age of 16. It features works by children for children. It seeks to help children develop an appreciation of the printed book by exposing them to the publishing process. The winners of the competition ultimately get to see their work appear in print. The competition usually opens in April.

Web: www.marshallcavendish.com/education/buddingwriters/

Facebook: Budding Writers Project

– Chapter 10 –

LONG SCHOOL BREAK ACTIVITIES

The long break begins...some parents dread it, some actually enjoy it. Others are fortunate to have enough help so that life continues without worry or disruption. For local schools, the long break starts in November, with school resuming in January. A further mid-year break follows in May for about four weeks. International schools start their summer holidays in June or so, with school resuming in August or September. Either way, the perennial problem (or challenge depending on your outlook) is how to occupy the kids, preferably in a meaningful and mutually beneficial way. For the expatriate community, a popular choice is an exodus to home countries overseas. But for those remaining in Singapore (us included), a more proactive plan is required and fortunately, particularly over the last few years, the choices have expanded, both in depth and quality. My days spent searching the classifieds and trawling the great, hot outdoors in search of kiddy fulfilment are rapidly disappearing...

Any initial research into school holiday activities should start with your child's school and your local Community Centre/Club which runs some excellent programmes. Newspapers and periodicals such as *The Finder* are also worth looking at. On an ad hoc basis, some of the shopping malls offer excellent entertainment and activities specially scheduled for the school holidays. Other possibilities include sightseeing venues such as the Zoo and Bird Park, both of which often take into account holiday demand and conduct worthwhile extra activities. For example, the Zoo Explorer Camp (which runs during the end-of-year break) spans five days and four nights of animal interaction and relevant activities. Many of the private and specialist schools run programmes but I have only listed these when they do not promote an academic or school-oriented curriculum. For parents interested in such programmes, look out for advertisements or contact the schools directly.

The following suggestions are primarily applicable to the May to September and/or November to January school breaks. The details of the courses and camps listed may change from year to year but their basic format is unlikely to alter. In each instance, I have given information based upon the most recent courses/camps held.

FAST FACTS

Community Centres

Community Centres are your most convenient and probably cheapest option for holiday programmes. Do note that holiday courses fill up quickly. Look under the Lifeskills and Lifestyle section of the website.

Web: www.pa.gov.sg

Singapore's Museums

A number of the museums hold workshops and programmes for children during the school holidays. More information can be obtained by contacting the National Heritage Board.

Web: www.nhb.gov.sg / Facebook: I Love Museums

Hotline: 1800-2255-642

Email: nhb_feedback@nhb.gov.sg

Metropolitan YMCA

Metro-Y holds a wide variety of holiday camps during May/June and November/December. Activities include swimming, soccer, adventure camp and crafts.

Tel: 6839 8355

Email: programmes@mymca.org.sg

Web: www.mymca.org.sg / Facebook: MYMCA

(see also the Y Children's Holiday Camp at the YMCA, p. 313)

Singapore American Community Action Council (SACAC)

SACAC runs a range of programmes from June to August that are open to everyone. The emphasis is on sports.

Tel: 6363 6454

Location: 40 Woodlands St 41 H216 Singapore 738547

Email: sacacs@sas.edu.sg

Web: www.sacac.com

Schools

A number of international schools and local schools offer quality holiday programmes, which are open to everyone. The Canadian International School (www.cis.edu.sg) offers an extensive programme during June and July for all ages. Go to the website and click under "Summer School". Some of the courses can earn high school credits, whereas others are for fun and skill development, e.g. drama, pottery and art.

Location: Tanjong Katong Campus (Early Childhood to Grade 9)
371 Tanjong Katong Road Singapore 437128 /
Toh Tuck Campus (Early Childhood to Grade 3) 5 Toh Tuck Road
Singapore 596679
Tel: 6345 1573 (Tanjong Katong) / 6467 1732 (Toh Tuck)

The United World College of South East Asia (www.uwcsea.edu.sg) usually offers a multi-sports camp during the breaks (including the half-term), which will expose your child to rock climbing, kayaking and Brazilian capoeira, etc.

Location: Dover Campus 1207 Dover Road
Singapore 139654 / Tampines Campus
1 Tampines Street 73 Singapore 528704
Tel: 6775 5344 (Dover) / 6305 5344 (Tampines)
Email: info@uwcsea.edu.sg (Dover) /
uwcseaeast@uwcsea.edu.sg (Tampines)

Also worth contacting are ISS International School (Tel: 6235 5844 / www.iss.edu.sg) , Singapore American School (Tel: 6363 3403 / www.sas.edu.sg), Overseas Family School (Tel: 6738 0211) / www.ofs.edu.sg) and the Chinese International School (Tel: 6254 0200 / www.cnis.edu.sg).

For younger children, try your local kindergarten, White Lodge Kindergarten (Tel: 6468 8846 / www.white-lodge.org), The Playground Preschool (Tel: 6469 5045/ www.theplayground.edu.sg/) or EtonHouse International Preschool (Tel: 6746 3333, www.etonhouse.com.sg),

Singapore Zoological Gardens

Contact direct for holiday activities and camps. Look out too for its special Sleep with the Beasts initiative, which allows you and your family to spend a night under the stars in the company of the animals!

Tel: 6269 3411
Email: info@zoo.com.sg
Web: www.zoo.com.sg

Jurong BirdPark

Contact direct for holiday activities.

Tel: 6265 0022

Email: info@birdpark.com.sg

Web: www.birdpark.com.sg

Libraries

Most of Singapore's libraries run programmes for children throughout the year and are well worth contacting to find out about activities during the school holidays. Try both the Public Libraries and the regional libraries. Admission is usually free or parents pay a nominal fee for all programmes which can take the form of storytelling, craft workshops, video screenings, shows and sing-a-long sessions, to name but a few.

For more details about libraries, see Reading and Resources, pp. 280 – 294.

Email: helpdesk@nlb.gov.sg

Web: www.nlb.gov.sg

ART

Artistic activities are generally popular with children as they not only provide instant results but also foster creativity and self-fulfilment. As a mother of a very active child, I would be a more troubled soul without the close proximity of a box of crayons and a drawing pad! That said, there are artistic programmes available that are attractive to most children and the prospect of having their work displayed within the home or available for public viewing is attractive to just about every boy or girl.

Creative Hands

This retailer of artists' materials is a useful contact when looking for children's holiday workshops/ courses as it has tie-ups with freelance artists and craftspeople. Previous workshops have lasted five days and covered topics such as printmaking and papier-mâché.

Age group: 6 to 12 years

Location: Ngee Ann City,
#04-20B/C, 391 Orchard Road,
Singapore 238872
Tel: 6738 1690 (crafts)

Gradsign Art School

This popular art school runs short-term courses during the June and December holidays.

Courses: Puppet making, clay making, paper sculpture and cartooning, etc.
Age group: 4 years and above

Location: Block 151, #03-254,
Bukit Batok Street 11,
Singapore 650151
Tel: 6563 8012

Isadora's Workshop

This peaceful studio conducts arts and craft camps in the privacy of its own garden, during both the local and international school holidays. Activities may include clay sculpture, mask making, T-shirt decorating and basic drawing techniques.
Age group: 6 years and above (3 years and above with an adult in attendance)

Location: 102 Gardenia Road
Singapore 578 873
Tel: 9273 4991
Web: www.isadoraworkshop.com

Note: Regular art and craft classes are available.

Nanyang Academy of Fine Arts (NAFA)

NAFA runs cultural camps (with visits to Little India and Chinatown) and art-based activity camps. These take the form of lectures, hands-on sessions and demonstrations. These one-off camps are usually held in November/December. Look out too for other workshops during the year.
Age group: 5 to 12 years

Location: NAFA Campus 1,
HQ and School of Visual Arts
Building (Level 3), 80 Bencoolen
Street, Singapore 189655
Tel: 6512 4159 (Junior Art) /
6512 4209
Email: Junior_art @nafa.edu.sg
Web: www.nafa.edu.sg

Sculpture Square

> *I painted an ostrich egg. We had to be careful not to break it. The best thing was getting to take it home afterwards but now I have to keep it out of the reach of my baby brother...*
>
> **—Michaela, age 7**

Sculpture Square is a non-profit, independent arts organisation that seeks to promote, develop and stimulate the regional exchange of contemporary 3-D art. It also caters for the interests of children by promoting a 4-day annual arts carnival that is packed with inexpensive workshops and free fringe activities. The carnival is held in late May with a follow-up exhibition in September. Popular workshops include ostrich egg decoration, mask-making, tie-dye, puppet-making and mobile sculptures. Workshops are also conducted in November/December.

Age group: Varies but typically 4 years up

Location: 155 Middle Road, Singapore 188977
Tel: 6333 1055
Email: arts@sculptures.com.sg
Web: www.sculpturesq.com.sg

Note: As well as holiday workshops, Sculpture Square holds talks and conducts meet-the-artist sessions throughout the year.

Singapore Art Museum

The Singapore Art Museum often runs children's programmes in May/June and November. Participants get to experiment with different media and learn various art techniques during a week-long programme. You must register beforehand and places fill up quickly. It is also worth keeping an eye out for special weekend activities that run throughout the year. For example, balloon sculpting, mime, sculpture and face and henna painting have all been conducted during August weekends.

Location: 71 Bras Basah Road, Singapore 189555
Tel: 6332 3222
Email: NHB_SAM@nhb.gov.sg
Web: www.nhb.gov.sg/SAM

Studio Miu

This art studio holds a wide range of craft activities, e.g., candle-making, T-shirt painting, making jewellery using paper beads, mosaic art, creating greeting cards and batik. Programmes run from June through early August and again in November/ December

> *The T-shirt painting was a lot of fun. I think I will try to do this at home. The instructions were easy to follow and I was very pleased with the result!*
>
> **—Aiko, age 9**

Price Guide: Fees start from $42 per session for children's holiday art classes.

Age group: All ages

Location: #04-20V, Ngee Ann City, 391 Orchard Road, Singapore 238872
Tel: 6733 0917
Email: studiomiu_art@pacific.net.sg
Web: www.studiomiu.com.sg

UniqArts and Technologies

As well as offering a wide range of art courses throughout the year, UniqArts also conducts some intensive courses (generally five lessons) during the long school breaks.

Courses: Programmes have included robotic invention, Pokemon Sculpture and Art, Fun 3-D Animation, Drawing and Manga Art.

Age group: 5 years and above

Location: Roxy Square 1,

50 East Coast Road, #02-32
Singapore 428769
Tel: 6344 1670
Email: uniqArts@yahoo.com
Web: www.uniqarts.com.sg

Note: UniqArts also runs an e-Learning site that offers art courses on the Internet. It can be found at www.onlineartclass.com

MUSIC

I started my son with music lessons during a long break. It was an excellent opportunity for him to enjoy a family tradition during a time when the academic demands upon him were minimal. It proved a success because he had the time, space and aptitude to develop an interest in a particular instrument/musical activity. However, not all children want to be musical and the best advice is probably to let them choose rather than make the decision for them. That said, I would recommend school breaks as a time to explore or certainly initiate your child's musical dreams and schemes. Listed below are a number of possibilities that may help you and your child achieve this goal.

Kawai Music School

From time to time, this well established music school offers holiday workshops, as well as regular classes during the local school breaks.

Activities: Dancing, singing, performance, music history and recreational activities

Age group: 5 to 12 years

Contact: The Paragon #05-49/51, 290 Orchard Road, Singapore 238859 / Parkway Parade #03-07/08, 80 Marine Parade Road, Singapore 44926 / Millenia Walk #02-33/36A, 9 Raffles Boulevard, Singapore 039596 (venue may not be at the music school)
Tel: 6732 0031 (Paragon) / 6344 1903 (Parkway) / 6333 9495 (Millenia Walk)
Email: info@robertpiano.com
Web: www.robertpiano.com

Methodist School of Music

This school runs a music camp during the June break that includes dance, movement and day trips to places of relevant interest. It has also held a choir camp during the December holidays that included excursions, vocal training, Solfeggio sight-seeing and music theory and appreciation.

Age group: Usually between 7 and 12 years

Location: #03-20 John Wesley Centre, 496 Upper Bukit Timah Road, Singapore 678099
Tel: 6767 5258
Email: msm@msmusic.edu.sg
Web: www.msmusic.edu.sg

SPEECH AND DRAMA

Popular activities amongst children, speech and drama are useful ways of developing self-confidence and general presentation skills. School breaks present an ideal opportunity to focus on what might otherwise be considered luxury or secondary pastimes. There is a wide variety of courses and workshops available in Singapore and the annual Singapore Arts Festival is the flagship of a nation that is increasingly focusing on its role in the Southeast Asian arts scene.

Act3 International

> I come here for drama lessons as well but I really look forward to the holiday courses because we get to act and dress up all day! On the last day, we usually do a play in front of our families. It's great fun but I am always a bit nervous beforehand.
>
> **—Emily, age 9**

This leading children's theatre company offers June, September and November/December holiday programmes. Workshops concentrate on a particular topic such as *Mother Goose* stories, *Alice in Wonderland* and *West Side Story*. Drama techniques such as improvisation, characterisation and mime are explored (according to the age group), culminating in a stage performance at the end of the workshop. In addition, Act3 International often holds Open Days and theatre performances during the school breaks.

Age group: 3 and above (including teenagers)

Location: ONE-TWO-SIX Cairnhill Arts Centre, 126 Cairnhill Road, Singapore 229707
Tel: 6735 9986
Email: act3@act3international.com.sg
Web: www.act3international.com.sg

Centre Stage School of the Arts

Centre Stage predominantly follows the international schools' timetable and runs holiday programmes accordingly. In these programmes, children become involved in producing a piece of theatre, TV or film or create a variety of other projects. All aspects of production are examined, including set painting and prop preparation.

Location: Block 15 Woking Road Singapore 138694
Tel: 6732 7211
Email: info@centre-stage.com
Web: www.centre-stage.com

Note: Drumming workshops may also be available.

Julia Gabriel Centre for Learning

This popular centre runs a wide range of programmes in English and Mandarin during the June and November breaks.

Activities: Many programmes are theme-related, e.g., birds, pets, puppets, money, Chinese culture and fairy tales. Within these themes, children enjoy arts and crafts, music, drama, writing activities and more. Some of the programmes involve trips to outside places of interest.

Age group: Typically from 6 months to 12 years

Location: #04-00, Forum – The Shopping Mall, 583 Orchard Road, Singapore 238884 / 26 Evans Road #01-08 Singapore 259367
Tel: 6733 4322 (Forum) / 6737 5348 (Evans Road)
Email: enquiries@juliagabriel.com
Web: www.juliagabriel.com

Practice Performing Arts School

Activities: Drama, movement and creative expression are taught in a fun environment. Day trips are also on the agenda. Courses are conducted in English and Mandarin.

Age group: 4 to 12 years

Location: #02-08 Stamford Arts Centre, 155 Waterloo Street, Singapore 187962
Tel: 6337 2525
Email: ppas@practice.org.sg
Web: www.ppas.edu.sg

Young People's Performing Arts Ensemble

The YPPAE holds a Mandarin Performing Arts Camp for children during the May/June holidays and at the year end. The camp consists of theatre games, singing, speech, calligraphy and making props.

Age group: 4 to 12 years

Location: #03-28, Block 261, Waterloo Street, Singapore 180261
Tel: 6336 6776
Web: www.yppae.org
Email: hotline@yppae.org

SPORTS

School breaks are an excellent time to develop sporting interests and introduce new pastimes. There are many excellent, high-quality sporting programmes available that are run by trained professionals and it is advisable to book early once you have made your choice. For further details about individual activities, please see the chapter on Sports (pp. 79 – 127).

Gymnastics

Gymnastics can be an attractive sport for both child and parent. For the child, it offers physical freedom within set challenges while for the parent it presents a definite means of ensuring a child's fitness. The benefits of gymnastics are well established — increased flexibility, greater balance, better coordination and improved strength and agility. Like all sports, when taught well, self-confidence and self-discipline should result.

Above & Beyond Gymmastics and Sport

Activities: Gymnastic skills, trampolining, tumbling safety, jump roping, various ball sports and water activities

Age group: 4 years and above

Locations: Venues islandwide including Bishan Sports Hall, 5 Bishan Street 14, Singapore 579783 / Hollandse Club 22 Camden Park (off Adam Road) Singapore 299814 / Katong CC, 51 Kampong Arang Road Singapore 438178 / Pasir Ris East CC, #01-08, 1 Pasir Ris Drive 4, Singapore 519457 / Singapore Sports School 1 Champions Way, Singapore 737913
Postal address: 54 Genting Lane, Ruby Land Complex, Blk 2, #06-01/E6, Singapore 349562
Tel: 9762 2175
Email: email@abgymsport.com
Web: www.abgymsport.com

JWT Kids Gym

Activities: Gymnastic activities as well as games, art and enjoying a discovery centre

Age group: 4 to 9 years

Locations: United Square #02-12, 81 Clemenceau Avenue, Singapore 239917 / Eastgate Building, 46 East Coast Road, Singapore 428766
Tel: 6333 8511 (Clemenceau Ave) / 6348 1889 (East Coast Road)
Email: funnergym@jwtkids-singapore.com
Web: www.jwtkids-singapore.com

Sporty Joe's

As well as regular gymnastic classes throughout the year, Sporty Joe's also offers Sports and Adventure Camps during the Christmas and June/July school breaks.

Activities: Gymnastics, basketball, track and field events, obstacle courses and activity games

Age group: 4 to 12 years

Location: Turf City, #02-10, 200 Turf Club Road, Singapore 287994
Tel: 6468 1103 / 9749 8137
Email: admin@sportyjoe.com
Web: www.sportyjoe.com

Ice Skating

Kallang Ice World

An ice rink is a good place to spend time during the hot, humid holiday season. Skating is always a popular choice and young children in particular can benefit from learning something new. Kallang Ice Palace runs courses during some of the school breaks.

Age group: All ages

Location: 5 Stadium Walk, Leisure Park Kallang Singapore 397693

Tel: 6348 1123
Email: kallangiceworld@jackinv.com.sg
Web: www.leisurepark.com.sg/ice_skating.html

Rugby

Centaurs Sports

In addition to regular rugby classes and training sessions, Centaurus also conducts holiday camps. They manage and maintain four Mini/Touch rugby pitches and a full-sized floodlit rugby pitch.

Course: As well as rugby, these camps offer volleyball, handball, soccer and other sports for boys and girls.

Age group: 5 to 14 years

Location: Turf City #02-05, 200 Turf Club Road, Singapore 287994
Tel: 6468 9851
Email: vickidaniels@centaursgroup.com
Web: www.centaursgroup.com/

Skiing

Snow City

It's hot and humid, the school holidays are upon you and your children are restless and bored. Okay, so it's freezing in Europe and the winter sports season is in full swing...but you can ski here despite the Singaporean sun. Snow City offers some special winter sports packages that ensure your child's talents on the piste won't go unnoticed.

Location: 21 Jurong Town Hall Road, Singapore 609433
Tel: 6560 2306 (Mondays to Fridays, 9.00 a.m. – 6.00 p.m.) / 6560 4773 (Saturdays and Sundays and Public Holidays)
Email: contact@snowcity.com.sg
Web: www.snowcity.com.sg

Soccer

Soccer/football is big news in Singapore and it will come as no surprise to learn that there are a number of programmes on offer during the school holidays. These programmes offer children the opportunity to pick up basic skills like passing, trapping and ball control. All of the following organisations have offered soccer programmes during the year-end school break (mainly in December) but they are also useful contacts for school holiday programmes in June and July. It is also worth contacting your local S-League Football Club, e.g. Home United, for clinics that may be held during the year-end break.

International Soccer Academy (ISA)

This academy runs camps in November/December, during the half-term breaks and in June.

Age group: Boys and girls of all ages

Postal address: 39 Arab Street, #02-01, Singapore 199738
Tel: 6291 2337 / 9630 7552 (Mr. Ismail)

Email: isasoccer@pacific.net.sg
Web: www.isa.com.sg

JSSL Arsenal

This centre runs weekday soccer camps during the major holiday periods. Contact it direct for further details.

Age group: 3 years and above

Location: Victoria Junior College, Marine Vista, 449035
Tel: 6348 5780 / 9137 4657 (Rina) / Weather Line: 9640 9047
Email: john@jsoccerleague.com / faulkner@gala.com.sg
Web: www.jssl-arsenal.com
Facebook: www.facebook.com/people/Jssl-Arsenal/100001160243321

Little League Soccer

As well as running regular classes and training sessions, Little League Soccer holds holiday programmes.

Age group: 4 to 16 years old

Locations: Various venues including Tanglin Trust School, Portsdown Road, Singapore 139299/
Mailing address: 2 Kim Chuan Drive #08-01 CSI Distribution Centre Singapore 537080
Tel: 6487 5185
Email: info@littleleaguesoccer.com
Web: www.littleleaguesoccer.com

Young Eagles Soccer Camp

This stay-in camp has operated since 1997 under the guidance of Geylang United Football Club. It offers basic soccer skills training in a fun environment for aspiring young footballers. The camp takes place every November/December with professional coaches in attendance. Competitions, games and educational trips all feature in this highly popular holiday camp.

Age group: 7 to 13 years

Location: 5 Bedok North St. 2
2nd Level Sports For Life Centre
Singapore 469645
Tel: 6441 7873
Web: www.gufc.org.sg

Tennis

If your child is interested in learning to play tennis or improve his/her skills, keep a lookout in the newspapers and various periodicals because this is one sport that is widely available and has new openings every year. The following venues are a sure bet for high-quality, established training.

The ClayCourts @ Singapore

The coaches for these camps are professionals who are used to training children. Kids' tennis clinics are held on weekdays throughout the year.

Courses: Tennis in the morning is followed by indoor sports (e.g. golf, archery and rock climbing) in the afternoon.

Age group: 6 years and above

Location: The ClayCourts, 10A

Winchester Road, Alexander Park,
Singapore 117784
Tel: 8112 1447 (Simon Harvie)
Email: summertennis@hotmail.com
Web: www.theclaycourts.com

Savitar

Savitar has a long tradition of providing tennis coaching to both adults and children. It operates after-school programmes for some of Singapore's international schools as well as runs programmes in private clubs and at other venues. All coaches are internationally certified tennis professionals.

Courses: Junior Camps for beginners to tournament standard are available. These consist of both half-day and full-day camps. Students are expected to know the basics of tennis.

Age group: 8 to 16 years

Locations: Various private clubs and schools throughout Singapore
Office Address: Willow Stream Spa Tennis Facility Level 8 Fairmont Hotel 80 Bras Basah Road Singapore 189560
Postal address: Savitar, Bras Basah Post Office, PO Box 302, Singapore 911811
Tel: 6837 3705 / 917 35142
Email: tennis@savitargroup.com
Web: www.savitargroup.com/
Facebook: Savitar Tennis, Singapore

Note: Camps run during the mid-year break, during the international schools' summer break, in December and at other times.

TFL (Total Fitness Leisure)

TFL hosts a regular Junior Tennis programme throughout the year, as well as tennis camps during the long school holidays.

Age group: 5 years and above

Address: TFL Training Consultants, 7 Pine Grove, #03 - 04, Singapore 597592
Tel: 6733 3689 / 9021 6245 (Todd)
Email: Info@tfl-training.com
Web: www.tfl-training.com

Note: TFL also runs swimming camps.

Wakeboarding/ Water-Skiing

Wakeboarding/water-skiing is something that can be initiated over a relatively short period and is a sport that does not require long-term commitment.

Extreme Sports and Marketing

Age group: Although there are skiers aged 3 and above, the beginner's course is only guaranteed for children 7 years and above.

Tel: 6344 8813
Email: cowabung@pacific.net.sg
Web: www.extreme.com.sg

Note:

- Skiers do not have to be able to swim.
- The beginner's course is guaranteed provided you are over the age of 7

and complete it within 2 weeks (i.e., the course can be extended for up to a fortnight until you pass).
• Equipment for children is available.

VARIETY PROGRAMMES

The programmes below are more broad-based in what they offer, so if your child does not have a particular interest in mind and would like to take part in several activities, this section is for you.

Alliance Française de Singapour

The Alliance Française de Singapour was established in 1949 and all its teachers are qualified French speakers.
Activities: French language courses
Age group: 7 to 9 years / 10 to 12 years / 13 to 15 years

Location: 1 Sarkies Road,
Singapore 258130
Tel: 6737 8422
Web: www.alliancefrancaise.org.sg
Email: courses@alliancefrancaise.org.sg

Camp Magic

This well-established annual camp is run by storyteller Katherine McLeod.
Activities: Camps revolve around a theme, e.g. recyling. Storytelling, performance and art are just some of the activities on offer.
Age group: 4 to 10 years
Price Guide: For a half-day camp (for 3 to 4 years old, for 5 days, from 9.00 a.m. to 12.30 p.m., is $385). For a full-day camp (for 3 to 11 years old, for 5 days, from 9.00 a.m. to 3.15 p.m., is $560)

Location: Block 10 Woking Road, just off of Portsdown Road (venue may vary)
Tel: 9008 5484
Email: enquiries@katherinemcleod.com
Web: www.katherinemcleod.com

Camp SAFRA

SAFRA's June and December camps offer physical challenges within a team environment. The camps are open to non-members.
Activities: Previous activities have included hiking at Bukit Timah Hill, going to an indoor air weapons range, rock climbing, bowling, traditional games and kids' boxercise. Team building, sporting activities, educational visits and group performances are all key components of a SAFRA camp.
Age group: 7 to 12 years

Location: Various
Tel: 6377 9835
Email: hq@safra.sg
Web: safra.sg

Note: SAFRA also conducts camps for younger children.

Children's Technology Workshop

Founded in Canada in 1997, this education centre teaches children technological concepts through hands-on activities.

Activities: icamp (operates throughout the year and as a short course during the main school breaks). Projects are based on themed adventures involving engineering and robotics, video game creation, animation and graphic design.

Age group: 7 to 14 years

Location: 583 Orchard Road, #02-K1 Forum The Shopping Mall, Singapore 238884
Tel: 6887 4547
Email: enquire@ctworkshop.com.sg
Web: www.ctworkshop.com.sg
Facebook: www.facebook.com/pages/Childrens-Technology-Workshop-Singapore/142576464251

IT Leisure and Education

This IT training company stationed at the Omni-Theatre at Singapore Science Centre conducts multimedia and robotics workshops. There is a wide range of robotics workshops and there are robotic kits for kindergarten children as well.

Age Group: 5 to adult

Location: 21 Jurong Town Hall Road, Singapore 609433
Tel: 6222 4081
Email: enquiries@itleisure.com
Web: www.itleisure.com

CRCE - Summer Youth Employment Program

Only children of American Association members who attend local international schools can participate in this programme.

Activities: A minimum of 4 weeks' paid employment in positions in industries such as retail, catering, fast food, hospitality and corporate

Age group: 14 to 18 years

Locations: Islandwide
Tel: 6738 0371
Email: yep@aasingapore.com
Web: www.aasingapore.com (look under Career Resource Centre ® Youth Internship Programs)

Crestar Learning Centre – Kinderplay

something for preschoolers!

Some of Crestar's branches conduct a Kinderplay holiday programme during the year-end break.

Activities: Language activities and games, KinderMusic and art and craft.

Age group: 18 months to 4 years

Locations: Islandwide
Tel: Head Office: 6342 5600
Web: www.crestar.com.sg

Note: Crestar runs holiday programmes (usually commencing late November) for children aged 4 to

12. These include instrumental music, ballet, art, Chinese and speech and drama programmes. Contact your nearest outlet for further details or visit Crestar's website.

Gymboree

something for preschoolers!

If you have preschool children, you can check what's on at Gymboree during the long school break.

Activities: Music and movement, sports, use of equipment, arts and crafts, games and make believe and more

Age group: 2 to 4 years

Location: Tanglin Mall #03-17/18, 163 Tanglin Road, Singapore 247933 / Harbourfront Centre 1 Maritime Square #03-09/10 Harbourfront Centre Singapore 099253

Tel: 6735 5290 (Tanglin Mall) / 6271 1545 (HarbourFront Centre)

Email: gymboree@singnet.com.sg (Tanglin Mall) / harbourfront@gymboree.com.sg (HarbourFront Centre)

Web: www.gymboree.com.sg

Learning Horizon

Learning Horizon runs 1-week themed holiday camps in June and December. These feature science, geography, drama, nature and sports. Expect also related activities (e.g., games, quizzes and storytelling) and outings to places of interest.

Age group: 4 to 12 years

Location: The Grassroots Club, 190 Ang Mo Kio Ave 8 #03-02 Singapore 568046

Tel: 6552 4142

Email: grassroots@learninghorizon.com.sg

Web: www.learninghorizon.com.sg

Lifeskills & Lifestyle @ People's Association

Singapore's neighbourhood Community Centres run a wide variety of programmes during the long breaks under the remit of PA Kiddies within the Lifeskills and Lifestyle programme. These courses offer value for money and are run by professionals. Previous workshops have included Christmas cooking and card-making, dough craft, ribbon art and science activities.

Activities: Creative arts, sciences and personal development

Age group: Nursery and above

Locations: Selected Community Centres

Contact: Visit your nearest Community Centre/Club to register or request more information.

Web: www.pa.gov.sg (look under Courses® Lifeskills & Lifestyle Courses® PA Kiddies)

Outward Bound Singapore

OBS runs holiday programmes, particularly during the year-end break. Check out the Open Enrolment page on its website. Courses aim to equip students with effective communication, teamwork and leadership skills in an adventurous environment.

Courses: Children and Family Programmes (8 years and above), Pre-Teen Camps (10 years and above) and Youth Programmes (older children)

Age group: 10 years and above

Tel: 6545 9008
Email: PA_Outward_Bound@pa.gov.sg
Web: www.obs.pa.gov.sg
Facebook: Outward Bound Singapore

SPARKc@Marine Parade

see Adventure Singapura!, p. 64 – 65

Spartacus

Spartacus has successfully run camps during the school holidays since 2002. Check out its website for its latest schedule.

Activities: Camps vary in length and content but are generally multi-interest with a focus on sport. Camps are usually held in Singapore and do not involve overnight stays.

Age group: 5 to 12 years

Location: Contact for details
Tel: 6467 6210 or 9840 1974
Email: andrewguest@spartacuscamps.com

Note: Spartacus also organises parties.

Straits Times School Holiday Programme

The Straits Times runs a school holiday programme during both the mid-year break and at Christmas. The programme aims to give teenagers living in Singapore the opportunity to learn about an activity that is outside their regular school curriculum. It is open to all teenagers and placements are highly sought after, with thousands registering for about 30 places per course. Details are published in *The Straits Times* nearer the time of the school holidays (usually under the listings for Events in the *Life* section).

Activities: Music journalism, photography, rock climbing, kayaking, wakeboarding, abseiling, acting, scuba diving, snorkeling and sailing are among the available courses. Some lucky participants have even interviewed musical celebrities.

Age group: 13 to 19 years

Tel: 6319 6319 (main line)
Web: www.straitstimes.com (nearer the time of the event)

SuperCamp

SuperCamp has its roots in the United States where it has been run by the Learning Forum Company since 1982. SuperCamp places emphasis on teaching students how to learn and is considered to be a leading academic and life skills programme. SuperCamp first came to Singapore in 1990, with Julia Gabriel Centre for Learning coordinating programmes every December.

Activities: Life skills courses include effective communication, building relationships, listening skills and problem solving. The study skills curriculum includes memory, Quantum reading, Quantum writing and mind mapping.

Age group: Senior Team (13 to 17 years), Leadership Team (15 to 17 years), Junior Forum (9 to 12 years), Graduate Coaching Program (9 to 17 years), Get Smart (Junior Holiday with Success Program) (6 to 9 years)

Office Address: 31 Ubi Road 1 #03-01 Aztech Building Lobby A Singapore 408694
Tel: 6590 9803 / 9863 0033 (Sheryn)
Email: enquiries@qln.com.sg
Web: www.supercamp.sg

Tumble Tots

something for preschoolers!

As well as regular classes, Tumble Tots also offers activities for very young children during the long school break.

Activities: Conversational, physical and creative play and playing with letters and numbers

Age group: 2 to 3½ years

Location: Tampines No. 495 Tampines Ave 5 #02-27/28 Tampines Sports Hall Singapore 529649 / Jurong East Blk 134 Jurong East St 13 #04-309E Singapore 600134 / Choa Chu Kang 1 Choa Chu Kang St 53 #02-10 CCK Sports Complex Singapore 689236
Tel: 6784 0241 (Tampines) / 6897 0413 (Jurong East) / 6760 6306 (Choa Chu Kang)
Email: enquiry@tumbletotscck.com
Web: www.tumbletots.com.sg

Note:

- Discounted rates are available to members.
- Transport may be available.

Very Special Arts Singapore

This non-profit charity runs an arts camp in November during the school break. It is open to children both with and without disabilities.

Activities: The main elements include dance, music, art and physical activities.

Age group: 7 to 11 years (June) / 12 upwards (November)

Location: Various venues are used (e.g., Temasek Polytechnic)
Postal address: 133 Bedok North Avenue 3 #01-138 Singapore 460133
Tel: 6448 6275
Email: general@vsa.org.sg / theo@vsa.org.sg
Web: www.vsa.org.sg

Note: Non-disabled volunteers are always needed.

Y Children's Holiday Camp

The YMCA offers a multi-faceted programme during the year-end break (usually late November/early December). This ranges from 1-day to 3-day activity-specific camps. Other activities and camps may be available during the June holidays.

Activities: LEGO, art, cooking, crafts, creative maths, robot design, sport, drama and adventure, etc.
Age group: 4 years and above

Location: YMCA, 1 Orchard Road, Level 2, Singapore 238824 (and other venues)
Tel: 6586 2222
Email: eductr@ymca.org.sg
Web: www.ymca.edu.sg (look under Announcement)

Note: Camps for the physically and intellectually challenged may also be available.

HOLIDAY CAMPS AWAY

The day eventually comes for every child to welcome the opportunity to escape the confines of the home environment and explore the world without parental presence. Holiday camps can help prepare for this because of the emphasis they place on team spirit, self-confidence and leadership skills. Holiday camps may also appeal because of the fun and opportunities they offer. However, the choice must rest with your child because, regardless of age, some will be reluctant to leave home and should not be coerced into a situation they might find intimidating.

Most of the camps listed here have been running for a number of years. They are considered good quality, established ventures that may appeal to the older child (i.e., 8 years and above). Any camp serious in its intentions should welcome parental enquiries and make a clear commitment to safety and supervision.

Camp Castaway

This holiday camp has been running since 1983 and children from international schools in Kuala Lumpur, Singapore and Jakarta have all attended. The camp is located on Pulau Besar, which offers an idyllic setting with white, sandy beaches, colourful coral reefs and dense tropical rainforest.
Activities: Programmes typically feature water sports (such as surfing, snorkelling and water-skiing), competitions, crafts, hiking, talent shows and storytelling by the campfire at the end of the day. More adventurous and challenging packages may also be available.
Age group: 9 to 14 years

Location: Pulau Besar (near Mersing in Malaysia)
Organisers: Jim and Junia Baker
Castaway Recreational Program
3 Jalan Anak Bukit, #15-02
Singapore 588998
Tel: 6468 7615
Email: junia@pacific.net.sg
Facebook: Camp Castaway, Pulau Besar

Edu Outdoor Activities (EOA)

EOA's camps and tours promise an eco experience. They are particularly attractive to outdoors enthusiasts, with the prime objectives being spending time outdoors and gaining an appreciation of nature. As participants are led through the wilderness by experienced wardens, they learn to recognise birds, mammals, plants and trees as well as acquire outdoor skills such as campcraft, first aid, orienteering, jungle survival and conservation. Holiday camp sites are located in Johor, Bintan and on the Riau Islands. You will need to organise or join a group to experience these camps.

In Singapore, you can also join a half-day eco tour (children will need an adult to accompany them) to Sungei Buloh Wetland Reserve, Pulau Ubin, Labrador Nature Reserve or the Kranji farms in the company of an experienced guide (other destinations are available).

Activities: Nature educational walks and camps, adventure activities and adventure sports

Age group: Varies according to the camp (most are not recommended for children aged 3 and below)

Postal address: 37A Lowland Road, Singapore 547440
Tel: 6487 2950
Email: info@edu-sg.org
Web: www.edu-sg.org

Note: EDU also runs camps at venues regionwide throughout the year.

LooLa Adventure Resort

LooLa runs weekly camps for seven weeks during the international schools' summer break. Students from Singapore's international and local schools go to the resort, which has accommodation consisting of bungalows set on stilts in the sea.

Activities: Kayaking, climbing, cycling, orienteering and team games

Age group: 8 to 14 years

Location: Bintan, Indonesia
Organisers: Open since August 1999, with holiday camps operative since summer 2001, LooLa is developed and owned by two teachers.
Tel: 6764 6496
Email: info@loola.net
Web: www.loola.net

Rider's Lodge

Rider's Lodge provides a wonderful introduction to horse riding, both in terms of facilities offered and by virtue of its location. Accommodation is in a beautiful country-style manor house and lessons are given by internationally qualified instructors. Camps are available throughout the year with more options during the long school holidays. Budding riders and those seeking to improve their equestrian techniques will enjoy this opportunity.

Activities: The Beginner Riders Camp (3-days/2-nights and 2-days/1-

night)) features riding lessons, horse feeding and care, saddling, mounting and grooming. The Young Riders Camp (3-days/2-nights) features mounted riding lessons, dressage and equitation, horse grooming and other social activities.

Age group: 8 years and above

Location: Rider's Lodge at The Legends Golf and Country Resort, Lot 1302 Kebun Sedenak, 81000 Kulai, Johor, Malaysia
Tel: 607 652 5330
Email: riders@riderslodge.com.my
Web: www.riderslodge.com.my

Note: Special rates are available for parents who wish to accompany their children.

SPECIAL EVENTS AND VENUES

Listed below are venues worth checking out during the school breaks as well as some special events that take place during these periods. For more information about these and other events, refer to the chapter on Annual Events (pp. 233 – 245).

Asian Children's Festival

When? November

D'Marquee at Downtown East

Look up this venue for shows, particularly for young children. Typically, the shows will feature plenty of music, colourful costumes and lots of interaction. Character shows have included Hello Kitty, Barney, Sesame Street and the Russian Lilliputian Circus.

When? All year round, but especially in December and June

Location: Downtown East, 1 Pasir Ris Close, Singapore 519599
Tel: 6589 1688
Web: www.downtowneast.com.sg

National Day

When? August

Omni-Theatre

Films are shown here throughout the year, but typically the most recent animated IMAX children's movie is shown during the school breaks, e.g. Bugs! You can tie this in with a visit to the latest exhibition at the Singapore Science Centre.

When? All year round

Location: Singapore Science Centre, 15 Science Centre Road, Singapore 609081
Tel: 6425 2500 (Science Centre). Tickets are also usually sold through SISTIC (www.sistic.com.sg)
Web: www.omni-theatre.com.sg

The Singapore Arts Festival/Kidsfest

When? May/June

For more information, *see* Music and Movement, pp. 173 – 174

Singapore Dragon Boat Festival

When? June

Singapore Expo Hall

Although this venue hosts a variety of events throughout the year, it often holds shows and entertainment for children during the school breaks. Whether it's Bob the Builder, Hi-5, a Children's Day Carnival or a massive book sale, there is bound to be something to interest your child.

When? All year round, but especially December, March (see Disney on Ice in The Performing Arts, p. 171 – 172) and June

Location: #01-01, 1 Expo Drive, Singapore 486150
Tel: 6580 8308
Web: www.singapore-expo.com.sg

Singapore River Regatta

When? November/December

SHOPPING CENTRE ACTIVITIES

With shopping being a national pastime, it is perhaps inevitable that Singapore's shopping centres accommodate the needs of its younger customers by providing entertainment when school is out. Such events should not be readily dismissed because the quality and variety of children's entertainment is generally exceptional. Many activities pull in large audiences and participation can be both passive and interactive. Below are just a few of the places that conduct special kids' activities. These can vary from movie-making workshops (Forum) to professionally staged Christmas shows (Raffles City) and an animal mini zoo at Great World City.

Centrepoint

Previous activities: Play area, Santa Express Train and character shows

Location: 176 Orchard Road, Singapore 238843
Tel: 6737 9000
Web: www.centrepoint.com.sg

Compass Point

Previous activities: Snowflake workshops, Santa Meet and Greet, Christmas shows and competitions

Location: 1 Sengkang Square, Singapore 545078
Tel: 6881 2707
Web: www.compasspoint.com.sg

Forum — The Shopping Mall

Previous activities: Circus workshops, Mr Men and Little Miss shows, face painting, Christmas shows and science workshops.

Location: 583 Orchard Road, Singapore 238884
Tel: 6732 2479

IMM Building

Previous activities: Children's shows

(e.g. Clifford the Dog, SpongeBob SquarePants, Hi-5 celebrations), Christmas train rides, cartoon character photo sessions and tea parties

Location: 2 Jurong East Street 21, Singapore 609601
Tel: 6536 1188
Web: www.imm.sg

Marina Square

Previous activities: Little Robots shows, art sessions, acrobatic performances and children's book sales

Location: 6 Raffles Boulevard, Singapore 039594
Tel: 6339 8787
Web: www.marinasquare.com.sg

Novena Square

Previous activities: Acrobatic shows, ice skating displays, Lion Dance performances and various activities for children

Location: 238 Thomson Road, Singapore 307683
Tel: 6358 0700
Web: www.novenasquare.com

Plaza Singapura

Previous activities: Pokemon shows, Blue's Holiday Clues shows and meet-and-greet cartoon characters, Singapore F1 Exhibition

Location: 68 Orchard Road, Singapore 238839
Tel: 6332 9298
Web: www.plazasingapura.com.sg

Raffles City

Previous activities: Disney shows, Christmas carolling, Barbie exhibitions and LEGO events

Location: 252 North Bridge Road, Singapore 179103
Tel: 6318 0238
Web: www.rafflescity.com

Tanglin Mall

Previous activities: Magic shows, balloon sculpting, fancy dress contests, meet-and-greet Father Christmas encounters and the perennial favourite — snowfall at Christmas time

Location: 163 Tanglin Road, Singapore 247933
Tel: 6736 4922

United Square

Previous activities: Barney show, photo sessions, Chinese New Year performances and competitions

Location: 101 Thomson Road, Singapore 307591
Tel: 6251 5885
Web: www.unitedsquare.com.sg

ION Orchard

Previous Activities: Largest Christmas tree along Orchard Road during the Christmas season — one can step inside and admire the decorations.

Location: 2 Orchard Turn Singapore 238801
Tel: 6238 8228
Web: www.ionorchard.com

City Square Mall

Previous Activities: Rock-climbing competitions

Location: 180 Kitchener Road, Singapore 208539

Tel: 6595 6565

Web: www.citysquaremall.com.sg

Nex Mall

Previous Activities: Tigger and Pooh playland and merchandise

Location: 23 Serangoon Central Singapore 556083

Tel: 6416 6366

Web: www.nex.com.sg

Funan DigitaLife Mall

Previous Activities: IT Gaming Competitions, IT Exhibitions

Location: 109 North Bridge Road, Singapore 179097

Tel: 6336 8327

Web: www.funan.com.sg

VivoCity

Previous Activities: Exhibitions, Concerts on Level 3, Giant Christmas tree on Level 3 at Christmas season

Location: 1 HarbourFront walk

Tel: 6376 9117

Web: www.vivocity.com.sg

NOTES

NOTES